Corpus Linguistics on the Move

Language and Computers

STUDIES IN DIGITAL LINGUISTICS

VOLUME 79

The titles published in this series are listed at *brill.com/lc*

Corpus Linguistics on the Move

Exploring and Understanding English through Corpora

Edited by

María José López-Couso, Belén Méndez-Naya,
Paloma Núñez-Pertejo, and Ignacio M. Palacios-Martínez

TUTA SUB AEGIDE PALLAS 1683

BRILL
RODOPI

LEIDEN | BOSTON

Cover photo: Morguefile.

Library of Congress Cataloging-in-Publication Data

Names: López-Couso, María José, editor. | Méndez-Naya, Belén, editor. | Núñez-Pertejo, Paloma, editor. | Palacios-Martínez, Ignacio M. (Ignacio Miguel), 1959– editor.
Title: Corpus linguistics on the move : exploring and understanding English through corpora / edited by María José López-Couso, Belén Méndez-Naya, Paloma Núñez-Pertejo, and Ignacio M. Palacios-Martínez.
Description: Leiden ; Boston : Brill, [2016] | Series: Language and computers; 79 | Includes bibliographical references and index.
Identifiers: LCCN 2016016589 (print) | LCCN 2016027308 (ebook) | ISBN 9789004308077 (hardback : alk. paper) | ISBN 9789004321342 (e-book) | ISBN 9789004321342 (E-book)
Subjects: LCSH: Corpora (Linguistics) | English language—Data processsing. | Linguistic analysis (Linguistics) | Computational linguistics.
Classification: LCC P128.C68 C677 2016 (print) | LCC P128.C68 (ebook) | DDC 420.1/88—dc23
LC record available at https://lccn.loc.gov/2016016589

Typeface for the Latin, Greek, and Cyrillic scripts: "Brill". See and download: brill.com/brill-typeface.

ISSN 0921-5034
ISBN 978-90-04-30807-7 (hardback)
ISBN 978-90-04-32134-2 (e-book)

Contents

Preface

This volume contains a selection of the research presented at the General Session of the 34th ICAME conference, which was held in Santiago de Compostela in May 2013, and is a faithful reflection of the major areas of interest to the ICAME community. The conference was organized jointly by two research groups at the Department of English and German of the University of Santiago de Compostela, the Research Unit *Variation, Linguistic Change, and Grammaticalization* (VLCG; http://www.usc-vlcg.es/) and the *Spoken English Research Team at the University of Santiago de Compostela* (SPERTUS; http://www.spertus.es/). We would not have been able to organize the conference without the valuable collaboration of our colleagues Teresa Fanego, Mario Cal, and Francisco Javier Fernández-Polo, who worked side by side with us as part of the organizing committee both before and during the conference. To the three of them, our most heartfelt thanks. Thanks are also due to all our student helpers, who diligently assisted us during those hectic days.

We would also like to express our gratitude to all the participants of ICAME 34 for helping to make the conference such a success and to all the authors for their unfailing cooperation in the edition of the volume. We are also deeply indebted to a number of colleagues who acted as anonymous external reviewers, and whose insightful comments and suggestions have greatly contributed to the quality of the volume: Bas Aarts, Annelie Ädel, Leszek Berezowski, Ana Bocanegra, Laurel J. Brinton, Claudia Claridge, Peter Collins, Mark de Vries, Belén Díez-Bedmar, Francisco Javier Fernández-Polo, Cristiano Furiase, Gaëtanelle Gilquin, Gunther Kaltenböck, Daphné Kerremans, Barbara Kryk-Kastovsky, Christian Mair, Iain McGee, Hilary Nesi, Paul Rayson, Ute Römer, Marco Schilk, Doris Schönefeld, Elena Seoane, Cristina Suárez-Gómez, Eivind Torgersen, Graeme Trousdale, Salvador Valera, Bertus van Rooy, Ignacio Vázquez Orta, Anja Wanner, and Laura Wright.

Finally, we would like to thank our extremely efficient editorial assistant, Pilar Castillo, and the editorial staff of Brill, especially Eric van Broekhuizen; without their help, *Corpus Linguistics on the Move* would never have become a reality.

List of Figures

List of Tables

Notes on Contributors

Bas Aarts

is Professor of English Linguistics and Director of the Survey of English Usage, University College London. He has published books and articles on English grammar and corpus linguistics, most recently the *Oxford Modern English Grammar* (O.U.P., 2011), *The Verb Phrase in English* (C.U.P., 2013, edited with Joanne Close, Geoffrey Leech, and Sean Wallis), and the *Oxford Dictionary of English Grammar* (O.U.P., 2014).

Siân Alsop

teaches academic writing at Coventry University. She has an MA in Early Modern English Literature from the University of Warwick and is currently completing a PhD on the pragmatic annotation of the *Engineering Lecture Corpus* (ELC). She has worked as a research assistant on the project to develop the *British Academic Written English* (BAWE) corpus, and as web editor for the Warwick Medical School. She was recently a visiting scholar at the University of Tübingen to develop the ELVis language visualization software.

Anita Auer

is Professor of English Linguistics at the University of Lausanne and Principal Investigator of the Emerging Standards Project. She is a (socio)historical linguist with a special interest in diachronic and synchronic aspects of language variation and change. Her current research focuses on both alternative histories of the English language (i.e. the role of historical urban vernaculars in standardization processes and the language of the labouring poor in Late Modern England) and the historical development of English subjunctive constructions.

Jill Bowie

is an Honorary Research Fellow at the Survey of English Usage, University College London, where she has worked on the Changing English Verb Phrase project and the Teaching English Grammar in Schools project. Her research interests include English grammar, corpus linguistics, language evolution and change, and the analysis of spoken discourse. She has published on recent change in the English perfect and modals.

Eduardo Coto-Villalibre

holds a PhD in English Linguistics from the University of Santiago de Compostela (2014) with a dissertation on *get*-constructions in World Englishes. He works on corpus linguistics and World Englishes, and his publications focus mainly on the passive voice in East and South East Asian varieties of English.

Pieter de Haan

is Senior Lecturer of English Language and Linguistics at Radboud University in Nijmegen. He teaches BA courses on English proficiency, grammar, syntax, translation English-Dutch and Dutch-English, as well as MA courses on advanced grammar and use, information structure, and advanced translation English-Dutch. His research interests include corpus linguistics, syntactic patterns in native and non-native English writing, syntactic differences between native speech and writing, and the development of very advanced Dutch EFL writing. He is an active member of the Learner Corpus Association.

Johan Elsness

is Professor of English Language at the University of Oslo. He has published widely, especially on tense and aspect, and on nominalizations, and is the author of *The Perfect and the Preterite in Contemporary and Earlier English* (Mouton de Gruyter, 1997). He has been a visiting scholar at various universities: Brown University, Rhode Island; University College London; Macquarie University, Sydney; University of Cape Town.

Moragh Gordon

is a PhD student in the Department of English and the Institute of Linguistics at Utrecht University. She received a BA in English Language and Culture (2011) and an MA in Linguistics (2012) from Utrecht University. Her research interests include language variation and change, historical sociolinguistics, language and dialect contact, and corpus linguistics with a particular reference to historical data. Her PhD research examines the urban vernacular of Bristol during the period 1400–1700, which includes the compilation of a multi-genre corpus of texts written in Bristol.

Hilde Hasselgård

is Professor of English Language at the University of Oslo. Her research interests lie within functionally-oriented corpus linguistics, particularly contrastive and interlanguage studies. Publications include *Adjunct Adverbials in English* (C.U.P., 2014) and a number of edited volumes, most recently *Cross-Linguistic Perspectives on Verb Constructions* (Cambridge Scholars Publishing, 2015, co-edited with Signe O. Ebeling). She is on the editorial team of *Languages in*

Contrast and *Functions of Language*, and also participates in the compilation of the Norwegian component of the *Varieties of English for Specific Purposes dAtabase* (VESPA) learner corpus.

Turo Hiltunen

works as a university lecturer in English Philology at the University of Helsinki. His main areas of research are theoretical and applied corpus linguistics, phraseology, and English for Academic Purposes. He is one of the compilers of *Early Modern English Medical Texts* (Benjamins, 2010), *Late Modern English Medical Texts* (forthcoming), and the *Hanken Corpus of Academic Written English for Economics*.

Magnus Huber

is Professor of English Linguistics and the History of English at Justus Liebig University Giessen. His main research interests are historical linguistics and (historical) sociolinguistics, corpus linguistics, dialectology, New Englishes, and pidgins and creoles. Together with his team he compiled the *Old Bailey Corpus 1720–1913*. He is also interested in the historical evolution and structure of English-based contact languages as well as New Englishes. He co-edited the *Atlas and Survey of Pidgin and Creole Languages* (O.U.P., 2013) and a volume on *The Evolution of Englishes. The Dynamic Model and Beyond* (Benjamins, 2014).

Marianne Hundt

is Professor of English Linguistics at Zurich University. She has (co-)authored three monographs (*New Zealand English Grammar—Fact or Fiction*, Benjamins, 1998; *English Mediopassive Constructions*, Rodopi, 2007; *Change in Contemporary English*, C.U.P., 2007) and (co-)edited nine volumes on various topics of English linguistics. Jointly with Daniel Schreier, she is editor of *English World-Wide*. Her research interests include variation and grammatical change in contemporary and Late Modern English, varieties of English as a first language (with a focus on English in New Zealand, Britain, and the US), second-language varieties of English (especially in Fiji and South Asia), and language in the Indian Diaspora.

Mikko Laitinen

is currently Professor of English at the University of Eastern Finland. He has also worked at Linnaeus University, Sweden. His background as a researcher is from the *Research Unit for Variation, Contacts, and Change* (VARIENG), University of Helsinki. His research interests include quantitative approaches to language variation and change, English as a Lingua Franca from a diachronic perspective, variationist sociolinguistics, linguistic diversity, and globalization.

He is the author of *Agreement Patterns in English* (Société Néophilologique, 2007), one of the co-authors of the *National Survey on the English Language in Finland: Uses, Meanings and Attitudes* (VARIENG, 2011), and the co-editor of *Dimensions of Sociolinguistic Landscapes: Materials and Methodological Solutions* (Peter Lang, 2015).

María José López-Couso
is Senior Lecturer at the University of Santiago de Compostela and a member of the Research Unit *Variation, Linguistic Change, and Grammaticalization.* Her main research areas are morphosyntactic and pragmatic change and grammaticalization processes in the history of English, with specific interests in the fields of clausal complementation, existential constructions, negation, and parentheticals. She has published extensively on these and other topics in international journals and edited volumes. She has co-edited *English Historical Syntax and Morphology* (Benjamins, 2002), *Rethinking Grammaticalization: New Perspectives* (Benjamins, 2008), *Theoretical and Empirical Issues in Grammaticalization* (Benjamins, 2008), and *Information Structure and Syntactic Change in the History of English* (O.U.P., 2012). She co-edits the journal *Research in Corpus Linguistics* (RiCL) and is a member of the ICAME Executive Board.

Martti Mäkinen
is Senior Lecturer of English at the Centre for Languages and Business Communication at Hanken School of Economics, Helsinki. He received his doctorate in 2007 from the University of Helsinki. He then worked on the *Middle English Grammar Corpus* at the University of Stavanger, before taking up his current position in 2010. His research interests include English for Academic Purposes, English for Specific Purposes, corpus linguistics, history of scientific writing, and manuscript studies. He is also one of the compilers of the *Corpus of Early English Medical Writing* and the *Hanken Corpus of Academic Written English for Economics*.

Beatriz Mato-Míguez
holds an MA in English Language and Literature from the University of Santiago de Compostela and is currently pursuing doctoral research in English Linguistics. Her main research interests include the interconnections between grammar and discourse, with a special focus on insubordinate conditional clauses and their differences in usage in British and American English, as well as their variation with other types of directives.

Belén Méndez-Naya
is Senior Lecturer at the University of Santiago de Compostela and a member of the Research Unit *Variation, Linguistic Change, and Grammaticalization*. Her main research interests are grammaticalization processes in the history of English, in particular clausal complementation, the development of English intensifiers, parentheticals, and pragmatic markers. She has published widely in these areas both in international journals and edited volumes. Her editorial work includes the volume *Sounds, Words, Texts and Change* (Benjamins, 2002, with Teresa Fanego and Elena Seoane) and a special issue on English intensifiers (*English Language and Linguistics* 12/2, 2008). She is a member of the Editorial Board of *Folia Linguistica* (Mouton) and *Selim*.

Paloma Núñez-Pertejo
is Senior Lecturer at the University of Santiago de Compostela and a member of the Research Unit *Variation, Linguistic Change, and Grammaticalization*. Her main research interests include grammaticalization processes in the history of English, applied linguistics, corpus linguistics, and the teaching and learning of English. She has published on the development of the aspectual system (*The Progressive in the History of English with Special Reference to the Early Modern English Period: A Corpus-Based Study*; Lincom Europa, 2004), youth language, intensification, and pragmatic markers. She is a member of the Editorial Board of *English Linguistics Research* (Sciedu Press).

Mike Olson
is currently working as a Ruby on Rails developer in Madison, Wisconsin, while completing his PhD on seventeenth-century Dutch at the Institute of Linguistics at Utrecht University. He received a BA in English and German at Georgia State University in 2002 and an MA in German with a focus on historical sociolinguistics at the University of Wisconsin-Madison in 2006. His research interests include language variation and change, especially as a result of language and dialect contact, historical sociolinguistics, and corpus linguistics with a focus on historical data. In addition, he is involved in software development with specific interests in natural language processing.

Ignacio M. Palacios-Martínez
is Senior Lecturer at the University of Santiago de Compostela and Director of SPERTUS (*Spoken English Research Team at the University of Santiago*). His main research areas are spoken English, youth language, and English language teaching, with particular interests in the fields of intensifiers, quotatives, vague

language, negative polarity, and language learning factors and strategies. He has published extensively on these and other topics in international journals. He has also co-edited several volumes in the area of English language teaching (*Diccionario de enseñanza y aprendizaje de lenguas*, enClave-ELE, 2007; *Current Issues in English Language Teaching. An International Perspective,* Cambridge Scholars Publishing, 2010). He serves on the Editorial Board of *Miscelánea, RESLA,* and *VIAL*.

Antoinette Renouf
is Emeritus Professor of English Language and Linguistics at Birmingham City University (BCU). She is a pioneer in the field of corpus linguistics, with research interests that include lexis and lexical semantics, particularly textual word patterning and meaning, and automated text analysis. In the 1980s, she co-directed the COBUILD lexicographic project. From 1990 to 2009, she directed major UK government-funded projects in lexical and semantic change, lexical attraction, and repulsion; she also developed WebCorp and WebCorpLSE. She was a board member of ICAME from 1984, and Chair of its Executive Board for six years. She is widely published, and an international speaker and advisor on corpus linguistics.

Bianca Widlitzki
is a research assistant in English Linguistics at Justus Liebig University Giessen. She is currently writing her PhD on morphosyntactic variation and change in Late Modern British English from a sociolinguistic perspective. Her more general research interests include language variation and change, sociolinguistics, and corpus linguistics.

CHAPTER 1

From the Fringe to the Mainstream: English Corpus Linguistics Moving Ahead

María José López-Couso, Belén Méndez-Naya, Paloma Núñez-Pertejo, and Ignacio M. Palacios-Martínez

Setting the Scene

Although corpus linguistics is a relatively young discipline, it has undoubtedly experienced exponential growth in just a few decades, moving from fringe to mainstream linguistics. In a context dominated by generative grammar, the establishment of the Survey of English Usage at University College London by Randolph Quirk in 1959–1960, and the compilation of the pioneering Brown Corpus (1961–1964) by W. Nelson Francis, paved the way for the founding of the International Computer Archive of Modern and Medieval English (ICAME) in Oslo on 12th February 1977. This momentous landmark is intimately associated with the names of Geoffrey Leech, Jan Svartvik, Stig Johansson, and Arthur O. Sandved, in addition to that of W. Nelson Francis himself. In its origins, ICAME aimed to archive, document, and distribute computerized English corpora as well as to promote the coordination of research initiatives in the field (see Leech and Johansson 2009, 10). With these aims in mind, shortly after came the publication of the first issue of the ICAME newsletter (*ICAME News*, 1978, which would subsequently become the *ICAME Journal*) and the organization of the first ICAME symposium, in Bergen (1979).

Many things have changed since the early days of ICAME. In comparison to the small bunch of resources stored at Bergen in the 1970s, an impressive range of corpora is now available to contemporary corpus linguists, as reflected in catalogues such as the Corpus Resource Database (CoRD; <www.helsinki.fi/varieng/CoRD/>). We can now use not only corpora including written texts and/or transcribed spoken material, but also multi-modal corpora; small and neat collections of data across the three circles of English, together with mega-corpora containing several hundreds of millions words; and reference corpora side by side with different types of specialized corpora, both synchronic and diachronic, native and non-native, raw and annotated for linguistic (e.g. tagging, parsing, etc.) and non-linguistic marking (metadata). Such a wealth of

 | DOI 10.1163/9789004321342_002

corpora invites a wide array of applications, from lexical, grammatical, and pragmatic studies to the analysis of register, geographical, and historical variation, as well as to implications for the learning and teaching of English as a foreign language. The exponential technological advances of the last couple of decades have also greatly influenced the discipline. Corpus linguistics has moved from "huge machines located inside glass doors and operated by engineers dressed in white coats" (Svartvik 2007, 13) to new-generation laptops from which we can search a variety of corpora by means of user-friendly data retrieval tools with a mere tap of the touchpad.

The first ICAME symposium back in 1979, with 37 participants from 10 different countries, initiated an uninterrupted series of successful ICAME conferences which have kept alive the spirit of early ICAMERs for almost forty years now. *Corpus Linguistics on the Move: Exploring and Understanding English through Corpora* offers a representative sample of the research presented at the 34th ICAME conference, held in Santiago de Compostela in May 2013. The meeting gathered over 200 participants from more than 100 universities in 24 different countries, thus testifying to the unstoppable expansion of English corpus linguistics across the globe. From the rich programme of the general session of the conference, the fourteen contributions selected here, which are conveniently summarized below, reflect major areas of interest to the ICAME community and to specialists in corpus linguistics in general.

Various aspects of corpus development are discussed in Part I of the volume, which introduces us to different kinds of resources created as a response to new research needs. The three chapters in this section introduce, respectively, a corpus which stems from a project on historical urban English dialectology (Auer, Gordon, and Olson), a corpus of English for Specific Purposes (Mäkinen and Hiltunen), and two new corpora of advanced learner English in the globalization context (Laitinen).

Part II provides new insights into register variation, as represented by academic writing and news texts. The articles by de Haan, Hasselgård, and Hiltunen, on the verb phrase, metadiscourse, and the passive, respectively, deal with variation in academic writing in native and learner corpora across various disciplines (both hard and soft), genres (research articles, essays), and levels of writer's expertise (novices, experts), and therefore contribute significantly to our knowledge of the academic register, while also having important pedagogical implications. In turn, Renouf, with her study on adverbial hapaxes in two British newspapers, draws our attention to the fascinating creativity characteristic of the journalistic register.

The remaining chapters of the volume explore various grammatical and pragmatic features of English in a variety of corpora. Two areas of study which have attracted increasing attention among the corpus linguistics community are world Englishes and the spoken language. It comes as no surprise therefore that Parts III and IV of the volume are devoted to variation in space and to the pragmatics of spoken English. Part III contains four contributions on the domain of grammar in varieties of English from both the inner and the outer circles. Elsness and Coto-Villalibre adopt a contrastive perspective with studies on the verb phrase (past referring forms and constructions with *get*, respectively), and compare their results for South African English and for Hong Kong English with those obtained for other varieties of the language. Chapters 11 and 12, on the other hand, look at the two reference varieties, examining change in article use with role nouns in the recent history of American English (Hundt) and clause fragments in spoken British English (Bowie and Aarts). As with the latter article, the three chapters in Part IV are concerned with the analysis of spoken British English, present and past, though with a stronger emphasis on pragmatics. Mato-Míguez focuses on various ways of expressing directive meaning in the contemporary language, while Widlitzki and Huber's contribution deals with the speech act of swearing in the Late Modern period. The volume closes with Alsop's study on the pragmatic functions of humour in university lectures in three different cultural settings.

Although the fourteen studies that make up the present volume have been conveniently grouped together according to their main thematic focus (corpus compilation, register variation, grammatical variation across Englishes, and the pragmatics of the spoken language), an intricate network of connections can easily be established across chapters from different sections. A particularly telling example is Alsop's contribution (chapter 15), which is included in Part IV, devoted to insights into pragmatics, but also pays attention to issues of corpus compilation and annotation (cf. Part I) and analyses a particular register, namely spoken academic discourse (cf. Part II), as represented in a specialized corpus, which contains material from three geographical varieties of English (cf. Part III). Thematic links can also be established between chapters dealing with linguistic change in either the long or the short diachrony (Auer, Gordon, and Olson; Laitinen; Hundt; Widlitzki and Huber), those focusing on the verb phrase (Laitinen; de Haan; Elsness; Coto-Villalibre), those discussing cohesive devices (Hasselgård; Bowie and Aarts), or those which have obvious pedagogical applications (Mäkinen and Hiltunen; de Haan; Hasselgård; Hiltunen; Alsop).

All in all, *Corpus Linguistics on the Move: Exploring and Understanding English through Corpora* faithfully reflects the spirit of ICAME conferences, which year after year serve as a meeting point for linguists of different persuasions and with different interests under the common umbrella of English corpus linguistics. It is precisely in such a context that fruitful cross-fertilization and positive synergies are likely to occur.

Issues in Corpus Compilation

Recent advances in corpus linguistics and in linguistic studies in general call for the compilation of new materials which enable scholars to deal with their research questions in a more efficient way and which, once available, open new avenues for research. Chapter 2, "English urban vernaculars, 1400–1700: Digitizing text from manuscript", by *Anita Auer, Moragh Gordon, and Mike Olson*, introduces us to the innovative research project of the Emerging Standards (ESt), presently under development at the Universities of Lausanne and Utrecht. The ESt project highlights the contribution of four rising regional urban centres (York, Bristol, Coventry, and Norwich) to the standardization of English in the medieval and post-medieval period, thus questioning the validity of the Chancery Hypothesis, centered solely in London, along the lines suggested by Wright (2000) and Benskin (2004). In order to achieve its goals, the first step in the ESt project is the compilation of a multi-genre corpus organized into four subcorpora, one for each of the aforementioned localities, covering the time span 1400–1700. The ESt corpus contains texts from a number of existing corpora and collections, as well as new materials which the corpus compilers have retrieved from manuscripts and early prints. The chapter offers a detailed description of the digitization of the ESt corpus, explaining the process of decision-making aimed at keeping a balance between faithfulness to the original (e.g. by maintaining the manuscript spelling and punctuation, scribal edits, etc.) and technical feasibility. The texts are transcribed into XML following the TEI guidelines, by using the XML-editor Oxygen especially adapted by Mike Olson to meet the requirements of the project. Alongside meticulous paleographic and philological information, the corpus provides extremely valuable archival details, with links to the facsimiles of the texts, together with extra-linguistic information (origin of the text, gender, occupation, and life times of the authors, among others) essential for the study of emerging standards. On the whole, the ESt corpus is a most welcome addition to the existing wealth of corpora covering the crucial period of the standardization of the English language, by shifting the focus towards less documented localities.

Another research area which has undergone remarkable growth over the last few years is English for Academic Purposes, no doubt as a result of the increasing internationalization of higher education and of the use of English as a vehicle of instruction. Corpus linguistics has played a particularly prominent role here, through the development of various academic English and learner corpora. Chapter 3 by *Martti Mäkinen and Turo Hiltunen*, "Creating a corpus of student writing in economics: Structure and representativeness", reports on the ongoing compilation of a specialized learner corpus of academic English, the *Hanken Corpus of Academic Written English for Economics*, a joint effort of the Centre for Languages and Business Communication at Hanken (Mäkinen) and the University of Helsinki (Hiltunen). The corpus represents the written production of students in economic sciences at the Hanken School of Economics (Helsinki, Finland) and currently contains over 0.5 million words. At present, it focuses on one particular genre, end-of-term papers, collected from a course on Academic Writing for Business Studies. The compilers envisage the future extension of the corpus to other genres (in particular, earlier versions of end-of-term papers, which will enable scholars to assess the influence of the instructor's intervention on the learning process) and the periodic addition of new texts, so that the *Hanken Corpus* becomes a monitor corpus. The corpus is annotated in XML according to the TEI Initiative P5. Each file includes both metadata (e.g. age, gender, linguistic background, phase of studies of the authors) and the text of the essay itself. The text has been tagged for part-of-speech using CLAWS and the C7 tagset and is divided into paragraphs and sentences following the conventions of the *British Academic Written English* (BAWE) corpus, which has served as a point of reference.

One of the most valuable features of the *Hanken Corpus* is that it can be fruitfully employed for both research and applied purposes. On the one hand, it has been devised as a source of data for studies on learner academic English. As such, it enables comparative and contrastive studies when used with 'exemplar corpora' illustrating expert output in economics (e.g. the relevant sections in the *British National Corpus* (BNC) and the *Corpus of Contemporary American English* (COCA), or ECON-PUB, a 0.5 million word corpus of economics journals also compiled by the authors) or with 'analogue corpora' of student writing (e.g. BAWE, which contains student texts from various disciplines produced by native speakers). Alongside research, the *Hanken Corpus* also constitutes an extremely helpful teaching resource which facilitates the identification of characteristic patterns in the writing of L2 learners, thus allowing teachers to detect errors and improve syllabus design.

The globalization of English poses a further important challenge for English corpus linguistics, since expanding circle varieties are not so well represented in corpora as those of the inner and outer circles. In this context, the starting point of Chapter 4, "Ongoing changes and advanced L2 use of English: Evidence from new corpus resources" by *Mikko Laitinen*, is that advanced L2 English constitutes "one stage in the long continuum of Englishes", and is therefore susceptible of being analysed with the methods applied to recent and ongoing grammatical change in native use. However, this research objective faces a methodological problem, since existing learner corpora are mostly designed to meet the aims of research on interlanguage and on various levels of proficiency in language acquisition in instructional environments, and are typically restricted to one single genre (e.g. student essays). In this scenario, Laitinen's chapter presents two multi-genre corpora currently being compiled at Linnaeus University, the *Corpus of English in Sweden* (SWE-CE) and the *Corpus of English in Finland* (FIN-CE). The innovation of these two resources is that they contain a variety of written genres which have emerged as a result of the diversification and expansion of English, and focus on non-instructional environments. Moreover, SWE-CE and FIN-CE allow comparisons with native material, since their architecture is similar to that of well-established corpora for the inner and outer circles, such as the Brown family or the *International Corpus of English* (ICE).

The usefulness of these newly-developed resources is tested in the second part of the chapter by means of three pilot studies which deal with variables recently investigated for inner and outer circle varieties, namely the conjunctive use of ANY/EACH/EVERY+TIME, -ONE/-BODY indefinite pronouns, and changes in the modal auxiliary system. Interestingly, the results of the first two case studies show that advanced L2 learners participate in the changes to a similar extent as native speakers. Therefore, the evidence from the advanced L2 corpora introduced in the chapter helps to qualify the findings derived from conventional learner corpora, which do not normally reflect the adoption of newly grammaticalized forms (such as *-time* conjunctions). On the other hand, the analysis of ongoing changes in core and emergent modals show that advanced L2 lags behind American English (the most advanced variety), but is ahead of both British English and outer circle varieties. Laitinen's chapter testifies to the increasing need for new corpus resources such as SWE-CE and FIN-CE which makes possible the investigation of grammatical changes in the expanding circle.

The potential applications of the new materials presented in Part I of the volume for historical sociolinguistics and dialectology, on the one hand, and for the study of English in the expanding circle in both instructional and non-instructional settings, on the other, will no doubt bear fruit in the near future.

Investigating Register Variation through Corpora

Advanced L2 English is also examined in the first chapter of Part II of the volume. In "Verbs and verbs phrases in advanced Dutch EFL writing: Case studies in quantitative and qualitative EFL analysis" (chapter 5), *Pieter de Haan* continues a line of research initiated by de Haan and van der Haagen (2014) and de Haan (2015) into the syntactic development of advanced L2 writing. The author reports the results of a longitudinal study on the acquisition of verb phrase complexity by four Dutch students of English as a Foreign Language. Using written assignments from the LONGDALE (Longitudinal Database of Learner English) project and starting from the premise that formal academic writing is characterized by a more nominal style (i.e. more noun phrases and fewer verbs, as opposed to speech), de Haan examines how the use of verbs and verb phrases develops in the students' writing over a five-month period in order to test whether such a development can be used as an indicator of their syntactic control and of a more mature EFL production. Quantitatively, the data suggest an overall decline in the number of verb phrases, which can be seen as indicative of the gradual acquisition of a more academically appropriate written style. On the other hand, the qualitative analysis shows a great deal of variation in the internal make-up of the verb phrases, with over one hundred different constituent patterns, the most common consisting of only two constituents and hardly any containing more than three. The enormous variation in the structure of the verb phrases attested in the corpus makes it difficult to associate any specific feature of verb phrases with mature EFL writing. In view of this, the author concludes that relating the use of verb phrases in advanced EFL writing to the development of syntactic control on the part of advanced learners, and hence to the level of sophisticated EFL production, "is a highly complex and problematic affair", which shows that "there can be a wide gap between (passive) knowledge and (active) control".

The interactional resources used by both L1 and L2 writers to organize academic discourse is the topic of *Hilde Hasselgård*'s contribution "Discourse-organizing metadiscourse in novice academic English" (chapter 6). Drawing on data from four corpora, the Norwegian component of *Varieties of English for Specific Purposes dAtabase* (VESPA-NO), the *British Academic Written English* (BAWE), the *Michigan Corpus of Upper-Level Student Papers* (MICUSP), and the *Corpus of Research Articles* (CRA), the author sets out to compare the use of metadiscourse in two disciplines, linguistics and business, across three different writer groups: Norwegian learners of English, novice L1 writers (both British and American), and expert writers. For her purposes, Hasselgård operationalizes Ädel's (2010) taxonomy of functional categories of metadiscourse (introducing topic, concluding topic, enumerating, previewing, reviewing, endophoric marking, delimiting topic, adding to topic, marking asides, and contextualizing), to which she adds two further categories (current text reference and *I will/have*). The comparisons across disciplines and groups of writers yield interesting quantitative and qualitative results. To begin with, it is shown that discipline clearly conditions the frequency and types of metadiscourse used in L1 writing, with linguistics using metadiscursive expressions to a greater extent than business. This is probably due to the "more explicit attention to discourse structure and perhaps also to a more writer-responsible approach to writing" found in linguistics texts. When Norwegian learners and L1 writers are compared, the results show that the former use more metadiscourse than the latter. This suggests that non-native speakers may need more explicit metadiscourse devices to construct a text so as to compensate for possible weaknesses in their command of the language. The novice vs. expert variable also proves relevant, since the level of expertise of the writer and of the reader seems to reduce the need for metadiscourse. It can therefore be concluded that metadiscourse is closely connected not only with linguistic proficiency level but also with the degree of expertise and authority in the field. These results open new paths in the teaching and training of academic English for both L1 and L2 writers and call for future work on the complex network of factors which may determine the use of metadiscourse.

Academic writing and variation across disciplines and degree of writer's expertise are also the concern of *Turo Hiltunen*'s "Passives in academic writing: Comparing research articles and student essays across four disciplines" (chapter 7). The cross-disciplinary focus of this chapter adds significantly to our understanding of the use of the passive, one of the staples of academic English, on the part of novice and expert writers in both hard (medicine and physics) and soft sciences (law and literary criticism). Making use of a self-compiled 2-million-word corpus of published research articles and of a selection of student essays from the BAWE corpus, the author shows that, on the whole, passives are more frequent in the hard than in the soft disciplines, but also detects individual differences within these two groups, with passives being more common in physics than in medicine and in law than in literary criticism. The tendency to use the passive in scientific articles is only partially replicated in student essays, since in the hard disciplines student texts contain fewer passives than research articles, while the balance is reversed in the case of the soft disciplines. As to the type of passive (bare, i.e. without *be* vs. verbal), Hiltunen's results are in line with the observations made in earlier studies on the high relative frequency of use of bare passives in scientific writing (over 20% in the eight subcorpora). The corpus data also reveal that bare passives are consistently less frequent in student essays than in research articles, where they are particularly useful to introduce metadiscursive elements of the kind discussed by Hasselgård in chapter 6. In the author's opinion, the lower rate of bare passives in essays could signal "inadequate register awareness" on the part of students and their tendency to use a more informal style. Finally, as regards degrees of passivization, the analysis of lexical patterning in the corpora brings to light various trends which reflect the purpose of each discipline; for example, verbs reporting activities performed during the research process (e.g. *use*, *compare*) are more common in texts from the hard sciences, while those denoting cognitive and communicative acts (e.g. *understand*, *write*) prevail in law and literary criticism articles. In view of the informative findings reported on in this chapter and of their pedagogical applications, further work on the passive and other grammatical patterns is certainly needed for other disciplinary settings.

From academic English, we move to the journalistic register with the article "Adverbial hapax legomena in news text: Why do some coinages remain hapax?" (chapter 8), where *Antoinette Renouf* presents the results of a study on non-recurring adverbial formations with data from *The Independent* and *The Guardian* published between 1984 and 2012. The candidate adverbs were first retrieved automatically by means of the APRIL and WebCorp Linguist's Search Engine systems and then manually trawled, which allowed the author to establish a set of *bona fide* adverbial hapaxes, comprising forms created mostly through regular processes of derivation with the suffixes *-ly*, *-style*, *-wards*, and *-wise*. Through the detailed analysis of these hapaxes Renouf identifies a number of inhibiting qualities that may go a long way towards explaining the lack of productivity of certain formations. Thus, it is shown that adverbial neologisms have few chances of recurring if their base elements are rare or context-determined (e.g. *goatily*), are grammatically irregular (e.g. *antiquities-wise*), or if the resulting adverbs show non-standard orthography representing particular phonological features of speech (e.g. *strrrrictly*, which evokes the Scottish rhotic trill). Furthermore, singletons which are semantically specific (e.g. Irving Wardle's coinage *undeflatably*), genre-specific (e.g. *monocularly*, characteristic of the genre of arts reviews), or quoted from a specialized textual domain (e.g. the technical adverb *pneumonically*) are also likely to remain hapax in journalistic texts. Similarly, adverbs which have arisen as the result of creative play (e.g. *self-excusingly*, formed by analogy with *self-accusingly*, which occurs in the nearby context) are also unlikely to recur. Finally, the author shows how the existence in the lexicon of a well-established semantic competitor may block the institutionalization of a coinage (e.g. *indirectedly* vs. *indirectly*) and how multi-word adverbial strings (e.g. *not-so-subtly*) have a low likelihood of recurrence, their chances diminishing with increasing length. All in all, Renouf's study contributes significantly to the study of neologisms by shifting the focus from successful adverbial formations to the "silent majority" of hapax legomena and highlights the role of such creative devices in the journalistic register.

Corpora and Grammar: Examining Grammatical Variation in Space

From variation in register discussed in the chapters in Part II of the volume, Part III moves on to variation in space. In chapter 9, "English in South Africa: The case of past referring forms", *Johan Elsness* explores the preterite-present perfect alternation in South African English, and compares his results on this variety with those obtained in his earlier research on other inner circle Englishes, namely British English, American English, New Zealand English, and Australian English (Elsness 1997, 2009a, 2009b). The chapter opens with a useful overview of South Africa's unique linguistic ecology. Although English is the L1 of just a minority of (mostly white) speakers, it nevertheless enjoys a strong position in the country, being used as an L2 by other ethnic groups, in particular by the majority black population, among which a new 'crossover' L1 variety has emerged in the post-apartheid era. Elsness' study combines data from an elicitation test carried out at the University of Cape Town with corpus data from the *Corpus of Global Web-Based English* (GloWbE). The analysis discloses striking differences between white and black speakers as regards the use of the two variants. While White South African English patterns very much like British English, thus showing higher scores for the present perfect, Black South African English aligns with the American English norm, thus privileging the preterite in most of the structures studied. The author suggests that the similarities between White South African English and the British norm are accounted for by the British heritage of the white L1 speakers. He also hints at the potential influence of Afrikaans, which uses the perfect construction to cover the spectrum of both the English perfect and the preterite. Speakers of Black South African English, on the other hand, seem to be more sensitive to the general dominance of American English globally and, in particular, to the pervasive influence of American popular culture in the media.

Another study on the verb phrase in varieties of English world-wide is "A look at participial constructions with *get* in Hong Kong English" (chapter 10), by *Eduardo Coto-Villalibre*. The chapter, which is part of a larger cross-varietal project on '*get* + past participle' constructions, offers new data on Hong Kong English, as represented in the *International Corpus of English* (ICE-HK), and compares them with the results obtained by the author in his earlier research on British English (ICE-GB) and Indian English (ICE-IN). Coto-Villalibre proposes a data-driven gradient for '*get* + past participle' sequences according to their degree of 'passiveness' and classifies them into central passives, pseudo, adjectival, idiomatic, and resultative constructions. The analysis of the parameters relevant to the use of *get*-constructions (among them, frequency, information status of the subjects, and semantic prosody) serves to confirm earlier observations on the syntactic, semantic, and pragmatic characteristics of *get*-constructions, but also contributes new insights into the topic. In terms of frequency, *get*-constructions are less common in Hong Kong English than in the other two varieties considered, adjectival *get* being the dominant type, as also happens in British English. In this respect, Hong Kong English and British English differ from Indian English, where central *get*-passives prevail, possibly due to the substrate influence of Hindi. In the three varieties studied, *get*-constructions are predominantly agentless and their subjects tend to convey given information, are responsible for initiating the action (especially in Hong Kong English), and are typically animate and human. Curiously enough, however, central *get*-passives seem to be undergoing change in the direction of *be*-passives; thus, they show a preference for non-responsible subjects in all three varieties and can occur with inanimate subjects, especially in Indian English (about 75% of the total), which may point to ongoing grammaticalization. As for semantic prosody, *get*-constructions as a whole seem to convey neutral meanings, i.e. with neither beneficial nor adversative effects on the subject, which is particularly striking in the case of Hong Kong English, since passives in Cantonese (the substrate language) are commonly associated with adversative meaning. The shift from adversative contexts to more neutral ones is more advanced in the ICE-IN material, a rather unexpected result given the conservative character of Indian English.

Rather than offering cross-varietal analyses of Englishes world-wide, the next two chapters focus on the reference varieties, American and British English. In "*Who is* the/a/Ø *professor at your university?* A construction grammar view on changing article use with single role predicates in American English" (chapter 11), *Marianne Hundt* presents empirical data on the variation in the use of articles with role predicate nominals like *professor*, as in the example included in the title of her chapter. Starting from the results of the scant previous quantitative research (Biber et al. 1999, 262; Berezowski 2009), according to which such nouns typically occur in bare noun phrases, Hundt moves on to a very careful analysis of article use with five role nouns (*professor, president, governor, manager*, and *director*) using twentieth-century data from the *Corpus of Historical American English* (COHA). Her study, which combines Construction Grammar with a variationist approach, takes into account the three potential variants, namely bare, definite, and indefinite noun phrases, plotting them against grammatical determinants (type of copula, occurrence/non-occurrence of modification) and over time. The different factors are considered both individually and in combination by means of a multivariate analysis. The big picture is that bare noun phrases are generally on the decrease with the selected nouns. A more nuanced picture, however, emerges when focusing on the individual items: some single role nouns (e.g. *professor*, *director*, and *manager*) show diachronic variation in the use of articles, while others remain stable. With *professor*, indefinite noun phrases constitute the dominant pattern and increase over time, especially when no modification is present. In turn, *director* and *manager* yield mirror images in their diachronic development, the former patterning increasingly with bare noun phrases and the latter moving from bare to (in)definite noun phrases, especially in the absence of modification and with *be* as copula. Prototypical title nouns, such as *president* and *governor*, by contrast, show stable variation over time, with bare noun phrases as the preferred variant. The different behaviour of the five nouns under study as regards article use suggests that membership in the single role category is gradient, with nouns designating professions (e.g. *professor*) being on the periphery and those which allow only one person to occupy the role (e.g. *president*) corresponding to the prototype. The data from COHA reveal that bare noun phrase use, originally associated with single role holders, has come to be extended from these to title nouns, and from them to pseudo-titles, whereas ordinary nouns can be interpreted as single role holders when slotted in a title or pseudo-title construction. Hundt labels the mechanism underlying this extension 'constructional bootstrapping', that is, items undergoing change are slotted into established constructions and the extension works analogically.

The attention shifts from American English to British English in chapter 12, where *Jill Bowie and Bas Aarts* examine "Clause fragments in English dialogue", a common feature of spoken interaction which has not yet been studied in detail from an empirical, corpus-based perspective. Fragments are non-sentential units of discourse which typically convey propositional meaning and which are interpreted through their grammatical links with the surrounding context (the antecedent structure). An example is *this week* in the following dialogue: A: *I am going to try and have Wednesday off* B: *Yeah /* ***This week***. ['You are going to try and have Wednesday off this week?']. Using data drawn from the spoken dialogues in the British component of the *International Corpus of English* (ICE-GB), the authors catalogue four different grammatical types of fragments, namely (i) extensions, which add a constituent to an already complete antecedent structure; (ii) matches, which provide an alternative constituent to an antecedent structure; (iii) match-and-extensions, a combination of the two earlier types; and (iv) completions, that is, constituents that complete an incomplete antecedent structure in context. Each of these types can show other-speaker (OS) or same-speaker (SS) linkages on the discourse-pragmatic dimension. The quantitative analysis shows that matches and extensions predominate in the data, and are therefore the focus of the qualitative analysis that follows. In the case of os extensions, Bowie and Aarts explore the grammatical functions of the added constituents, both at the level of the clause (generally clausal adjuncts, as *this week* in the example above) and at the level of the phrase (e.g. B: *Is uh <,> Giles being energetic about life at the moment* / A: ***Oh very yes yeah*** /, where the fragment realizes a pre-modifier function ['Giles is being very energetic about life at the moment']). os matches, the most frequent type of fragment in the sample, are shown to have a wide range of grammatical functions in the antecedent structure, as well as a variety of discourse functions, being commonly used to answer polar and *wh*-questions (e.g. A: *What time is it* <,> B: ***Twenty past eight*** / [matching *what time*]), to posit questions, to indicate agreement/disagreement with the other speaker, and to express acknowledgement/reaction to what the other speaker has said. All these functions serve as cohesive devices in dialogue. The authors also highlight the similarities between ss and os fragments, though admitting that there is a fuzzy boundary between ss fragments and loose attachments ('theticals' in Kaltenböck et al.'s 2011 terminology). Finally, in the line of Culicover and Jackendoff (2005), Bowie and Aarts' chapter provides suggestive empirical evidence against the so-called 'strict ellipsis' account of fragments (i.e. the idea that every elliptical utterance has to be an underlying sentence), since the interpretation of fragments frequently requires adjustments in the antecedent structure (e.g. changes in the illocutionary force or in pronouns) and cannot therefore be directly recovered from the preceding context.

Corpus Insights into the Pragmatics of Spoken English

Bowie and Aarts' discussion on clause fragments serves as a suitable link with the first chapter in Part IV of the volume, devoted to corpus insights into pragmatic aspects of the spoken language. Drawing also on data from spoken British English, in "The expression of directive meaning", *Beatriz Mato-Míguez* (chapter 13) examines a construction which could, in principle, be characterized as somewhat 'fragmentary', namely so-called insubordinate clauses introduced by *if* of the type *If you could go to the next page*. As shown in this example, insubordinate *if*-clauses have the formal appearance of conditional subclauses, but lack the corresponding apodosis. Though occasionally discussed in earlier work (cf., among others, Stirling's 1999 research on 'isolated' *if*-clauses in Australian English), in the last few years, especially since the publication of Evans' (2007) seminal article, insubordination has become a remarkably productive area of research cross-linguistically. Mato-Míguez's article represents a further contribution to our understanding of the fascinating cross-linguistic phenomenon of insubordination. Since the focus of the chapter is on the pragmatic uses of directives, the author explores the variation between insubordinate *if*-clauses and other (more canonical) constructions used for the expression of directive meaning, such as imperatives, including both ordinary imperatives (e.g. *Go to the next page*) and certain types of *let*-clauses (e.g. *Let's go to the next page*), and conditional structures only marginally conditional or with no conditional meaning at all (e.g. *If you go to the next page, I will start my explanation*). The first part of the chapter provides a detailed description of all these constructions, paying careful attention to the most salient features of insubordinate constructions and conditional clauses with directive meaning, from which the former seem to have derived historically. As in earlier work by the author (cf. Mato-Míguez 2014), insubordinate *if*-directives are considered here as having non-subordinate status, rather than as resulting from a process of ellipsis. The chapter then moves to a corpus-based study of the three constructions in contemporary spoken British English as represented in the *Diachronic Corpus of Present-Day Spoken English* (DCPSE). The overall results reveal a considerably higher incidence of *let*-imperatives than of the remaining directive types under discussion, while ordinary imperatives and insubordinate *if*-clauses show similar rates of occurrence. The analysis of the directive constructions according to the speech act categories they typically convey suggests that some of these patterns have specialized for specific pragmatic functions. Thus, while *let*-imperatives are exclusively found in the data to express suggestions and to guide the hearer through an argument ('expository directive'), insubordinate *if*-clauses and conditional structures with directive meaning are more closely associated with the issuing of requests. Since these constructions are more indirect and less intrusive than ordinary imperatives, they prove to be particularly useful devices for the avoidance of potential face-threatening acts.

Politeness (or rather, impoliteness) in the spoken language is also in the spotlight in *Bianca Widlitzki and Magnus Huber*'s contribution "Taboo language and swearing in eighteenth and nineteenth century English: A diachronic study based on the *Old Bailey Corpus*" (chapter 14). The chapter examines bad language in the Late Modern English period with data from the *Old Bailey Corpus 1720–1913* (OBC). The OBC allows researchers to access the spoken language of past stages (as recorded in trial proceedings), its detailed annotation scheme providing invaluable sociolinguistic information (e.g. social class, age, and gender), pragmatic information (speaker role in the courtroom), and textual information (e.g. printer, publisher). Widlitzki and Huber set out to trace potential diachronic changes in three different domains: the sociolinguistics of swearing, its types and functions, and its representation in print. After a careful process of identification and codification of both censored (e.g. *b--y*) and uncensored (e.g. *bloody*) tokens of offensive language in the OBC, the chapter discloses interesting trends in the use of swearing and taboo in eighteenth and nineteenth century spoken English. First, the data reveal an increasing disapproval of bad language over the period, which is reflected in an overall drop in frequency of use, especially in the latter part of the eighteenth century. The authors explain how this decrease is closely related to crucial socio-cultural changes taking place in Late Modern England, which also led to stricter censoring and the gradual concealment of swearing in print. Second, the chapter shows how bad language is almost exclusively found in quotes when speakers report the language produced by others. As expected, lower-class speakers account for a higher proportion of taboo language in the OBC, whereas (unexpectedly) much higher rates are obtained by females than by males. This gender difference is probably due to the tendency for women to use more reported speech than men, though the authors suggest that it well mask a social class effect. Finally, the OBC data also show remarkable diachronic shifts in the functions and themes of offensive language. Thus, cursing, the most common function in the early eighteenth century, declines drastically over time, while slot fillers experiment just the opposite development. As regards themes, family terms (e.g. *bastard*) and, especially, *bloody* gain ground at the expense of religious swearing, a symptom of the growing secularization of the British society of the time.

The volume closes with another contribution which explores specific pragmatic features through the analysis of the spoken language. In "The 'humour' element in engineering lectures across cultures: An approach to pragmatic annotation" (chapter 15), *Siân Alsop* discusses on the use of humour in the *Engineering Lecture Corpus* (ELC), a corpus currently under development at the University of Coventry. The ELC is a cross-cultural multi-modal corpus of engineering lectures delivered in English at three universities in the United Kingdom (UK), New Zealand (NZ), and Malaysia (MS), therefore representing both English as an L1 (UK and NZ subcorpora) and as an L2 (MS component). The corpus is annotated for a number of pragmatic features, among them humour.

Understanding humour requires a high degree of cultural adjustment, to such an extent that, in the context of the internationalization of higher education, British universities mention it in their support materials for foreign students. In this scenario, one of the aims of Alsop's chapter is to account for the functions of humour as a pragmatic device in three different cultural settings. The author discovers interesting differences between the subcorpora with regard to both the incidence of humour itself (humour episodes being most frequent in the UK material) and the preferences for individual types of humour. Thus, while playful and joke are widespread in all three subcorpora, some other humour types are characteristic of particular components of the corpus (e.g. irony/sarcasm is most common in the UK lectures, self-deprecating humour takes up more space in the NZ material, and, unexpectedly, wordplay is most salient in the L2 Malaysian component). Alsop is also concerned with the functions of the different types of humour in spoken academic discourse, which range from correcting behaviour (e.g. irony/sarcasm, and teasing/mock-threatening), to creating solidarity and bonding (irony/sarcasm and disparaging humour), stressing the power position of the lecturer (bawdy, word-play, and self-deprecation), and helping to cope with serious, life-threatening issues (black humour). In the globalized world with English as the major medium for higher education, a study such as this one, which sheds light on the cultural significance of certain pragmatic features, is relevant to both students and lecturers. An added value of Alsop's work lies in the original type of pragmatic annotation implemented in the ELC corpus for humour. As opposed to the common practice in previous studies on the same topic (e.g. Nesi 2012; Reershemius 2012), where humour is retrieved from the structural mark-up of laughter, here humour and laughter are not taken to be co-extensive, and therefore the former is annotated irrespective of the presence of the latter in the context.

We believe that the fourteen contributions included in this volume bear witness to the relevance of corpus methodology in a wide range of areas in English language studies and together demonstrate that English corpus linguistics is a vibrant field of research which is definitely *on the move*.

References

Ädel, Annelie. 2010. "*Just to Give You a Kind of Map of Where We Are Going:* A Taxonomy of Metadiscourse in Spoken and Written Academic English." *Nordic Journal of English Studies* 10/2: 69–97.

Benskin, Michael. 2004. "Chancery Standard." In *New Perspectives on English Historical Linguistics*, edited by Christian J. Kay, Carole A. Hough, and Irené Wotherspoon, 1–40. Amsterdam and Philadelphia: John Benjamins.

Berezowski, Leszek. 2009. *The Myth of the Zero Article*. London: Continuum.

Biber, Douglas, Stig Johansson, Geoffrey Leech, Susan Conrad, and Edward Finegan. 1999. *Longman Grammar of Spoken and Written English.* London: Longman.

Culicover, Peter W., and Ray Jackendoff. 2005. *Simpler Syntax.* Oxford: Oxford University Press.

de Haan, Pieter. 2015. "Nouns and Noun Phrases in Advanced Dutch EFL Writing: From Quantitative to Qualitative Longitudinal Data Analysis." In *Studies in Learner Corpus Linguistics: Research and Applications for Foreign Language Teaching and Assessment*, edited by Erik Castello, Katherine Ackerley, and Francesca Coccetta, 127–42. Bern: Peter Lang.

de Haan, Pieter, and Monique van der Haagen. 2014. "A Longitudinal Study of the Syntactic Development of Very Advanced Dutch EFL Writing." In *Recent Advances in Corpus Linguistics: Developing and Exploiting Corpora*, edited by Lieven Vandelanotte, Kristin Davidse, Caroline Gentens, and Ditte Kimps, 335–49. Amsterdam and New York: Rodopi.

Elsness, Johan. 1997. *The Perfect and the Preterite in Contemporary and Earlier English.* Berlin: Mouton de Gruyter.

Elsness, Johan. 2009a. "The Present Perfect and the Preterite." In *One Language, Two Grammars? Differences between British and American English*, edited by Günter Rohdenburg, and Julia Schlüter, 228–45. Cambridge: Cambridge University Press.

Elsness, Johan. 2009b. "The Perfect and the Preterite in Australian and New Zealand English." In *Comparative Studies in Australian and New Zealand English: Grammar and Beyond*, edited by Pam Peters, Peter Collins, and Adam Smith, 89–114. Amsterdam and Philadelphia: John Benjamins.

Evans, Nicholas. 2007. "Insubordination and its Uses." In *Finiteness: Theoretical and Empirical Foundations*, edited by Irina Nikolaeva, 366–431. New York: Oxford University Press.

Kaltenböck, Gunther, Bernd Heine, and Tania Kuteva. 2011. "On Thetical Grammar." *Studies in Language* 35/4: 852–97.

Leech, Geoffrey, and Stig Johansson. 2009. "The Coming of ICAME." *ICAME Journal* 33: 5–20.

Mato-Míguez, Beatriz. 2014. "*If You Would Like to Lead*: On the Grammatical Status of Directive Isolated *If*-Clauses in Spoken British English." In *Diachrony and Synchrony in English Corpus Linguistics*, edited by Alejandro Alcaraz-Sintes, and Salvador Valera-Hernández, 259–83. Bern: Peter Lang.

Nesi, Hilary. 2012. "Laughter in University Lectures." *Journal of English for Academic Purposes* 11/2: 79–89.

Reershemius, Gertrud. 2012. "Research Cultures and the Pragmatic Functions of Humor in Academic Research Presentations: A Corpus Assisted Analysis." *Journal of Pragmatics* 44/6–7: 863–75.

Stirling, Lesley. 1999. "Isolated *If*-Clauses in Australian English." In *The Clause in English: In Honour of Rodney Huddleston*, edited by Peter Collins, and David A. Lee, 273–94. Amsterdam and Philadelphia: John Benjamins.

Svartvik, Jan. 2007. "Corpus Linguistics 25+ Years On". In *Corpus Linguistics 25 Years On*, edited by Roberta Facchinetti, 11–25. Amsterdam and New York: Rodopi.

Wright, Laura, ed. 2000. *The Development of Standard English (1300–1800)*. Cambridge: Cambridge University Press.

PART 1

Issues in Corpus Compilation

CHAPTER 2

English Urban Vernaculars, 1400–1700: Digitizing Text from Manuscript*

Anita Auer, Moragh Gordon, and Mike Olson

Abstract

This paper presents the recently launched research project "Emerging Standards: Urbanisation and the Development of Standard English, c. 1400–1700", which aims at illuminating the complex processes involved in the emergence and development of Standard English. To this end, the project systematically investigates the urban vernaculars of York (North), Bristol (Southwest), Coventry (West Midlands), and Norwich (East Anglia) over the period 1400–1700, with a specific focus on factors such as time, text type, and migration patterns. A comparison of the results of these longitudinal studies of urban vernaculars (as well as findings from London) is expected to clarify our understanding of the origin and spread of formal written English.

In the current chapter we introduce this project in historical urban dialectology, with a particular focus on the empirical data that serve as the basis for the investigation. Research into the four urban vernaculars will be based largely on self-compiled corpora that contain a variety of texts from the different urban centres. It is the digitization process from manuscript to searchable corpus in the Text Encoding Initiative (TEI) format that will be described here.

Keywords

historical sociolinguistics – historical dialectology – urban vernaculars – TEI – Late Middle English – Early Modern English – supralocalization – language variation and change

* We want to thank two anonymous reviewers for their suggestions and comments on an earlier version of this chapter.

 | DOI 10.1163/9789004321342_003

Introduction to the Research Project

This study serves to introduce the recently launched research project "Emerging Standards: Urbanisation and the Development of Standard English, c. 1400–1700", which is being conducted at the University of Lausanne (Switzerland) and Utrecht University (The Netherlands). As the title of the project indicates, the focus is on the early stages of the standardization of written English and the role that different urban centres in England played in this development. Ultimately, the aim is to illuminate the complex processes that are involved in the emergence and development of Standard English. On the one hand, we explore the role that authorities with power and prestige play in the standardization processes (language history "from above"), but we are also particularly interested in uncovering more covert factors, such as the effects of national and international trade, work migration, and the book trade. It is thus the role of such factors in the origin and spread of a formal written standard to which we pay particular attention.

In histories of the standardization of English the focus has traditionally been on the pre-eminent urban community—London—and has been associated primarily with the Chancery Standard. This also continues to be reflected in academic work, although today mainly in student course books. The Chancery English hypothesis has been convincingly challenged by Wright (2000), who shows that the so-called single-ancestor theory, which can refer to a single dialect, text type, place, or point in time, cannot possibly hold true; similar arguments are found in Benskin (2004). Nevertheless, we still need to shed light on the exact mechanisms involved in the emergence and diffusion of a supralocal norm of English and its spread throughout England. The traditional account of the development of written Standard English attributes an important role to London in shaping the standard form, in that the city was the national seat of government and justice. The eminent position that the language in London had gained by the late sixteenth century, in particular concerning literature, is attested in Puttenham's *Arte of English Poesie* (1589, 120):

> This part [i.e. language] in our maker or Poet must be heedyly looked vnto, that it be naturall, pure, and the most vsuall of all his countrey: and for the same purpose rather that which is spoken in the kings Court, or in the good townes and Cities within the land, then in the marches and frontiers, or in port townes, where straungers haunt for traffike sake, or yet in Vniuersities where Scholers vse much peeuish affectation of words out of the primatiue languages, or finally, in any vplandish village or corner of a Realme, where is no resort but of poore rusticall or vnciuill people: neither shall he follow the speach of a craftes man or carter, or

> other of the inferiour sort, though he be inhabitant or bred in the best town and Citie in this Realme, for such persons do abuse good speaches by strange accents or ill shapen soundes, and false ortographie.

Puttenham promotes the language of London gentlemen and of the Royal Court, while explicitly warning against other social and regional varieties of English, and those from beyond the borders (1589, 120). However, such stigmatized varieties must not be ignored when investigating the diffusion of a supralocal norm. Indeed, regional varieties need to be taken into consideration when illuminating processes of language standardization, as well as the socio-economic factors that Puttenham warns against. In this project we therefore explore an alternative history of language standardization in England by shifting the focus to regional centres. In order to do so, the Emerging Standards (henceforth EmSt) project investigates the language used in important regional centres, notably York (North), Bristol (Southwest), Coventry (West Midlands), and Norwich (East Anglia), which fulfilled many roles, such as administrative and institutional functions, as well as being used in manufacturing and marketing, and in domestic and international trade. From medieval times to the seventeenth century, these four cities constituted the largest communities in England other than the pre-eminent urban centre of London (cf. Kermode 2000, 442; Trudgill 2010, 53). Given that the four cities were economically vital and of regional significance, levels of literacy were also significantly higher than was typically the case in small towns and rural areas. Thus, the urban vernaculars of major regional centres with high levels of literacy and text production (manuscripts as well as printed texts from 1476 onwards) will be systematically investigated over the period 1400–1700, looking at factors such as time, text type, and migration patterns. A comparison of the results of these longitudinal studies of urban vernaculars (plus findings from London) is expected to clarify our understanding of the origin and spread of formal written English. In order to do so, we compile multi-genre corpora covering the period 1400–1700 for all the cities under investigation. In the following section, we describe the corpus compilation process, focusing in particular on the process of producing digitized texts from manuscripts.

The *Emerging Standards Corpus*

The empirical basis of the project incorporates both manuscript and printed material. We work with (a) data that are readily available from existing collections and corpora, and (b) data collected from archives and record offices in the four cities under investigation and archives/libraries elsewhere. Existing collections and corpora from which material has been extracted or has been of other use in the investigation are:

(a) Late Middle English:
Helsinki Corpus (ME IV 1420–1500)
Middle English Grammar Corpus (1100–1500)
Linguistic Atlas of Late Medieval English (1350–1500)
Corpus of Early English Correspondence (1417–1681)
Corpus of Middle English Medical Texts (1375–1500)
Middle English Dictionary (1100–1500)

(b) Early Modern English:
Helsinki Corpus (1500–1710)
Corpus of Early English Correspondence (1417–1681)
Corpus of English Dialogues (1560–1760)
Lampeter Corpus of Early Modern English Tracts (1640–1740)
Corpus of the Project "Language and Linguistic Evidence in the 1641 Depositions"
Old Bailey Corpus (from 1674 onwards)
Early English Books Online (1473–1700)

From these corpora and collections material originating from York, Coventry, Norwich, and Bristol has been selected. However, a large amount of newly collected material will also be included, and will form the basis of a newly compiled corpus, consisting of four subcorpora, one for each of the respective towns. As regards the 'origins' of the texts, it is important to us that the text was produced in the specific town/city, e.g. that the text was written in York and/or printed in York. We are aware that the authors of the texts may have come from a different place, e.g. scribes who worked on a memorandum book and/or scribes who wrote down depositions may have been trained in and/or have come from London; however, it is precisely the use of different dialects in writing (and thus linguistic variants) that allow us to reveal in what way the supralocalization processes proceeded. In line with recent sociolinguistic studies (cf. Kerswill and Williams 2000; Cheshire et al. 2011), we are interested in dialect levelling as a result of migration.

The *Emerging Standards Corpus* contains a variety of text types covering the time span 1400–1700. The text types that have been collected so far are: ordinances, accounts (guilds, cathedrals, etc.), other civic records, court leet documents, depositions, wills, plays (mystery plays), letters (private, business), and diaries.

A substantial amount of material was photographed in the Borthwick Institute in York, the York City Record Office, the archive of the York Merchant

Adventurers' Hall, the Herbert Coventry History Centre, the Norfolk Record Office, and the Bristol Record Office. Editions exist of some of the materials that were collected, e.g. *The Little Red Book of Bristol*, the *Coventry Leet Book; or Mayor's Register*, and the *York Mystery Plays*. However, some of these are not very recent transcriptions and are often heavily edited, making them less reliable for linguistic analyses. For the purpose of the EmSt project, the editions will therefore be checked against the originals and re-transcribed to suit the project's specific research aims.

As regards the number of texts included in the corpus and its overall representativeness, the ultimate choice of texts very much depends on the availability of texts from the different urban centres. Our original plan was to compile, in the first instance, subcorpora of c. 100,000 words each, where the token number is fairly equally distributed according to the text type in the individual urban centres. As is often the case with historical data, some text types have survived in greater numbers than others. We are currently still at an early stage in the corpus compilation process, i.e. investigating what texts are available in the different archives and collecting the first sets of texts. Exact details regarding word counts per text type will thus be known in due course.

The Transcriptions

The transcriptions are based on the photographs of the original manuscripts. The texts are transcribed by one person, then checked by two other members of the project, and finally re-checked by the original transcriber. The main aim is to digitalize the texts so that they can be searched easily and facilitate linguistic research. Considering the philological approach that we take in this project, it is essential that the original spelling and punctuation be maintained. The manuscript material is being transcribed into XML format (Extensible Markup Language), based on TEI XML specifications (version P5). The advantages of using mark-up are that it allows for widespread compatibility, shareability, and easily convertible data. The TEI (Text Encoding Initiative) provides guidelines and a wide range of tags that can be used to provide the digital transcriptions with practically any kind of semantic or typographic rendering or annotation that is required. The wide range of possibilities allows us to render the manuscripts into very faithful transcriptions. However, this wide range of possibilities is also where the challenge lies. In standard XML-editors, most of the tagging has to be done manually, and the more complex the set of tags used, the more time-consuming is the transcription task. For the EmSt corpus, decisions have been made as to what subset of tags should be used. It should be noted that the team agreed to adhere to the TEI guidelines as strictly as possible while also producing transcripts that are as diplomatic as humanly feasible, i.e. with respect to time and effort required. This also allows for comparability with other existing corpora, even if they contain less diplomatic transcriptions, e.g. places in other corpora where they decided not to indicate where they have expanded abbreviations, brevigraphs, etc. Ultimately, the aim is to obtain a minimal subset that provides a maximum of research possibilities, while still maintaining feasibility. An example of the decisions that had to be made here had to do with orthography. For instance, we want to retain the graphs thorn <þ> and eth <ð> in the EmSt corpus. Although there is no problem representing these graphs in TEI, since the graphs are available in Unicode, the implications for search entries had to be considered. If the spelling had been normalized to the modern digraph <th>, searches would be easier because only one spelling variant had to be entered and retrieved. However, if all spelling variants were maintained, either all different graphs would have to be entered in a search in order to retrieve all variants of <th>, or the programmer would have to find a way to make sure that a search entry with modern spelling <th> would also retrieve the other variants. Similar issues arose with brevigraphs such as the crossed <p> for *par*, *per*, or *pro*. Here we have decided to use modern-day spellings. Given that the digitized text indicates that an expansion has been made, we know that the original contained a brevigraph and/or abbreviation. People interested in brevigraphs and/or abbreviations can check the facsimile, which is linked to the TEI version. Although these brevigraphs can be represented within TEI, it would be more complex than with graphs that are readily available in Unicode, and would also complicate searches, not least because some brevigraphs seem author-specific. To transcribe the original texts in TEI XML format the XML-editor Oxygen was used, which allows for a relatively rapid and error-free editing of TEI texts.

When using Oxygen in the first instance, it turned out that the encoding slowed the transcription process down significantly, particularly because many tags still had to be typed in manually. Figure 2.2 below shows the transcription of Figure 2.1 in Oxygen's text mode. As can be seen in Figure 2.2, the text contains many tags, most of which are only conveying very basic text lay-out features, such as line breaks, superscript, deletions, and insertions. In order to facilitate and speed up the transcription process of the texts in this particular project, the Oxygen editor tool has been customized by Mike Olson (Utrecht University). At this point, the customized version is being specifically designed for this project, with buttons for many of the tags that are required for the transcription of historical texts. It is therefore easier to maintain consistency within the team, since all team members have the same set of buttons to choose from. This way everybody uses the same mark-up, and errors are less likely to occur. In the author view of Oxygen, most of the features to be captured in the transcriptions can now be easily encoded by way of using

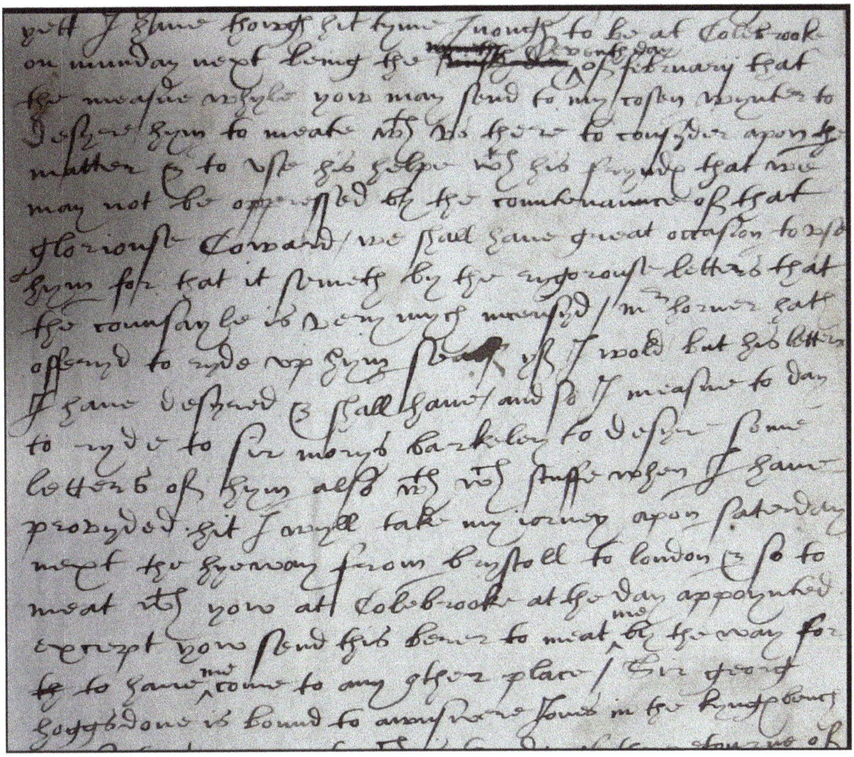

FIGURE 2.1 *Image of the original text. Letter by Hugh Smyth, Bristol, 31 January 1563 (Bristol Record Office, AC/C7_3).*

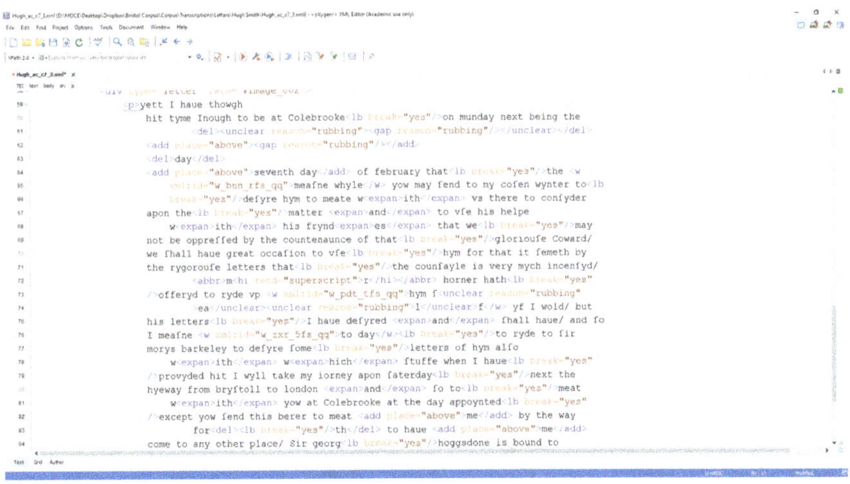

FIGURE 2.2 *Screen shot of TEI transcription in Oxygen.*

buttons and shortcut keys. Moreover, in the author mode the encodings are visualized, i.e. expansions appear in italics. This makes editing less strenuous, as the reading of long sequences of tags that intersperse text can be avoided. The customized author mode thus makes it possible to transcribe historical texts in a word processor-like view (cf. Figure 2.3). The non-customized author mode of Oxygen (cf. Figure 2.4) also has some basic mark-up buttons, such as for Bold and Italics, but for historical texts many more different features are required.

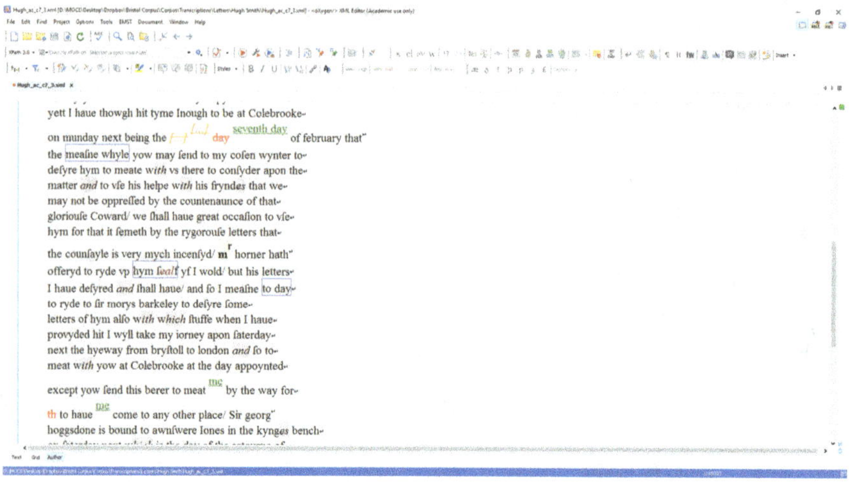

FIGURE 2.3 *Customized author mode in Oxygen.*

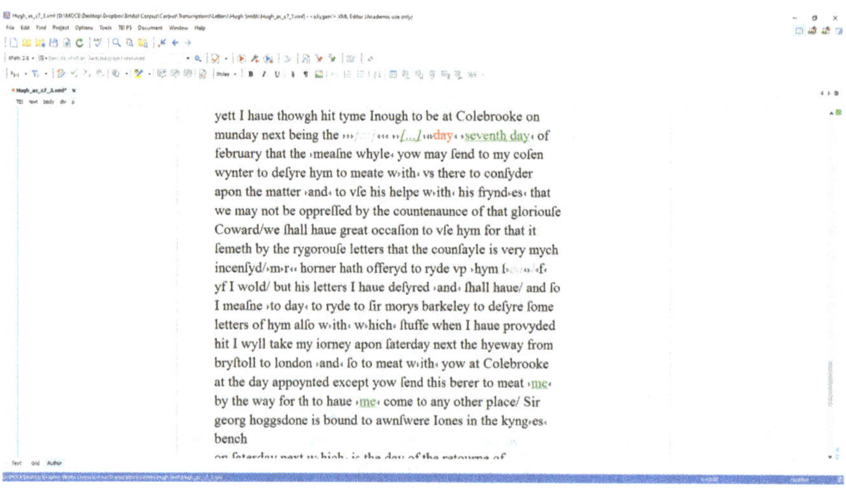

FIGURE 2.4 *Non-customized author view of transcription in Oxygen.*

Figure 2.4 above shows that many buttons, e.g. for line breaks, deletions, and insertions, have been added. In the following section, concerning text encoding, some of the new features of the customized version are illustrated and explained.

Text Encoding

As pointed out earlier, the aim was to come up with a minimal set of tags to encode the transcriptions and to obtain transcriptions that are as close to the original as possible. As for the general lay-out, capitalization and original punctuation, spelling, and line breaks are maintained. Additions and deletions are marked up as such and cases of uncertainty in readings are indicated. In what follows, a selection of the encodings that were picked for this project will be demonstrated, to illustrate the possibilities that the customized version offers for the transcription and representation of historical texts.

Orthography

In the transcriptions, the graphs used in Middle and Early Modern English texts, such as ash, thorn, eth, yogh, and long <s> are maintained and can easily be inserted by using the special character buttons or corresponding shortcut keys. As with a word processor, when the cursor is held on the button, the corresponding shortcut key will appear (cf. Figure 2.5).

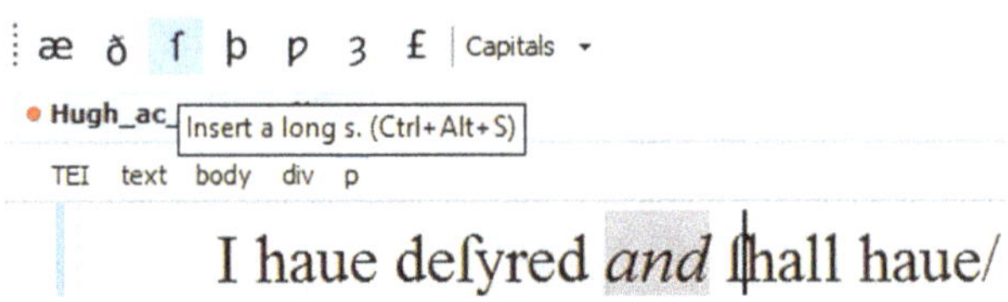

FIGURE 2.5 *Special graphs tool bar: Inserting long <s>.*

Line Breaks and Word Divisions Across Line Breaks

In the non-customized version of Oxygen a tag for each line break has to be inserted manually with the <lb/> tag. In addition to inserting the tag, it also has to be indicated whether a word is broken up across the line break, since for searching purposes the word still has to be recognized as a whole word. In the example in Figure 2.6, the line break does not divide a word, so it can be seen as a 'real' line break. In the unmodified version, this requires a great amount of manual labour.

```
be at Colebrooke<lb break="yes"/>on munday next
```

FIGURE 2.6 *Line breaks in text mode.*

In the customized version, the enter key as well as the line break button in the tool bar insert line breaks. When the enter key is hit, a dialogue box will appear, as shown in Figure 2.7:

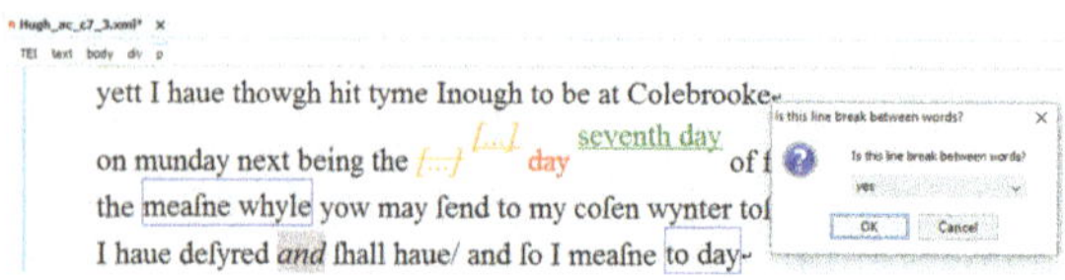

FIGURE 2.7 *Line breaks in the customized author mode.*

The default setting is a 'real' line break and pressing the enter key twice will result in the insertion of a line break. If a word is divided, 'no' can be chosen from the drop-down menu. The change from having to enter each line break manually to just clicking enter twice in most cases has sped up the transcription process considerably.

Additions, Deletions, and Uncertainties

Additions

The aim is to indicate when words are inserted between lines or in the margins. In Figure 2.8, the word *good* has been inserted above the line:

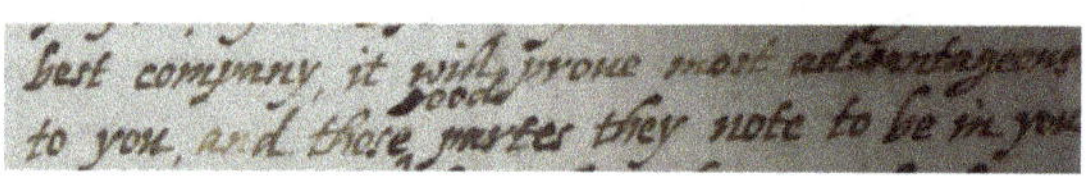

FIGURE 2.8 *Letter by Elizabeth Smyth, Bristol, 22 September 1624 (Bristol Record Office, AC/C48_2).*

We consider additions/insertions very important as self-corrections can indicate a scribe's awareness of variant forms and reveals the conscious choices the writer made. In order to make sure that this will be displayed correctly, the following tags are needed:

```
to you, and these <add place="above">good</add> partes they note
```

FIGURE 2.9 *Additions, example 1.*

In the customized editor, the green *add* button is used and the tags are supplied automatically. A drop-down menu allows the editor to indicate the place where the original word was inserted, as well as a hand-ID in case the text was written by multiple hands. The word will be displayed above the line in green and underlined, as shown in Figure 2.10:

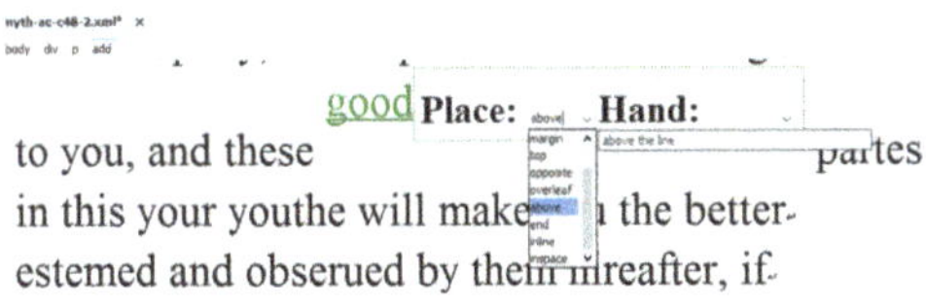

FIGURE 2.10 *Additions, example 2.*

Deletions

In the customized version it is possible to select words or sections to indicate that they were deleted in the original text (cf. Figure 2.11):

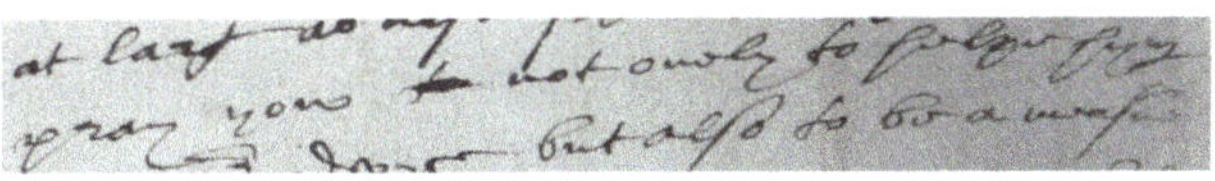

FIGURE 2.11 *Letter by Hugh Smyth, Bristol, 28 April 1580 (Bristol Record Office AC/C18_4).*

As illustrated in Figure 2.12, the deleted word will be displayed in red and struck through (the shortcut key is shown when hovering the cursor over the button):

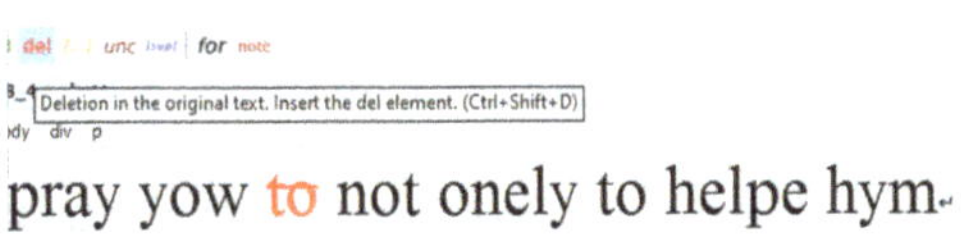

FIGURE 2.12 *Inserting deletions.*

In some cases only parts of the deletions are legible. In those cases a gap element can be inserted for the part that is illegible. Supposing that the deleted word shown above contained more letters with a middle part that was illegible, it would be displayed like this:

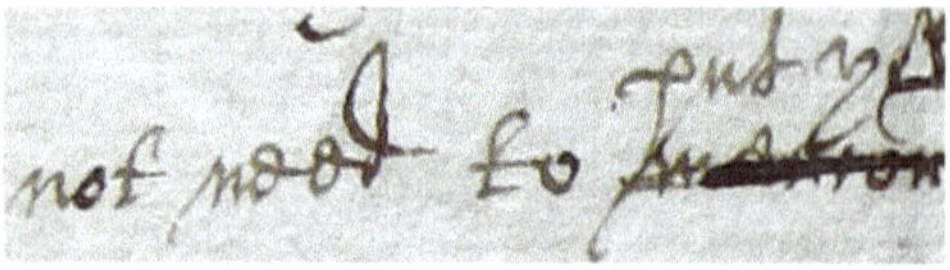

FIGURE 2.13 *Excerpt from letter by Thomas Smyth, Bristol, 16 March 1639 (Bristol Record Office 36074/153).*

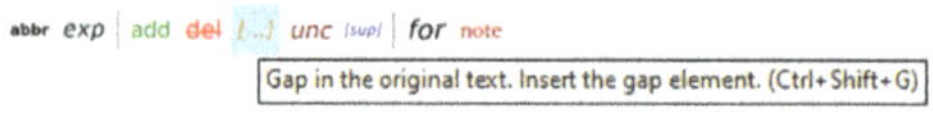

FIGURE 2.14 *Partially illegible words, example 1.*

Again, if this had to be done by inserting the tags manually instead of using a button, a lot of typing would be involved:

```
not need to <del>m<gap reason="rubbing"/>or</del>
```

FIGURE 2.15 *Partially illegible words, example 2.*

The gap element can also be used on its own when something is illegible for some reason.

In Figure 2.16 below the page is torn:

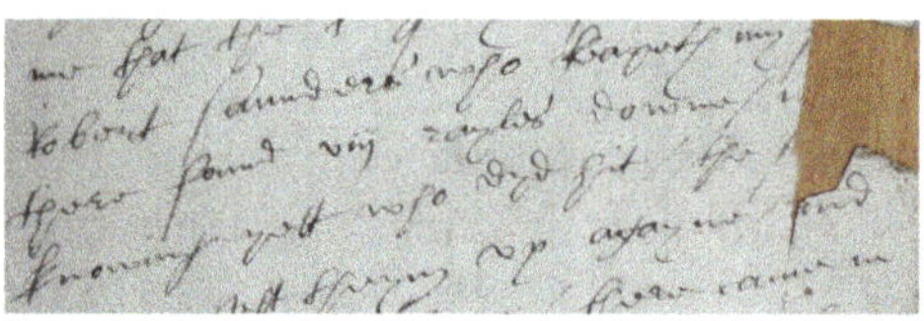

FIGURE 2.16 *Excerpt from letter by Hugh Smyth, Bristol, 28 June 1579 (Bristol Record Office, AC/C18_1).*

The gap element will be inserted and the reason for illegibility will also be given, which can be picked from a drop-down menu. When floating the cursor over the selected choice, an explanation is given:

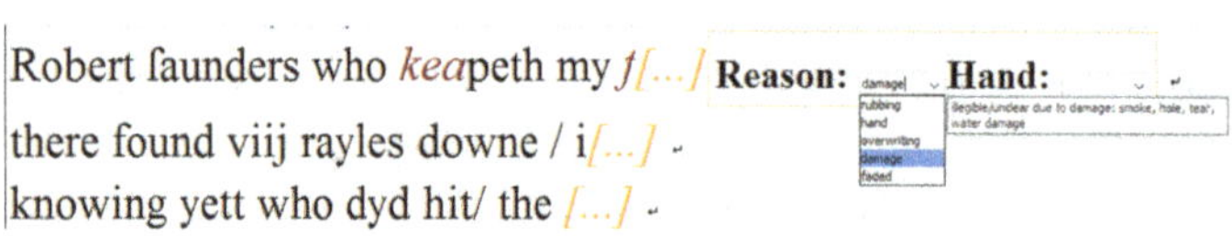

FIGURE 2.17 *Illegible material.*

Uncertainties

Another important feature that was added includes a button for uncertain readings, which displays the uncertain reading in purple and italics and allows for choosing a reason in the drop-down menu, as illustrated in the example for the gap element in Figure 2.17 above. In Figure 2.18 below, one graph was blotted. It seems to be an <l>, but this is of course conjectural.

FIGURE 2.18 *Letter by Hugh Smyth, Bristol, 1 January 1563 (Bristol Record Office, AC/C7_3).*

In the transcription this graph is thus marked as unclear and a reason is given:

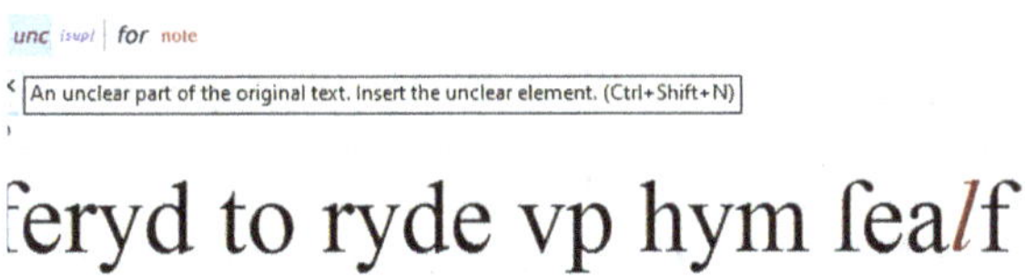

FIGURE 2.19 *Unclear readings.*

FIGURE 2.20 *Supplying reason for unclear reading.*

Abbreviations, Suspensions, Contractions, and Brevigraphs

Suspension marks such as macrons and tildes are very common in our material. However, they vary in the way they are applied and it is sometimes not even clear if a graph, or which one, was indeed intended. Some suspension marks and brevigraphs are very hard to transcribe as there is no suitable symbol readily available. To solve this, brevigraphs and suspensions were expanded and marked as expansions with an expansion button. This is important because some suspension marks and brevigraphs are open to different interpretations and it should thus be possible to exclude those from searches. Examples are brevigraphs for –*es* and *and*, where the inclusion of a vowel and the alternation between *and* spelled with an <a> or <o> might play an important role in the analyses (Carredano et al. 2008). There are buttons in the customized XML-editor to mark up quickly both abbreviations and expansions. Brevigraphs such as a crossed <p> for *par*, *per*, or *pro*, and suspension marks, such as macrons and tildes, which, for example, indicate double <m> as shown in the word *commendations* in Figure 2.21 below, were thus expanded:

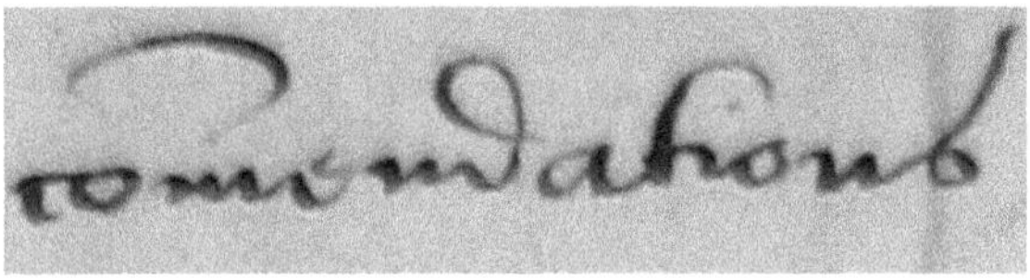

FIGURE 2.21 *Letter by Hugh Smyth, Bristol, 31 January 1563 (Bristol Record Office, AC/C7_3).*

Some abbreviations are not expanded. This mainly concerns abbreviations that are very common, as with titles such as *Mr*, *Mrs*, *sir*, and *Esq.* These abbreviations are marked up as abbreviations so that these can be excluded from searches. Abbreviations for any kind of word that may be of relevance for morphosyntactic analyses, such as relative pronouns, are expanded and marked up as expansions.

Extra-Textual Information

In addition to textual mark-up, the project is also concerned with the provision of extra-textual information, such as archival information, links to the facsimiles, but also possible extra-linguistic social variables such as the following: place of origin of a text, gender of the author, life dates of the author, birthplace of the author, occupation, and date when the text was written.

Considering that we are taking a variationist approach to language change, i.e. particularly the development of more uniform written English, all of these external variables will be important at the analysis and interpretation stage of the project and will provide us with a more nuanced view of the process as it unfolds. Thus, all TEI transcriptions come with a header containing some compulsory elements as provided by the TEI, and elements specially required for the EmSt project. Different templates are being created for each text type. In Figure 2.22 below, a header for letters is illustrated.

```xml
<?xml version="1.0" encoding="UTF-8"?>
<TEI xml:id="TEI_c1z_vbh_ln" xml:lang="en" xmlns="http://www.tei-c.org/ns/1.0">
    <teiHeader xml:lang="en">
        <fileDesc>
            <titleStmt>
                <title>Hugh Smythe to Matthew Smythe 1563</title>
            </titleStmt>
            <publicationStmt>
                <authority>EMST</authority>
                <idno>Bristol_correspondence_BRO_Ashton Court_44</idno>
            </publicationStmt>
            <notesStmt>
                <note/>
            </notesStmt>
            <sourceDesc>
                <msDesc>
                    <msIdentifier>
                        <repository ref="org:org_n3w_ldf_dn"/>
                        <collection>Ashton Court</collection>
                        <idno>AC/C7/1</idno>
                        <altIdentifier>
                            <idno/>
                        </altIdentifier>
                    </msIdentifier>
                </msDesc>
            </sourceDesc>
        </fileDesc>
        <profileDesc>
            <creation>
                <date type="sent" when="1563-01-31" cert="medium"/>
                <date type="received"/>
                <persName type="sender" ref="psn:person_czq_tqh_ln"/>
                <persName type="addressee" ref="psn:person_kfh_fsh_ln"/>
                <settlement type="sent" ref="plc:place_etc_ldf_dn"/>
                <settlement type="received" ref="plc:place_vll_lzk_hn"/>
            </creation>
            <textClass>
                <catRef target="gen:CORRESPONDENCE"/>
            </textClass>
            <handNotes>
                <handNote xml:id="hand_001" scope="sole" scribeRef="psn:person_czq_tqh_ln"/>
            </handNotes>
        </profileDesc>
    </teiHeader>
```

FIGURE 2.22 *Header of a letter.*

Figure 2.23 shows a more user- and reader-friendly version of the header, as displayed in the customized editor.

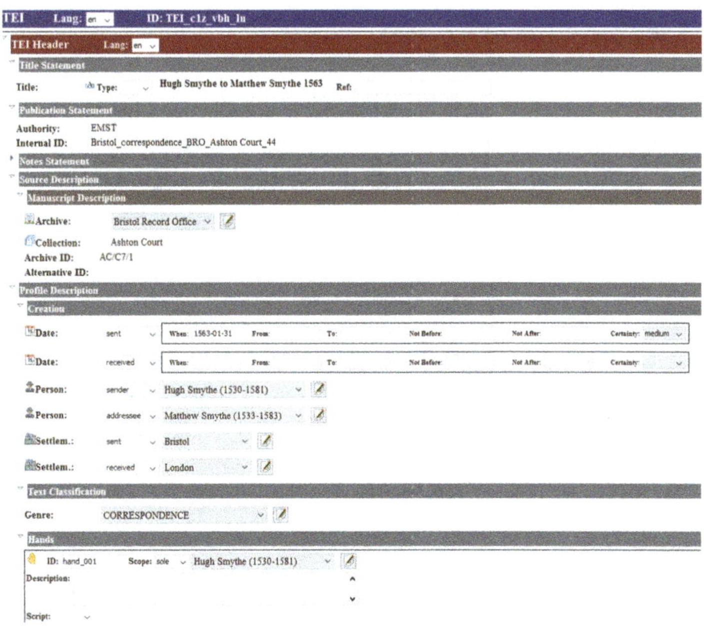

FIGURE 2.23 *The header in the customized author view.*

Here the fields can be filled in as one would do with an online form. For the letters, the title in the title statement consists of the sender, the recipient, and date of the letter, as shown in Figure 2.24.

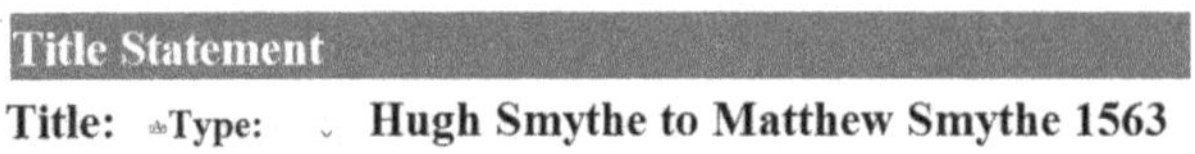

FIGURE 2.24 *Title statement in the customized author view.*

The publication statement (cf. Figure 2.25) contains information as to the publication and/or availability of the TEI text (TEI consortium). Authority indicates what institution or who makes the material available, which in this case is the EmSt project. The internal ID consists of an identifier given to each transcription, which is used as an identifier within the project and also gives each text a unique ID. The Note Statement allows the transcriber or editor to add any kind of additional remarks or information.

FIGURE 2.25 *Publication statement in the customized author view.*

The source description section contains the information related to the archive from which the photographic image and ultimately the digital version is derived (cf. Figure 2.26). These digital versions are so far mainly transcriptions of manuscripts, which is why the source description contains a manuscript description box:

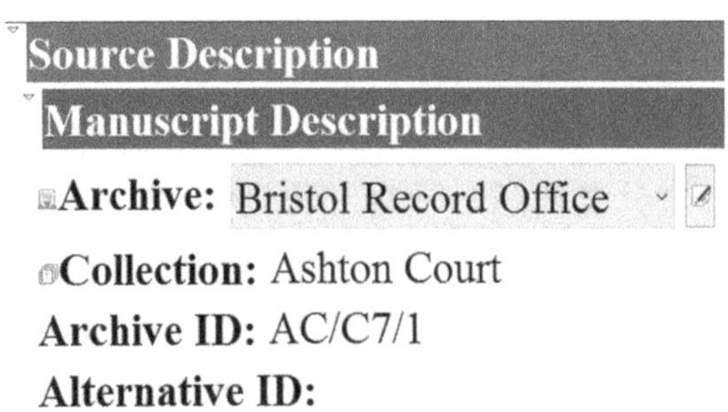

FIGURE 2.26 *Source description in the customized author view.*

The manuscript description provides information as to where the original is held, what collection it may be part of, the shelf mark as given by the archive that holds it, and a possible alternative identification number. The archive can be chosen in the drop-down menu, and a new one can be added by clicking on the pencil icon. The archive information is stored in a separate file, containing lists of repositories. When adding an archive in the header, a reference number will be inserted automatically that links the file to the information stored in the archive list. The great advantage of this is that if the archival information were to change, all files that are associated with it will update that information at the same time.

The profile description (cf. Figure 2.27) contains information about the creation of the letter, i.e. date of sending and receiving, sender and recipient, place of the sender, and place of the receiver. The people and places can be selected from the drop-down menu or added by clicking the pencil icon. Like the archival information, person information and places are stored in separate files. In the special person file, specific information can be filled in, such as life dates, settlements, gender, and occupation. As in the archive files, the reference inserted in the TEI header is linked to the information in the person file.

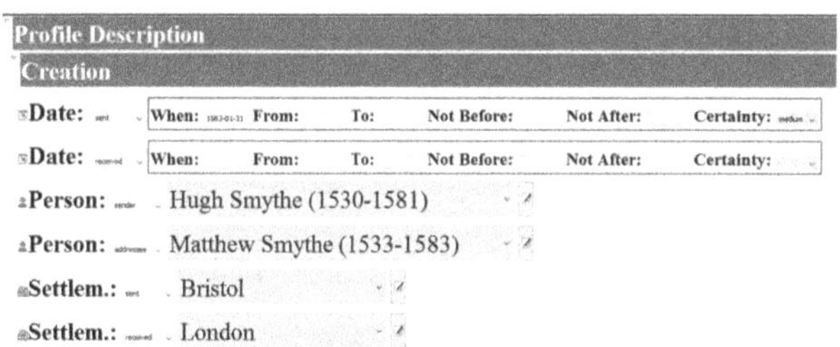

FIGURE 2.27 *Profile description in the customized author view.*

The precise date can be filled in if known. When only a rough indication can be given as to the date the 'Not before (a specific point in time)' and 'Not after (not after a specific point in time)' fields can be filled in to express a time range. The 'From' and 'To' fields are not relevant here but can be used to indicate a time span in which a certain event took place. In the person files, for instance, these fields can be used to express how long a person lived or worked at a certain place.

The text classification (cf. Figure 2.28) contains information as to what genre the transcribed text belongs. Here the genre can be picked from the drop-down menu which contains a list of pre-defined genres.

FIGURE 2.28 *Text classification in the customized author view.*

In the hands section (cf. Figure 2.29), a description of a hand used in the text can be added in the notes field, and when a text contains more than one hand, they can be added by clicking the hand icon in the tool-bar. In addition to that, the scope of the hand can be indicated. In the case of this letter, there is only one hand and the scope is thus 'sole'.

FIGURE 2.29 *Hand information in the customized author view.*

In the facsimile section, by clicking on the folder icon and selecting images from a pre-defined base directory, the images will be linked to the file. By clicking on the small icons on the left of the image IDs, the image will be displayed, as shown in Figure 2.30.

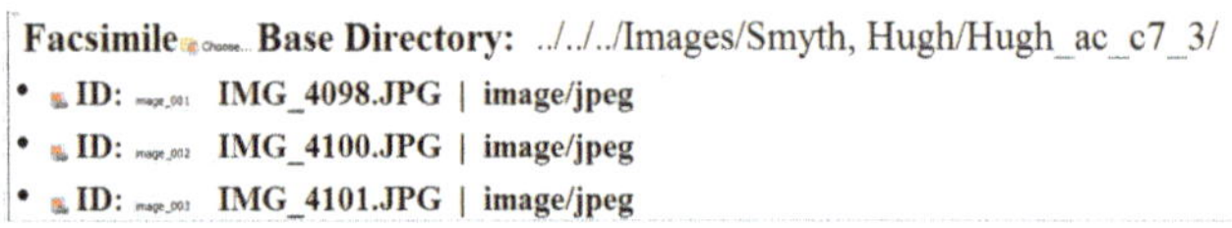

FIGURE 2.30 *Facsimile section in the customized author view.*

This is very helpful during the transcription process and also when editing and correcting the transcriptions, as the corresponding image is always close at hand. In addition to that, the images can be linked to the page breaks in the transcriptions, so that each page in the transcription has the page of the original text associated with it.

Concluding Remarks

In this chapter an insight has been given into the basic corpus outline for EmSt. At the same time, some of the features of the customized XML-editor have been demonstrated. At this stage, the aim is to obtain searchable transcriptions that represent the originals as closely as possible and to store the associated metadata. Future plans for the project are (1) the normalization of spelling (which is an inherent issue with historical texts), for which we are planning to use VARD (Baron et al. 2011), and (2) POS-tagging, which will be evaluated and decided on once the normalization process has been completed. Once the information has been enriched with this level of linguistic detail, we will use Orange Textable (Xanthos 2014) to conduct a wide variety of linguistic analyses. Because this tool is so flexible and user-friendly, it allows linguists to analyse their data in many different ways quickly and answer their research questions efficiently, which is, ultimately, the aim of this project.

References

Baron, Alistair, Paul Rayson, and Dawn Archer. 2011. "Quantifying Early Modern English Spelling Variation: Change over Time and Genre." Paper presented at the Conference on New Methods in Historical Corpora, Manchester, April 29–30.

Benskin, Michael. 2004. "Chancery Standard." In *New Perspectives on English Historical Linguistics*, edited by Christian J. Kay, Carole A. Hough, and Irené Wotherspoon, 1–40. Amsterdam and Philadelphia: John Benjamins.

Carredano Amores, José Gabriel, Julia Fernández Cuesta, and Luisa García García. 2008. "Compilation of an Electronic Corpus of Northern English Texts from Old to Early Modern English." Paper presented at the Sixth International Conference on Middle English (ICOME6), Cambridge, July 24–26.

Cheshire, Jenny, Paul Kerswill, Sue Fox, and Eivind Torgersen. 2011. "Contact, the Feature Pool and the Speech Community: The Emergence of Multicultural London English." *Journal of Sociolinguistics* 15/2: 151–96.

Kermode, Jennifer. 2000. "The Greater Towns 1300–1540." In *The Cambridge Urban History of Britain. Volume I. 600–1540*, edited by David M. Palliser, 441–65. Cambridge: Cambridge University Press.

Kerswill, Paul, and Ann Williams. 2000. "Creating a New Town Koine: Children and Language Change in Milton Keynes." *Language in Society* 29: 65–115.

Olson, Mike. HisTEI. (Vers. 0.3) [Oxygen Framework]. Unpublished, Utrecht Institute of Linguistics OTS, Utrecht University, Utrecht, M.Olson@uu.nl.

Puttenham, George. 1589. *The Arte of English Poesie*. London.

SyncRO Soft SLR. 2014. Oxygen XML Editor (Vers. 15.2). [Computer software]. SyncRo Soft. http://www.oxygenxml.com/xml_editor/download_oxygen_xml_editor.html.

TEI Consortium, eds. TEI P5: Guidelines for Electronic Text Encoding and Interchange. 1.0. October 2007. TEI Consortium. Retrieved March 15, 2014. http://www.tei-c.org/Guidelines/P5/.

Trudgill, Peter. 2010. *Investigations in Sociohistorical Linguistics. Stories of Colonisation and Contact.* Cambridge: Cambridge University Press.

Wright, Laura, ed. 2000. *The Development of Standard English (1300–1800)*. Cambridge: Cambridge University Press.

Xanthos, Aris. 2014. "TEXTABLE: Programmation Visuelle pour l'Analyse de Données Textuelles." In *JADT 2014: Proceedings of the Twelfth International Conference on Textual Data Statistical Analysis, June 3–6, 2014 = Actes, 12es Journées Internationales d'Analyse Statistique des Données Textuelles, Juin 3–6, 2014,* edited by Emilie Née, Jean-Michel Daube, Mathieu Valette, and Serge Fleury, 691–703. Paris: Jadt.org.

CHAPTER 3

Creating a Corpus of Student Writing in Economics: Structure and Representativeness

Martti Mäkinen and Turo Hiltunen

Abstract

This chapter describes the ongoing compilation of an economics learner corpus, the *Hanken Corpus of Academic Written English for Economics*. The corpus is a joint effort between the Hanken School of Economics and the University of Helsinki, and the intention is to create a research and teaching resource with a focus on the writing of economics students. The chapter argues for the need of such a corpus, and discusses compilation issues. The annotation and tagging of the corpus is also described, using illustrative examples from the corpus itself.

Keywords

English for Academic Purposes – economics – corpus design – learner corpus – annotation

Introduction

Despite the recent proliferation of learner corpora covering various L1s in different settings, there is currently no academic learner corpus representing the discipline of economics (see Granger and Goossens 2012). This chapter reports on the compilation of such a corpus, the *Hanken Corpus of Academic Written English for Economics* (*Hanken Corpus*), addresses some issues related to its compilation, and illustrates how it can be used in research.

The *Hanken Corpus* is a collection of student texts in business studies and economics written by learners of English as part of their studies at the Hanken School of Economics, Helsinki (Hanken). The corpus has two aims: to function as a source of data for studies on learner academic writing and as a resource in corpus-aided teaching of academic writing.

 | DOI 10.1163/9789004321342_004

The project is a joint enterprise, launched in 2013 by the authors, who work at the Centre for Languages and Business Communication at Hanken (MM) and at the Department of Modern Languages, University of Helsinki (TH). The impetus for compiling this corpus arose from the need to obtain an analytical tool for learner English in academic writing at Hanken, partly for the abovementioned reason (there was no such corpus), and partly due to the interesting linguistic background of Hanken students, most of whom are bilingual in Swedish and Finnish.

As in any corpus compilation, the core issues include the encoding, mark-up, annotation, and distribution of the texts of the corpus. Moreover, in this specific case, drawing the boundaries between economics and related disciplines is particularly challenging (Massey 1999) and bears on the issue of representativeness but also on the choice of a suitable reference corpus. On the one hand, data from the *Hanken Corpus* can be compared to published research articles, either extracted from general reference corpora or collected separately. On the other hand, the *Hanken Corpus* can be compared to those student texts written by native English speakers which are available, for example, in the *British Academic Written English Corpus* (BAWE) and the *Michigan Corpus of Upper-Level Student Papers* (MICUSP). With such reference corpora it is possible to obtain information about differences between texts by students of different linguistic backgrounds and differences between novice and expert writing in the discipline of economics (see Hiltunen and Mäkinen 2014).

The aim of this chapter is to provide information about the current stage of the project and establish links with other, related research; to address some issues that have emerged over the course of compilation and to describe the solutions to these; and, finally, to outline some ways of using the corpus.

Background

Although a large number of English corpora are currently freely available, there are many situations where researchers need to build a new 'do-it-yourself' corpus (McEnery et al. 2006, 71) in order to investigate their specific research questions. Such situations are particularly common in an English for Academic Purposes (EAP) context, where there is considerable variation between different teaching settings. For example, courses offered at university language centres commonly aim at teaching either general academic skills, such as reading or listening in a foreign language, or more specific ones, such as discipline-specific writing skills. These objectives obviously require different teaching approaches. On the other hand, individual courses may vary greatly in terms of size, number of contact hours, as well as students' background and language skills.

The fact that higher education has become increasingly international also has a bearing on EAP teaching. In the UK in particular, higher education institutions have a large population of foreign students. Krishnamurthy and Kosem (2007) report that non-UK students made up nearly 14% of the student population in 2004–2005, and that by 2011–2012 the percentage had increased to 17.4%.[1] However, this development is not exclusive to the UK. While the number of foreign degree students is much lower in Finland, it is steadily growing, as shown by recent statistics: according to the Ministry of Education, in 2012 foreign students accounted for 5.7% of all students in Finnish universities, but over 12% of new students.[2]

This is likely to mean that in EAP teaching groups are becoming increasingly varied in terms of students' backgrounds. This being the case, if teachers want to develop their teaching towards successfully targeting the specific characteristics of their teaching settings, it may be necessary to compile a corpus based on self-collected data representing the relevant situations. This has been one of our aims in compiling the *Hanken Corpus*.

At the same time, despite the variety of teaching contexts, there is still value in making one's own corpus data available to the community of EAP researchers and teachers. The most obvious reasons are verifiability and replicability of research. Whenever corpus data are made publicly available, any findings based on them can be verified by others. Moreover, it enables teachers and researchers to perform comparisons between different types of data, in order to explore factors that cause variation. In this respect, Krishnamurthy and Kosem (2007) also lament the fact that while many EAP practitioners are involved in corpus-based research and teaching, "their work frequently goes unreported" (2007, 359), as a result of which any experiences and insights tend to remain within local institutional settings; the same point is made by Alsop and Nesi (2009, 72). However, fortunately there are also excellent descriptions of corpora that are publicly available, which we have found extremely useful and inspiring (see e.g. Nesi 2008; Römer and Brook O'Donnell 2011). For this reason, the current chapter provides a detailed description of the *Hanken Corpus* and reflects critically on the practices we have adopted, acknowledging our intellectual debt to previous work.

---

1 Higher Education in Facts and Figures: Summer 2013, <http://goo.gl/MNSmem>.

2 Higher Education in Facts and Figures: Summer 2013, <http://goo.gl/zqYdD7>. The percentage of enrolled foreign students per the number of enrolled Finnish students at Hanken in 2012 was about 8%; the same year, new foreign students made up 11.3% of first-year students.

The Hanken Corpus *and Other Corpora*

Like many EAP corpora, the *Hanken Corpus* focuses on written English (for a list of such corpora, see e.g. Krishnamurthy and Kosem 2007, 360–362). The *Hanken Corpus* represents the written production of students in economic sciences (most of them Masters students) enrolled at the Hanken School of Economics, in Helsinki, Finland. From a linguistic point of view, Hanken is an interesting case: it is a Swedish-speaking business school where the majority of students are native speakers of Swedish, a minority language in Finland. In addition, the student population at Hanken includes L1 speakers of Finnish, as well as foreign students representing a variety of linguistic and cultural backgrounds.[3] As discussed below, these demographics are also reflected in the composition of the *Hanken Corpus*.

Using McEnery et al.'s (2006, 60) classification and terminology, the *Hanken Corpus* is a 'specialized corpus' representing texts in a specific domain, student writing in the field of economics. At present, the corpus contains texts representing a single genre, the end-of-term paper on an academic writing course, whose goal is to provide the students with communicative skills and knowledge required to write their Master's thesis. In the classification proposed by Thompson (2006), the *Hanken Corpus* would thus be an example of an ESAP—English for *Specific* (as opposed to *general*) Academic Purposes—corpus, in that its objective is to provide tools for teaching discipline-specific skills in economics and business studies.

In addition, given that the *Hanken Corpus* contains texts written by non-native speakers of English, it is also a 'learner corpus', defined by Pravec (2002, 81) as a "computerized textual database of the language produced by foreign language learners".[4] Gilquin et al. (2007) point out that learner corpora can contribute to EAP research and materials design, which have been dominated by the use of native corpora, by helping researchers identify and target

---

3 The Hanken School of Economics is the smallest university in Finland, comprising of over 2,000 students and about 200 staff. The school is divided into two campuses, one in Helsinki and another in Vaasa, thus serving the two major concentrations of Swedish-speakers in Finland, South and West coasts of Finland. There are five departments at Hanken—Finance and Statistics, Management and Organization, Marketing, Economics, and Accounting and Commercial Law—and they provide students with studies in 11 programmes: Accounting; Commercial Law; Economics; Entrepreneurship, Management, and Organization; Finance; Information Systems Science; Marketing; Management and Organization; Politics and Business; Statistics; and Supply Chain Management and Corporate Geography.

4 Gilquin et al. (2007, 320) specify that the notion 'learner' in this context covers both foreign and second language learners.

problems specific to non-native speakers. The *Hanken Corpus* thus shares many aspects of design and objectives with other learner corpora, and findings based on it can therefore be usefully contrasted with them. That said, the *Hanken Corpus* is also unique among learner corpora. For one, unlike the 2.5-million-word *International Corpus of Learner English* (ICLE), which contains learner essays representing general English (Granger 2003, 540), the *Hanken Corpus* contains samples of discipline-specific writing tasks. While there are other corpora which follow similar principles, none of them, as far as we know, concentrates on learner academic writing in the discipline of economics.

The *Hanken Corpus* is designed to be a dynamic 'monitor corpus', in the sense that new texts will periodically be added to it. At this stage, this means that a new set of essays is processed and annotated at the end of each academic term, after which they will be included in the corpus. Later on, we intend to include texts representing other student genres, such as theses, as well as coursework from other instructors' courses. Eventually, the corpus will be made publicly available online through a dedicated server, and mirrored in an international corpus repository.

From the perspective of research, the design of the *Hanken Corpus* allows for two basic uses. First, it can be used to investigate patterns of writing which are characteristic of the student population at Hanken; such information can be used, among other things, for error detection and syllabus design locally. Second, it can be used in tandem with other corpora, in order to carry out comparisons. Using the terminology in Tribble (2011), the *Hanken Corpus* may either be contrasted with an 'exemplar' corpus, representing expert output in the field of economics (i.e. published academic writing), or an 'analogue' corpus, a largely similar set of data which nevertheless differs from it in some respect (e.g. in terms of genre).

There are a number of options, as far as exemplar corpora are concerned. Most general corpora (including the *British National Corpus* (BNC) and the *Corpus of Contemporary American English* (COCA)) contain many texts that fit the bill. In our previous work, we have used a small, self-compiled reference corpus of research articles in economics (ECON-PUB) to explore differences between student and expert writing in this discipline. What constitutes a suitable analogue corpus for the *Hanken Corpus* also depends on the research question. For example, in order to explore how economics students' writing may differ from other kinds of student writing, it is useful to compare the *Hanken Corpus* with such corpora as BAWE and MICUSP, both of which contain texts representing a variety of disciplines and genres. When contrasted with essays specifically by native speakers, data from the *Hanken Corpus* also allow for the detection of learner's misuse of lexical items and phraseological patterns, using the framework of contrastive interlanguage analysis (e.g. Granger 2003, 541–542).

Economics, One Discipline or Many?

The classification of academic disciplines is known to be a difficult task, one in which consensus is not always reached (see e.g. Krishnamurthy and Kosem 2007, 363 and Hiltunen 2010, 11–16). The discipline of economics, which the *Hanken Corpus* attempts to represent, is a case in point: there are inevitable questions that we as corpus compilers have had to tackle, such as "is economics a 'hard' or 'soft' science, or both?", "how does *economics* relate to *business studies*?", "what are the decisive criteria for defining a discipline?", and finally, the question presented in the title of this section: "is economics one discipline or many?".

In a popular undergraduate textbook, Allsopp (1995, 5) defines economics as a discipline which is interested in human behaviour—in cooperation, competition, and in conflicts, all arising from decisions regarding resources—and as such it would be closer to human and soft sciences. However, the scrutiny of masses and individuals alike in economics does not, of course, rule out empirical approaches, i.e. both qualitative and quantitative methods are equally useful, and therefore the discipline also maintains characteristics of hard sciences.

Even though economics attests to the characteristics of both hard and soft sciences, this does not answer the questions as to the relationship of the term to business studies or other disciplines. On the one hand, economics is often used as an umbrella term to cover several subjects in the economic sciences, of which economics, paradoxically, is one, as is exemplified by the Hanken School of Economics syllabuses; on the other hand, other business schools use business studies as the top category, one that may itself comprise economics (cf. Corder 1990).

In most universities the primary aim of business studies degrees is the production of graduates to fulfil the needs of employers. However, Macfarlane (1997, 7–8, 19) argues that issuing a general definition of the concept of business studies is in fact difficult, in that it is a discipline that draws methodologically and culturally on both sciences and humanities, and thus is attested in different permutations from one business school to another, just as is the case with economics. Accordingly, his four-field model distinguishes between programmes that are *about* business or *for* business, which in addition can be either humanities- or science-based.

As this brief discussion has shown, the terms 'economics' and 'business studies' seem to overlap and can thus, in certain contexts, be used interchangeably, as is seen in the study programmes of various business schools. While economics can be seen as a single discipline, we treat it as an umbrella term for a variety of closely related areas of study. Faced with these multi-purpose, multi-level terms, we find our use of the term justified.

The informants of the *Hanken Corpus* are first and foremost students majoring in subdisciplines of economics. As can be seen in the list of subjects taught (cf. footnote 3 above), they require different combinations of approaches, both for and about business, hard and soft.

Compilation of the *Hanken Corpus*

Currently, the *Hanken Corpus* contains 142 texts and 516,000 words. In what follows we introduce the compilation, composition, and encoding of the corpus in detail.

Genres in the Hanken Corpus

Alsop and Nesi (2009, 72) mention two types of texts typically included in student writing corpora, namely general essays produced for a writing course, and discipline-specific student writing, produced for assessment in the students' own departments. Texts in the *Hanken Corpus* represent a middle point between these two poles. The current version contains end-of-term papers submitted for the completion of an academic writing course. As defined in the assignment, students are required to produce research reports on a minor study which they design and carry out. In spite of this, there is some variation between texts in terms of genre, caused by the students' main subject of study within the economic sciences. Using the classification in Moore and Morton (2005, 48–51), the majority of texts would represent the genre of 'research report', but there are also occasional papers which would perhaps be better categorized as 'feasibility studies' or 'literature reviews'. However, we decided not to make this distinction at the level of genre, since the assignment was the same in all cases.

Data Collection and Text Processing

The current data have been collected from a course called *Academic Writing for Business Studies*, which is an optional, advanced course offered by the Centre of Languages and Business Communication at Hanken. Most of the students taking the course are enrolled in Master's programmes, even though there are occasional undergraduate students in the teaching groups. The course runs for fourteen weeks (one full term). At the beginning of the course, students are made aware that their texts may be used for research purposes if they sign a form of consent; this they have done almost invariably. No remuneration has been offered to students in exchange for their consent. In addition to the form of consent, certain demographics have been collected for each writer: age, sex, linguistic background (mother tongue, years of English studies, other languages known), major subject, and phase of studies (undergraduate/graduate/postgraduate). The grade of the paper does not play a role in choosing the material for the corpus, even though we do record the grade. After linking the texts to the collected metadata, they have been anonymized.

The texts are fairly uniform in length (3,500–4,500 words) as defined in the assignment, even though a few papers extend beyond 5,000 words. Students submit a shorter first draft of their essay in the middle of the course, which is read and commented on by the instructor; however, the final version usually contains more text than the draft, thus the final version also contains text which has not previously been reviewed.

A few texts have been unusable due to file formatting issues; however, no texts have been discarded due to their academic quality: the *Hanken Corpus* represents student written production 'as is', as long as the grade is a bare pass or better. Not all parts of the text have been included in the corpus: any front and back matter, including tables of content, references, notes, and appendices have been excluded.[5] Also tables and graphs have been replaced by a place holder in the corpus texts. This decision was made partly to normalize the kind of text included, and partly to facilitate the tagging process.[6] The resulting text files retain paragraph and section division (with titles and subtitles), but not line division.

Files are named according to the author ID; hence the author with the ID 0050 has written texts 0050a, 0050b, 0050c, etc. File names thus do not indicate that there would be any relationship between the texts, only an affiliation with an author (see below on including drafts in the corpus). The text files are also split into sentences and POS-tagged, using CLAWS. The published version of

5 Both front matter (title, table of contents, abstract) and back matter (references, appendices) are parts of academic papers that differ from the actual content of the text stylistically and in the proportions of parts of speech, and therefore they are considered as text that should be excluded. The kinds of texts found in notes (mostly footnotes) varied between additional comments and Cambridge style citations. While the former type may have been valuable additions to an author's argumentation, the benefits of retaining that text would have been minor as compared to processing difficulties.

6 The problem with tables is that they contain almost solely numerical data and as such they would be ignored in linguistic studies in any case; also, tables add to the number of words significantly, and this skews frequencies and statistics.

the corpus will include different flavours, including plain text and XML; the finalized texts will be UTF-8 encoded.

XML Annotation

The *Hanken Corpus* is currently being XML-annotated according to the Text Encoding Initiative *P5: Guidelines for Electronic Text Encoding and Interchange* (TEI P5). The aim is to include all the relevant meta-information on the authors and the texts in the actual files themselves. XML annotation provides ease of use for corpus users, and it enables database-like filtering and searching without the need to go beyond the ubiquitous plain text format and regular text processing tools in the preparation of the files. The structure and content of the TEI-encoded files are explained below.

Each text file in the corpus contains one student text. The texts are made unique by their file names, but also by the metadata provided in the file headers. The *Hanken Corpus* XML-annotated text files present the metadata and structure of texts in a hierarchy, with several nodes under the root node.

The root element of the text files contains two sub-elements, a TEI-conformant header, and the text part that carries the metadata on the paper and the text of the submitted paper, respectively. As the texts in the *Hanken Corpus* were stripped of the front matter, back matter, and comments, the text element only shows the text body.

TEI Header Element in the *Hanken Corpus*

The TEI header includes the metadata on the text, organized in hierarchically nested nodes, so that there is never an overlap between two nodes on the same level of the hierarchy. The header holds hierarchically equal nodes 'File description', 'Encoding description', and 'Profile description', which are further divided into sub-nodes. Table 3.1 below shows the structure of the *Hanken Corpus* TEI header with its nested nodes, and explains what kind of information is included in each node.

XML-encoded Text Element in the *Hanken Corpus*

The 'Text' element in the *Hanken Corpus* only contains one nested node, 'Body'. The nodes which are usual in text representation in XML, 'Front' and 'Back' (for front and back matter, respectively), are not relevant for the *Hanken Corpus* files, as those parts have been edited out in the file preparation process.

'Body' is divided into 'p' and 's' elements, corresponding to paragraphs and sentences. At the moment, our XML annotation does not extend beyond the 's' element, even though the word elements are acknowledged in the POS tagging.

TABLE 3.1 *The* Hanken Corpus *TEI header*

TEI Header		
File description		
Title statement	The title of the paper in a nested title element as found in the submitted version of the text	
Publication statement	Information on the distributor of the *Hanken Corpus*, and about the conditions of use	
Notes statement	Any additional notes on the text not covered by other parts of the TEI header	
Source description	Free-format information about the texts of the corpus	
	Date	The date of submitting the paper, given in the format *yyyy-mm*
	Course title	The name of the course or module as indicated by the Hanken School of Economics study guide
	Course code	The code used for the course internally at the Hanken School of Economics; a free-format string of characters
	Genre	Identified by a descriptive label; often *research report.*
	Paper topic	The area of economics the paper represents, as identified by its author
	Text status	*Draft* or *final* version
	Related text	Information on the draft or final version of the same text: *none* or text ID as given in the TEI header of the related text, e.g. *0051*
	Grade	The grade range of the paper (if available) in the upper (*U*), middle (*M*), or lower third (*L*) of the accepted grades
	Number of words	The number of words of the text body as an integer
	Number of s	The number of sentence units in the body of text
	Number of p	The number of paragraph units in the body of text
	Referencing style	The referencing style used (e.g. *APA*, *Harvard*, or *Oxford*)

Encoding description	A note on the encoding standard used (*TEI P5*)
Profile description	
Participation description	
Person	
Author ID	The unique identification code for every writer, in four digits, e.g. *0050*
Gender	Male (*m*) or female (*f*)
Year of birth	A four digit integer, *yyyy*
First language	The first language of the writer, as reported by themselves
Other languages known	Other languages known by the writer, as reported by themselves
English studies, years	The number of years the student has studied English
Level	Undergraduate (studying for the degree of BSc in Economics, encoded as *UG*), graduate (for the degree of MSc in Economics, encoded *G*), or doctoral student (encoded *PG*)
Major subject	The author's major subject at the Hanken School of Economics; a descriptive label: *Accounting*; *Commercial Law*; *Economics*; *Entrepreneurship, Management, and Organization*; *Finance*; *Information Systems Science*; *Marketing*; *Management and Organization*; *Politics and Business*; *Statistics*; *Supply Chain Management and Corporate Geography*

Example TEI Header for the *Hanken Corpus*

The header described above is illustrated in example (1), with information from an actual corpus text (this example is complemented by the TEI element, which provides the text ID).

(1) TEI header for a *Hanken Corpus* file

```
<TEI id=“0003a” n=“version 1.0”>
<teiHeader>
  <fileDesc>
    <titleStmt>
      <title>Postponement strategy for global business: Sustaining
      competitiveness in uncertain market conditions. Case: Benetton
      Group</title>
    </titleStmt>
    <extent/>
    <publicationStmt>
      <distributor>Hanken Corpus of Academic Written English for
      Economics (Hanken Corpus) </distributor>
      <availability>
        <p>[forthcoming Information about distribution and
        availability]</p>
      </availability>
    </publicationStmt>
    <notesStmt>
      <note>[additional notes on the text not covered by other parts of the
      TEI header]</note>
    </notesStmt>
    <sourceDesc>
      <p n=“date”>2011-11</p>
      <p n=“course title”>Academic Writing for Business Studies</p>
      <p n=“course code”>5125</p>
      <p n=“genre”>Research report</p>
      <p n=“paper topic”>Supply chain management</p>
      <p n=“text status”>final</p>
      <p n=“related text”>none</p>
      <p n=“grade”>U</p>
      <p n=“number of words”>3841</p>
      <p n=“number of s-units”>205</p>
      <p n=“number of p-units”>21</p>
      <p n=“referencing style”>Harvard</p>
    </sourceDesc>
```

```
  </fileDesc>
  <encodingDesc>
    <p>TEI P5</p>
  </encodingDesc>
  <profileDesc>
    <particDesc>
      <person>
        <p n=“student ID”>0003</p>
        <p n=“gender”>f</p>
        <p n=“year of birth”>1989</p>
        <p n=“first language”>swe</p>
        <p n=“other languages known”>fin,eng,fre</p>
        <p n=“English studies, years”>12</p>
        <p n=“level”>UG</p>
        <p n=“major subject”>Supply Chain Management and Corporate
        Geography</p>
      </person>
    </particDesc>
  </profileDesc>
</teiHeader>
```

POS-Tagging

The *Hanken Corpus* has been part-of-speech (POS) tagged using the CLAWS tagger. POS tagging is a well-known type of annotation which makes it possible to carry out many types of analyses. With the help of grammatical tags, it is possible to disambiguate homograph words, count the rates of occurrence for different word classes, as well as to filter a given word's collocates based on word class (Manning and Schütze 1999, 154; McEnery et al. 2006, 34). Our specific aim has been to increase the usefulness of the *Hanken Corpus* for the study of phraseology, as POS tagging enables the retrieval of potential phraseological units with a good level of precision (see below, as well as Hiltunen and Mäkinen 2014).

The *Hanken Corpus* was tagged with the stand-alone version of CLAWS4 (Garside and Smith 1997), using the C7 tagset. Along with tagging, the software also performs automatic sentence-splitting. We employ the standard horizontal output, illustrated in (2), where a word is immediately followed by an underscore (_) and a grammatical tag.[7] The tagged sentence in its entirety is enclosed within sentence tags, to which we have added information about the

7 At present, grammatical tags are not integrated into the XML encoding, but the current format allows us to make full use of them in linguistic analysis.

number of the paragraph and the sentence within the paragraph; this useful convention is adopted from the BAWE corpus.

(2) CLAWS7-tagged sentence from the *Hanken Corpus*

> <s n="s2.5;p1.20"> The_AT word_NN1 strategy_NN1 is_VBZ used_VVN in_II management_NN1 ,_, accounting_VVG ,_, finance_VV0 ,_, marketing_NN1 and_CC personnel_NN2 policy_NN1 with_IW seemingly_RR different_JJ meanings_NN2 depending_II21 on_II22 the_AT discipline_NN1 that_CST uses_VVZ it_PPH1 ._. </s>

The passage quoted in (2) also illustrates another aspect of automatic annotation, namely accuracy. According to the tagger website, CLAWS is normally able to achieve 96–97% accuracy, although this obviously varies somewhat depending on the characteristics of the text.[8] This means that the tagged output inevitably contains errors. In (2), for instance, *accounting* has been mistakenly tagged as an *-ing* participle of a lexical verb, even though it is clearly a noun. The following word, *finance*, is also a noun, yet it has been tagged as a base form of a verb. While these errors are unfortunate, we do not currently have the resources to correct them individually. Despite these limitations, we have found grammatical annotation extremely useful.

The *Hanken Corpus* in Use: Future Plans

As already mentioned, a learner corpus can be contrasted with analogue and exemplar corpora. For this task we have used partly existing, partly self-compiled corpora, as described in this section, in which we will also report on our plans regarding corpus compilation and research.

BAWE, ECON-PUB, and First Studies

In a previous study using the *Hanken Corpus* we compared the use of formulas (as defined by Simpson-Vlach and Ellis 2010) in student texts by native (BAWE) and non-native speakers (*Hanken Corpus*), and by professional scholars (ECON-PUB) (Hiltunen and Mäkinen 2014). The BAWE corpus (Nesi 2008; see also Alsop and Nesi 2009), which has also been a point of reference in the compilation of the *Hanken Corpus*, is a large collection of 2,761 student texts produced for assessment in British universities in 2005–2007. The corpus was compiled to enable research into student writing across a wide range of genres

8 See further <http://ucrel.lancs.ac.uk/claws/>. The error rate of the tagging of the *Hanken Corpus* has not yet been determined.

and disciplines, including economics and business studies. We have used these two subsections of BAWE as a close analogue to the *Hanken Corpus*. Together, they contain 242 texts (93 by native speakers of English) and with a total word count of 540,000. The main 'genre families' represented in these subsections are case study, critique, and essay.

ECON-PUB was used as a reference point at the other end of the scholarly continuum, that is, published economics texts. ECON-PUB is a self-compiled expert corpus of economics research articles. The texts, 50 in all, are from five journals,[9] published between the years 2007–2011, and they comprise over 500,000 words. ECON-PUB corpus files were produced in the same way as the texts in the *Hanken Corpus*, as described above.

Our immediate findings show that both native and non-native students of economics seem to know how to produce formulaic language for an academic setting, but that they still lack knowledge of the multiple functions in which specific formulas can be used.[10] These findings have been useful in course development and in planning future research.

In the near future we will be looking into the development of student writing through the study of formulaic language in both earlier and later versions of the same text; that is, we will examine drafts and final versions of the texts. This will entail extending the *Hanken Corpus* to include the former type of texts.

Extending the Hanken Corpus

With the *Hanken Corpus*, our long-term goal is to create a resource that is maximally useful both as a teaching tool and as a resource for research. In our view, this involves building a corpus that is not limited to just one type of writing, but which contains several texts by the same student, produced at different stages in their studies. Using Schmied's (2007) terminology, such a corpus could be described as a 'parallel corpus', though not in the traditional sense of the term, which refers to a corpus containing versions of the same text in different languages. Instead, a corpus representing the written production of the same student at three different stages of their studies, and produced under different constraints.

We are currently complementing the existing corpus by adding the first draft of those final essays already included. In this way, we intend to enhance the usefulness of the corpus by allowing access to two kinds of texts, created before and after the first teacher intervention. By consulting these two versions,

9 The journals sampled are *Journal of Economic Literature*, *Journal of Financial Economics*, *Journal of Marketing*, *Quarterly Journal of Economics*, and *Strategic Management Journal*.

10 For example, the formula *according to the* has several functions in published economics articles, only one of which is attested in student data (Hiltunen and Mäkinen 2014, 365).

it is possible to assess how the students' writing evolves during the teaching term as a result of a teacher's formative assessment (Nesi and Gardner 2012, 26). Also, as all the informants in this corpus have produced a supervised end-of-term paper written for an academic communication course, one can also use the corpus to observe the persistence of learning outcomes by contrasting the end-of-term papers with later texts, e.g. Master's theses. While theses are, of course, different from other types of coursework in terms of length and the writing and editing process (Alsop and Nesi 2009, 74), they are nonetheless interesting from the point of view of monitoring a student's progress.

We have also sent out a call-for-papers to subject teachers at Hanken in order to obtain student texts submitted for the completion of economics courses. This will provide us with texts that have not been written on communication courses or supervised by language teachers. Contrasting these texts with the texts currently included in the *Hanken Corpus* will allow us to determine how the intervention of the language teacher influences the texts.

There are also plans to extend the XML annotation to the POS tagging: as mentioned above, our current XML encoding identified the sentence as the smallest unit of text, thus the current POS tags are structurally just parts of words for an XML query engine. In the future, our annotation will identify words according to TEI P5, and with this we will be able to nest information about the POS tag and the lemma of a word in the word element.

Conclusion

This chapter has provided information about the current stage of the *Hanken Corpus* project, and has established links with other, related research. It has also discussed the issues that have emerged over the course of the compilation work, has described solutions to them, and, finally, has outlined some of the ways of using the corpus in earlier and in forthcoming studies.

In research, the *Hanken Corpus* has considerable potential in comparative and contrastive studies, when juxtaposing student texts with published economics articles. The information gleaned from such studies will be directly applicable in the teaching of academic writing. The corpus can also be used as a reference corpus, by teachers and students alike, when searching for examples of typical student performance in an easily definable context. For such usage one does need an exemplar corpus (as was noted earlier) in order to form a picture of accepted or prevailing performance in academic writing.

The compilation project is still a work in progress, not least due to the fact that the *Hanken Corpus* is also a monitor corpus. Nevertheless, we will provide access to the corpus to any interested parties upon request, even before the official online publication.

Corpora

BAWE	*British Academic Written English Corpus*. 2008. Compiled by Hilary Nesi, Sheena Gardner, Paul Thompson, and Paul Wickens. http://www.coventry.ac.uk/bawe.
BNC	*British National Corpus*, version 3 (BNC XML Edition). 2007. Distributed by Oxford University Computing Services on behalf of the BNC Consortium. http://www.natcorp.ox.ac.uk/.
COCA	Davies, Mark. 2008–. *The Corpus of Contemporary American English: 520 million words, 1990-present*. http://corpus.byu.edu/coca/.
MICUSP	*Michigan Corpus of Upper-Level Student Papers. 2009*. Ann Arbor, MI: The Regents of the University of Michigan. http://micusp.elicorpora.info/.
Hanken Corpus	*Hanken Corpus of Academic Written English for Economics*. 2013–. Compiled by Martti Mäkinen, and Turo Hiltunen. https://github.com/dcrhc20/HankenCorpus/.

References

Allsopp, Vicky. 1995. *Understanding Economics*. Florence, KY: Routledge.

Alsop, Sian, and Hilary Nesi. 2009. "Issues in the Development of the British Academic Written English (BAWE) Corpus." *Corpora* 4/1: 71–83.

CLAWS Part-of-Speech Tagger for English. University Centre for Computer Corpus Research on Language (UCREL). Lancaster University. http://ucrel.lancs.ac.uk/claws/.

CLAWS7 Tagset. University Centre for Computer Corpus Research on Language (UCREL). Lancaster University. http://ucrel.lancs.ac.uk/claws7tags.html.

Corder, Colin. 1990. *Teaching Hard, Teaching Soft*. Aldershot: Gower.

Garside, Roger, and Nick Smith. 1997. "A Hybrid Grammatical Tagger: CLAWS4." In *Corpus Annotation: Linguistic Information from Computer Text Corpora*, edited by Roger Garside, Geoffrey Leech, and Tony McEnery, 102–21. London: Longman.

Gilquin, Gaëtanelle, Sylviane Granger, and Magali Paquot. 2007. "Learner Corpora: The Missing Link in EAP Pedagogy." *Journal of English for Academic Purposes* 6/4: 319–35.

Granger, Sylviane. 2003. "The International Corpus of Learner English: A New Resource for Foreign Language Learning and Teaching and Second Language Acquisition Research." *TESOL Quarterly* 37/3: 538–46.

Granger, Sylviane, and Diane Goossens. 2012. "Learner Corpora around the World." UCL Centre for English Corpus Linguistics. Accessed November 30, 2014. https://www.uclouvain.be/en-cecl-lcworld.html.

Hiltunen, Turo. 2010. *Grammar and Disciplinary Culture: A Corpus-Based Study*. Helsinki: Department of Modern Languages. http://urn.fi/URN:ISBN:978-952-10-6464-7.

Hiltunen, Turo, and Martti Mäkinen. 2014. "Formulaic Language in Economics Papers: Comparing Novice and Published Writing." In *Corpus Analysis for Descriptive and Pedagogic Purposes: ESP Perspectives*, edited by Maurizio Gotti, and Davide S. Giannoni, 347–68. Bern: Peter Lang.

Krishnamurthy, Ramesh, and Iztok Kosem. 2007. "Issues in Creating a Corpus for EAP Pedagogy and Research." *Journal of English for Academic Purposes* 6/4: 356–73.

Macfarlane, Bruce. 1997. "In Search of an Identity: Lecturer Perceptions of the Business Studies First Degree." *Journal of Vocational Education and Training* 49/1: 5–20.

Manning, Christopher, and Hinrich Schütze. 1999. *Foundations of Statistical Natural Language Processing*. Cambridge, MA: MIT Press.

Massey, Doreen. 1999. "Negotiating Disciplinary Boundaries." *Current Sociology* 47/5: 5–12.

McEnery, Tony, Richard Xiao, and Yukio Tono. 2006. *Corpus-Based Language Studies: An Advanced Resource Book*. London: Routledge.

Moore, Tim, and Janne Morton. 2005. "Dimensions of Difference: A Comparison of University Writing and IELTS Writing." *Journal of English for Academic Purposes* 4/1: 43–66.

Nesi, Hilary. 2008. "BAWE: An Introduction to a New Resource." In *Proceedings of the 8th Teaching and Language Corpora Conference*, edited by Ana Frankenberg-Garcia, Tawfiq Rkibi, Maria do Rosário Braga da Cruz, Ricardo Carvalho, Cristina Direito, and Diogo Santos-Rosa, 239–46. Lisbon: Instituto Superior de Línguas e Administração.

Nesi, Hilary, and Sheena Gardner. 2012. *Genres across Disciplines: Student Writing in Higher Education*. Cambridge: Cambridge University Press.

Pravec, Norma A. 2002. "Survey of Learner Corpora." *ICAME Journal* 26: 81–114.

Römer, Ute, and Matthew Brook O'Donnell. 2011. "From Student Hard Drive to Web Corpus (Part 1): The Design, Compilation and Genre Classification of the *Michigan Corpus of Upper-Level Student Papers* (MICUSP)." *Corpora* 6/2: 159–77.

Schmied, Josef. 2007. "The Chemnitz Corpus of Specialised and Popular Academic English." In *Towards Multimedia in Corpus Studies*, edited by Päivi Pahta, Irma Taavitsainen, Terttu Nevalainen, and Jukka Tyrkkö. Accessed October 19, 2014. http://www.helsinki.fi/varieng/series/volumes/02/index.html.

Simpson-Vlach, Rita, and Nick C. Ellis. 2010. "An Academic Formulas List: New Methods in Phraseology Research." *Applied Linguistics* 31/4: 487–512.

Thompson, Paul. 2006. "Assessing the Contribution of Corpora to EAP Practice." In *Motivation in Learning Language for Specific and Academic Purposes*, edited by Zoe Kantaridou, Iris Papadopoulou, and Ifigenia Mahili, CD-ROM. Macedonia: University of Macedonia.

Tribble, Christopher. 2011. "Revisiting Apprentice Texts: Using Lexical Bundles to Investigate Expert and Apprentice Performances in Academic Writing." In *A Taste for Corpora. In Honour of Sylviane Granger*, edited by Fanny Meunier, Sylvie De Cock, Gaëtanelle Gilquin, and Magali Paquot, 85–108. Amsterdam and Philadelphia: John Benjamins.

CHAPTER 4

Ongoing Changes and Advanced L2 Use of English: Evidence from New Corpus Resources

Mikko Laitinen

Abstract

This chapter approaches the global spread of English by charting new ways of studying the expansion and diversification of English to non-native contexts. The research builds on the idea that the ongoing globalization of English calls for new empirical approaches to contact, variability, and the interplay of the established varieties and new forms of English. It tests the methods of recent and ongoing grammatical change in investigating advanced non-native use. This methodology, combining historical linguistics and variationist sociolinguistics in a statistically sensitive corpus-based framework, has previously been used in the study of native varieties, but not in non-native contexts. The chapter first presents the compilation of a new multi-genre corpus of advanced English texts in non-instructional settings in Sweden and Finland, and then provides three case studies which examine how various lexico-grammatical variables currently undergoing change are adopted in non-native contexts. The results show substantial differences between traditional learner evidence and advanced non-native English in use, and indicate that the non-native evidence lands somewhere in-between the most advanced variety, standard American English, but ahead of other native and non-native inner and outer circle varieties. The findings therefore suggest that the processes and mechanisms of variability emerging in the globalization of English are more complex than previously thought.

Keywords

corpus compilation – ongoing grammatical change – English in the expanding circle – second language use – ANY/EACH/EVERY+TIME as conjunctions – -ONE and -BODY indefinite pronouns – modals and emergent modal auxiliaries

 | DOI 10.1163/9789004321342_005

Introduction

The study of ongoing grammatical change in the recent history of English is undoubtedly one of the success stories of English corpus linguistics. Various studies have provided information on "frequency drifts" in grammar (Leech et al. 2009, 270) and have shown not only how writers make use of (often) gradient grammatical resources, but also how the purpose of text and the discourse situation influence variability. Leech (2003), Mair and Leech (2006), Leech et al. (2009), and Leech (2013) have suggested various sociolinguistic processes that underlie these changes, namely grammaticalization, Americanization, and colloquialization. According to Mair (2008), the methodological basis in these studies lies in combining historical linguistics and variationist sociolinguistics, and their evidence is drawn from systematically-collected corpora, both small and large, that offer equidistant observation points at certain intervals. The various Brown siblings now offer observation points from 30-year intervals from the early twentieth century to the early 2000s and contain texts from a range of genre categories, thus providing tools for tracing diachronic and diatopic variability.[1] Much of the focus has so far been on the norm-providing main metropolitan varieties of English, but scholars have also turned to investigating how changes are adapted in use in the outer and expanding circles (Collins 2009, 2014; Filppula 2012; Laitinen and Levin 2016; Laitinen in press).

The objective of this chapter is to test the methods of ongoing grammatical change for investigating advanced L2 use of English in the expanding circle contexts. This approach is motivated by recent research on bridging the paradigm gap between second and foreign language use which has suggested that the increased globalization of English requires innovative empirical studies of how the established native varieties and the new Englishes overlap (Mukherjee and Hundt 2011). It is suggested here that such a theoretically-informed diachronic approach provides empirical insights into the spread of English in general (Mair 2013) and strengthens the role of corpus-based studies in understanding English in the expanding circle (cf. Schneider 2014). Such an approach implies seeing advanced L2 English as one stage in the long continuum of Englishes. Similar efforts have recently been suggested in the study of indigenized postcolonial Englishes, with Noël et al. (2014) arguing that the study of World Englishes should highlight the study of grammar from a diachronic perspective.

1 The British English 2006 (BE06) is the exception, offering an observation interval of 15 years. On the BE06 corpus, see Baker (2009).

The approach suggested in the present study is new, since previous research on learner English has focused on interlanguage phenomena and various levels of proficiency in language acquisition (Granger 2008). Similarly, in studies of interactions in English as a Lingua Franca (ELF) (Jenkins et al. 2011; Seidlhofer 2011; Mauranen 2012), time and processes of change have often been overshadowed by a focus on meaning making.[2] Moreover, the approach here could also provide insights into understanding ongoing change in English in general. A case in point is colloquialization, the gradual spread of speech-like characteristics to written genres, which is often cited as the driving force of recent change (Leech et al. 2009, 239–249). An analogy could be made to learner varieties which, according to Aijmer (2002, 55), exhibit "register interference" and show overrepresentation of speech-like characteristics. It suggests that ongoing grammatical change involving speech-like characteristics is accelerated by speakers/writers in today's globalized linguistic marketplace (cf. Cheshire et al. 2011 on language change in unguided second language acquisition in urban multi-ethnolects).

The main argument here concerns corpus resources and the globalization of English. As pointed out by Hundt and Vogel (2011, 160), larger learner "corpora capturing different levels of proficiency would provide more insight" into the global spread of English. My argument is that in addition to size, new resources should be broad in the scope of texts represented. Since the existing learner corpora only cover one genre, their usability in diachronic analyses is limited. To carry out systematic studies on advanced L2 English, there is a need for new corpus materials, these designed so that they make textual comparisons with the existing native English corpora possible (cf. Rissanen 2008 on the general principles of evidence-based historical linguistics), and extending the textual coverage from learner essays to texts outside school settings.

The following section describes the ongoing multi-genre corpus collection which concentrates on English texts in two Nordic countries, Sweden and Finland. Previous research has shown that the role of English has changed considerably in these two countries (Leppänen et al. 2011; Bolton and Meierkord 2013), and they are used as a case for developing new corpus resources and for testing how advanced L2 English could be understood through diachronic linguistics. Then I present three case studies of ongoing change that involve grammaticalization, and which have been selected since they contain variables with varying discourse frequencies (cf. the frequency benchmarks in Biber et al. 1999, 38–40). The first one deals with low-frequency items of

2 The fact that historical linguistics plays a role here means answering Seidlhofer's (2011, xi) call for historical linguists to put the present-day ELF in a diachronic perspective.

adverbial conjunctive use of ANY/EACH/EVERY+TIME, whose recent history has been described in Brinton (2007). The second concerns mid-frequency items of human compound indefinite pronouns, -ONE/-BODY (D'Arcy et al. 2013; Laitinen forthcoming). The third describes changes in modal auxiliary verbs (Leech 2003, 2013) and focuses on broad quantitative patterns of modals and emergent modals in advanced L2 data.

The case studies first establish recent developments and then provide new evidence of variability in advanced L2 English. The research question here addresses the role of corpus data from the expanding circle contexts. The first two case studies investigate what types of quantitative evidence can be gained using the learner essays in the *International Corpus of Learner English* (ICLE), i.e. traditional learner corpus data, and then look at how this evidence could be amended by multi-genre corpus evidence from non-instructional environments. The third investigates the diachronic fortunes of modals by comparing spoken and written advanced L2 English data with the results from the inner and outer circles as presented in Collins (2009, 286) and Leech (2013).

Towards New Corpus Resources

The focus on advanced L2 English here stems from insights in ELF research. Its key feature, distinguishing it from Second Language Acquisition, is not "seeing learners as deficient communicators who struggle with difficulties" (Mauranen 2012, 5), but rather as speakers who make use of the various linguistic resources for their own communicative purposes and whose divergent forms are not seen as deficiencies but rather as adaptations of variability (Seidlhofer 2011, 18; Mauranen 2012, 246). This chapter focuses on exploring quantitative patterns rather than establishing certain language forms as varieties (i.e. the English as a Second Language focus) or finding deficiencies in use (i.e. learner research).

On the methodological level, this study aims not merely at repeating what has been done in the study of native varieties, but also at developing the empirical basis for investigating advanced L2 grammar from the perspective of historical linguistics. According to Leech et al. (2009, 24–31), "short-term diachronic comparable corpus linguistics" is based on corpora that cover a comparable set of genres. The various Brown corpora consist of 15 genres, and even though this division was not originally aimed at diachronic investigations, it has been used in studying recent changes in the core varieties. As for the expanding circle, the ICLE consists of one genre of argumentative and literature essays by advanced learners of English (Granger 2008). Since it is designed for interlanguage research, this one-genre approach has turned out to be sufficient. The two ELF corpora, VOICE (*Vienna-Oxford International Corpus of English*) and ELFA (*English as a Lingua Franca in Academic Settings*), contain material from spoken interactions from institutional and formal contexts, and the VOICE corpus contains non-scripted face-to-face interactions in which English is used "as a common means of communication among speakers from different first-language backgrounds" (Seidlhofer 2011, 23). The interactions represent a range of speech events, such as interviews, press conference, service encounters, and workshop discussions (Seidlhofer 2011, 23–24; for ELFA, see Mauranen 2012, 73–74).

Space does not allow for a comprehensive analysis of these resources, but suffice it to say that since the existing expanding circle corpora have by and large been designed for synchronic studies, new multi-genre corpus resources are needed. Corpora containing a wide range of texts on the written-spoken continuum would enable real time studies of how grammatical structures undergoing changes are adapted in use. Textual variation enables determining direction of change and examining to what extent the various sociolinguistic processes in recent changes continue in the expanding circle.

The new corpus sources could complement the existing sources of evidence and include written texts other than purely argumentative learner essays, as in ICLE, and should focus primarily on written texts, as the existing ELF corpora contain a variety of spoken situations. It is, however, equally clear that there is no need to reinvent the wheel in corpus design, since the existing inner and outer circle corpora, which enable diachronic approaches, offer a model that could be modified for contexts in which English texts appear not only in print (such as student theses), but also in various mediated online genres, such as personal and professional blogs, fan fiction, micro-blog (Twitter) messages, and other web-based genres.

Our corpus building work is carried out on the following broad principles:

(a) these corpus materials should enable quantitative comparisons with the existing corpora from which much of the evidence of the recent history of English is drawn, and
(b) their corpus design should enable diachronic approaches of exploring how recent and ongoing changes are adapted in use;
(c) the new corpus resources should take into account the diversity of English uses in the two countries used as a case;
(d) even though Sweden and Finland are used as a testing ground, the sampling frame should ideally be replicated elsewhere where the role of English is changing.

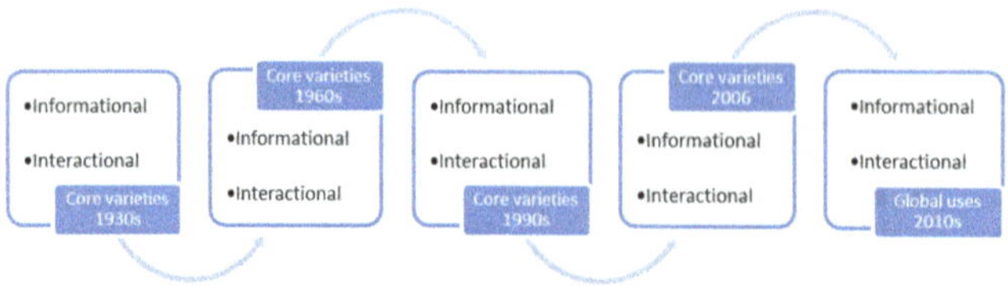

FIGURE 4.1 *Tracing recent and ongoing grammatical changes in advanced L2 use of English.*

The corpora which we are currently compiling are synchronic, covering texts from 2009–2015, but, similarly to Collins (2009), it is assumed that the patterns of variability in the channels (spoken-written) and genre, when compared with other corpora, could also be used to draw diachronic conclusions. It goes without saying that ideally such corpora could allow us to trace how long-term processes of change are reflected in advanced L2 use.[3] Figure 4.1 visualizes what is meant by the diachronic approach, tracing how ongoing change is adapted to advanced L2 English.

The case studies below are based on two corpora that are being compiled at Linnaeus University in Sweden. Their working titles are the *Corpus of English in Sweden* (SWE-CE) and the *Corpus of English in Finland* (FIN-CE). The objective is that they should cover a representative sample of English use in non-instructional environments in these two countries. It is important to highlight the notion of use, since learner texts from both countries are included in the ICLE, and the *Uppsala Learner English Corpus* consists of Swedish high school student writing collected between 1999 and 2001 (Johansson and Geisler 2009). In addition to being countries in which the role and nature of English is shifting, Sweden and Finland also provide an interesting testing ground because the main languages of these two countries, i.e. Swedish and Finnish, are typologically different.

The corpus design builds on the idea that the corpora will be small and tidy (Hundt and Leech 2012); our target is one million words per corpus. If the Brown siblings were collected through a randomized stratified sampling from publication catalogues of specific time frames, the collection process of these two corpora could be best described as opportunistic sampling, since the domains where English is used need to be charted through ethnographic work. We aim for tidy collections, meaning that we can identify all the informants

3 Examples of such long-term processes include variability in progressive structures, which involve both token and type level changes (Laitinen and Levin 2016), changes in passive structures, and frequency increases in non-finite structures such as FOR+NP+TO-infinitives (Laitinen 2011).

TABLE 4.1 *The sampling frame of texts used in the collection of* FIN/SWE-CE

	1. Business/civil administration	**2. Education**	**3. Media**	**4. Personal globalization**
Dimension 1 (information density vs. interactional content)	(Annual results publications) (Annual results presentations) (Spoken)	Academic theses		
			Organizational blogs	Professional blogs
	(Municipal webpages)		Online newspapers	
		Administrative e-mails		
	(Tourism discourse)			(Fiction)
			(Media interviews) (Spoken)	Personal blogs
		(Student interaction) (Spoken)		Micro blogs, tweets (Fan fiction)
				(Face-to-face interviews) (Spoken)

and collect a set of sociolinguistic background information, and can have knowledge of the extent to which the materials have been subjected to normative language checking by professional editors/translators and native speakers. Preference is given to texts that are not edited, but our working hypothesis is that the more informationally-oriented (see Table 4.1 above) a text is, the more likely it is to have undergone language checking. Materials edited by native speakers are excluded.

The textual domains are visualized in Table 4.1. These domains are adapted from Appadurai's (1996, 33–36) discussion of the "five dimensions of global flows" of social and cultural landscape through which globalization could be observed. They are used as a tool in operationalizing the material collection, and his five "scapes"[4] have been simplified into four broad domains: (1) business and civil administration, (2) education, (3) media, and (4) personal

4 These are: (a) ethnoscapes, (b) technoscapes, (c) financescapes, (d) ideoscapes, and (e) mediascapes.

globalization. On the vertical axis, the sampling frame makes use of Biber's (1988, 104–108) multi-dimensional analysis of textual variation, and we use dimension 1 as the basis for placing various texts in the matrix. This dimension refers to information density and exact content in contrast to interactional and generalized content. At this stage of the compilation, it is used as a heuristic tool in the material collection and is not yet empirically validated.

Table 4.1 shows the corpus design in late 2014, and the bracketed types are materials which we know exist, but which are not yet included in the corpus. The corpus design focuses primarily on written texts (see the discussion on the existing ELF corpora above); yet, we envisage that in some domains, such as media, select spoken materials are easily accessible and could be included in the corpus in the future.

The two corpora are currently in compilation, and the following case studies are based on a sample of 1,050,649 words of texts from three genres with varying levels of formality. They are (a) informationally dense academic prose texts (i.e. student theses from disciplines other than language studies), available through public databases: 456,510 running words; (b) news texts written by journalists for online news platforms; we have confirmed with the authors that these news texts have not undergone native speaker intervention (164,271 words);[5] and (c) 429,868 words of personal/professional blogs (freely available in the blogosphere) that could be expected to reflect colloquialization and represent spoken-like written texts (cf. Sand 2013).

New Corpus Evidence from Advanced L2 English

Towards ANY/EACH/EVERY+TIME as Conjunctions

The first study focuses on conjunctive uses of ANY/EACH/EVERY+TIME. Brinton (2007) shows that this structure is undergoing change: conjunctive uses, roughly paraphrasable by WHENEVER, as in (1)–(3), have gradually increased their share, whereas adverbial uses[6] (4)–(6) are decreasing.

(1) "[...] It's like somebody's always trying to get you." *Any time* he wants, Davis can get a minimum estimate of the number of Hoosiers [...] (COHA, 2008, MAG)

5 News texts in general are described as agile and economic by Hundt and Mair (1999).

6 Including both prepositional uses and uses as nominal complements that are fixed collocates to verbs such as GIVE and HAVE.

(2) [...] patient's condition is critical but not hopeless. IT COMES as a shock *each time* you hear the phrase. (COHA, 1958, MAG)
(3) It might be tempting to update your drivers *every time* a new version becomes available [...] (COHA, 2002, NF)
(4) You can get me *anytime* on my cell phone, here's the number. (COHA, 2003, NF)
(5) The charges on my evening calls were only somewhat better than AT & T's,; saving me 6 cents on an 8-minute call to California—not enough to warrant my dialing five extra digits *each time.* (COHA, 1997, NEWS)
(6) It was a point he got to with every one of the leaders and he meant it *every time.* (COHA, 1991, MAG)

The adverbial uses are "historically prior to the conjunctive use" for all three items (Brinton 2007, 78). EVERY TIME, which dates back to Middle English, begins to increase in the sixteenth century and forms the majority in Present-day English (PDE). EACH TIME develops in the late seventeenth century, and the variable is equally split today. Finally, ANY TIME appears in early/mid-nineteenth century American English (AmE), and its conjunctive uses are in the minority in PDE.

Figure 4.2, supporting Brinton's (2007) primarily qualitative observations, shows quantitative evidence from COHA. It provides evidence from the observation points in roughly 50-year intervals. The search string consisted of the following items (the bracketed figures show the raw counts):[7] ANY TIME, ANYTIME (2,421 in total), EACH TIME, EACHTIME (1,041), EVERY TIME, EVERYTIME (2,221). Since the [cs] tag (i.e. subordinating conjunction in the CLAWS7 tagset) used with the items did not result in any hits, the raw results were pruned to extract the relevant cases. The relevant cases conform to the definition used by Brinton (2007), i.e. operating over a (typically finite) clause, having no main syntactic function, and having a fixed left-margin position in the clause. In addition, they express temporal contingency and/or simultaneity overlap in interclausal relations (Kortmann 1997, 80–81).

As shown in Figure 4.2, the three items display distinct trajectories in which the conjunctive senses increase at the expense of adverbial adjuncts. The conjunctive senses of EVERY+TIME undergo rapid growth which is nearing completion in the twentieth century. Similarly, EACH+TIME increases heavily so that the incoming uses account for just over half of the cases in PDE. In turn,

7 The univerbated spellings account for less than 10% of the cases for ANY+TIME, are rare with EVERY+TIME, and do not exist for EACH+TIME.

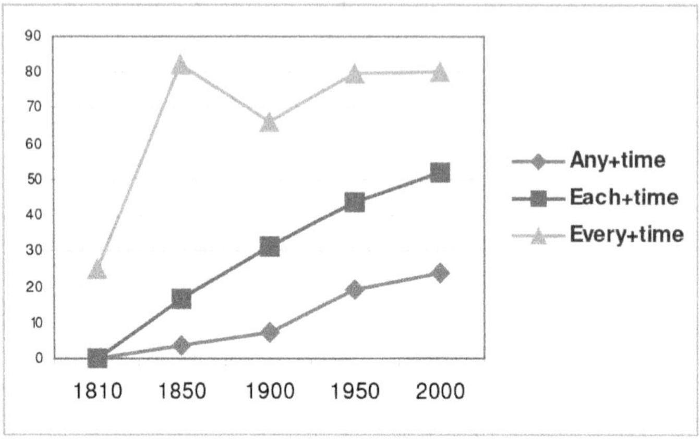

FIGURE 4.2 *The conjunctive senses of* ANY/EACH/EVERY+TIME *in* COHA (*N*=2,566).

the developments in ANY+TIME are slower than in the other two, yet its diachronic path is similar.

This structure offers an interesting case study for tracing change in advanced L2 English. It is unarguable that the change is ongoing, and the new uses are brought about by grammaticalization whereby complex prepositional phrases develop into conjunctions (Brinton 2007). The origins of the conjuctive uses are at the informal end of communication, as they appear first in fictional dialogues (colloquialization).

In what follows, the results first illustrate the developments in two native varieties in the second half of the twentieth century, and then illustrate in detail the differences and similarities between ICLE and the new multi-genre corpus materials. Figure 4.3 visualizes the share of the incoming adverbial conjunctive variant in (a) six Brown corpora (LOB, Brown, F-LOB, Frown, BE06, and AE06) and examines evidence drawn from (b) ICLE and (c) FIN/SWE-CE. It shows, unexpectedly, that the share of the conjunctives gradually increases in AmE and British English (BrE). The total share of the conjunctive use in the Freiburg versions increases to around 60%, and the increase continues in the 2006 versions. The figure in the 2000s is slightly higher than the total of the incoming conjunctive use in the 2000s subcorpus in COHA, in which it is 56% (1,312 out of 2,355).[8]

8 The absolute figures for the variant forms are the following: AmE (Brown, Frown, AE06): 76; BrE (LOB, F-LOB, BE06): 89; LearnerE (ICLE): 66; Advanced L2E (FIN/SWE-CE): 41.

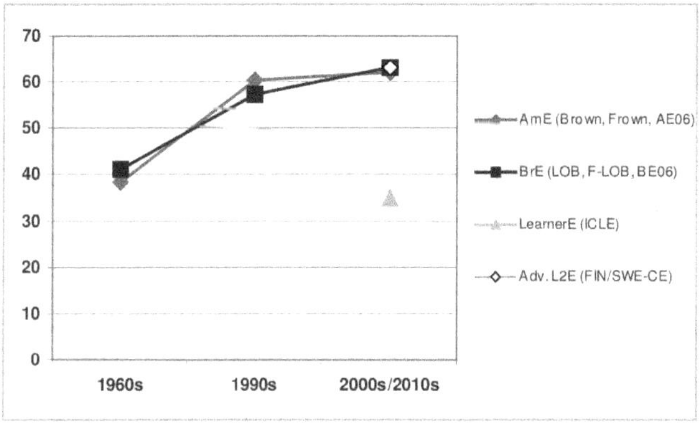

FIGURE 4.3 *The share of the incoming conjunctive variant in eight corpora (N=272).*

In ICLE, the proportions of the incoming variant forms are considerably lower (35%) than in the two native varieties and also in the advanced L2 material. The differences between the absolute figures in ICLE and BE06/AE06 are statistically significant at 1% level (contingency table test, chi-square values range between 5.771 and 15.235, df=1). Moreover, the share of the incoming conjunctives in the FIN/SWE-CE material clearly exceeds that of ICLE, and the proportions are comparable to those in the two metropolitan varieties. The differences between ICLE and FIN/SWE-CE are statistically significant (chi-square value 15.235, $p<0.001$, df=1).

The conclusions at this stage are mixed and call for further analysis. It should be pointed out that the corpora are roughly of the same size, with the exception of ICLE.[9] On the one hand, learner corpus texts clearly trace the two native varieties. It is perhaps fair to say that they lag behind the two main metropolitan varieties by one or two generations.[10] Considering the register interference mentioned in the introduction, this is unexpected because the incoming variable (i.e. the conjunctive sense) has colloquial origins, and the ICLE data in general tend to contain speech-like characteristics (Granger and Rayson 1998). A more likely explanation stems from the nature of the variable which has emerged through grammaticalization. Hundt and Vogel (2011, 160),

9 The decision to use the ICLE in its entirety (c. 2.7 million words) is based on the fact that the samples from various countries are small (cf. Hundt and Vogel 2011) and thus not suitable for analysing low-frequency variables. The Brown siblings are roughly one million words; FIN/SWE-CE results are based on 1,050,649 words.

10 What brings about this diachronic difference is unknown, and calls for further analysis.

exploring the uses of the progressive, point out that learners' attention in classroom settings tends to be on "grammaticality issues", and they are therefore less likely to stretch lexico-grammatical structures to new contexts and adopt newly-grammaticalized forms. On the other hand, the written FIN/SWE-CE evidence indicates that advanced L2 users of English in non-instructional settings participate in this change, and that the share of the incoming sense is even with the BE06 and AE06 results. The differences here are not statistically significant.

The tendencies observed in this one variable are clear, as the multi-genre FIN/SWE-CE material is closer to the edited materials in BE06 and AE06 than the learner essays in ICLE. The following examples illustrate some of the conjunctive uses from FIN/SWE-CE.

(7) I am a bit concerned, Jimmie Åkesson, because *each time* I attend the Committee of EU-Affairs to discuss measures of international co-operation in order to prevent extremism, Sweden Democrats are per definition against. (SWE-CE, new media, 2011)

(8) P1 thought that *every time* a contracting manager goes to a new destination he/she must sell his/her company, the services <proper name> provides [...] (FIN-CE, education, 2011)

As noted above, the objective of this corpus project is to build resources that allow for the study of advanced L2 English as one stage in the continuum of Englishes. This means tracing variability not only in one genre, such as learner essays, but in a range of texts, covering the continuum of discourse situations.

Figure 4.4 below, showing the shares of the incoming conjunctive sense, illustrates the results (2000/2010s) divided into four broad genres: (1) academic texts (J in the 2006 versions of the Brown family and the education texts in FIN/SWE-CE); (2) non-fiction texts (texts D-H in the 2006 versions of the Brown family and the new media texts in FIN/SWE-CE); (3) news texts (A-C in Brown and the news section in FIN/SWE-CE); and (4) fictional texts (K-R) which do not have a corresponding category in the expanding circle corpus.[11]

The absolute numbers are obviously low, and without quantitative evidence from mid-/high-frequency variables it is wise to exercise caution in interpreting the results, but the data nevertheless enable a close focus on textual variability, in particular on the expanding circle, beyond traditional learner essays. The pattern is clear, since the shares for the incoming variant are greater in non-fiction and news than in academic texts. If one relied only on

11 The figure for connective uses in the academic texts in BE06 is zero.

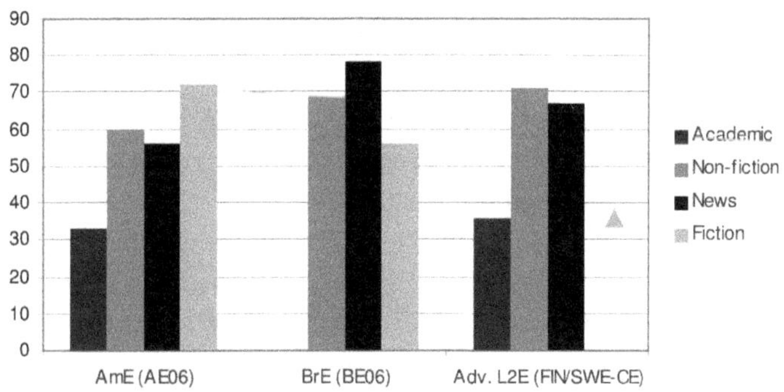

FIGURE 4.4 *The share of the incoming variant form divided into genres (N=181).*

the ICLE evidence (indicated with a triangle), the view in variability would be substantially narrower. It is, however, important to note that the formal argumentative essays in ICLE actually conform to the broad pattern in which the share of the conjunctive sense is lower in formal texts than in other genres.

Ongoing Change in Compound Indefinite Pronouns -ONE and -BODY

This section focuses on compound indefinite pronouns of personal reference which consist of two morphemes, a set of determiners (EVERY, ANY, SOME, NO) and two nominal elements, -ONE and -BODY. According to Raumolin-Brunberg and Kahlas-Tarkka (1997, 75), the nominal elements have been variable since the sixteenth century.[12] They are typically seen to be in free variation, but -ONE is held to be more elegant, yet these stylistic differences are not subject to metalinguistic comments in PDE (D'Arcy et al. 2013) nor were they commented upon in early prescriptive grammars (Laitinen forthcoming). Corpus evidence shows that -ONE is more frequent in written registers than -BODY, which is favoured in conversation and in AmE (Biber et al. 1999, 352–353).

As in the case of ANY/EACH/EVERY+TIME as conjunctions, the variable makes an interesting case study for tracing variability in advanced L2 English. Firstly, the variable characterizes involved style (Biber 1988, 102) and should therefore be overrepresented in traditional learner essays (cf. register interference). Secondly, D'Arcy et al. (2013) show that the indefinites are undergoing

12 The variable in Early Modern English consisted of not only -ONE/-BODY but also of the -MAN indefinites, which disappeared by the early eighteenth century except in set phrases, and the simple forms (see Laitinen forthcoming on the sociolinguistic embedding in this process).

change in progress in which the more formal variant -ONE is gradually ousting -BODY. Their apparent time dialect evidence from contemporary British dialects shows sociolinguistic differences in which younger speakers prefer -ONE at statistically significant levels, and the results from the *British National Corpus* (BNC) indicate clear differences between newspaper data and spoken material. The process is constrained by the four determiners, and NO favours -BODY more than the other three. Thirdly, D'Arcy et al.'s (2013) data illustrate substantial differences between the various native varieties around the world. New Zealand English (NZE) shows greater use of -ONE than BrE, which is not as advanced as Canadian English, but is clearly more advanced than AmE. They suggest that "one possible interpretation of this difference is that NZE is more innovative than the other varieties" investigated (2013, 304).

These previous results indicate that the spread of English in the modern period has increased variability, and I investigate the variant proportions in the same set of corpora as in the previous case study to determine whether the two non-native corpora differ from each other, and whether advanced L2 writers polarize the change further. The variable includes only personal references of the compound indefinites in which -ONE/-BODY can be used interchangeably, and I have manually excluded determiner+head sequences, e.g. NO ONE ANSWER, -ONE post-modified by OF-phrases, and other irrelevant instances, such as -BODY compounds in the sense of *every human body* or *That person was a nobody*.

Figure 4.5 shows the proportions of -ONE in these corpora, and illustrates a recent increase of -ONE in both AmE and BrE, but this increase is more considerable in AmE. The log-likelihood (LL) values suggest that the share of -ONE in the 1960s corpora is lower than in the 2006 corpora, and this difference is statistically highly significant at 0.01% level. The LL values, 47.81 in AmE and 46.71 in BrE, exceed the critical value of 15.13.[13] As for the differences in the entire variable, a contingency table test suggests that the recent change has been more considerable in AmE (chi-square value 67.07, p<0.001) than in BrE, in which the chi-square value falls short of the critical value at 5% level (3.83). Therefore, in terms of ongoing change, an increase of -ONE takes place in both varieties, but is coupled with a decrease of -BODY in AmE, though not in BrE.

Figure 4.5 also shows the proportions in ICLE and in FIN/SWE-CE and suggests considerable quantitative differences between these two corpora. These differences are similar to those presented above for ANY/EACH/EVERY+TIME as conjunctions, since the advanced L2 texts collected from non-instructional

13 The LL calculator used is Paul Rayson's tool at the UCREL website <http://ucrel.lancs.ac.uk/llwizard.html>.

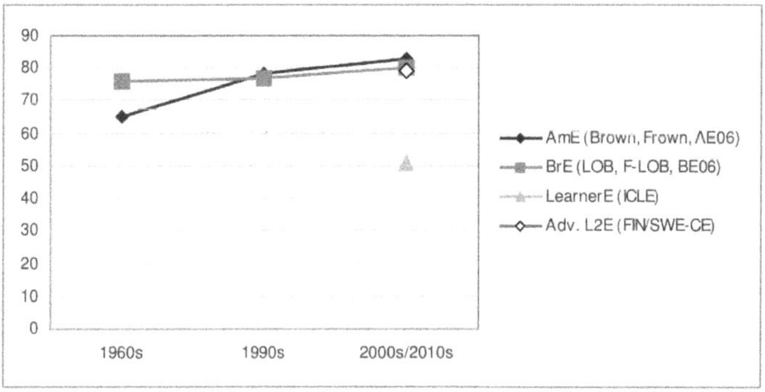

FIGURE 4.5 *The share of the incoming variant -ONE in eight corpora (N=9,874).*

settings (FIN/SWE-CE) are more similar to the two metropolitan varieties than those of ICLE. In FIN/SWE-CE, the proportion of -ONE is 79% (633/797), on par with the two native varieties, whereas the variable is equally split in ICLE (-ONE accounts for 51% of the cases; 2,138/4,225). The differences are statistically highly significant (chi-square value 57.960, p<0.001).

These findings provide further evidence that, not surprisingly, traditional learner data exhibit overrepresentation of speech-like characteristics, but more importantly for the purposes of this chapter, similar overrepresentation is not seen in the advanced L2 texts from non-instructional settings. This overrepresentation is also observable in the normalized frequencies of the compound indefinites. In the two metropolitan varieties, they increase 40% in BrE (from 623 per million words to 873 per million words) and 19% in AmE (690 to 810 per million words). As a characteristic of involved speech style, there is a considerable overuse in ICLE (1,608 per million words), but the figure in FIN/SWE-CE is similar to that of the Brown siblings (759 per million words) (genre differences are discussed below).

As shown by D'Arcy et al. (2013), -ONE and -BODY exhibit variability depending on the internal constraint of the determiner forms. Figure 4.6 illustrates a snapshot of the situation in 2000s/2010s and shows the share of -ONE correlated with the four determiners in BE06 and AE06 and in the two non-native corpora. The data provide another angle on the overall results, showing that the patterns are highly similar in three of the four corpora. In BE06/AE06 and in FIN/SWE-CE, two determiners (ANY, SOME) attract over 85–90% share of -ONE, and the share for EVERY is slightly lower (c. 80%), and the distribution is more variable with the negative NO, with the proportions of -ONE ranging from 64% in BrE to 75% in AmE, with FIN/SWE-CE in the middle at 66%. More importantly, none of these differences are statistically significant when the variable is tested with a contingency table test.

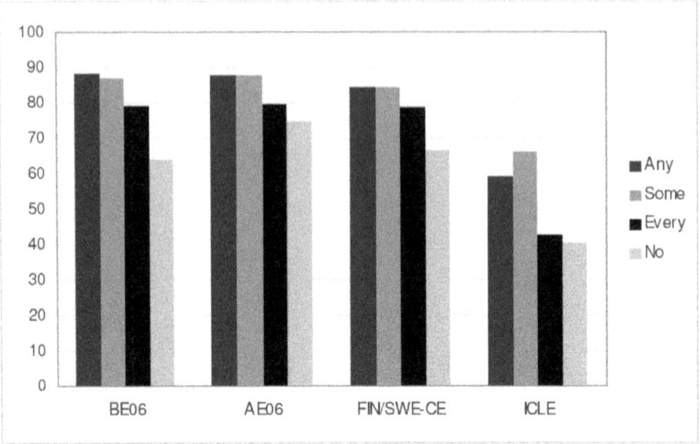

FIGURE 4.6 *The share of the incoming variant -ONE in four PDE corpora correlated with the determiners (N=6,976).*

The evidence from ICLE is different, as the incoming -ONE occurs most often with SOME and ANY, similarly to the three other corpora, but the shares are naturally lower. The differences are accentuated with EVERY and NO, where the shares drop to below 50%. A contingency table test shows that the differences between the distributions between the incoming -ONE in traditional learner data, on the one hand, and in the 2006 versions of Brown corpora and in FIN/SWE-CE, on the other, are highly significant (chi-square values range between 29.314 and 137.545, $p<0.001$).

As shown above, one of the advantages of the multi-genre corpus design of FIN/SWE-CE is that it enables us to look into genre differences in advanced L2 English, which thus far has not been possible on a large scale when using learner corpus evidence. Recall that in ICLE the proportion of the incoming -ONE is 51% (cf. Figure 4.5 above). Table 4.2 sets out the order of genres according to their prevalence of -ONE.

Table 4.2 shows that in BE06 and AE06 the share of -ONE is highest in the learned subsection (J). There are a few -BODY forms in this subsection, but they come from direct quotes in spoken interviews and are excluded here. For instance, J54 in BE06 is an extract from a study on social and welfare policies based on interview material, and similarly, in AE06, the majority of the excluded -BODY forms come from J26, an oral history of the South African AIDS epidemic. The next highest shares occur in News (A-C), Fiction (K-R), and general non-fictional prose (D-H). In FIN/SWE-CE, the order is similar, with the highest share in news (88%; 72/82), followed by academic texts, from which all direct quotes were removed (84%; 179/212), and the new media texts, in which the share is the lowest (76%; 382/503).

TABLE 4.2 *The share of the incoming -ONE according to genre in four corpora*

Corpus					
BE06	Learned (100%)	News (84%)	Fiction (81%)	Non-fiction (77%)	
AE06	Learned (100%)	Fiction (84%)	News (83%)	Non-fiction (80%)	
FIN/SWE-CE		News (88%)	Acad. (84%)	New media (76%)	
ICLE					Learner essays (51%)

The conclusion at this stage adds to the evidence presented in the previous case study. The results of this mid-frequency variable show that advanced L2 data from non-instructional settings show few traces of overrepresentation of speech-like characteristics, and the patterns observed in Figures 4.5 and 4.6 and Table 4.2 are similar in three out of the four corpora. These quantitative differences between FIN/SWE-CE and the traditional learner essays further strengthen the idea that there are differences in the two types of non-native material. It is worth noting that these quantitative differences are visible on two levels. Firstly, in the internal constraint of the determiner forms, the two metropolitan varieties and the advanced L2 evidence exhibit similar patterns of variability, which are different from ICLE at statistically significant levels. Secondly, the genre differences in Table 4.2 suggest that adding evidence of textual variation from learner contexts provides a more detailed picture of how this ongoing change is adapted in advanced L2 English use.

Ongoing Changes in Core Modals and Emergent Modals

My final case study is concerned with the ongoing changes in core and emergent modals, which have been investigated extensively in various inner circle Englishes and increasingly also in (non-)native outer circle varieties (Leech 2003, 2011, 2013; Collins 2009; Noël et al. 2014). Previous studies have identified two general quantitative trends. On the one hand, Leech (2013) has shown that core modals have decreased throughout the twentieth century, and this decrease is also visible in the 2006 versions of the Brown family of corpora. This process is more marked in AmE than in BrE, as the former is "roughly one generation in advance of the British decline, which is following in its wake" (Leech 2013, 100). On the other, emergent modals, verbal idioms which share semantic and syntactic similarities with modal auxiliaries, have increased significantly. Their increase, however, is not as fast as the decrease in the core modals, and Leech (2013) hints at "modality deficit" in the present-day core native varieties. These two developments are far from straightforward, and the core modals form three distinct groups in which the high-frequency items (WILL, WOULD, CAN) have been least subject to the drop; the mid-frequency forms have decreased slightly, whereas the least frequent ones (SHALL, NEED, OUGHT) have been subject to a heavy decrease. This decline is also supported by evidence from COHA (Leech 2013). Results from spoken language suggest that these developments are changes from below, as both the decline and the increase are steeper in spoken than in written corpora. As for possible causes, Leech (2013) points out that these changes have most likely been brought about by the colloquialization of genres and the grammaticalization of the various emergent modals. Additionally, various outer circle varieties have also been investigated, and a recent special issue (Noël et al. 2014) presents four case studies of inner and outer circle varieties. The results in Collins (2009, 2014) show that Australian English (AusE) evolves in the same direction as the inner core varieties, since it "behaves most like AmE, while BrE and NZE are the most 'conservative'" (2009, 285). He also suggests that AusE speakers disfavour modals to a greater extent but do not adopt the emergent modals as eagerly, which, he explains, is brought about by their endonormative independence.

This case study tests the extent to which the same methodology sheds light on language variability in the expanding circle contexts. As in the two previous sections, the material consists of FIN/SWE-CE, but instead of ICLE, I use the spoken corpus VOICE, available as a POS-tagged version online. The learner essay material is excluded, since the studies in the preceding sections show substantial differences with the advanced L2 corpus, so that the focus here moves to comparing differences and similarities in recent diachronic shifts in inner/outer circle varieties and advanced L2 English. The results first compare the evidence from FIN/SWE-CE and VOICE with the ratios of core and emergent modals in written and spoken BrE and AmE, as reported in Leech (2009, 283, 286; 2013), and then extend Collins' (2009) results on the "diachronic fortunes" of a subset of emergent modals in various inner and outer circle varieties to advanced L2 English.

As for the methods, the relevant instances of core modals have the four N(egation)I(nversion)C(ode)E(mphasis) properties. The emergent modals have emerged through grammaticalization, and have idiomatic meanings which are salient through the meanings of their parts (e.g. BE GOING TO in expressing future intention), and are semantically related to the core modals (Leech 2013). Following the practice in Collins (2009), the results are presented in ratios, and I concentrate on quantitative, form-based patterns, and leave qualitative analyses for future work (Laitinen in press).

TABLE 4.3 *Ratios of core and emergent modals in spoken and written AmE and BrE compared with spoken and written advanced L2 evidence*

	Core modals	Emergent modals	Ratio (cm/em)
AmE	32,188	13,264	2.4
BrE	34,621	9,986	3.5
Advanced L2	29,697	9,870	3.0

Table 4.3 shows the ratios of core and emergent modals from various written and spoken corpora and compares how the diachronic trends mentioned above continue in advanced L2 use. The new evidence from the two advanced L2 English corpora is based on 2,073,731 words, and they are compared with the results from F-LOB and Frown and from the demographic subcorpus of the BNC (5.2 million words) and the *Longman Spoken American Corpus* (5 million words). All figures show results normalized per one million words.

The ratios in Table 4.3 vary between 2.4 in AmE and 3.5 in BrE, meaning that the former variety contains more emergent modals than the latter. The new evidence presented here is noteworthy, as the ratio in the advanced L2 corpora, 3.0, is between the two metropolitan varieties. A contingency table test shows that the differences are highly significant ($p<0.001$).

Even though these results show broad quantitative patterns, they illustrate what types of evidence new corpora could offer for the study of ongoing change. This quantitative finding shows that the driving force of this change is, unexpectedly, AmE and, in particular, spoken AmE. Yet advanced L2 speakers and writers participate in this diachronic shift and have lower ratios than BrE. It might be the case that the prominent role of spoken AmE in general (cf. Mair 2013) brings about the result in Table 4.3, but this needs to be verified in future studies, looking at what types of patterns of variability emerge in individual modals.[14]

14 Laitinen (2014, in press) focuses on quantitative and qualitative patterns in advanced L2 use of those items which undergo the largest frequency changes in recent history, i.e. either decreases or increases in the native varieties.

This finding should also be approached with some degree of caution. The first limitation is that the texts in the corpora used are separated by one or two decades, in that the native materials come from the 1990s and the advanced L2 data from the 2000s/2010s. Leech (2013) presents evidence from BE06/AE06, but unfortunately his article does not include absolute numbers, and his spoken and written comparisons are limited, since there are no spoken native corpora from the 2000s. This diachronic difference is partly counterbalanced by the fact that VOICE consists of recordings from formal professional settings, whereas the native evidence comes from spontaneous dialogues. The second limitation is that I am not comparing exactly like with like in the written corpora, and there are qualitative differences in the materials, since the native varieties come solely from edited, published materials and are not directly comparable with my advanced L2 corpora. Recall from the sections above, however, that the FIN/SWE-CE corpora contain texts from multiple genres.

Nevertheless, these results merit further study because they provide a different view to Collins' (2009) findings from the ICE corpora. He reports that in the native and non-native outer circle varieties the ratios of emergent modals are substantially lower than in any of the four native varieties examined. The final section of this chapter, then, focuses on a set of emergent modals used by Collins to see how new findings from advanced L2 use fare with the inner and outer circle evidence.

Collins' (2009) results are based on a set of five emergent modals (HAVE TO, HAVE GOT TO, NEED TO, BE GOING TO, WANT TO) which he draws from eight ICE corpora and one specifically-tailored AmE corpus. He compares the relative preference of these items in speech and writing to determine their "diachronic fortunes" in various language varieties. He points out that the motivation stems from the need to find out whether the change in the modals in general is from below, i.e. from "informal spoken genres" (Collins 2009, 286). He draws a scale which shows that these emergent modals are most frequent in the inner circle varieties (on average 3.08 emergent modals per one core modal). This frequency is higher than the ratio in the three native South East Asian varieties studied (2.89) and in the two non-native outer circle varieties, Indian English and Kenyan English (2.93).

I extracted the same set of emergent modals from the two advanced L2 corpora used here. To make the samples equally balanced with Collins' (2009) findings, I discarded the new media texts from the sample. The results show that the ratio for the advanced L2 English is 3.02 (the normalized frequencies per one million words are 2,000 in writing and 6,040 in speech), this frequency being well below the ratio in AmE (5.44), but considerably higher than that of BrE (2.58) in Collins (2009, 286). More importantly, if one uses the scale established above, it indicates that advanced L2 English is not as advanced as the inner circle varieties, but more advanced than the outer circle varieties.

It should be noted here that these are preliminary results and should therefore be interpreted tentatively, but together with the results from low/mid-frequency items, they nevertheless offer a more thorough multi-genre view to grammatical variability in advanced L2 English than has previously been possible. Their value stems from the fact that they are based on material collected from naturalistic settings which represent a variety of texts in the expanding circle, and they enable systematic study of advanced L2 English as one stage in the long continuum of Englishes.

Conclusions

Various scholars have recently suggested that the ongoing globalization of English calls for new empirical ways of approaching contact, variability, and the interplay of the established varieties and new forms of English (Mukherjee and Hundt 2011; Mair 2013; Schneider 2014). This chapter has presented a study which tests the methods used for the analysis of ongoing grammatical change for exploring advanced L2 English in the expanding circle contexts. The main line of reasoning concerns the need for new corpus materials, containing a representative sample of genres which have emerged and are emerging as a result of the expansion and diversification of English. The argument suggested is that systematic studies on advanced L2 English require new corpora, which should be based on existing good practice in corpus collection, but which nevertheless should not only be larger in size than the existing learner English resources but also represent texts by speakers/writers who use English as an additional tool in their daily activities in non-instructional settings. Most importantly, these new corpus resources should offer access to a range of genres and be designed so that they allow comparisons with existing native English corpora. All in all, such multi-genre corpus resources could provide a much-needed diachronic dimension to the study of English as a Lingua Franca.

The corpora presented here are in compilation, and our experience is that new solutions are needed to make the materials comparable with the corpora from which much of the evidence on the recent history of English is drawn. A case in point is fiction and fictional texts, which in the expanding circle contexts only exist to a very limited degree, often in forms found on the Internet, which makes it difficult to establish authors' identities (i.e. for instance fan fiction). However, what is clear is that these new corpus sources, which are representative of the diversity of English texts in the expanding circle, could provide additional information on what happens to the core grammar of English in this globalization process.

The results of the three case studies have allowed us to answer the research question posed in the introduction. The first two case studies set traditional learner corpus evidence side by side with advanced L2 data, and the results suggest quantitative differences between these materials. The evidence from advanced L2 data shows similar variant frequencies as in the various Brown corpora from the second half of the twentieth century and the early twenty-first century. The data are different from the ICLE results to a statistically significant degree, which merits further investigation of other quantitative and qualitative differences between the corpora. The third case study suggests that advanced L2 evidence is situated in the middle of the most advanced variety, AmE, but ahead of BrE, and also ahead of native and non-native outer circle varieties, thus suggesting that the global expansion of English calls for additional empirical research. All in all, the results show that advanced L2 speakers/writers participate in adopting recently grammaticalized structures, an observation which we have also found when investigating special uses of the progressive in Laitinen and Levin (forthcoming).

Corpora

AE06 *The American English 2006 corpus*. Compiled by Paul Baker. https://cqpweb.lancs.ac.uk/ame06/.

BE06 *The British English 2006 corpus*. Compiled by Paul Baker. https://cqpweb.lancs.ac.uk/be2006/.

BNC *British National Corpus*, version 3 (BNC XML Edition). 2007. Distributed by Oxford University Computing Services on behalf of the BNC Consortium. http://www.natcorp.ox.ac.uk/.

Brown *A Standard Corpus of Present-Day Edited American English, for Use with Digital Computers*. 1964, 1971, 1979. Compiled by W. Nelson Francis and Henry Kučera. Brown University. Providence, Rhode Island.

COHA Davies, Mark. 2010–. *The Corpus of Historical American English: 400 million words, 1810–2009*. http://corpus.byu.edu/coha/.

FIN-CE *The Corpus of English in Finland. A Multi-Genre Corpus Resource of Advanced Non-Native English Texts*. In compilation. Compiled by Mikko Laitinen, Linnaeus University.

F-LOB *The Freiburg-LOB Corpus* (original version). 1999. Compiled by Christian Mair, Albert-Ludwigs-Universität Freiburg.

Frown	*The Freiburg-Brown Corpus* (original version). 1999. Compiled by Christian Mair, Albert-Ludwigs-Universität Freiburg.
ICLE	*International Corpus of Learner English*. 2002. Project director: Sylviane Granger. Centre for English Corpus Linguistics. Université Catholique de Louvain. http://www.uclouvain.be/en-cecl-icle.html.
LOB	*The Lancaster-Oslo/Bergen Corpus* (original version) 1970–1978. Compiled by Geoffrey Leech, Lancaster University, Stig Johansson, University of Oslo (Project leaders), and Knut Hofland (Head of computing), University of Bergen.
LSAC	*The Longman Spoken American Corpus*. Compiled by Jack Du Bois and his team at the University of California at Santa Barbara (UCSB). Pearson Education.
SWE-CE	*The Corpus of English in Sweden. A Multi-Genre Corpus Resource of Advanced Non-Native English Texts*. In compilation. Compiled by Mikko Laitinen, Linnaeus University.
VOICE	*The Vienna-Oxford International Corpus of English* (version 2.0 XML). 2013. Director: Barbara Seidlhofer. Researchers: Angelika Breiteneder, Theresa Klimpfinger, Stefan Majewski, Ruth Osimk-Teasdale, Marie-Luise Pitzl, and Michael Radeka. http://voice.univie.ac.at.

References

Aijmer, Karin. 2002. "Modality in Advanced Swedish Learners' Written Interlanguage." In *Computer Learner Corpora, Second Language Acquisition and Foreign Language Teaching*, edited by Sylviane Granger, Joseph Hung, and Stephanie Petch-Tyson, 55–76. Amsterdam and Philadelphia: John Benjamins.

Appadurai, Arjun. 1996. *Modernity at Large: Cultural Dimensions of Globalization*. Minneapolis: University of Minnesota Press.

Baker, Paul. 2009. "The BE06 Corpus of British English and Recent Language Change." *International Journal of Corpus Linguistics* 14/3: 312–37.

Biber, Douglas. 1988. *Variation Across Speech and Writing*. Cambridge: Cambridge University Press.

Biber, Douglas, Stig Johansson, Geoffrey Leech, Susan Conrad, and Edward Finegan. 1999. *Longman Grammar of Spoken and Written English*. London: Longman.

Bolton, Kingsley, and Christiane Meierkord. 2013. "English in Contemporary Sweden: Perceptions, Policies, and Narrated Practices." *Journal of Sociolinguistics* 17/1: 93–117.

Brinton, Laurel J. 2007. "Rise of the Adverbial Conjunctions {Any, Each, Every} Time." In *Connectives in the History of English*, edited by Ursula Lenker, and Anneli Meurman-Solin, 77–96. Amsterdam and Philadelphia: John Benjamins.

Cheshire, Jenny, Paul Kerswill, Sue Fox, and Eivind Torgersen. 2011. "Contact, the Feature Pool and the Speech Community: The Emergence of Multicultural London English." *Journal of Sociolinguistics* 15/2: 151–96.

Collins, Peter. 2009. "Modals and Quasi-Modals in World Englishes." *World Englishes* 28/3: 281–92.

Collins, Peter. 2014. "Quasi-Modals and Modals in Australian English Fiction 1800–1999, with Comparisons Across British and American English." *Journal of English Linguistics* 42/1: 7–30.

D'Arcy, Alexandra, Bill Haddican, Hazel Richards, Sali A. Tagliamonte, and Ann Taylor. 2013. "Asymmetrical Trajectories: The Past and Present of *-Body*/*-One*." *Language Variation and Change* 25/3: 287–310.

Filppula, Markku. 2012. "Convergent Developments between 'Old' and 'New' Englishes." Paper presented at the Seventeenth International Conference on English Historical Linguistics (ICEHL 17), Zurich, August 20–25.

Granger, Sylviane. 2008. "Learner Corpora." In *Corpus Linguistics: An International Handbook*, edited by Anke Lüdeling, and Merja Kytö, 259–75. Berlin: Mouton de Gruyter.

Granger, Sylviane, and Paul Rayson. 1998. "Automatic Profiling of Learner Texts." In *Learner English on Computer*, edited by Sylviane Granger, 119–31. London: Longman.

Hundt, Marianne, and Geoffrey Leech. 2012. "'Small is Beautiful.' On the Value of Standard Reference Corpora for Observing Recent Grammatical Change." In *The Oxford History of the English Language*, edited by Terttu Nevalainen, and Elizabeth C. Traugott, 175–88. Oxford: Oxford University Press.

Hundt, Marianne, and Christian Mair. 1999. "'Agile' and 'Uptight' Genres: The Corpus-Based Approach to Language Change in Progress." *International Journal of Corpus Linguistics* 4/2: 221–42.

Hundt, Marianne, and Katrin Vogel. 2011. "Overuse of the Progressive in ESL and Learner Englishes—Fact or Fiction?" In *Exploring Second-Language Varieties of English and Learner Englishes: Bridging a Paradigm Gap*, edited by Joybrato Mukherjee, and Marianne Hundt, 145–65. Amsterdam and Philadelphia: John Benjamins.

Jenkins, Jennifer, Alessia Cogo, and Martin Dewey. 2011. "Review of *Developments in Research into English as a Lingua Franca*." *Language Teaching* 44/3: 281–315.

Johansson, Christine, and Christer Geisler. 2009. "The Uppsala Learner English Corpus: A New Corpus of Swedish High School Students' Writing." In *Multilingualism: Proceedings of the 23rd Scandinavian Conference of Linguistics: Uppsala University,*

1–3 October 2008, edited by Anju Saxena, and Åke Viberg, 181–90. Uppsala: Acta Universitatis Upsaliensis.

Kortmann, Bernd. 1997. *Adverbial Subordination: A Typology and History of Adverbial Subordinators Based on European Languages*. Berlin: Mouton de Gruyter.

Laitinen, Mikko. 2011. "Contacts and Variability in International Englishes: Compiling and Using the Corpus of English in Finland." In *Methodological and Historical Dimensions of Corpus Linguistics*, edited by Paul Rayson, Sebastian Hoffmann, and Geoffrey Leech. Accessed February 27, 2014. http://www.helsinki.fi/varieng/journal/volumes/06/.

Laitinen, Mikko. 2014. "Ongoing Changes in English Modals: On the Developments in Advanced L2 Use of English." Paper presented at the Third Conference of the International Society for the Linguistics of English (ISLE 3), Zurich, August 24–27.

Laitinen, Mikko. In press. "Ongoing Changes in English Modals: On the Developments in ELF." In *New Approaches in English Linguistics: Building Bridges*, edited by Olga Timofeeva, Sarah Chevalier, Anne-Christine Gardner, and Alpo Honkapohja. Amsterdam and Philadelphia: John Benjamins.

Laitinen, Mikko. Forthcoming. "Indefinite Pronouns with Singular Human Reference in the Long 18th Century." In *Linguistic Change in its Social Contexts in Eighteenth-Century English*, edited by Minna Palander-Collin, Terttu Nevalainen, and Tanja Säily. Oxford: Oxford University Press.

Laitinen, Mikko, and Magnus Levin. 2016. "On the Globalization of English: Observations of Subjective Progressives in Present-day Englishes." In *World Englishes: New Theoretical and Methodological Considerations*, edited by Elena Seoane, and Cristina Suárez-Gómez, 229–52. Amsterdam and Philadelphia: John Benjamins.

Leech, Geoffrey. 2003. "Modals on the Move: The English Modal Auxiliaries 1961–1992." In *Modality in Contemporary English*, edited by Roberta Facchinetti, Frank Palmer, and Manfred Krug, 223–40. Berlin: Mouton de Gruyter.

Leech, Geoffrey. 2011. "The Modals ARE Declining. Reply to Neil Millar's "Modal Verbs in TIME: Frequency Changes 1923–2006," *International Journal of Corpus Linguistics* 14/2 (2009): 191–220." *International Journal of Corpus Linguistics* 16/4: 547–64.

Leech, Geoffrey. 2013. "Where Have All the Modals Gone? An Essay on the Declining Frequency of Core Modal Auxiliaries in Recent Standard English." In *English Modality: Core, Periphery and Evidentiality*, edited by Juana I. Marín-Arrese, Marta Carretero, Jorge Arús Hita, and Johan van der Auwera, 95–115. Berlin: Mouton de Gruyter.

Leech, Geoffrey, Marianne Hundt, Christian Mair, and Nicholas Smith. 2009. *Change in Contemporary English. A Grammatical Study*. Cambridge: Cambridge University Press.

Leppänen, Sirpa, Anne Pitkänen-Huhta, Tarja Nikula, Samu Kytölä, Timo Törmäkangas, Kari Nissinen, Leila Kääntä, Tiina Räisänen, Mikko Laitinen, Päivi Pahta, Heidi Koskela, Salla Lähdesmäki, and Henna Jousmäki. 2011. *National Survey on the English Language in Finland: Uses, Meanings and Attitudes*. Accessed February 27, 2014. http://www.helsinki.fi/varieng/journal/volumes/05/.

Mair, Christian. 2008. "Corpora and the Study of Recent Change in Language." In *Corpus Linguistics: An International Handbook*, edited by Anke Lüdeling, and Merja Kytö, 1109–25. Berlin: Mouton de Gruyter.

Mair, Christian. 2013. "The World System of Englishes: Accounting for the Transnational Importance of Mobile and Mediated Vernaculars." *English World-Wide* 34/3: 253–78.

Mair, Christian, and Geoffrey Leech. 2006. "Current Changes in English Syntax." In *The Handbook of English Linguistics*, edited by Bas Aarts, and April McMahon, 318–42. London: Blackwell.

Mauranen, Anna. 2012. *Exploring ELF: Academic English Shaped by Non-Native Speakers*. Cambridge: Cambridge University Press.

Mukherjee, Joybrato, and Marianne Hundt, eds. 2011. *Exploring Second-Language Varieties of English and Learner Englishes: Bridging a Paradigm Gap*. Amsterdam and Philadelphia: John Benjamins.

Noël, Dirk, Bertus van Rooy, and Johan van der Auwera. 2014. "Diachronic Approaches to Modality in World Englishes: Introduction to the Special Issue." *Journal of English Linguistics* 42/1: 3–6.

Raumolin-Brunberg, Helena, and Leena Kahlas-Tarkka. 1997. "Indefinite Pronouns with Singular Human Reference." In *Grammaticalization at Work. Studies of Long-Term Developments in English*, edited by Matti Rissanen, Merja Kytö, and Kirsi Heikkonen, 17–86. Berlin: Mouton de Gruyter.

Rissanen, Matti. 2008. "Corpus Linguistics and Historical Linguistics." In *Corpus Linguistics: An International Handbook*, edited by Anke Lüdeling, and Merja Kytö, 53–68. Berlin: Mouton de Gruyter.

Sand, Andrea. 2013. "Singapore Weblogs: Between Speech and Writing." In *Corpus Linguistics and Variation in English: Focus on Non-Native Englishes*, edited by Magnus Huber, and Joybrato Mukherjee. Accessed February 27, 2014. http://www.helsinki.fi/varieng/series/volumes/13/.

Schneider, Edgar W. 2014. "New Reflections on the Evolutionary Dynamics of World Englishes." *World Englishes* 33/1: 9–32.

Seidlhofer, Barbara. 2011. *Understanding English as a Lingua Franca*. Oxford: Oxford University Press.

PART 2

Investigating Register Variation through Corpora

CHAPTER 5

Verbs and Verb Phrases in Advanced Dutch EFL Writing: Case Studies in Quantitative and Qualitative EFL Analysis

Pieter de Haan

Abstract

This chapter reports on a study of the development of syntactic control in English as a Foreign Language (EFL). Formal academic writing is characterized by a nominal, rather than a verbal style, implying that more mature writers will use fewer verb phrases (VPs). At the same time, formal writing tends to be more complex, suggesting that VPs used by more mature writers will be more complex. The writings of four individual Dutch first-year university students of English with varying scores on grammar placement tests and grammar exams were analysed. VPs were examined in terms of complexity and in terms of occurrence in main clauses or subclauses. The four students were shown to behave differently on two separate occasions with a three-month interval, suggesting the beginning of a development into more mature writers; but they were also shown to behave differently from each other, suggesting that some of them developed at a greater speed than others. A comparison of the writing of the students discussed in this chapter suggests that a wide gap can exist between (passive) knowledge and (active) control.

Keywords

EFL development – LONGDALE – verb phrase complexity – syntactic control – qualitative analysis

Introduction

It has been claimed recently that writing instruction is crucial in English as a Foreign Language (EFL) teaching, in that it facilitates language development (Reichelt et al. 2012; Williams 2012). Reichelt et al. (2012) observe that students' writing skills are often poor in both their native language (L1) and their second or foreign language (L2), so that a focus on writing instruction is generally

 | DOI 10.1163/9789004321342_006

beneficial to the development of their L2 proficiency, while Williams (2012, 328) argues that this development is crucial for "knowledge internalization, modification, and consolidation". Given the nature and the availability of written L2 data, studies that address L2 writing skills and their development have typically focused on lexical matters, although the variety of language features that can be successfully studied has expanded in the last few years. Thus, Chen and Baker (2010) compared native academic writing with L1 and L2 student writing on the basis of the study of lexical bundles (cf. Biber et al. 1999), and concluded that the student writings contain more verb phrase (VP) based lexical bundles while the native academic writings contain more noun phrase (NP) based lexical bundles. Laufer and Waldman (2011) compared the use of English verb-noun collocations used by native Hebrew writers to that by native student writers, finding that the non-native writers underproduce verb-noun collocations at all levels of language proficiency.

Murphy and Roca de Larios (2010) explored the strategic use of the L1 by a group of Spanish EFL learners, looking specifically at how advanced L2 learners solve lexical problems. They expressed concern at the large amount of variation within writers' production (Schoonen 2005), and called for the inclusion of multiple tasks in research designs. Finally, Thewissen (2013) studied language development in terms of accuracy, using data from the *International Corpus of Learner English* (ICLE), and concluded that error patterns tend to stabilize or improve, and that improvement usually occurs between the Common European Framework of Reference (CEFR) levels B1 and B2.

Thus far there have been few longitudinal case studies into L2 writing development, two notable exceptions being Li and Schmitt (2009), and Kobayashi and Rinnert (2013). Both these studies reported on single L2 student writers and addressed issues such as the textual, social, and cultural aspects of writing. Springer (2012) studied the discourse competence of Dutch EFL writers with reference to the CEFR levels C1 and C2, comparing longitudinal Dutch written EFL data with published native literary and linguistic research articles. The LONGDALE (*Longitudinal Database of Learner English*) project (Granger 2009) was launched to create a large amount of longitudinal EFL data produced by learners with various language backgrounds that can be used for EFL development studies. The LONGDALE project currently includes data of EFL learners from five different native language backgrounds (Granger 2009).

In terms of writing quality, Silva (1993), after studying 72 research articles on English as a Second Language (ESL) writing, found that non-native writing is distinctly less sophisticated than native English writing. This lack of sophistication was found to be due not only to such things as grammatical and lexical errors, but also to an erroneous or immature use of cohesive devices, resulting in unclear logical relationships in the writing. Syntactically, ESL writing was generally found to be characterized by less complex sentence and phrase structures and more coordinated sentences.

The current chapter reports on continued research into the way in which written L2 English, and more particularly written EFL produced by native speakers of Dutch, develops over time. Longitudinal written EFL data produced by Dutch university students of English have been collected at the English Department of Radboud University since 2002 with a view to improving the department's EFL writing courses. The study of these longitudinal data has enabled us not only to confirm many of Silva's (1993) conclusions, but also to make observations about how Dutch students' written EFL develops in the direction of native written English.

De Haan (2015) sums up the most recent findings of the project. Advanced Dutch students' EFL written production undeniably develops towards native-like production, but the measures on which these findings are based do not all point unambiguously in the same direction. For instance, Grant and Ginther's (2000) observation that more advanced L2 writers are generally more fluent (in terms of production), use longer words, and write longer sentences is confirmed by the Dutch EFL data. However, their observation that more advanced L2 writers have a higher type/token ratio (indicating, in their view, a more mature vocabulary control) is not confirmed by the Dutch EFL data. Type/token ratio is shown to be a good indicator of progress in initial stages of learning, but not at more advanced stages (cf. also de Haan and van Esch 2005).

Likewise, lexical density, which is generally assumed to be an indicator of vocabulary knowledge and therefore associated with maturity of writing, is shown not to increase in the Dutch EFL writers as they become more advanced. On the contrary, it tends to decrease with advancement. It is therefore argued that a higher lexical density does not indicate a growth in vocabulary knowledge, but rather that a decreased lexical density is an indication of a more advanced syntactic control, because it corresponds to the writer's more advanced use of grammatical words to build more complex syntactic constructions.

De Haan (2015) therefore seeks to find other indicators of a more mature EFL production, and looks at the use of nouns and noun phrases in advanced Dutch written EFL production. Comparing the written production of two students over a five-month period, he relates form and function of noun phrases in their writing to other indicators of mature writing, such as those mentioned above. He finds a clear relation between the use of noun phrases and the command of an appropriate academic writing style.

The current chapter is a continuation of a study, started by de Haan and van der Haagen (2014) and de Haan (2015), into the syntactic development of advanced Dutch EFL writing. De Haan and van der Haagen find that the distribution of nouns and verbs becomes increasingly native-like over time, although they observe a great amount of variation in the way individual students develop. The more frequent use of verbs and VPs has been shown to be characteristic of native British English speech, while native writing, especially academic writing, can be characterized as more nominal (Biber et al. 1999; de Haan 2001, 2002). Formal academic writing features more complex phrase structures and fewer verbs in general, and more noun phrases, while speech has a more verbal style, with fewer noun phrases, fewer complex phrase structures in general, and more verbs (de Haan 2002). More recently, Biber et al. (2011) have shown that grammatical complexity in academic writing is fundamentally different from that in speech. They argue that academic writing is a skill that is acquired much later in both L1 and L2 development, and involves "many types of complex phrasal embedding [which] are produced in only the more specialized circumstances of formal writing" (Biber et al. 2011, 29). The aim in the current chapter is to study the way in which the use of verbs and VPs develops in four Dutch students' written production. More specifically, I wish to find out if the differences observed in the use of verbs and VPs can be used as indicators of the development of students' syntactic control. What I would like to see is a gradual move towards a more academically appropriate nominal style.

Method

The methodology adopted in this study is comparable to that of de Haan (2015). For the current study I examined data collected for the LONGDALE project (Granger 2009) from a single cohort of students of English at Radboud University, who started their studies in September 2011. Radboud University has been involved in the project since 2008, when the first student data were collected from the 2008 cohort of students. Increasingly more data have been collected since then, starting in the academic year 2009–2010, and we are currently collecting the data of the seventh cohort of students (2015–2016). The total number of words of the Dutch part of the LONGDALE project is now well over two million, and continues to increase.

Dutch university students of English are generally considered to be advanced EFL learners because of their institutional status (Melissen 2007; Verheijen et al. 2013). The English Department at Radboud University has been applying a home-made placement test for many years and incoming students' scores have displayed a constant test score distribution. In order to relate these placement test scores to the CEFR levels, the new cohort of incoming students were also subjected to the Online Oxford Placement Test (OOPT) in September 2013. Over 90% of the students that took the test had average OOPT test score results that placed them at CEFR level C1 or C2 (de Vries and de Haan 2013). Their scores on the home-made placement test were comparable to those of previous cohorts. I am therefore confident that the first-year students of English at Radboud University are advanced, or even very advanced, EFL learners.

English students take writing courses in each of the three years of BA study. A remedial grammar course and an introductory English syntax course are taught in the first year. The writing classes focus specifically on things like the formulation of thesis statements, the construction of paragraphs, avoiding logical fallacies, and avoiding possible plagiarism. The first-year writing course, in particular, pays special attention to the use of cohesive devices and logical connectors. The writing course itself does not pay explicit attention to the syntactic make-up of the sentences in the students' written work, other than the correct positioning of adverbials, although students do practice sentence embedding and the use of relative clauses in the grammar course. In the second- and third-year courses, less attention is paid to such mechanics of the language, with attention gradually shifting towards issues concerning more complex and demanding essay topics and research papers.

The issue of longitudinal EFL data collection has received some attention in the past. De Haan and van Esch (2004, 2005, 2007, 2008) collected longitudinal data of a number of cohorts of Dutch students of English and Dutch students of Spanish, in an attempt to chart basic quantitative foreign language writing development features (these data were not part of the LONGDALE project). Although they found clear signs of development in the writing of the students of Spanish, in terms of word length, sentence length, and type/token ratio scores, they did not witness any such development in the writing of the students of English, with the exception of mean sentence length. Differences between students of Spanish and English were attributed to the fact that the latter were very advanced EFL users, as opposed to the former, who had not had any training in Spanish prior to university. Any development of basic features was hard to establish at the English students' more advanced level of proficiency.

Earlier, it had been suggested (Shaw and Liu 1998; Ortega 2003) that collecting longitudinal data at relatively short intervals (i.e. shorter than nine months) might not be useful for the study of syntactic development, as students seldom display a more advanced syntactic behaviour at such intervals. However, de Haan and van der Haagen (2014) showed that syntactic development can be observed in individual students over a three-month period. Also, Hayes et al. (2000) argued that students are unlikely to show their full potential in any arbitrarily selected writing assignment, and therefore the aim should be to collect as many written data as possible. It is with the latter in mind that I decided to collect as many writing assignments as possible from our students, with a minimum of three texts per year. Following another suggestion by Hayes et al. (2000), I also decided to collect writing assignments that cover a wide variety of tasks and topics, in order to confirm earlier findings (de Haan and van der Haagen 2012, 2013) that the writing task and the topic tend to influence the students' lexical and syntactic behaviour. This latter observation had also been made for L2 French, Italian, and Dutch (Kuiken and Vedder 2007, 2008; Michel et al. 2007).

I collected six written assignments over a period of five months, starting with a personal paper in September, during the students' first writing class. Three of these were in-class assignments and the other three were home assignments (cf. the scheme presented in Table 5.1 below). The in-class assignments were completed in thirty minutes; there were no time limits for the home assignments. The total number of words in this sample is 234,255. The general mean essay length for the essays in this sample is 467 words. The mean essay lengths for the various writing tasks reflect the timed conditions in texts 1, 2, and 5. The topics for the writing assignments were as follows:

September Text 1 "My expectations of the coming year"
September Text 2 "First-year students can take specific steps to become successful in college"
October Text 3 British literature—analysis of a short story
November Text 4 British literature—analysis of student's own sonnet
December Text 5 "The Dutch government should spend more money on primary/less money on tertiary education"
January Text 6 Take home exam American literature—American Romanticism

Basic statistics, such as mean word length, mean sentence length, and type/token ratio, were calculated by means of Mike Scott's WordSmith Tools version 6.0. The data were automatically parsed with the Stanford Parser (Klein and Manning 2003). They were subsequently postprocessed with Corpus Studio (Komen 2011b) and Cesax (Komen 2011a). Since the EFL writing produced by Dutch university students is virtually error-free (de Haan and van Esch 2005), it can be assumed that the Stanford Parser performs equally reliably on this

TABLE 5.1 *Data collection and basic statistics*

	Text 1 Sep. 2011 in class	Text 2 Sep. 2011 in class	Text 3 Oct. 2011 at home	Text 4 Nov. 2011 at home	Text 5 Dec. 2011 in class	Text 6 Jan. 2012 at home
# essays	96	94	86	82	66	78
# words	27,911	36,526	47,114	45,880	19,477	57,347
mean # words/essays	291	389	548	560	295	735
mean # VPs/100 words	17	17	14	13	14	13

EFL material as on native English data. The Stanford Parser analyses verbal groups consisting of more than one verb as VPs with embedded VPs (one extra VP for each verb); therefore, I selected only those VPs that were not dominated by a VP node. This yielded a total number of 33,725 VPs for the six texts written by all the students in the cohort. The total number of words produced for these texts is 234,255, so the overall number of VPs per 100 words is 13.9. There is some variation in the number of VPs per 100 words in the various texts, as is shown in Table 5.1, but the general trend appears to be towards a decrease in the number of VPs.

As I was particularly interested in the linguistic behaviour of individual students, I selected the work of the first four students who completed all six assignments. These students are referred to here as RAD1101, RAD1102, RAD1111, and RAD1113. RAD1101 is a male student; the other three are female. The students were in their late teens when they registered as first-year students at Radboud University. Table 5.2 sets out the basic numerical data for these four students.

The first two students had average scores on an initial English grammar and usage placement test, taken in September 2011, with RAD1101 having a slightly higher score than RAD1102 (the median score for the entire cohort being 37). RAD1111 was clearly a below-average student, while RAD1113 was an above-average student. The first-year practical English grammar exam in October 2011 yielded comparable results, with RAD1102 doing marginally better than RAD1101 (the median score for the entire cohort being 6.5 on the Dutch 10-point scale), while RAD1113 performed much better, and RAD1111 actually failed this exam (the lowest pass mark being 5.5). The first two students can therefore be regarded as average students in terms of grammatical knowledge of English; RAD1111 is below average, and RAD1113 is above average.

TABLE 5.2 *Basic quantitative data for the four students selected*

Student ID	Placement Test Score (max. 50)	Grammar Exam Score (max. 10)	Total # words in all six texts	# VPS per 100 words overall	# words in text 2	# VPS per 100 words in text 2	# words in text 5	# VPS per 100 words in text 5
RAD1101	38	6.2	2,809	12.2	367	17.2	349	11.2
RAD1102	36	6.3	2,529	14.5	314	17.8	246	15.4
RAD1111	27	4.6	2,567	15.0	349	15.5	255	17.3
RAD1113	42	7.2	3,239	12.6	413	13.1	579	16.8

If we look at the total number of words produced in all six texts, we see that RAD1113 is clearly the most fluent student, but that RAD1111 is not necessarily the least fluent. This is not only true overall, but also for the two texts selected. RAD1111's scores are consistently higher than RAD1102's. The mean number of VPS produced in the six texts by all the students in this cohort was 13.9 per 100 words. RAD1101 produced 12.2 VPS per 100 words; RAD1102 produced 14.5; RAD1111 produced 15; RAD1113 produced 12.6. This suggests that RAD1101 and RAD1113 use a less verbal style than the other two students.

Results and Discussion

Quantitative Results

Figure 5.1 shows the number of VPS used per 100 words in each of the six texts examined. Each of these four students has a different distributional pattern. The most regular pattern is observed in RAD1113, whose VP use steadily decreases until text 5, which shows a sudden increase, after which the decreasing pattern appears to resume. I will return to this phenomenon below.

As I indicated in the introduction, the students wrote on a variety of topics, including academically motivated essays, personal papers, and argumentative essays. Texts 2 and 5 are both representative of in-class argumentative essays written under the same conditions, both of them having the same time limit, and both requiring the student to respond to a prompt that called on their own resources. They could not rely on any specific course reading that they might have done (unlike text 6, which was a take-home exam for American literature, involving a good deal of secondary course reading). The remainder

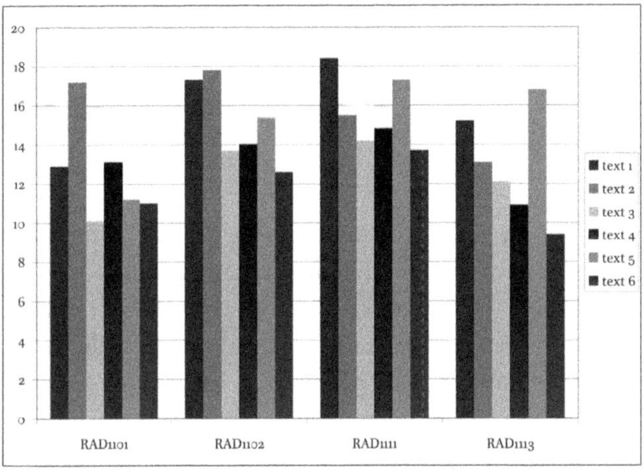

FIGURE 5.1 *Distribution of VPs per 100 words in various texts produced by the four students.*

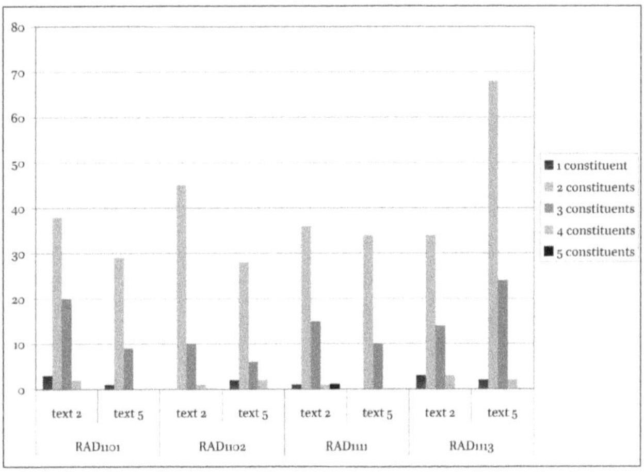

FIGURE 5.2 *Distribution of VP size in text 2 and text 5 (percentage scores per student).*

of this chapter will therefore be devoted to a comparison of these four students' use of VPs in texts 2 and 5, which were produced at an interval of three months (mid-September and mid-December).

Figure 5.2 shows the relative distribution of VPs in text 2 and text 5 broken down for the number of constituents. VPs consisting of more constituents can be assumed to be more complex. The majority of VPs used, ranging from 60% to 80%, consist of two constituents, and there are hardly any VPs that consist of more than three constituents. Also, there is no clear development that points to more complex VPs. On the contrary, all the students have fewer 3-constituent VPs in text 5 than in text 2, and in three of them, the number of 2-constituent VPs is greater in text 5 than in text 2.

Qualitative Analysis

There is a great deal of variation in the internal make-up of the VPs produced by the four students. Over a hundred different constituent patterns are distinguished. The three most common types make up about 30% in each of these four students. They all consist of two constituents, and they are the same three patterns in the four students, namely *to* VP (the infinitive complement clause), VBZ NP (a present tense verb complemented by a noun phrase), and MD VP (a modal auxiliary complemented by a VP), and they all come in this order, except for RAD1113, who used slightly more the MD VP pattern than the VBZ NP pattern.

The *to* VP pattern has a large variety of verbs in the VP. Corpus examples are *to climb them* (RAD1113, t2) or *to quit school* (RAD1111, t5). The VP in this pattern can itself, of course, be a complex VP, as in *to adapt the study materials to the needs of a child* (RAD1113, t5). The verb form that occurs most often in the pattern VBZ NP is the present tense form *is*, as shown in examples (1)–(4).

(1) is enough time for other projects or outside interests (RAD1101, t2)
(2) is a lack of time and money (RAD1102, t5)
(3) is one of the best ways to learn (RAD1111, t2)
(4) is focus—focus derived from motivation (RAD1113, t2)

The pattern MD VP is exemplified in examples (5)–(7). In this pattern, also, the VP can be complex, as in (7).

(5) might be useful in the future (RAD1102, t2)
(6) can be a wonderful opportunity for students (RAD1113, t5)
(7) should be used to give children an ideal basis for the rest of their lives (RAD1101, t5)

The great diversity of structures of the VPs used in these texts, as well as their realizations, make it problematic to link any specific characteristic VP feature to something like EFL development or mature EFL use. I cannot but conclude that at this stage, on the basis of these data, it is not possible to point to VP use as an indicator of the quality of EFL use, other than in the broadest terms: there appears to be a gradual decrease in the use of VPs, which suggests that the students are moving from a spoken to a written style. Now consider the excerpts from the students' second texts below. In text 2 they had to argue that first-year students can take specific steps to become successful in college.

> Furthermore, trying to put as much interest in a study as possible is very important in developing a certain joy in studying. This should not always be a drought, but instead be somewhat of a nice experience. More input automatically means more output, so results will definitely improve if a student starts to enjoy doing assignments and studying texts. There will always be certain aspects of a study which one does not really fancy, but that is understandable. (RAD1101, t2)

> First of all, work hard. It is said very often, but it is true. You cannot pass your exams if you do not do anything. Keeping up with your assignments is half the work, so make sure you know what you have to do every week and do your assignments with care, so you will actually learn something.
>
> To attend your classes is also a good idea. Make sure you are seated somewhere in the front, so you can hear and see what your teacher is talking about. Make sure you make notes and read them again later. (RAD1102, t2)

> The step to begin with, is to make sure you are in one of the front rows in your classroom, this way you can actively participate in class. You will not miss any important information and you will be motivated to think about the questions the teacher asks. In one of the front rows, the PowerPoint presentation or whiteboard will be closest to you, so you will be forced to make notes during class and really pay attention to what is said. Interaction with your fellow students and teacher is one of the best ways to learn. (RAD1111, t2)

> Between the temptations of television, films, games, the unimaginable depths of the internet and the long-winding labyrinth of social networks, procrastination is without question the first and foremost obstacle to a successful academic career. Of course, who wouldn't rather be watching comedy clips on Youtube, or slaying zombies on the console than settle down to the assigned reading for the upcoming lecture? It is only natural that we would prefer activities from which we derive pleasure to those that are tedious, laborious or place a heavy demand on our time. How, then, to combat procrastination? (RAD1113, t2)

These short excerpts show how RAD1101 and RAD1113 produce different language from RAD1102 and RAD1111. Admittedly, RAD1101 is extremely formal

(*… certain aspects of a study which one does not really fancy…*), but this student's complex VP constructions, like *starts to enjoy doing assignments,* simply do not occur in RAD1102 and RAD1111, who in fact both address an implied reader directly. RAD1113 steers away from directly addressing the reader by using impersonal constructions, a rhetorical question, and the pronoun *we*. Note also that RAD1102 uses shorter sentences than the other students.

Both RAD1102 and RAD1111 mention external conditions (sitting in the front row, making notes), while RAD1101 and RAD1113 stress the student's own intrinsic motivation (develop a certain joy, combat procrastination). The latter two students interpret the steps in a totally different way from the former two. This may be a reflection of a more mature thinking process, expressed in more mature language.

Below are the excerpts from text 5, written three months after text 2. Over these three months the students took a remedial English grammar course, an oral communication course (including advanced English vocabulary training), and a writing course, which dealt specifically with text structuring. They also took courses in British culture and history, English literature, and philosophy. In text 5 the students were asked to support (or reject) the claim that the Dutch government should spend more money on primary education and less on tertiary education.

> Furthermore, primary school is to serve as a fluent transition with secondary school and therefore primary education is important in the future of the life of a child. Not only should primary school provide children with knowledge, it should also be helpful when making a decision which type of secondary education to choose. In contrast, tertiary education is optional and does not play a role in a person's life who is not smart enough to go to university.
>
> Finally, primary education should create equal chances for every child. Since primary school is compulsory for every child, it should encourage children to get the most out of their lives, even when there is a limit in knowledge. Tertiary education can be a wonderful opportunity for students but in comparison to primary education, it is optional and thus should not be so much of a factor in one's life. (RAD1101, t5)

> In primary school there are many children who have difficulties with learning, and if the primary schools had more money, they could help those children better. Now, the children often do not get enough support from their teachers, because there is a lack of time and money. If the primary schools got more money, they could solve this problem.

Universities could do with less money, because the people that go to university are the people that earn most money. They have the means to pay for the high education, or to pay the money back later. They could also lend more money from DUO. If the universities get less money, they could easily raise the college money and still be fine. (RAD1102, t5)

The current Dutch government decided to spend less money on universities, they want to spend less money on bachelor and master studies by forcing students to pay for their own education and by letting them pay a fine when they do not graduate for their bachelor within three years.

The Dutch government instead wants to spend more money on primary education because this is much more important than university. Primary education is the basis for further education and it is obligatory for all children living in the Netherlands. In the Netherlands you cannot leave school legally till you are eighteen. It is necessary to teach children as much as possible in primary school so that they can easily proceed to secondary school. Most children that finish secondary school are already eighteen and thus have the legal age to quit school. (RAD1111, t5)

My personal primary school experience makes me wonder whether there are not factors other than money that play a more important role in the success of a primary school education. I spent some of my years in primary school in an emergency building consisting of what was, basically, a carpeted container, but because we had a teacher who was very enthusiastic (and willing to adapt the study materials to the needs of a child) our class did very well. The kids who picked things up easily got to work on their own, even allowed to skip parts of the textbooks if they could make the tests without trouble, while attention was re-directed to those kids who needed it most. We even got to help other kids a couple years younger than us learn how to read and write, and we got a lot of experience outside of the regular curriculum by being allowed to work on a number of projects, such as interviewing people for a paper or planning and preparing to turn the classroom into a restaurant for an afternoon or writing and putting on a play. (RAD1113, t5)

A number of observations can be made here. First, RAD1113 writes from a personal experience, which may be the reason why her fifth text is much longer than her second text (the reverse is true for the other three students). Writing from this personal experience may also explain why she uses a curious mix of formal language (*... attention was redirected to ...*) and informal language (*We* *even got to help other kids a couple years younger than us* ...). Second, RAD1111 continues to address the reader directly, while RAD1102 no longer does so. However, RAD1111 does not appear to be arguing a point at all, but merely stating a presumed fact, and giving reasons for it. I will return to this below.

RAD1102 again uses relatively short sentences, which, especially in the second paragraph cited here, are repetitive (*They have*... *They could*...). The writing here is by no means flawless. RAD1101, for instance, produces an awkward construction in an attempt at relative clause formation in ... *does not play a role in a person's life who is not smart enough to go to university*. In the case of RAD1102 we can detect interference from Dutch, as in *children who have difficulties with learning* (where the preposition is directly taken from the equivalent Dutch expression), which suggests that RAD1102's grammatical control in English is to some extent dictated by grammatical patterns in her native language.

What is also noticeable in RAD1102 is the repeated use of embedded *if*-clauses. In text 5 there are no fewer than five, three of which occur in the excerpt above, and they are invariably of the type *if the*... *had/get/got more/less money*.... In contrast, RAD1101 does not use a single conditional clause in the entire text; meanwhile, RAD1111 uses only one. RAD1113 uses six *if*-clauses (one of which occurs in the excerpt above), but these are never as repetitive as in the case of RAD1102.

RAD1101 and RAD1102 display an interesting difference in their approach to argumentation. RAD1101 is more inclined to highlight logical consequences, as in the second sentence of the second paragraph cited above (*Since primary school is compulsory for every child, it should encourage children* ...), and to convey a sense of urgency by means of the use of *should*, which indeed occurs fifteen times in this student's text 5. RAD1102, on the other hand, does not use *should* at all, and the two occurrences of *because* (both occurring in this excerpt) are not used to support an argument, but rather to justify an assumption. In contrast, RAD1102 uses *could* five times (all occurring in the excerpt cited above); this, coupled with the relatively large number of *if*-clauses, gives RAD1102's text 5 a speculative, rather than an argumentative character.

In view of the assignment for text 5, it would appear that none of the other three students is as successful as RAD1101, although the reasons are different. RAD1102's text is speculative, rather than argumentative. RAD1111's text explains a presumed fact, rather than arguing in favour of a claim. Finally, RAD1113 presents an entirely different point of view, namely that the amount of money devoted to (primary) education may not necessarily be related to the quality of education. She does this from her own personal experience, and eventually comes to the conclusion that she rejects the claim in the essay prompt.

Conclusion

This study has shown that relating the use of VPs in advanced EFL writing to the development of syntactic EFL control, and hence the level of sophisticated EFL use, is a highly complex and problematic affair. An overall sparse use of VPs points to an appropriate expository style, while an abundance of VPs is more typical of speech. Inevitably, the use of relatively short sentences results in more VPs, although the occurrence of long sentences does not necessarily imply the occurrence of fewer VPs, as sentences can derive their length and complexity from the presence of embedded clauses. In practice, however, much of the complexity of long sentences is caused not (only) by embedded clauses, but (particularly) by the occurrence of embedded noun phrases and prepositional phrases. Much of what constitutes mature or academically appropriate EFL writing lies outside syntactic control.

However, a number of problems remain. This study is based on the analysis of texts produced by only four individual EFL learners, and it is not easy to determine at this stage exactly what accounts for their grammatical control. Personal characteristics of these learners, for instance, have not been taken into consideration. The excerpts in the previous section, for example, might suggest that RAD1101 is perhaps more inclined to show off his knowledge of formal style (as in the use of the formal *one* in both texts). Likewise, RAD1113 may have a tendency to write generally from a personal perspective. This can only be confirmed by a qualitative analysis of more texts and of the work from a larger number of EFL learners.

A further problem is the behaviour of the Stanford Parser, which occasionally yields unexpected output. For instance, the distinction between main clauses and subclauses is not entirely unproblematic. This has meant that manual post-editing of the parser output has proved necessary in order to deal with the presence of modal auxiliaries. Nor has the Stanford Parser output given me a reliable picture of the occurrence of VPs in main clauses and subclauses, so I have had to exclude this from the analysis. The parser's way of analysing multi-verb groups as a series of embedded VPs is not entirely satisfactory either. So, rather than looking at a phrase like *might have been done* as (might (have (been (done)$_{VP}$)$_{VP}$)$_{VP}$)$_{VP}$, one would like to see it analysed as (might have been done)$_{VP}$. As it is, these cases had to be manually sorted out at the beginning of the analysis. The use of the Stanford Parser output, and subsequent processing in Corpus Studio and Cesax, also revealed that complexity can be hidden on a deeper level in a relatively simple structure.

The students performed with varying degrees of success in the initial placement test in September and in the grammar exam in October, which indicates differences in grammatical knowledge. The findings presented in this paper fail to show unambiguously how students' grammatical knowledge relates to their grammatical control and/or discourse competence. Comparing the writings of the students discussed in this chapter suggests that there can be a wide gap between (passive) knowledge and (active) control. Still, the qualitative analysis of these texts did not refute any of the findings based on the numerical data; indeed, these data pointed in a direction that could be explored further in the qualitative analysis. I feel confident that more detailed research will confirm these provisional findings. Such research will have to include the comparison of in-class assignments with home assignments and a comparison of written EFL characteristics with written native Dutch characteristics.

Corpora

ICLE *International Corpus of Learner English*. 2002. Project director: Sylviane Granger. Centre for English Corpus Linguistics. Université Catholique de Louvain. http://www.uclouvain.be/en-cecl-icle.html.

LONGDALE *Longitudinal Database of Learner English*. 2008. Project director: Fanny Meunier. Centre for English Corpus Linguistics. Université Catholique de Louvain. http://www.uclouvain.be/en-cecl-longdale.html.

References

Biber, Douglas, Bethany Gray, and Kornwipa Poonpon. 2011. "Should We Use Characteristics of Conversation to Measure Grammatical Complexity in L2 Writing Development?" *TESOL Quarterly* 45/1: 5–35.

Biber, Douglas, Stig Johansson, Geoffrey Leech, Susan Conrad, and Edward Finegan. 1999. *Longman Grammar of Spoken and Written English*. London: Longman.

Chen, Yu-Hua, and Paul Baker. 2010. "Lexical Bundles in L1 and L2 Academic Writing." *Language Learning and Technology* 14/2: 30–49.

de Haan, Pieter. 2001. "Aspects of the Syntax of Spoken English." In *A Wealth of English. Studies in Honour of Göran Kjellmer*, edited by Karin Aijmer, 47–56. Gothenburg: Gothenburg University Press.

de Haan, Pieter. 2002. "The Non-Nominal Character of Spoken English." In *From the COLT's Mouth… and Others'. Language Corpora Studies in Honour of Anna-Brita Stenström*, edited by Leiv E. Breivik, and Angela Hasselgren, 59–69. Amsterdam and New York: Rodopi.

de Haan, Pieter. 2015. "Nouns and Noun Phrases in Advanced Dutch EFL Writing: From Quantitative to Qualitative Longitudinal Data Analysis." In *Studies in Learner Corpus Linguistics: Research and Applications for Foreign Language Teaching and Assessment*, edited by Erik Castello, Katherine Ackerley, and Francesca Coccetta, 127–42. Bern: Peter Lang.

de Haan, Pieter, and Monique van der Haagen. 2012. "Modification of Adjectives in Very Advanced Dutch EFL Writing: A Development Study." *The European Journal of Applied Linguistics and TEFL* 1/1: 129–42.

de Haan, Pieter, and Monique van der Haagen. 2013. "Assessing the Use of Sophisticated EFL Writing: A Longitudinal Study." *Dutch Journal of Applied Linguistics* 2/1: 16–27.

de Haan, Pieter, and Monique van der Haagen. 2014. "A Longitudinal Study of the Syntactic Development of Very Advanced Dutch EFL Writing." In *Recent Advances in Corpus Linguistics: Developing and Exploiting Corpora*, edited by Lieven Vandelanotte, Kristin Davidse, Caroline Gentens, and Ditte Kimps, 335–49. Amsterdam and New York: Rodopi.

de Haan, Pieter, and Kees van Esch. 2004. "Towards an Instrument for the Assessment of the Development of Writing Skills." In *Applied Corpus Linguistics: A Multidimensional Perspective*, edited by Ulla Connor, and Thomas Upton, 267–79. Amsterdam and New York: Rodopi.

de Haan, Pieter, and Kees van Esch. 2005. "The Development of Writing in English and Spanish as Foreign Languages." *Assessing Writing* 10: 100–16.

de Haan, Pieter, and Kees van Esch. 2006. "Assessing the Development of Foreign Language Writing Skills: Syntactic and Lexical Features." In *Corpus Linguistics beyond the Word: Corpus Research from Phrase to Discourse*, edited by Eileen Fitzpatrick, 185–202. Amsterdam and New York: Rodopi.

de Haan, Pieter, and Kees van Esch. 2007. "Measuring and Assessing the Development of Foreign Language Writing Competence." *Porta Linguarum* 9: 7–21.

de Vries, Rina, and Pieter de Haan. 2013. "CEFR B2 to C2: Charting a Long and Winding Road." Paper presented at the Learner Corpus Research Conference, Bergen, September 11–13.

Granger, Sylviane. 2009. LONGDALE. Retrieved October 20, 2010. http://www.uclouvain.be/en-cecl-longdale.html.

Grant, Leslie, and April Ginther. 2000. "Using Computer-Tagged Linguistic Features to Describe L2 Writing Differences." *Journal of Second Language Writing* 9/2: 123–45.

Hayes, John R., Jill A. Hatch, and Christine M. Silk. 2000. "Does Holistic Assessment Predict Writing Performance? Estimating the Consistency of Student Performance on Holistically Scored Writing Assignments." *Written Communication* 17/1: 3–26.

Klein, Dan, and Christopher D. Manning. 2003. "Accurate Unlexicalized Parsing." In *Proceedings of the 41st Annual Meeting of the Association for Computational*

Linguistics, edited by Erhard W. Hinrichs, and Dan Roth, 423–30. Stroudsburg, PA: Association for Computational Linguistics.

Kobayashi, Hiroe, and Carol Rinnert. 2013. "L1/L2/L3 Writing Development: Longitudinal Case Study of a Japanese Multicompetent Writer." *Journal of Second Language Writing* 22: 4–33.

Komen, Erwin. 2011a . "Cesax (Coreference Editor for Syntactically Annotated XML corpora)." Retrieved April 26, 2013. http://erwinkomen.ruhosting.nl/software/Cesax/.

Komen, Erwin. 2011b. "Corpus Studio." Retrieved April 25, 2013. http://erwinkomen.ruhosting.nl/software/CorpusStudio/.

Kuiken, Folkert, and Ineke Vedder. 2007. "Task Complexity and Measures of Linguistic Performance in L2 Writing." *IRAL* 45/3: 261–84.

Kuiken, Folkert, and Ineke Vedder. 2008. "Cognitive Task Complexity and Written Output in Italian and French as a Foreign Language." *Journal of Second Language Writing* 17/1: 48–60.

Laufer, Batia, and Tina Waldman. 2011. "Verb-Noun Collocations in Second Language Writing: A Corpus Analysis of Learners' English." *Language Learning* 61/2: 647–72.

Li, Jie, and Norbert Schmitt. 2009. "The Acquisition of Lexical Phrases in Academic Writing: A Longitudinal Case Study." *Journal of Second Language Writing* 18/2: 85–102.

Melissen, Melis. 2007. *Exameneisen havo-vwo nieuwe stijl 2007*. Alphen aan den Rijn: Kluwer.

Michel, Marije, Folkert Kuiken, and Ineke Vedder. 2007. "The Influence of Complexity in Monologic versus Dialogic Tasks in Dutch L2." *IRAL* 45/3: 241–59.

Murphy, Liz, and Julio Roca de Larios. 2010. "Searching for Words: One Strategic Use of the Mother Tongue by Advanced Spanish EFL Writers." *Journal of Second Language Writing* 19/2: 61–81.

Ortega, Lourdes. 2003. "Syntactic Complexity Measures and their Relationship to L2 Proficiency: A Research Synthesis of College-Level L2 Writing." *Applied Linguistics* 24/4: 492–518.

Reichelt, Melinda, Natalie Lefkowitz, Carol Rinnert, and Jean M. Schultz. 2012. "Key Issues in Foreign Language Writing." *Foreign Language Annals* 45/1: 22–41.

Schoonen, Rob. 2005. "Generalizability of Writing Scores: An Application of Structural Equation Modelling." *Language Testing* 22: 1–30.

Shaw, Philip, and Eric Ting-Kun Liu. 1998. "What Develops in the Development of Second-Language Writing?" *Applied Linguistics* 19/2: 225–54.

Silva, Tony. 1993. "Toward an Understanding of the Distinct Nature of L2 Writing: The ESL Research and its Implication." *TESOL Quarterly* 27: 657–77.

Springer, Philip E. 2012. *Advanced Learner Writing: A Corpus-Based Study of the Discourse Competence of Dutch Writers of English in the Light of the C1/C2 Levels of the CEFR*. Oisterwijk: BOXPress.

Thewissen, Jennifer. 2013. "Capturing L2 Accuracy Developmental Patterns: Insights from an Error-Tagged EFL Learner Corpus." *The Modern Language Journal* 97/S1: 77–101.

Verheijen, Lieke, Pieter de Haan, and Bettelou Los. 2013. "Information Structure: The Final Hurdle? The Development of Syntactic Structures in (Very) Advanced Dutch EFL Writing." *Dutch Journal of Applied Linguistics* 2/1: 92–107.

Williams, Jessica. 2012. "The Potential Role(s) of Writing in Second Language Development." *Journal of Second Language Writing* 21/4: 321–31.

CHAPTER 6

Discourse-Organizing Metadiscourse in Novice Academic English*

Hilde Hasselgård

Abstract

This study concerns discourse-organizing metadiscourse in two disciplines of novice academic English: linguistics and business. It is based on the VESPA (*Varieties of English for Specific Purposes dAtabase*) corpus of discipline-specific texts in English by Norwegian learners compared to the *British Academic Written English* (BAWE) corpus and the *Michigan Corpus of Upper-Level Student Papers* (MICUSP). The following dimensions are compared: disciplines (linguistics vs. business), English L1 vs. L2, and British vs. American writers. An additional comparison is made with published research articles within the same disciplines. The learners have a significantly higher frequency of metadiscourse than L1 novice writers in both disciplines, though not all types of metadiscourse are equally different. Learners and L1 novices alike use more metadiscourse than the professional academics represented in the corpus of research articles. In the cross-disciplinary comparison, linguistics was found to use more metadiscourse than business in all the writer populations.

Keywords

metadiscourse – academic writing – student writing – disciplinary variation – discourse organization – Norwegian learners of English

Introduction

Do learners of English signal the organization of their academic papers in the same way as native speakers? The present study explores discourse-organizing

* I am grateful to the audience at my conference presentation at ICAME 34 for their input and to the reviewers of this chapter for constructive comments.

 | DOI 10.1163/9789004321342_007

metadiscourse among Norwegian learners of English within two academic disciplines: linguistics and business. The learners are compared to native speakers of English who are students in British and American universities. All these groups can be considered novice writers and novice academics. The aims are to survey the functional types of metadiscourse used by each group, and to discover to what extent and in what respects the two disciplines differ in their use of metadiscourse, and whether learners differ from native speakers in their choice of metadiscursive expressions and in the differentiation between disciplines. Finally, the novice writers will be compared to "expert writers" (authors of published research articles) to gauge the extent to which the students have acquired the norms for using metadiscourse within their disciplines.

The organization of academic papers and the use of metadiscourse have been shown to vary across languages and cultures (e.g. Clyne 1987; Crismore et al. 1993; Dahl 2004), genres (e.g. Hyland 2005; Bondi 2010), and disciplines (e.g. Hyland 1998; Hyland and Tse 2004; Dahl 2004). The present research design is intended to uncover variation along the following dimensions: discipline, L1 background, and writer expertise.

Theoretical Preliminaries

Defining Metadiscourse

Although various definitions have been given, most researchers seem to agree that "metadiscourse is text about the evolving text, or the writer's explicit commentary on her own ongoing discourse" (Ädel 2006, 20); that is, "metadiscourse represents the writer's awareness of the unfolding text as *discourse*" (Hyland and Tse 2004, 167). The attention to discourse can be related to the organization of the discourse or the writer's attitude to (and engagement with) the propositional content. According to Hyland (1998, 437), metadiscourse is an interactional resource for explicitly organizing the discourse, engaging the audience, and signalling the writer's attitude. The (interactional) resources of metadiscourse "are concerned with ways of organizing discourse, rather than experience, to anticipate readers' knowledge and reflect the writer's assessment of what needs to be made explicit to constrain and guide what can be recovered from the text" (Hyland and Tse 2004, 168). Hyland (2005, 37) offers the following definition of metadiscourse:

> Metadiscourse is the cover term for the self-reflective expressions used to negotiate interactional meanings in a text, assisting the writer (or speaker) to express a viewpoint and engage with readers as members of a particular community.

The term 'reflective' (or 'reflexive', e.g. Ädel 2010) specifies that expressions of metadiscourse are about "the evolving discourse itself or its linguistic form" (Ädel 2010, 75). Importantly, metadiscourse makes reference to the current text rather than other texts (Ädel 2010), and should not be confused with expressions of intertextuality. This is particularly pertinent to the analysis of linguistics texts, whose objects of study are often external texts. Thus, *paper* is metadiscursive in example (1), but not in (2).[1]

(1) My *paper* shows that a corpus search is a comprehensive task even with few returns [...]. (VESPA-LIN)

(2) Lillo's aims in the *paper* "Exploring rhyming slang in Ireland" are [...]. (VESPA-LIN)

Vande Kopple (1985, 83) claims that at "the level of metadiscourse, we do not add propositional material but help our readers organize, classify, interpret, evaluate, and react to such material". Though agreeing that metadiscourse is predominantly textual or interpersonal in nature (e.g. Hyland and Tse 2004, 167), Hyland insists that metadiscourse cannot be entirely divorced from the "propositional material" of the text: "Metadiscourse is an essential part of any text and contributes to the ways it is understood and acted upon: it is not a separate and separable set of stylistic devices that can either be included or not without affecting how a text is presented and read" (Hyland 2005, 23). This view is in line with Halliday's functional view of language, according to which the three metafunctions are always present simultaneously (e.g. Halliday and Matthiessen 2014, 83).

Previous Studies of Metadiscourse in Academic Writing

An early, still much cited, study of metadiscourse is Vande Kopple (1985). The contribution of his paper was to provide a taxonomy of metadiscourse which has been applied, modified, and elaborated by later scholars.[2] Vande Kopple's main categories are text connectives, validity markers, illocution markers, code glosses, narrators, attitude markers, and commentary (Vande Kopple 1985, 85), conveying both textual and interpersonal meanings (Vande Kopple 1985, 86).

Both Mauranen (1993) and Crismore et al. (1993) study the use of metadiscourse by Finnish and Anglo-American writers on the assumption that the use of metadiscourse will vary according to factors such as (first) language and

1 All examples are given as they appear in the corpora, with any infelicities intact.

2 For an overview of precursors to Vande Kopple, see Stainton (1996).

culture.[3] Mauranen, investigating economics articles published in English by Finnish and Anglo-American writers, finds less metadiscourse in the Finnish-produced sample. The difference is believed "to reflect different assumptions of shared knowledge in the communication process" (1993, 18); that is, more shared knowledge should diminish the need for metadiscourse. By contrast, in an investigation of argumentative writing by students writing in their L1, Crismore et al. (1993) find that Finnish writers use more metadiscourse than Americans. They also studied the effect of gender: the general trend was that females used more metadiscourse than men in both the Finnish and the American sample (Crismore et al. 1993, 66).

Stainton (1996) gives a review of metadiscourse studies up to the time of writing. One observation (presumably by Stainton's own team) deserves special mention: in a small study two groups of 20 native and non-native speakers were exposed to two versions of the 'same' text with different amounts of metadiscourse. Non-native speakers preferred the version with more metadiscourse, but native speakers preferred the other one (1996, 33). This is associated with the function of metadiscourse, namely to "provide guidance and direction for the reader" (Stainton 1996, 10). Presumably, native speakers are better equipped to make the necessary inferences with fewer explicit signals.

Metadiscourse has been the subject of numerous studies by Hyland and associates (for example, Hyland 1998, 2005; Hyland and Tse 2004). Hyland (1998) compares the use of metadiscourse across four disciplines: biology, astrophysics, applied linguistics, and marketing. He finds important disciplinary differences in the overall frequency of metadiscursive expressions as well as the internal distribution of textual vs. interpersonal metadiscourse and subtypes of these (1998, 446). Hyland and Tse (2004, 167) redefine metadiscourse as a primarily interpersonal feature of communication and present a revised model for classifying metadiscourse, in which many features that used to fall into the 'textual' category are reanalysed as 'interactive', while the formerly 'interpersonal' are renamed 'interactional' (Hyland and Tse 2004, 169). The framework is applied to a corpus of MA and PhD dissertations, spanning six disciplines. Doctoral dissertations are found to employ more metadiscourse than MA dissertations (Hyland and Tse 2004, 170). The disciplines differ markedly, with applied linguistics using the largest amount of metadiscourse and electronic engineering the lowest (Hyland and Tse 2004, 172). Hyland's (2005) monograph describes metadiscourse in relation to rhetoric, genre, culture, and community. Though to a great extent drawing on previous work by

3 See also Hyland (1998, 438), who argues that metadiscourse is "intimately linked to the norms and expectations of particular cultural and professional communities".

himself and others, Hyland shows that all these variables may influence the use of metadiscourse.

Dahl's (2004) study is based on a corpus of research articles spanning three disciplines (linguistics, economics, and medicine) and three languages (English, Norwegian, and French). The aim is to survey the influence of both language/culture and discipline on the use of textual metadiscourse. Dahl finds that Norwegian and English writers employ metadiscourse in similar ways, while French writers use much less, suggesting that French writing culture is more reader-responsible (cf. Hinds 1987). There is also a disciplinary difference: medicine uses markedly less metadiscourse than economics and linguistics (Dahl 2004, 1818).

Ädel (2006) studies metadiscourse in L1 and L2 English on the basis of the Swedish part of the *International Corpus of Learner Essays* (ICLE) and the *Louvain Corpus of Native English Essays* (LOCNESS). British and American texts in LOCNESS are kept apart, thus facilitating a three-way comparison of novice writing. The learners use more metadiscourse of both the personal (making direct reference to the writer or the reader; cf. 2006, 47) and the impersonal kind (mainly text-reflexive; cf. 2006, 98). British students use less than American students, particularly of personal metadiscourse (e.g. Ädel 2006, 190). Interestingly, Ädel raises the question of "the control corpus and the norm" in learner corpus research (2006, 205ff.), suggesting that learners should ideally be compared to *both* native-speaker student essays and professional texts, so as to measure them (justly) against writers at the same level of expertise, but also evaluating them against writing that "represents the norm that advanced foreign learner writers try to reach and their teachers try to promote" (2006, 207).

Ädel (2010) outlines a slightly different taxonomy of metadiscourse, which is the one adopted here. The model has the following categories: metalinguistic comments (repairing, reformulating, commenting on linguistic form/meaning, clarifying, managing terminology); discourse organization (see below); speech act labels; and references to the audience (2010, 83). The taxonomy is designed to be applicable to both speech and writing.

Lee (2009) studies metadiscourse in English L1 and L2 postgraduate student writing as well as expert writing (journal articles). The students came from Newcastle University, with the non-natives having mixed L1 backgrounds. Lee finds that non-native speakers use more textual metadiscourse and less interpersonal metadiscourse than native speakers (2009, 277). The student/expert comparison gave less conclusive results, with few differences in the overall frequency of metadiscourse, but some variation in the distribution of particular functional types.

Hypotheses of the Present Study

Against the background of previous studies it is possible to outline the following hypotheses for the present investigation:

(a) Disciplines will differ qualitatively and quantitatively in their use of metadiscourse (Dahl 2004).
(b) Learners will overuse metadiscourse compared to native speakers (Stainton 1996; Ädel 2006).
(c) American writers will use more metadiscourse than British writers (Ädel 2006).
(d) Novice writers will use more metadiscourse than expert writers. This is uncertain, however. Lee (2009) found little difference, but Mauranen's (1993) suggestion that more shared knowledge should diminish the need for metadiscourse might imply that experts writing for experts are less in need of metadiscourse.

The existence of examples such as (3), which consists almost exclusively of metadiscourse, lends support to the hypothesis of overuse in learner texts.

(3) In general, the outline of this paper will, in addition to this introduction, include a discussion on these N-grams concerning the features I mentioned above. (VESPA-LIN)

However, the findings of previous studies are sometimes conflicting. For example, Hyland and Tse (2004, 170) find that doctoral dissertations contain more metadiscourse than MA dissertations. This seems to contradict the hypothesis of a decrease in metadiscourse with the level of writer expertise. Similarly, those studies that compare linguistics and business writing report different findings: no difference (Dahl 2004), linguistics uses more (Hyland and Tse 2004), and linguistics uses less (admittedly compared to marketing rather than business; Hyland 1998). It is also interesting to note that Dahl (2004) found little cultural difference between Norwegian and English-language writers in their use of metadiscourse, which suggests that any differences between Norwegian learners of English and native speakers should be mainly due to the L1/L2 variable.

Material and Method

Corpora of discipline-specific writing allow comparisons of lexico-grammatical features across registers (in the vein of Biber 2006 and Hyland 2008). The bulk of this study is based on three corpora of novice academic writing, all of which comprise the disciplines linguistics and business/economics:

(a) The Norwegian component of the VESPA (*Varieties of English for Specific Purposes dAtabase*) corpus represents advanced learners of English. VESPA-NO consists of discipline-specific texts in English by university students whose first language is Norwegian. The linguistics component contains course assignments written by students of English, and the business component contains assignments by students doing an English-medium course as part of a business degree.
(b) The *British Academic Written English* (BAWE) corpus (Nesi and Gardner 2012) represents novice academic writing by students in British universities. The corpus consists of 'good-standard' assignments from BA and MA level.
(c) The *Michigan Corpus of Upper-Level Student Papers* (MICUSP) represents novice writing in the US and consists of A-graded student assignments at undergraduate and graduate level (Römer and O'Donnell 2011; Ädel and Römer 2012, 4–5).

Only English L1 texts were selected from BAWE and MICUSP to provide a native-speaker basis for comparison with the Norwegian learners. All three corpora contain texts from both BA and MA levels, which might facilitate a quasi-longitudinal study. However, in practice, the distribution of texts across the levels is relatively uneven, with a rather small proportion of MA papers in both BAWE and VESPA (cf. Nesi and Gardner 2012, 7). Since some of the subcorpora are quite small already (see Table 6.1), a subdivision according to levels was undesirable. Note that the L1 corpora contain assignments that have received favourable evaluation, while no such requirement was used in the VESPA compilation. This is a variable which unfortunately cannot be controlled for except by means of a post-hoc grading of the VESPA scripts.

The novice writing in BAWE and MICUSP may not represent the norms of the discipline, so a corpus of 'expert' academic writing was consulted for comparison, namely the *Corpus of Research Articles* (CRA). The corpus is searchable from the Hong Kong Polytechnic University's website and contains research articles from 39 academic disciplines, from which linguistics and economics were used.[4] The writers in CRA are not necessarily native speakers of English, but their articles have been published in English-medium journals with high impact ratios and can thus be assumed to represent the discourse of their disciplines.

4 See further <http://rcpce.engl.polyu.edu.hk/RACorpus/> (accessed January 2014).

This combination of corpora facilitates comparison across L1 background (English L1 vs. L2), registers (linguistics vs. business), and British vs. American English. Additionally, novice writers can be compared to experts in the field.

Table 6.1 shows the size and composition of the corpora. VESPA and BAWE have been annotated so that material such as tables, quotations, and linguistic examples can be excluded from corpus searches (see Ebeling and Heuboeck 2007). The word counts for these corpora in Table 6.1 are exclusive of such material. The average text length varies considerably across corpora, which may well have consequences for the use of metadiscourse; however, it has not been taken into account in the present study.

TABLE 6.1 *Overview of the corpora used for the study*

	Linguistics			Business/Economics		
	Texts	Words	Av. text length	Texts	Words	Av. text length
VESPA (L2)	239	267,855	1,120	70	47,335	676
BAWE (L1, UK)	76	167,437	2,203	64	141,249	2,207
MICUSP (L1, US)	34	118,476	3,484	16	49,088	3,068
CRA	20	174,684	8,734	20	232,303	11,615

The broad disciplines are the same in all the corpora, but the subdisciplines and topics may differ. This is particularly the case for the business/economics discipline: most of the VESPA papers concern cross-cultural business communication, the BAWE papers are mainly reports on company analyses, while the MICUSP papers are mainly reports and research papers within social economics.

All the corpora represent the register of academic prose, as defined according to Biber and Conrad (2009, 6), that is, a language variety "associated with a particular situation of use"—the communication of disciplinary knowledge in an academic setting (cf. also Ilie 2002, 10). As pointed out by Biber and Conrad (2009, 32), "there are also important register differences among academic disciplines"; thus, linguistics and business can be seen as subregisters of academic prose. Furthermore, the student papers differ from the published articles in their intended audience, namely (mainly) the teachers vs. (mainly) fellow academics (see further Ilie 2002 on register characteristics of published research). This difference comes to light in the comparison of student and expert texts since metadiscourse, even the discourse-organizing type, is interactive in that it guides the reader through the text (Hyland and Tse 2004).

Searches in BAWE and VESPA were performed using WordSmith Tools. Since these corpora have the same type of annotation (see above), searches excluded material not representing the students' own writing. WordSmith was also used for exploring MICUSP,[5] while CRA was searched online from its website. As MICUSP and CRA do not have any functional annotation, search hits that were clearly from quoted material were removed manually. In what follows, quantitative information is given as either raw frequencies or normalized frequencies per 10,000 words. Paul Rayson's log-likelihood calculator was used for the statistical comparisons, with the significance level set at $p<0.05$, critical value=3.84.[6]

The Taxonomy of Discourse-Organizing Metadiscourse and the Search Items

Several taxonomies of metadiscourse have been proposed. For useful reviews, see e.g. Stainton (1996), Hyland (2005, 32ff.), and Ädel (2006, 167ff.). The framework of Vande Kopple (1985) is generally acknowledged as an important influence on the study of metadiscourse. Subsequent frameworks thus have much in common. This study uses that of Ädel (2010), which was outlined in broad terms above. The functional categories of the framework for discourse-organizing metadiscourse are presented below (Ädel 2010, 85ff.):

(a) **Introducing topic** (used to open the topic; e.g. *in this paper I explore*).
(b) **Concluding topic** (used to close the topic; e.g. *we conclude that*).
(c) **Enumerating** (used to show how specific parts of the discourse are ordered in relation to each other; e.g. *in the following section*; *finally*).
(d) **Previewing** (points forward in the discourse; e.g. *as I discuss below*).
(e) **Reviewing** (points backward in the discourse; e.g. *as we have seen*).
(f) **Endophoric marking** (used to point to a location in the discourse, without specifying whether it is before or after the current point; e.g. *as we can see in*).
(g) **Delimiting topic** (used to explicitly state how the topic is constrained; e.g. *is outside the scope of this paper*).
(h) **Adding to topic** (used to explicitly comment on the addition of a topic or subtopic; e.g. *we might add that*).

5 I am extremely grateful to Ute Römer for access to the MICUSP files.
6 <http://ucrel.lancs.ac.uk/llwizard.html> (last accessed December 2014).

(i) **Marking asides** (used to open or close a 'topic sidetrack' or digression; e.g. *let me digress*).

(j) **Contextualizing** (used to comment on the conditions of speaking or writing; e.g. *I have said little about*).

Only categories (a)–(f) have been included in the analysis. This is for reasons to do with corpus findings: some types of expressions were not frequent enough across the corpora to make comparisons meaningful.

As Hyland points out, "there are no simple linguistic criteria for identifying metadiscourse" (2005, 27). The list of search terms used for the present study was arrived at from lists in previous studies (e.g. Hyland 2005, 218ff.; Ädel 2006, 98), close-reading of some corpus texts, and patterns that became apparent in connection with other searches. In addition to Ädel's (2010) categories of discourse-organizing metadiscourse, the following items were included:

(k) **Current text reference.** This category includes all references to the paper under production, not necessarily in phrases belonging to any of the functional categories in Ädel's (2010) list. Notably, the word *text* was not included, as preliminary searches indicated that *text* is rarely used metadiscursively.

(l) ***I will/have.*** These may belong in Ädel's category of speech act labels (2010, 88). However, *I will*, referring to the writer *qua* writer (Ädel 2010, 79), tends to occur in patterns that imply previewing, topic introduction, or topic delimitation, as shown in Figure 6.1. Similarly, *I have* occurs in patterns of reviewing or topic conclusion. Since many expert texts have multiple authors, *we will/have* were also included.[7]

7	on how the CEOs behaved,	I will look at intercultural
8	borders. </s><s n="s2.2;p2.9">	I will do so through the cultural
9	(RF) is expressive, but	I will now look at the most
10	dimensions that he discus, but	I will only say something about
11	and femininity/masculinity, but	I will only say something about a
12	the people involved in this case,	I will start this discussion by
13	, and to make this clear	I will use some example from
14	are made in companies	I will present four different
15	correct. </s><s n="s2.4;p1.5">	I will now reflect upon the
16	France are the three countries	I will use as examples, together
17	culture. </s><s n="s2.2;p1.14">	I will justify my answer after the

FIGURE 6.1 *Concordance of* I will *in* VESPA-BUS *(excerpt).*

7 Ädel (2012) explores the metadiscursive use of *you* referring to the reader *qua* reader. This use is clearly audience-oriented, while the writer reference implied by the expressions with *I will/have*, though presuming a reader, are more oriented towards discourse organization.

Table 6.2 presents the final selection of search terms, namely those that were frequent enough to make a cross-corpus comparison interesting. Each functional category is exemplified below.

TABLE 6.2 *Search terms included in the study*

Function	Term	Example
Introducing topic	*aim, purpose, begin*, start*, introduction, in this essay/paper/ article, of this essay/paper/article, this study, this essay/paper will, this paper is*	(4)
Concluding topic	*summary, summari*, conclud*, conclusion, sum up*	(5)
Enumerating	*initially, finally, firstly, secondly, thirdly,* sentence-initial *first, second, third*	(6)
Previewing	*as shown below, in the following, of the following, the* N *below, the below* N	(7)
Reviewing	*as mentioned above, in the preceding, the above* N, *the* N *above*	(8)
Endophoric marking	*as discussed, as mentioned, as noted, as referred*	(9)
Current text reference	*paper, essay, assignment, article*	(10)
I will/have	*I have, I will, we have, we will*	Fig. 6.1

(4) *The purpose of this paper* is to find indications as to whether Norwegian learners of English conform to convensions of academic writing [...]. (VESPA-LIN)

(5) *I conclude* that there are generational differences in attitudes to text language [...]. (BAWE-LIN)

(6) *Firstly,* employees do not own their companies, which tend to be multinationals [...]. (BAWE-BUS)

(7) *In the following text, I will discuss* some ethical dilemmas, based on the theories from Gesteland, Hall, Hofstede and Trompenaars. (VESPA-BUS)

(8) There is, *as mentioned above,* a difference in meaning between *money* and *currency* [...]. (VESPA-LIN)

(9) The idea of linguistic transfer leading to overhedging [...] is also demonstrated by Hinkel (1997), *as discussed* previously. (MICUSP-LIN)

(10) Linearization is discussed in detail later in the *paper.* (CRA-LIN)

There is some degree of overlap in the framework, particularly between 'Previewing'/'Reviewing' and 'Endophoric marking' and between 'Current text reference' and several other categories. For example, (9) contains a phrase that would not be picked up by the search terms under 'Reviewing', while in (10) a 'Current text reference' is part of a 'Previewing' expression. As most of the discussion treats the functional categories separately, this was not considered a serious problem.

Under 'Enumerating', only sentence-initial occurrences of *first*, *second*, and *third* were searched for, since they are more likely to be ordinals in other positions. The words *above*, *below*, *following*, and *preceding* were excluded from 'Previewing'/'Reviewing' because they had so many non-metadiscursive uses that it was considered more serviceable to identify discourse-organizing phrases which included them.

Hardly any of the items presented in Table 6.2 function exclusively as metadiscourse; therefore, they need to be seen in their proper context (cf. Hyland 2005, 25). Consequently, the concordances were post-edited manually to remove non-metadiscursive uses. Most of the figures presented in the next section are thus lower than those that emerge from simple corpus searches.

The Use of Metadiscourse Across Disciplines and Writer Groups

This section presents the use of discourse-organizing metadiscourse across disciplines within each corpus before comparing learners to native speakers and novice writers to experts. Comparisons are both quantitative and qualitative, giving details of the distribution of functional types of discourse-organizing metadiscourse as well as differences in preferred expressions.

Disciplinary Variation within L1 Groups

This section compares the linguistics and business/economic part of each of the novice corpora, to see whether the discipline colours the use of metadiscourse. Table 6.3 shows the patterns in VESPA. For each functional category, the frequency is significantly higher in linguistics than in business. Interestingly, the functional categories of metadiscourse have the same frequency rank in both disciplines. The most frequent category is *I will/have*, followed by 'Current text reference' and 'Introducing topic'. There is quite a leap in frequency between the third and the fourth most frequent category ('Enumerating') in both disciplines; i.e. the top three are clear favourites.

TABLE 6.3 *Disciplinary variation in VESPA (raw and normalized frequencies)*

	VESPA-LIN		VESPA-BUS		LL	p-value
	N	/ 10,000 W	N	/ 10,000 W		
Introducing topic	343	12.8	33	7.0	13.17	p<0.001
Concluding topic	140	5.2	10	2.1	10.00	p<0.01
Enumerating	186	6.9	12	2.5	15.50	p<0.0001
Previewing	102	3.8	3	0.6	17.33	p<0.0001
Reviewing	107	4.0	8	1.7	7.08	p<0.01
Endophoric marking	66	2.5	4	0.8	5.98	p<0.01
Current text reference	355	13.3	40	8.5	8.21	p<0.001
I will/have	618	23.1	86	18.2	4.58	p<0.01
Total	1,917	71.6	196	41.4	61.80	p<0.0001

A possible explanation for the more sparse use of metadiscourse in VESPA-BUS is that the texts are generally quite short (cf. Table 6.1), so there may be less need for explicit signals of text organization. On the other hand, if the need for metadiscourse is proportional to text length, we would expect little difference between linguistics and business in BAWE, which is not the case, as shown in Table 6.4.

TABLE 6.4 *Disciplinary variation in BAWE (raw and normalized frequencies)*

	BAWE-LIN		BAWE-BUS		LL	p-value
	N	/ 10,000 W	N	/ 10,000 W		
Introducing topic	133	7.9	36	2.5	43.95	p<0.0001
Concluding topic	100	6.0	48	3.4	10.89	p<0.001
Enumerating	106	6.3	139	9.8	11.84	p<0.001
Previewing	27	1.6	13	0.9	2.91	p>0.05
Reviewing	24	1.4	28	2.0	1.36	p>0.05
Endophoric marking	24	1.4	20	1.4	0.00	p>0.05
Current text reference	128	7.6	48	3.4	25.40	p<0.0001
I will/have	140	8.4	71	5.0	12.77	p<0.001
Total	682	40.6	403	28.4	28.22	p<0.0001

The discipline comparison in BAWE shows a similar trend to that of VESPA, although the pattern is not equally consistent. Linguistics contains more metadiscourse than business overall, but 'Enumerating' is used significantly more in business. 'Previewing', 'Reviewing', and 'Endophoric marking' are the least frequent categories in both disciplines and do not show significant differences.

Unlike VESPA, the disciplines in BAWE differ as to their top three categories: linguistics favours '*I will/have*', 'Introducing topic', and 'Current text reference'; business prefers 'Enumerating', '*I will/have*', and 'Concluding topic'. Compared to VESPA the functional categories are more evenly distributed in both disciplines in BAWE, at least among the most frequent five in Table 6.4. This may point to greater variation in the use of metadiscourse by native speakers.

Unexpectedly, MICUSP-LIN and MICUSP-ECO display very little difference in their use of metadiscourse, as detailed in Table 6.5. The overall frequency is slightly higher for linguistics, but not significantly so. However, three functional categories show significant frequency differences: '*I will/have*' and 'Previewing' are more common in linguistics, while 'Enumerating' is more common in economics, which is similar to the pattern in BAWE.

TABLE 6.5 *Disciplinary variation in MICUSP (raw and normalized frequencies)*

	MICUSP-LIN		MICUSP-ECO		LL	p-value
	N	/ 10,000 W	N	/ 10,000 W		
Introducing topic	75	6.3	27	5.5	0.40	p>0.05
Concluding topic	28	2.4	7	1.4	1.57	p>0.05
Enumerating	89	7.5	64	13.0	10.86	p<0.001
Previewing	45	3.8	3	0.6	16.12	p<0.0001
Reviewing	32	2.7	7	1.4	2.67	p>0.05
Endophoric marking	13	1.1	2	0.4	2.14	p>0.05
Current text reference	89	7.5	44	9.0	0.90	p>0.05
I will/have	101	8.5	20	4.1	10.64	p<0.01
Total	472	39.8	174	35.4	1.77	p>0.05

The top three categories in MICUSP-LIN are '*I will/have*', 'Enumerating', and 'Current text reference', the latter two with identical frequencies. MICUSP-ECO does not have '*I will/have*' among its top three categories, which are 'Enumerating', 'Current text reference', and 'Introducing topic'.

We may conclude that discipline matters for the use of metadiscourse, even if the picture is not clear for MICUSP. In VESPA, all types of metadiscourse are more common in linguistics. In BAWE and MICUSP, business/economics uses more 'Enumerating' than linguistics, but most other types are more frequent in linguistics. Unlike the native speakers, the learners had the same top three categories in both disciplines. In all three linguistics corpora, the most frequently used metadiscourse category is '*I will/have*'. This category is also relatively frequent in business/economics, but is superseded by 'Enumerating' in both L1 corpora. 'Introducing topic', 'Current text reference', and 'Previewing' are consistently more frequent in linguistics. These are exemplified in (11), (12), and (13).

(11) The *purpose* of this task is to explore the multimodality of a television advert for "Dr Pepper". (BAWE-LIN)

(12) Although *this study* demonstrates that cohesion is realized differently across genres, the text samples were small [...]. (VESPA-LIN)

(13) This is seen *in the following* two examples, from Sportiche (1988): [...]. (MICUSP-LIN)

Comparison of Learners and Native Speakers

For ease of presentation the tables in this section will report only normalized frequencies. However, the log-likelihood calculations are based on the raw frequencies reported in the previous section.

TABLE 6.6 *English L2 vs. L1, Linguistics (frequency per 10,000 words)*

	VESPA-LIN	BAWE-LIN	MICUSP-LIN	LL: V VS. B	LL: V VS. M
Introducing topic	12.8	7.9	6.3	23.28	35.19
Concluding topic	5.2	6.0	2.4	3.19	17.35
Enumerating	6.9	6.3	7.5	0.58	0.37
Previewing	3.8	1.6	3.8	18.29	0.00
Reviewing	4.0	1.4	2.7	25.00	4.03
Endophoric marking	2.5	1.4	1.1	5.57	8.43
Current text reference	13.3	7.6	7.5	30.77	25.52
I will/I have	23.1	8.4	8.5	147.36	107.87
Total	71.6	40.6	39.8	165.55	145.24

Table 6.6 shows that metadiscourse is almost consistently used more in VESPA-LIN compared to both BAWE-LIN and MICUSP-LIN.[8] The only category where VESPA does not differ significantly from either L1 corpus is 'Enumerating'. 'Concluding topic' is used more only in comparison to MICUSP, and is actually used more in BAWE than in VESPA (though the difference is not significant). 'Previewing' is used more in comparison to BAWE, but has the same frequency in VESPA as in MICUSP.

The total frequency of metadiscourse is similar between BAWE and MICUSP, though three functional categories differ: 'Concluding topic' is more frequent in BAWE (LL=27.84), while 'Previewing' and 'Reviewing' are more frequent in MICUSP (LL=12.92 and 5.58, respectively). The learners do not consistently resemble either UK or US usage: where BAWE and MICUSP are different, VESPA is closer to BAWE for 'Concluding topic' and 'Previewing', but closer to MICUSP for 'Reviewing.'

'*I will/have*' is almost three times as frequent in VESPA as in BAWE and MICUSP. Ädel (2006) found that American students used more personal metadiscourse than British students—this difference is not reflected in the use of '*I will/have*' in BAWE-LIN and MICUSP-LIN. This may point to a difference between general argumentative and discipline-specific writing in English as L1. The overuse of self-reference in L2 English by Norwegian learners was noted by Paquot et al. (2013). Investigations of L1 writing in Norwegian would be needed in order to ascertain if this is a feature of foreign-language writing or of cultural differences in text construction.

'Current text reference' is also frequent across the material. Incidentally, VESPA and MICUSP students generally refer to their texts as *paper*. In MICUSP this term is used almost invariably, while VESPA also uses *essay* and *assignment*. In BAWE *essay* occurs about twice as frequently as *paper* and *assignment* combined.

There are also different lexical preferences in the category 'Concluding topic'. The most frequent expressions involve *conclusion* or *conclude*, as in (14). An expression used only by the learners, though not very frequently, is *as a conclusion*, exemplified in (15).

(14) *In conclusion*, I have shown there are very specific ways in which these pronouns are used in Tony Blair's speeches. (BAWE-LIN)

8 Bold type in the table indicates significant differences between VESPA and BAWE or MICUSP. In the last two columns, V, B, and M stand for VESPA, BAWE, and MICUSP.

(15) *As a conclusion*, I found that text 1 is reader-friendly and easy to understand [...]. (VESPA-LIN)

'Previewing' is more frequent in VESPA than in BAWE, and 'Reviewing' and 'Endophoric marking' are more common in VESPA than in both L1 corpora. Especially *as mentioned* (*above*) seems to be more of a stock phrase in VESPA. It is possible that the Norwegian equivalent of this phrase, *som nevnt*, is more frequent than *as mentioned*, an assumption which is supported if we consult the *English-Norwegian Parallel Corpus* (ENPC).[9] The use of *as mentioned* in VESPA-LIN is illustrated in Figure 6.2.

34	in his claim about and ,	as mentioned	on page 2, I would have found it
35	CitroÃ«n Saxo. There are	as mentioned	seven questions in this text, all with
36	clause combinations and,	as mentioned	before, complex noun phrases. In
37	to its fuzzy definition and,	as mentioned,	its resemblance to the Norwegian
38	their linguistically aspects.	As mentioned,	they do share the same theme.
39	is most common in AusE.	As mentioned	above BrE is known to favour the
40	. Material processes are,	as mentioned	above, processes of , which means
41	questions one has asked.	As mentioned	above, I have chosen the ENPC and
42	them (Cook 2008: 21).	As mentioned	initially, lexical cohesion differ from
43	down to 44%.	As mentioned	above, the English framework
44		As mentioned	earlier, there are various different

FIGURE 6.2 *Excerpt of concordance of* as mentioned *in VESPA-LIN.*

The business/economics material varies less across the corpora, as seen in Table 6.7.[10] An overall tendency is that VESPA-BUS is more similar to MICUSP-ECO than to BAWE-BUS. The only differences between VESPA and MICUSP concern 'Enumerating' (underused) and '*I will/have*' (overused). These categories are also different between VESPA and BAWE. In addition, 'Current text reference' and 'Introducing topic' are overused in VESPA compared to BAWE, but not to MICUSP.

9 For information on this corpus, see <http://www.hf.uio.no/ilos/english/services/omc/enpc/>.

10 As in Table 6.6, bold type indicates significant differences between VESPA and BAWE or MICUSP.

TABLE 6.7 *English L2 vs. L1, Business/Economics (frequency per 10,000 words)*

	VESPA-BUS	BAWE-BUS	MICUSP-ECO	LL: V VS. B	LL: V VS. M
Introducing topic	7.0	**2.5**	5.5	**16.52**	0.87
Concluding topic	2.1	**3.4**	1.4	**6.91**	0.65
Enumerating	2.5	**9.8**	**13.0**	**29.73**	**37.20**
Previewing	0.6	0.9	0.6	0.37	0.00
Reviewing	1.7	2.0	1.4	0.16	0.11
Endophoric marking	0.8	1.4	0.4	0.99	0.75
Current text reference	8.5	**3.4**	9.0	**17.06**	0.07
I will/have	18.2	**5.0**	**4.1**	**62.58**	**46.71**
Total	41.4	**28.4**	35.4	**13.61**	2.23

The two L1 corpora do not differ significantly from each other regarding the total frequency of metadiscourse (LL=3.51). But four categories differ: MICUSP has more 'Introducing topic' (LL=8.61) and 'Current text reference' (LL=20.52), while BAWE has more 'Concluding topic' (LL=12.61) and 'Endophoric marking' (LL=3.95). The predominance of '*I will/have*' in VESPA-BUS is massive. However, if this category is excluded, frequencies per 10,000 words fall to 23.2 in VESPA-BUS, 23.5 in BAWE-BUS, and 31.3 in MICUSP-ECO, making the learners' overall use of impersonal metadiscourse the lowest in the material. Nevertheless, apart from the underuse of 'Enumerating', patterns in VESPA-BUS resemble those in MICUSP-ECO.

As in linguistics, learners and L1 speakers sometimes make different lexical choices in business writing too. This is conspicuous in the category of 'Enumerating': learners only use *first(ly)* and *finally.* No second or third points are marked explicitly, unlike all the other subcorpora. Example (16) is a case in point: the student uses *then* twice rather than *second(ly)* and *third(ly)*. This may be compared to (17). Note, however, that some L1 texts exaggerate their use of enumerating markers, as suggested by (18).

(16) *First* I will go through the task, using the terminology, and *then* analyse the situations between Hans and he's two becoming partners. *Then* I will use the dimensions of cultures to describe the differences between the Chinese culture and the Norwegian culture. (VESPA-BUS)

(17) *First of all,* its literacy rate is one of the highest in Latin America at 96 percent. According to the CIA World Factbook, the 2006 literacy rate in

Brazil is 88 percent, 91 percent in Mexico, and 67.5 percent in Nicaragua. *Secondly*, it has a young population [...]. (MICUSP-ECO)

(18) *Thirdly and finally*, MEDEF's proposed 'overhaul' of the French industrial relations system has recently demonstrated the fragility of joint action between the CGT and the CFDT [...]. (BAWE-BUS)

The learners are fonder of the expression *in this essay/paper* for topic-introducing than L1 writers are, while the postmodifying *of this essay/paper* is more common in L1 than in L2, as illustrated by (19) and (20).

(19) *In this essay* I will compare French and Chinese business culture to the Norwegian business style. (VESPA-BUS)

(20) The focus *of this essay* is to assess the extent of the labour theory if value's relevance in an analysis of the nature of employment under contemporary capitalism [...]. (BAWE-BUS)

Comparison with Expert Writers

The expert writers in CRA use discourse-organizing metadiscourse less frequently than all three novice groups, as shown in Table 6.8. Like the novice corpora, the expert corpus contains less metadiscourse in economics than in linguistics, in contrast to Dahl's (2004) findings. The novice L1 writers are thus situated in-between the learners and the experts with regard to the overall frequency of metadiscourse in both disciplines.

TABLE 6.8 *Total frequencies of discourse-organizing metadiscourse across the corpora*

	Linguistics		**Business/Economics**	
	N	/ 10,000 W	N	/ 10,000 W
VESPA	1,917	71.6	196	41.4
BAWE	692	41.3	422	29.9
MICUSP	472	39.8	174	35.4
CRA	574	32.9	569	24.5

Both BAWE and MICUSP differ significantly from CRA in linguistics (LL=16.58 for BAWE and 9.54 for MICUSP) as well as business/economics (LL=9.45 for BAWE and 17.00 for MICUSP). This suggests that neither of the L1 novice corpora matches the 'target norm' set by the published research articles as regards the general frequency of metadiscourse.

Figure 6.3 shows the pattern of metadiscourse categories across the linguistics subcorpora. The learners differ markedly from the expert writers in CRA on almost every point, particularly in the use of '*I will/have*'. The differences are all statistically significant, except for 'Enumerating'.[11] By contrast, the novice linguists represented in both BAWE and MICUSP are remarkably close to the CRA frequencies for most of the categories. Both have slightly more first-person references than CRA, but are nowhere near the overuse found in VESPA. In addition, BAWE shows a clear overrepresentation of topic-concluding metadiscourse compared to CRA (LL=23.76).

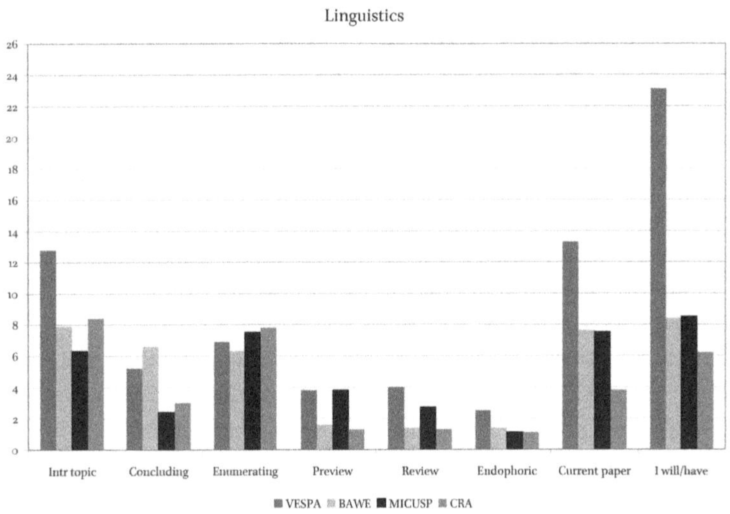

FIGURE 6.3 *Categories of metadiscourse in linguistics. Frequencies per 10,000 words.*

Figure 6.4 shows less convergence of the L1 novices and the expert writers in the business corpora. The most marked difference concerns 'Enumerating', which has very high frequencies in both BAWE and MICUSP, and where in fact the learners are closer to the experts. BAWE differs from both MICUSP and CRA in having fewer topic-introducing and more topic-concluding expressions. The learners use these types of metadiscourse more frequently than the experts, but not significantly so. As in linguistics, the Norwegian learners massively

11 The LL values are as follows: 'Introducing topic': 19.62; 'Concluding topic': 12.97; 'Enumerating': 1.02; 'Previewing': 25.83; 'Reviewing': 30.51; 'Endophoric marking': 10.17; 'Current text reference': 11.69; '*I will/have*': 21.71.

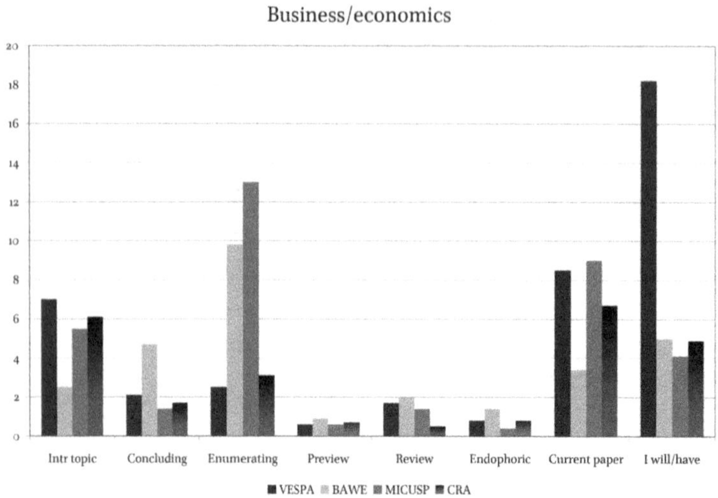

FIGURE 6.4 *Categories of metadiscourse in business/economics. Frequencies per 10,000 words.*

overuse '*I will/have*' compared to CRA as well as the other L1 corpora, and there is also an overuse of 'Reviewing' (LL=6.64), which is, however, matched by the other novice corpora. None of the other categories differ significantly between VESPA-BUS and CRA-ECO.

All the functional categories are more frequent in linguistics than in economics in CRA except 'Current text reference', which is more frequent in economics (LL=15.67, p<0.0001). '*I will/have*' and 'Endophoric marking' do not differ significantly between the disciplines, but the rest of the categories do.[12] Interestingly, 'Enumerating' is more frequent in linguistics than in economics in CRA (LL=43.48, p<0.0001), thus showing the opposite pattern to BAWE and MICUSP.

Discussion of Findings

Differences Across Writer Groups

The present investigation spans three different writer groups: Norwegian learners of English, novice L1 writers, and expert writers, each within two

12 LL and p-values are as follows: 'Introducing topic', LL=7.03, p<0.001; 'Concluding topic', LL=6.83, p<0.001; 'Previewing', LL=4.05, p<0.05; 'Reviewing', LL=7.54, p<0.001.

disciplines. Results show that language proficiency and professional expertise as well as discipline may influence the use of discourse-organizing metadiscourse, as hypothesized above.

The novice L1 corpora represented both British and American English. In contrast to Ädel's findings for argumentative writing (2006, 53, 100), this study has not found any great difference between these two groups as regards their overall use of discourse-organizing metadiscourse in discipline-specific writing, although a few functional categories differed, which raises the question as to whether disciplinary writing is less coloured by national culture than general argumentation.

The Norwegian learners use more metadiscourse than L1 novices and the experts in both disciplines. This was expected, but notably contradicts the results of Lee (2009), whose learner population had mixed L1 backgrounds. The L1/L2 difference is most pronounced for the markers of personal involvement, which clearly calls for a follow-up investigation of personal metadiscourse. Could the difference in the use of '*I will/have*' point to a difference in writing culture (e.g. Hyland 2002), or is it a sign of the writers' self-consciousness in constructing academic texts in a foreign language? Notably, Dahl (2004) did not find indications of cultural difference between English and Norwegian L1 writers in her study of textual metadiscourse in published research articles, which leaves the novice and the foreign-language factors as the most plausible explanations for the overuse of metadiscourse in VESPA.

Why do learners use more metadiscourse than native speakers? Stainton's (1996) report of non-native speakers preferring texts with more metadiscourse may hold a clue. If non-native speakers need more help in navigating through an academic text, they may, by analogy, also require more explicit devices when constructing one. However, learners who overuse metadiscourse risk producing unconvincing texts, as pointed out by Stainton (1996, 32): "if metadiscourse is used to excess, then the primary message can lose its discourse force; if an inappropriate type of metadiscourse is used then readers react negatively towards it".

The CRA texts are articles written by experts in their respective fields aimed at a readership of experts. This may mean that less metadiscourse is required by the typical readers of these texts—they will be able to make the appropriate inferences and follow the structure without much signposting. I would suggest that expert-to-expert writing is more reader-responsible (Hinds 1987). Furthermore, it presupposes a great deal of shared knowledge (Mauranen 1993), which presumably pertains not just to content but also to the way disciplinary discourse tends to be organized. If this is the case, it may explain the relative overuse of metadiscourse in novice texts; the novice writers are less familiar with the disciplinary landscape and therefore in greater need of a map of the unfolding text.

Methodological Issues

The design of this study highlights the often debated issue of reference corpora. The attested differences between the novice L1 corpora and the expert corpus indicate that novice L1 writing does not represent the target norm for learners of English. For example, if VESPA had been compared only to novice L1 corpora, a likely application of the findings would be to recommend that Norwegian business students use 'Enumerating' more. However, as frequencies in CRA match those of the learners, such advice is uncalled for.

This study places L1 novices at an intermediate stage between learners and experts in their use of discourse-organizing metadiscourse, indicating that the use of metadiscourse is connected to expertise and authority in the field as well as language proficiency. To measure the relative success of the learners *qua* novice academics, it makes good sense to compare them to L1 novices. However, the patterns of the expert corpus may represent a learning target for *both* groups of novice academics.

The corpora investigated in the present study have much the same design criteria, and are relatively comparable. However, the corpora differ in size (cf. Table 6.1): VESPA-BUS and MICUSP-ECO in particular are much smaller than the others. Thus, findings concerning these corpora may be less robust.

Another issue of corpus comparability concerns subdiscipline. As already indicated, this is particularly relevant for the business/economics corpora. The student texts across the three novice corpora have rather different topics and seem to come from rather different courses. Thus, it is debatable whether the business/economics texts really belong to the same discipline. Even within the broad discipline of linguistics, there may be differences of genre within the corpora, i.e. texts—or parts of texts—may be classified, for example, as essay, case study, or research report (cf. Nesi and Gardner 2012, 10). Such genres may require different repertoires of metadiscourse. Finally, as mentioned above, the VESPA scripts have not been graded. Thus, the students represented in this corpus may be less accomplished in their field than their British and American colleagues, although it is not clear whether (or how) this might affect their use of metadiscourse.

However, although the corpora are not ideal, they do represent the kinds of disciplinary writing that are available in the institutions where they were compiled. In practice it would be extremely difficult to provide large enough data sets which are truly comparable along all variables. Nevertheless, future studies would do well to take more variables into account, such as text length, text dispersion, subdiscipline, study level, and (sub)genre, to assess and refine the findings of the present study.

Concluding Remarks

A number of differences have been uncovered as regards the use of discourse-organizing metadiscourse across writer groups. The picture, though complex, indicates that writing in an L2 increases the use of (and possibly the need for) metadiscourse. In contrast, the level of expertise of the writer as well as of the reader seems to reduce the need for metadiscourse. Different disciplines seem to have different styles of metadiscourse. Of the two disciplines investigated here, linguistics consistently had a higher frequency of metadiscursive expressions than business/economics (although the difference in MICUSP was not significant). This suggests that the linguistics discipline generally involves more explicit attention to discourse structure and perhaps also a more writer-responsible (cf. Hinds 1987) approach to writing than business/economics.

Studies of metadiscourse have obvious applications for training in academic writing, for L1 and L2 writers alike. As argued by Vande Kopple (1985, 89), "exploration into the kinds and effects of metadiscourse might make our students more sensitive to the possibility that particular readers have more specific needs than most of them imagine". However, familiarity with metadiscursive expressions is not enough; successful writers should also be able to use an appropriate amount of these. While Vande Kopple's (1985) concern is that students might not use enough metadiscourse, it seems that Norwegian learners and L1 novice writers alike risk using it to excess.

Further avenues of research obviously include the need for more and better material within the disciplines studied, but also in other disciplines. In a language learning perspective, an important addition would be to analyse L1 texts in Norwegian, in order to investigate whether the Norwegian learners show evidence of a different writing culture than the L1 writers. In spite of Dahl's (2004) similar results for Norwegian and English research articles, it is still possible that cultural differences may manifest themselves in novice writing. Finally, the present results suggest that Norwegian learners of English and L1 writers may differ even more in their use of personal metadiscourse (see also Paquot et al. 2013). Thus, more types of metadiscourse should be added to the comparison to obtain a fuller picture of the ways in which these writers navigate through their texts.

Corpora

BAWE *British Academic Written English Corpus*. 2008. Compiled by Hilary Nesi, Sheena Gardner, Paul Thompson, and Paul Wickens. http://www.coventry.ac.uk/bawe.

CRA *Corpus of Research Articles*. The Hong Kong Polytechnic University. http://rcpce.engl.polyu.edu.hk/RACorpus/.

ENPC *The English-Norwegian Parallel Corpus*. 1994–1997. Compiled by Stig Johansson, Knut Hofland, Jarle Ebeling, and Signe Oksefjell. http://www.hf.uio.no/ilos/english/services/omc/enpc/.

MICUSP *Michigan Corpus of Upper-Level Student Papers*. 2009. Ann Arbor, MI: The Regents of the University of Michigan. http://micusp.elicorpora.info/.

VESPA-NO *Varieties of English for Specific Purposes dAtabase*, Norwegian component. 2014. Compiled by Signe O. Ebeling, and Hilde Hasselgård. http://www.uclouvain.be/en-cecl-vespa.html; http://www.hf.uio.no/ilos/english/services/vespa/.

References

Ädel, Annelie. 2006. *Metadiscourse in L1 and L2 English*. Amsterdam and Philadelphia: John Benjamins.

Ädel, Annelie. 2010. "*Just to Give You a Kind of Map of Where We Are Going*: A Taxonomy of Metadiscourse in Spoken and Written Academic English." *Nordic Journal of English Studies* 10/2: 69–97.

Ädel, Annelie. 2012. "'What I Want You to Remember Is ...': Audience Orientation in Monologic Academic Discourse." *English Text Construction* 5/1: 101–27.

Ädel, Annelie, and Ute Römer. 2012. "Research on Advanced Student Writing Across Disciplines and Levels. Introducing the *Michigan Corpus of Upper-Level Student Papers*." *International Journal of Corpus Linguistics* 17/1: 3–34.

Biber, Douglas. 2006. *University Language. A Corpus-Based Study of Spoken and Written Registers*. Amsterdam and Philadelphia: John Benjamins.

Biber, Douglas, and Susan Conrad. 2009. *Register, Genre and Style*. Cambridge: Cambridge University Press.

Bondi, Marina. 2010. "Metadiscursive Practices in Introductions: Phraseology and Semantic Sequences Across Genres." *Nordic Journal of English Studies* 10/2: 99–123.

Clyne, Michael. 1987. "Cultural Differences in the Organization of Academic Texts." *Journal of Pragmatics* 11/2: 211–47.

Crismore, Avon, Raija Markkanen, and Margaret S. Steffensen. 1993. "Metadiscourse in Persuasive Writing. A Study of Texts Written by American and Finnish University Students." *Written Communication* 10/1: 39–71.

Dahl, Trine. 2004. "Textual Metadiscourse in Research Articles: A Marker of National Culture or of Academic Discipline?" *Journal of Pragmatics* 36/10: 1807–25.

Ebeling, Signe O., and Alois Heuboeck. 2007. "Encoding Document Information in a Corpus of Student Writing: The British Academic Written English Corpus." *Corpora* 2/2: 241–56.

Halliday, M. A. K., and Christian M. I. M. Matthiessen. 2014. *Halliday's Introduction to Functional Grammar.* 4th edn. London and New York: Routledge.

Hinds, John. 1987. "Reader versus Writer Responsibility: A New Typology." In *Writing Across Languages: Analysis of L2 Text*, edited by Ulla Connor, and Robert B. Kaplan, 141–52. Reading, MA: Addison-Wesley.

Hyland, Ken. 1998. "Persuasion and Context: The Pragmatics of Academic Metadiscourse." *Journal of Pragmatics* 30/4: 437–55.

Hyland, Ken. 2002. "Authority and Invisibility: Authorial Identity in Academic Writing." *Journal of Pragmatics* 34/8: 1091–112.

Hyland, Ken. 2005. *Metadiscourse.* London: Continuum.

Hyland, Ken. 2008. "As Can Be Seen: Lexical Bundles and Disciplinary Variation." *English for Specific Purposes* 27/1: 4–21.

Hyland, Ken, and Polly Tse. 2004. "Metadiscourse in Academic Writing. A Reappraisal." *Applied Linguistics* 25/2: 156–77.

Ilie, Cornelia. 2002. "Who's Afraid of Paul Grice? The Role of the Cooperative Principle in Academic Metadiscourse." *RASK* 16: 3–32.

Lee, Seowon. 2009. "Metadiscourse in Academic Writing: A Corpus-Based Study of Expert, L1 and L2 Postgraduate Student Text." PhD diss., Newcastle University.

Mauranen, Anna. 1993. "Contrastive ESP Rhetoric: Metatext in Finnish-English Economics Texts." *English for Specific Purposes* 12/1: 3–22.

Nesi, Hilary, and Sheena Gardner. 2012. *Genres Across the Disciplines. Student Writing in Higher Education.* Cambridge: Cambridge University Press.

Paquot, Magali, Hilde Hasselgård, and Signe O. Ebeling. 2013. "Writer/Reader Visibility in Learner Writing Across Genres: A Comparison of the French and Norwegian Components of the ICLE and VESPA Learner Corpora." In *Twenty Years of Learner Corpus Research: Looking Back, Moving Ahead,* edited by Sylviane Granger, Gaëtanelle Gilquin, and Fanny Meunier, 377–87. Louvain: Presses Universitaires de Louvain.

Römer, Ute, and Matthew Brook O'Donnell. 2011. "From Student Hard Drive to Web Corpus (Part 1): The Design, Compilation and Genre Classification of the Michigan Corpus of Upper-Level Student Papers (MICUSP)." *Corpora* 6/2: 159–77.

Stainton, Caroline. 1996. "Metadiscourse: The Rhetorical Plane of Text." *Nottingham Working Papers* 2. Department of English Studies, University of Nottingham.

Vande Kopple, William J. 1985. "Some Exploratory Discourse on Metadiscourse." *College Composition and Communication* 26: 82–93.

CHAPTER 7

Passives in Academic Writing: Comparing Research Articles and Student Essays Across Four Disciplines*

Turo Hiltunen

Abstract

The passive is common in English academic prose, but the ways of using this construction varies between genres and disciplines. This corpus-based study investigates the extent of such variation in two kinds of academic texts—research articles and student essays—representing four different disciplines: medicine, physics, law, and literary criticism. The main focus is on the frequency of the construction, as well as its association with particular lexical verbs. The analysis shows that passives tend to be more frequent in the hard disciplines (medicine and physics). The lexical patternings suggest that this is due to passives being used to report research activities in these fields. Reported events are less common in the text-based humanities disciplines, which accounts for the comparatively lower frequency of the passive in law and literary criticism.

Keywords

grammar – passive voice – academic discourse – disciplinary differences – student writing

Introduction

Academic prose is characterized by a high frequency of passives (Biber et al. 1999, 476). In earlier research, the preference for passives in this register has

* I would like to thank two anonymous reviewers for their valuable comments and suggestions. Part of the data in this study comes from the *British Academic Written English* (BAWE) corpus, which was developed at the Universities of Warwick, Reading, and Oxford Brookes under the directorship of Hilary Nesi and Sheena Gardner (formerly of the Centre for Applied Linguistics [previously called CELTE], Warwick), Paul Thompson (Department of Applied Linguistics, Reading), and Paul Wickens (Westminster Institute of Education, Oxford Brookes), with funding from the ESRC (RES-000-23-0800).

 | DOI 10.1163/9789004321342_008

been linked with the need to obscure the author's identity (Rundblad 2007, 2008) and reduce his/her responsibility for the assertions being made in the text (Hyland 1996). Moreover, the use of the passive is frequently motivated by discourse needs (Dorgeloh and Wanner 2003; Wanner 2009), particularly when the agent is mentioned (Seoane 2009). The choice between the active and the passive voice is also connected to other paradigmatic choices, including the choice to use a particular lexical verb, tense, and aspect (Biber et al. 1999, 479). For example, as observed by Swales (2004a, 12), many commonly used verbs in academic texts vary greatly in their proportional preference for the passive voice (see also Huddleston 1971).

While the passive is known to occur frequently in academic English across the board, there is relatively little empirical work describing how its use varies in texts from different disciplines. Yet given that discipline has proved to be an important factor in accounting for variation in the relative frequency of many linguistic features (see e.g. Fløttum et al. 2006, 54), we can indeed expect it to play a role also in how passives are used. The hypothesis that the frequency of passives varies across disciplines is also supported by previous work on research article abstracts (Dorgeloh and Wanner 2003, 2009).

Another question which currently remains unanswered is whether student texts differ from professional texts with regard to how passives are used. This question is particularly interesting from the perspective of English for Academic Purposes (EAP): differences between students' production and expert performances may be indicative of problems in writing or argumentation, which could be targeted in specialized language teaching. In order to explore such differences, the current study compares research articles representing a particular discipline to corresponding student texts.

The study has two aims: first, to investigate how the use of the passive varies in research articles (RA) representing four different disciplines (medicine, physics, law, and literary criticism) and, second, to determine the extent to which RAs are similar to or different from student essays (SE) *within* the same discipline. I shall focus on the following two research questions:

(a) Do passives systematically occur at different rates in research articles (RAs) and student essays (SEs) representing four different disciplines (medicine, physics, law, and literary criticism)?
(b) What verbs are most commonly passivized in RAs and SEs?

The analysis presented in the following sections confirms that the frequency of the passive varies between disciplines, with published articles in the hard sciences exhibiting the highest rates of occurrence. A comparison of the lexical associations suggests that passives are strongly associated with reporting research activities, and this stylistic convention accounts for their high rates of occurrence in hard science RAs.

Theoretical Background

Using Corpora to Study Disciplinary Differences

Corpus-based research on disciplinary differences in academic writing has become a popular area of research in recent years. Much of this work has been inspired by the work of Ken Hyland, who has shown in numerous studies that there are many differences between disciplinary rhetorics, which are manifested in how often discourse phenomena such as hedging, boosting, and reporting occur in different kinds of texts (e.g. Hyland 1996, 1999, 2000, 2005). Along with discourse phenomena, similar bottom-up approaches have been applied to the analysis of grammatical constructions (e.g. Hyland and Tse 2005; Charles 2007; Hiltunen 2010); this is also the orientation of the present study, which focuses on disciplinary differences in the use of the passive. The broader aim in this type of research is to link accounts of disciplinary culture, based on work in sociology of science and higher education research, with the linguistic analysis of actual texts representing these disciplines. As Hyland (2000, 11) puts it:

> [t]he ways that writers choose to represent themselves, their readers, and their world, how they seek to advance knowledge, how they maintain the authority of their discipline and the processes whereby they establish what is to be accepted as a substantiated truth, a useful contribution and a valid argument are all culturally influenced practical actions and matters for community agreement.

The passive, as discussed in the following section, is clearly involved in a set of choices that writers make to present themselves in their texts.

Like many other previous studies, the present analysis relies on the influential classification of disciplines by Becher and Trowler (2001), which is based on the 'intellectual territory' that they cover. This classification employs two axes: hard/soft and pure/applied. Each of the disciplines studied here—medicine, physics, law,[1] and literary criticism—represents a different section

1 It is worth emphasizing that this category includes legal research writing, not legislative documents.

in the matrix, but this study primarily contrasts them in terms of whether they belong to the hard (medicine, physics) or soft sciences (law, literary criticism). While it is relatively straightforward to classify these four disciplines along the hard/soft dimension, such a binary classification is clearly not sensitive to all relevant characteristics of individual disciplines, and therefore any generalizations at this level need to be made with caution. Individual texts representing a given discipline may—and often will—be very different from each other, if they belong to different specialisms or advocate conflicting theories (cf. Becher and Trowler 2001, 186–188). This being the case, the way in which passives are used in legal and literary critical RAs does not necessarily apply to other soft disciplines (e.g. history or sociology), and the findings from medicine and physics RAs may not be generalizable to other hard science disciplines (e.g. chemistry or pharmacy).

Passives in Academic Prose

The passive has received a great deal of attention both in theoretical and applied linguistics (for an overview, see e.g. Wanner 2009, chapter 2), and its syntactic characteristics, functions, and register associations are therefore well understood. Along with nominalizations, the passive is also commonly seen as a staple of academic prose (e.g. Halliday and Martin 1993), and its use often attracts criticism from readers.[2] However, recent decades have clearly seen a trend towards reducing the number of passives in academic genres (Leech et al. 2009, 149). This shift, which is reflected in the submission guidelines of many academic journals (Wanner 2009, 164; Millar et al. 2013), has also been linked to increasing colloquialization observed across a variety of written English genres (e.g. Mair 2009), although this view is not supported by all studies (see in particular Seoane 2006, 2013).

Earlier studies also suggest that the link between the passive construction and academic English is more complex than often acknowledged. For one, while passives are commonly used in academic prose, their frequency is still lower than that of actives, if we measure the frequency as occurrences per number of words (Dudley-Evans and St. John 1998, 76) or per number of verb forms.[3] However, according to the *Longman Grammar*, roughly one fourth of

2 For instance, *Language Log* has published over 70 posts about the passive, many of which discuss non-linguists' views on the construction. See <http://www.lel.ed.ac.uk/grammar/passives.html#passivepostlist> and Pullum (2014).

3 In Seoane's (2006) analysis of British English scientific prose from the twentieth century, passives were proportionally more frequent than actives in transitive verb phrases (VPs).

finite verbs in academic prose are in the passive, whereas the percentage of passives is 15% for NEWS and 2% for conversation (Biber et al. 1999).

In addition, it is not straightforward to determine the motivations for using the passive in scientific prose. Various pragmatic functions have been identified for this construction: Dudley-Evans and St. John (1998) suggest, based on an early EAP study by Tarone et al. (1981),[4] that the passive is mainly used for reporting standard procedures and referring to previous research. Other studies have linked passives to impersonalization: they form one rhetorical resource that enables the author to remain absent while the reader is able to focus on the results being presented (Rundblad 2007, 251).[5] The passive can also be seen as having a hedging function, in that it allows writers to speculate about the interpretations without assuming explicit responsibility for them, which in Hyland's (1996) words helps them "protect their reputations and limit the damage which may be incurred from categorical commitments" (1996, 444). Finally, some passives may be motivated by discourse needs. The construction not only allows the writer to omit saying who the agent is, but it also makes it possible to order the information in such a way that is contextually suitable, taking into account the status of information and the weight of the sentence (Wanner 2009, 38). The passive can be used to move a non-agent constituent to be the topic of a clause, which may facilitate the flow of discourse from one sentence to the next.

That said, Seoane (2013, 89) is critical of the idea that most passives might be motivated by pragmatic functions. Instead, she argues that passives are mere "scientific-discourse markers" in Present-day English, conventionalized but functionally empty indices of academic writing style (Seoane 2013, 89)

Despite their prominence, passives have so far received relatively little systematic attention in corpus-based studies focusing on disciplinary variation in academic prose. Apart from Dorgeloh and Wanner's work on RA abstracts (2003, 2009),[6] the majority of EAP studies have focused on how passives are used in individual disciplines, e.g. astrophysics (Tarone et al. 1981) or medicine (Millar et al. 2013), or in the context of specific rhetorical functions such as reporting (Shaw 1992). With the exception of Millar et al. (2013), these studies tend to be based on relatively small data sets; Tarone et al. (1981), for instance,

4 A revised version of this paper was published as Tarone et al. (1998).

5 A similar effect can be achieved by using inanimate subjects such as *paper* or *study* (Seoane 2006; Dorgeloh and Wanner 2009).

6 The abstracts are from eight different journals representing humanities, social sciences, and natural sciences; see further Dorgeloh and Wanner (2003, 439–440) and Wanner (2009, 165–166).

only considers two articles. In addition, it is not clear whether passives occur at different rates in RAs and student writing, yet such information is clearly relevant from a pedagogical perspective, as it is potentially indicative of a gap between students' written production and the kind of discourse they aim to master (Tribble 2011). To provide a bird's-eye view of such differences, this study also compares frequencies of passives between student and expert texts in all four disciplines.

As for lexical associations of the passive construction in academic texts, Huddleston (1971) has shown that the relative frequency of passives is far from uniform across individual verbs. Instead, some verbs, like *associate, attach,* and *distribute* always occur in the passive, whereas others, like *act* and *reveal,* hardly ever do so. The findings of Huddleston's (1971) early corpus linguistic study were revisited, and largely confirmed, by Swales (2004a), using a larger corpus.

However, these studies leave open two important questions: does the propensity to occur in the passive remain constant across disciplines,[7] and do student texts exhibit similar lexical associations to those observed in RAs? The importance of the latter question is underlined by Swales (2004a), who qualifies the observed differences as "both substantial and of relevance for junior researchers with limited English language proficiencies" (2004a, 12). To provide some answers to these questions, the present study explores how lexical associations vary between different corpora, following the method described in the following section.

Methods and Materials

Source of Data

This study considers two kinds of academic writing: published research articles written by researchers, either individually or as part of a group, and student essays, written as part of coursework in higher education. In the majority of fields, the RA is the most important genre, which, according to Swales (1990, 177), brings together other research-oriented genres, such as monographs, dissertations, abstracts, and presentations. This being the case, it is essential for researchers to be able to master the conventions of this genre

7 Swales (2004a) does not specifically comment on disciplinary variation, even if his corpus covers four hard science disciplines (physics, cell biology, mechanical engineering, and electrical engineering) (Swales 2004a, 8). Millar et al. (2013) describe how lexical associations vary between sections of medical RAs.

irrespective of their area of research. The RA has received a great deal of scholarly attention, and its main characteristics are well documented, especially in the hard sciences (Swales 1990, 2004b).

Student essays constitute a much more varied group of texts. According to Nesi and Gardner (2012, 27), student writing assignments serve three main purposes: they demonstrate the student's disciplinary knowledge, produce new disciplinary knowledge, and prepare the student for professional practice. Depending on the emphasis of a given assignment, students therefore produce many different kinds of texts; along with research reports, they write argumentative essays, case studies, literature surveys, theses, as well as many other types of texts.

The data for this study come from two corpora, as summarized in Table 7.1. The first contains 256 published RAs (64 in each discipline) and ca. 2 million words.[8] This corpus is a 'specialized genre corpus', designed for exploring disciplinary differences in research writing (see Hiltunen 2010). Each discipline in focus represents one segment in Becher's four-fold typology of disciplinary groupings (e.g. Becher and Trowler 2001): physics: *hard-pure* discipline, medicine: *hard-applied* discipline, literary criticism: *soft-pure* discipline, and law: *soft-applied* discipline.[9] All the articles are taken from leading journals with a high impact factor.[10]

This corpus is contrasted with a second one, containing 'good-standard'[11] student essays extracted from the *British Academic Written English* (BAWE) corpus (Nesi 2008). To cast the net as wide as possible, all texts representing the four disciplines are included, irrespective of their genre type. The majority of texts in the two soft fields (English and law) are classified as 'essays', and most medical texts as 'case studies'; the physics subcorpus is more diverse, 'methodology recount' and 'explanation' being the main genres. Although the number of texts in this corpus is higher (388), they are on average much shorter, so that the aggregate word count is slightly under one million words. Both corpora were POS-tagged for this study using CLAWS (Garside and Smith 1997).

8 Each corpus text includes the main body of the text in its entirety, but not other text parts (i.e. abstracts, footnotes, references, tables, etc.). A full list of journals and articles included in the corpus is available in Hiltunen (2010, Appendix B).

9 For a more detailed discussion of the classification of these disciplines, see Hiltunen (2010, 16–22).

10 The selection of articles was not based on the authors' native language, so the corpus contains texts written both by native and non-native speakers of English (see Swales 2004b, 54 on this issue).

11 All BAWE texts have been graded either as 'merit' (M, equivalent to 60–69%) or 'distinction' (D, > 70%) (Nesi 2008).

TABLE 7.1 *Corpora used in this study*

Genre	Subcorpus	Discipline	Texts	Words
Student essay	MED-SE	Medicine	80	214,226
	PHY-SE	Physics	68	187,481
	LAW-SE	Law	134	346,139
	LC-SE	English	106	241,516
		Total	388	989,362
Research article	MED-RA	Medicine	64	248,693
	PHY-RA	Physics	64	363,294
	LAW-RA	Law	64	919,974
	LC-RA	Literary criticism	64	516,242
		Total	256	2,048,203

Retrieving Passive Constructions

Huddleston and Pullum et al. (2002, 1427) characterize the active and the passive voice as "contrasting forms [that] differ in the way semantic roles are aligned with syntactic functions". However, previous corpus studies have noted that the category of voice is difficult to operationalize for linguistic research (Svartvik 1966; Granger 1983). Typically, corpus studies (e.g. Seoane 2009; Millar et al. 2013) focus on *be* + past participle, which is the norm for the English passive construction (Xiao et al. 2006, 111).[12] This construction is illustrated in the following example.

(1) Wide excision *was performed* in 39 of 41 lesions. (MED-RA)

However, defining the passive in this way is possibly too restrictive if we are interested in the overall frequency of the passive. For one, participles are occasionally preceded by other verbs besides *be*, such as *get* (example (2)) and *become* (Xiao et al. 2006, 111).

(2) Indeed, the word Aristotle used that *gets translated* as genre is not *génos*. (LC-RA)

12 Granger (1983) explicitly states that she chooses to use the term '*be*+past participle construction', in order to avoid confusion over different understandings of the passive.

That said, such '*get*-passives' are extremely infrequent in academic prose, so that including them in the analysis would not have a major impact on the results. However, the passive can also occur without a finite verb in contexts where it is not necessary to mark features of tense and agreement (Wanner 2009), and these so-called 'bare passives' are fairly common in academic texts, as in (3).

(3) The process *initiated* by such a membership regime would provide multiple opportunities for framing human rights issues. (LAW-RA)

Wanner (2009, 85) makes the point that while bare passives are often excluded from studies for pragmatic reasons, they are functionally and syntactically similar to core passives, and should therefore be taken into consideration—especially in studies on scientific writing, which is "a type of discourse that values compact expressions" (Wanner 2009, 172). Despite their prominence, however, we do not know whether the rate of occurrence of bare passives is constant in different disciplinary contexts. For this reason, the present study covers both bare and verbal passives. This operationalization is consistent with Huddleston (1971) and Swales (2004a), but different from studies that only cover verbal passives (e.g. Granger 1983; Biber 1988; Xiao et al. 2006; Seoane 2009; Millar et al. 2013).

Bare and verbal passives were retrieved from the corpora by simply searching for the tag <VVN>, which stands for 'past participle of a lexical verb' in the C7 tagset. As the occurrence of the tag is not limited to passive constructions, it is necessary to remove all the instances that are not passives, including present perfect forms and items mistagged as participles.[13] The analysis also excludes participles which occur as pre-modifiers within an NP structure, as well as other instances where the participle is unambiguously adjectival (Wanner 2009).[14] However, Biber et al. (1999, 475) note that passive is a fuzzy category,

---

13 An example is (i), where the correct tag would have been <VVD> ('past tense of lexical verb').

(i) Generally my research *relied*_VVN on a research trail [...]

14 Various tests can be used to identify adjectival passives. According to Wanner (2009, 71), adjectival passives do not show implicit argument effects or license *by*-phrases. They are like adjectives in that they can be coordinated with adjectives and take prefixes such as *un-*. Huddleston and Pullum et al. (2002, 78–79) classify as 'adjectival' those participials which appear as complements of *seem, appear, look,* and *remain* or which can be modified by *very* or *too*. Following Biber et al. (1999, 937), idiomatic expressions like *be bound to*

and it is occasionally difficult to decide whether an instance of the construction represents an action (true passive) or a state (adjectival passive), and in many cases both readings are possible. This study adopts an inclusive approach and considers such instances in the analysis whenever the passive reading is theoretically possible.

After removing the false positives, the remaining instances were coded for two nominal linguistic variables, TYPE OF PASSIVE (*verbal/bare*) and VERB (multiple values), as well as for two nominal extra-linguistic variables: TEXT CATEGORY (*student essay/research article*) and DISCIPLINE (*medicine/physics/law/literary criticism*).

Determining the Frequency of Passives

The simplest way of comparing the frequency of passives across corpora is to normalize the counts to a common base of 1,000 words; this approach is referred to as a text-linguistic ('Type B') research design in Biber (2012). However, this baseline is also problematic, as it implicitly assumes that any corpora of the same length have exactly the same number of opportunities for using passives; this does not necessarily apply, and some scholars have therefore argued against using such overgeneral baselines (see e.g Ball 1994; Wallis et al. 2012).

The alternative approach would involve determining the frequency of passives relative to the number of situations where they could occur. This approach has been used in a diachronic study by Seoane (2009), who counts both normalized frequencies of passives (per 1,000 words) for different time periods and their ratios to all active verb phrases for which a passive counterpart would have been possible.[15] While conceptually this approach is preferable, with large corpora it very quickly becomes unwieldy. For this reason, this study follows the first approach.

However, to improve the accuracy of the chosen method, I also determine the frequency of passives relative to the total number of verb tokens. This baseline represents a "refinement" of the original baseline (see Wallis et al. 2012), because the occurrence of the passive is limited to verb phrases. Theoretically,

---

and participial adjectives denoting emotional states (e.g. *scared, excited*) have also been excluded.

15 This includes "active transitive structures with a patient or benefactive noun phrase eligible to become a subject of a passive clause" (Seoane 2009, 371).

this baseline is therefore more meaningful, and while it does not entirely remove non-alternating terms, it decreases their impact on the result.[16]

To test the statistical significance of the results, Kruskal-Wallis non-parametric ANOVA is used. Mann-Whitney test is used as a post-hoc test for pairwise comparisons (for more information, see e.g. Fløttum et al. 2006, 42–45).

Analysis of Verbs

To investigate the association between the passive construction and individual lexical verbs, I use two different measures adopted from Schmid (2000, 54), 'reliance' and 'attraction'. Reliance measures the degree to which the occurrence of a given word depends on a particular grammatical construction. In this case, the reliance score indicates how many per cent of the occurrences of a given verb are passives.[17] For instance, the verb with the highest token frequency in MED-RA, *use*, in fact has a relatively low reliance score compared to some other high-frequency verbs; it occurs in MED-RA a total of 808 times, out of which 329 are in the passive, yielding a reliance score of 329/808 × 100% = 40.7%. By contrast, the use of *see* and *perform* is much more dependent on the passive (reliance 85.1% and 80.0%, respectively).

Reliance is the sole measure used by Swales (2004a), and it is clearly useful for frequently occurring verbs, but less so with infrequent verbs. This is shown by the fact that most verbs with a reliance score of 100% only occur once in the entire corpus. For this reason, it is useful to incorporate into the analysis another measure, attraction. The verb's attraction is counted by dividing its frequency in the passive construction by the total number of passives in the subcorpus. For instance, given that the total number of passives in MED-RA is 7,525, the attraction score for *use* is 329/7,525 × 100% = 4.4% in this subcorpus.[18]

---

16 Yet another alternative would be to measure the frequency of passives in relation to the number of sentences. For instance, Millar et al. (2013) use the measure MPPS, which stands for 'mean number of passives per sentence'.

17 This measure is referred to as 'preference' by Millar et al. (2013, 14).

18 Attraction is thus directly proportional to the token frequency of passive forms of the verb.

Results

The results of the frequency analysis, followed by the analysis of passive type and lexical associations are presented in the sections below.

Frequency of Passives

The analysis of the data clearly shows that the frequency of passives in academic prose depends on the DISCIPLINE. Table 7.2 demonstrates that disciplinary differences are extremely marked in RAs. The table shows the raw frequency of passives in each subcorpus, as well as the means and standard deviations of normalized frequencies, counted using two different baselines: word baseline (Norm-1) and verb baseline (Norm-2). We can observe a clear split between hard and soft disciplines: passives are much more frequent in the former group. In both medicine and physics, the mean normalized frequency of passives, using word baseline (Norm-1), is over twice as large as in law and literary criticism. The difference between the means is statistically significant by the Kruskal-Wallis non-parametric ANOVA.[19]

TABLE 7.2 *Frequency of passives in RAs (SD = standard deviation)*

	Subcorpus			
	MED-RA	PHY-RA	LAW-RA	LC-RA
Passives	7,525	11,619	3,478	6,680
Norm-1: Mean	31.13	33.31	15.08	13.02
Norm-1: SD	6.28	7.13	3.22	3.03
Norm-2: Mean	39.24	38.89	14.50	13.62
Norm-2: SD	6.30	7.50	3.42	3.62

In addition, legal RAs employ more passives than literary critical RAs, and physics RAs more than medical RAs. However, post-hoc pairwise comparisons show that only the former difference is statistically significant.[20] These results are visualized as boxplots in the left panel of Figure 7.1.

19 Kruskal-Wallis chi-squared value=192.50, $p<0.001$, df=3, 1.

20 LAW–LC: U=2,729, $p<0.05$; MED-PHY: 1,731, $p>0.05$ (n.s.) (Mann-Whitney test).

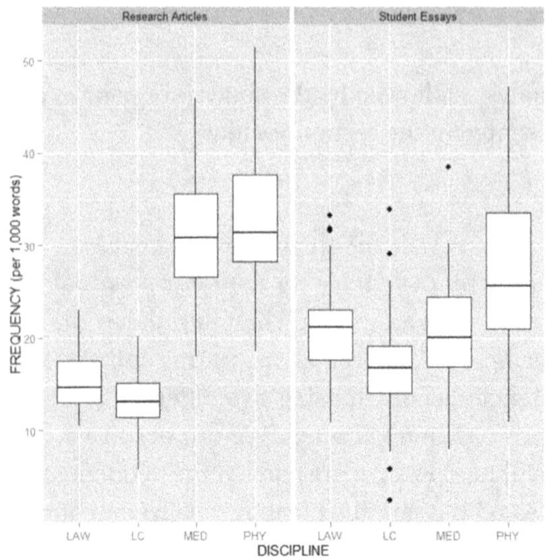

FIGURE 7.1
Frequency of passives in RAs *and* SEs *(word baseline), grouped by* TEXT CATEGORY.

Table 7.3 shows that the science writers' tendency to use the passive is partially replicated in student writing. There is a statistically significant difference between the means in different subcorpora.[21] The highest mean normalized frequency (using Norm-1) is found in physics, and the lowest in literary criticism, this difference being statistically significant. Interestingly, however, neither discipline is similar to medicine or law, which show very similar mean frequencies in student writing. These results are visualized as boxplots in the right panel of Figure 7.1.

TABLE 7.3 *Frequency of passives in* SEs *(*SD*= standard deviation)*

	Subcorpus			
	MED-SE	PHY-SE	LAW-SE	LC-SE
Passives	4,424	5,533	7,197	3,962
Norm-1: Mean	20.38	27.25	20.96	16.70
Norm-1: SD	5.27	7.93	4.31	4.77
Norm-2: Mean	24.10	30.26	23.40	17.02
Norm-2: SD	5.39	8.16	5.05	5.27

21 Kruskal-Wallis chi-squared value=99.21, p<0.001, df=3.

Tables 7.2 and 7.3 also show that word baseline (Norm-1) and verb baseline (Norm-2) provide similar results, offering further evidence that the observed trends are indeed correct. The only real difference between Norm-1 and the conceptually more meaningful Norm-2 is that the latter highlights the differences between the two disciplinary groupings. The reason is that scientific RAs tend to contain fewer verbs in general, and it is precisely in these texts that passives tend to be common.

Along with disciplinary variation, we can observe systematic differences in the data between SEs and RAs representing different disciplinary groupings. This is clearly shown in Figure 7.2, which plots the frequencies of passives in RAs and SEs using verb baseline, with DISCIPLINE as the grouping factor. As can be seen, in the hard disciplines, where passives are comparatively more frequent, student texts contain *fewer* passives than RAs (the lower left and lower right panels). By contrast, passives are comparatively infrequent in the soft disciplines, and student texts in these disciplines contain *more* passives than RAs (the upper left and the upper right panel). All four differences between RAs and SEs represented in Figure 7.2 are statistically significant.[22]

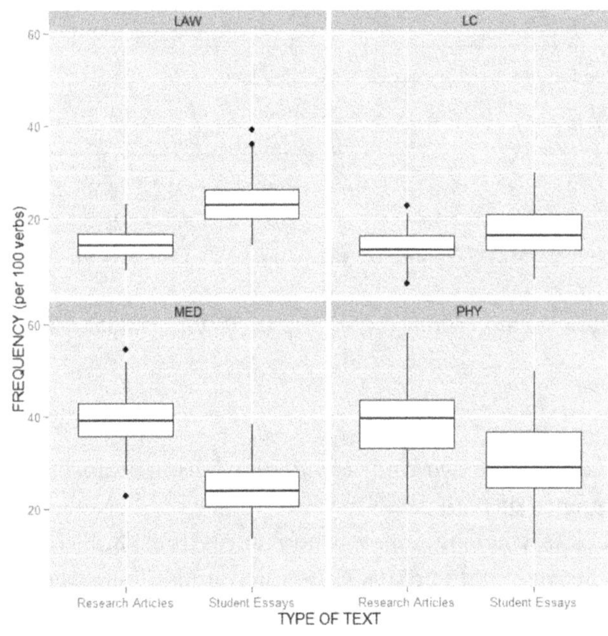

FIGURE 7.2 *Frequency of passives in RAs and SEs (verb baseline), grouped by DISCIPLINE.*

22 Medicine: U=4,943, $p<0.001$; Physics: U=3,396, $p<0.001$; Law: U=565, $p<0.001$; Literary criticism: U=2,110, $p<0.001$ (Mann-Whitney test).

The marked differences in published writing strongly suggest that the use of the passive voice is motivated by different factors depending on the disciplinary setting. Equally interesting is the finding that the frequency of passives varies significantly between SEs and RAs in all four disciplines, as such differences potentially carry pedagogical relevance. Based on Figure 7.1, SEs appear to form a more homogeneous collection than RAs, which may suggest that student writers have not become fully sensitive to the conventions of their disciplines. That said, these differences may also be attributable to differences in genre, audience, and the purpose of writing; further work is needed to determine the validity of this explanation.

Verbal vs. Bare Passives

Scientific writing has previously been found to exhibit a high relative frequency of bare passives, that is, passives without *be* (Wanner 2009, 170), and Table 7.4 confirms their importance in the data investigated here. In all subcorpora, bare passives constitute well over one fifth of all passives.

TABLE 7.4 *Verbal vs. bare passives*

		Medicine		Physics		Law		LC	
		RA	SE	RA	SE	RA	SE	RA	SE
Verbal passives	N	5,669	3,441	8,319	4,212	9,062	5,513	4,696	3,027
	%	76.4	75.3	77.8	71.6	76.1	67.2	76.1	70.3
Bare passives	N	1,856	983	3,300	1,321	4,416	1,682	1,984	935
	%	24.7	22.2	28.4	23.9	32.8	23.4	29.7	23.6
Total		7,525	4,424	11,619	5,533	13,478	7,195	6,680	3,962

At the same time, we can observe two kinds of variation between subcorpora. First, the relative frequency of bare passives varies somewhat between subcorpora, particularly in RAs, where their proportion ranges from 24.7% (medicine) to 32.8% (law). Second, and perhaps more interestingly, bare passives are consistently more frequent in RAs than SEs; the difference is statistically significant in all four disciplines.[23]

23 Medicine: chi-square value 9.19, $p<0.05$, df=1; Physics: chi-square value 39.02, $p<0.001$, df=1; Law: chi-square value 198.76, $p<0.001$, df=1; Literary criticism: chi-square value 46.51, $p<0.001$, df=1.

The high frequency of bare passives in LAW-RA appears to be caused mainly by the frequent use of metatextual links pointing to other locations in the text, as illustrated in (4) and (5). While similar links are occasionally found in MED-RA and PHY-RA, bare passives clearly have another function in these subcorpora: they are linked to the method sections, which are also rich in other types of passives (Heslot 1982, 88). Method sections are frequently extremely concise, and often merely label the method used in the study rather than characterize it in detail (Swales 1990, 167). In the data analysed here, bare passives are used mainly for packaging information and referring to other texts, as illustrated in (6) and (7).

(4) As *discussed* earlier in this essay, investments in patent-defeating prior art have increased significantly over this period as well. (LAW-RA)

(5) As we shift, however, from frictionless two-person models to a multiperson reality, information gaps like those *identified* in Table 1 often become too numerous and complicated for the parties to bridge on their own. (LAW-RA)

(6) Confidence intervals were estimated using the methods *described* by Simel et al. (MED-RA)

(7) The destabilizing effect of peroxynitrite can be evaluated in terms of transition free energy decrease (D+G+G) relative to the non-oxidized protein, *calculated* according to the fundamental equation as *reported* in literature. (PHY-RA)

The high relative frequency of bare passives across the board, together with the prominence of statements like (6) and (7) in MED-RA and PHY-RA, confirms the usefulness of the bare passive in research writing. The fact that the construction is systematically more frequent in RAs compared to SEs suggests, moreover, that student writers may not be using it as often as they could, and would therefore benefit from instruction in the functions of the passive, especially at the postgraduate level. Again, the issue of genre is likely to play a role: SEs are short and may contain less data commentary than RAs, therefore offering fewer opportunities for using metatextual location elements (examples (4) and (5)). The comparatively low frequency of passives may also reflect inadequate register awareness, given that student writing has been described as too informal (see Gilquin and Paquot 2008). It should be noted, however, that the effect size in all comparisons is relatively small, indicating that the variable PASSIVE TYPE does not play a major role in explaining the disciplinary differences observed above.

Verbs Used in Passive Constructions

The hypothesis that individual verbs vary as regards how often they occur in the passive (cf. Swales 2004a, 12) is immediately confirmed by corpus data. Figure 7.3 shows the verbs most closely associated with the passive in RAs representing different disciplines, with attraction plotted on the horizontal axis and reliance on the vertical axis. In order to keep the plot readable, only verbs with a reliance score higher than 10% and an attraction score higher than 0.4% are shown. This representation enables us both to observe parallels between subcorpora as well as to point out differences between then.

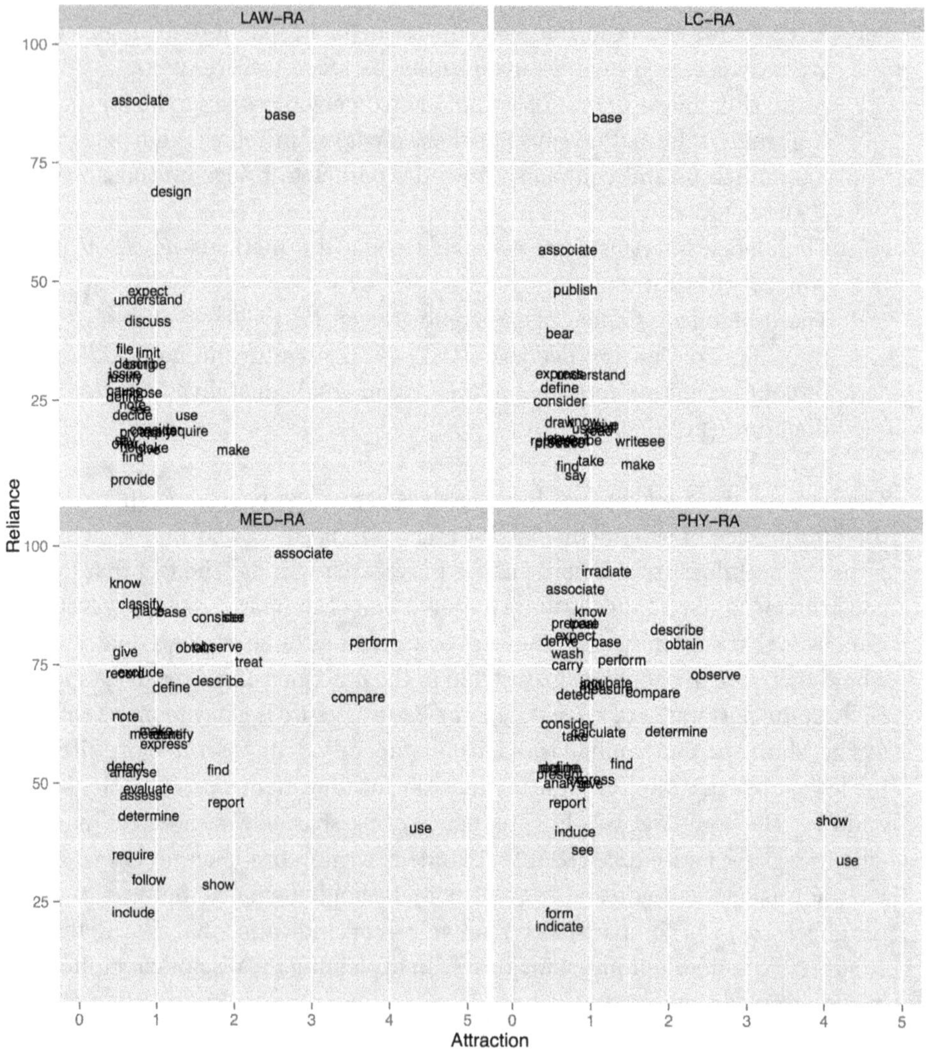

FIGURE 7.3 *Lexical association of the passive in RAs.*

As can be seen, in both MED-RA and PHY-RA (the lower left and the lower right panels), there are a few verbs on the right hand side of the plot which make up a considerable proportion of all instances of the passive. In MED-RA, for instance, a total of 729 different verbs are used in the passive, but over 10% of the tokens are made up of just three verbs: *use, compare*, and *perform*. Similarly, *use* and *show* have a high attraction score in PHY-RA. These lexical associations clearly reflect the purpose of using these disciplines. In the majority of cases, these verbs are used to represent real-world research acts, performed as part of the empirical research process (cf. Bunton 1999, 47); accordingly, the implied agent of the activity denoted by the passive form is the researcher (cf. Swales 1990, 167). This usage is illustrated in examples (8) and (9).

(8) Two different cell types *were used* to test the outcome of IL-2Ra blockade on T-cell function and IL-2R-mediated signaling. (MED-RA)
(9) The concentration of peroxynitrite *was determined* at 302 nm. (PHY-RA)

Other verbs that are commonly passivized in these subcorpora are also linked to the research process: *associate, treat, observe, determine*, and *obtain*. This finding suggests that the main factor accounting for the overall high frequency of passives in medicine and physics is that passives are commonly used for a particular function: reporting research activities. Such 'reported events', to borrow a term from Wanner (2009), are part and parcel of empirical research articles in the natural sciences, which in turn means that these texts offer many opportunities for using the passive as a marker of objectivity and neutrality in reporting. This explanation is consistent with previous studies on passives in academic prose (e.g. Tarone et al. 1998; Millar et al. 2013); in addition, it ties in with earlier work comparing the use of grammatical constructions between disciplinary discourses, which suggests that text-level differences are often due to the varying prominence of reported events in different disciplinary settings (see Hiltunen 2010).

The link between the passive and reporting statements also explains why passives tend to be less frequent in texts representing law and literary criticism: as a rule, reported events are much less common in the soft sciences, where the author's claims and interpretations are normally based on their own reasoning and consultation of sources, rather than on experimental results. For this reason, the research act verbs discussed above do not stand out in LAW-RA and LC-RA in terms of attraction (the upper left and the upper right panel in Figure 7.3). Instead, prominent verbs in these disciplines refer to other types of cognitive and communicative acts: making decisions or arguments (10), designing policies (11), or writing literary works (12).

(10) A plausible argument can be *made* that the consumption of institutional resources per appeal would be sharply reduced if a stricter standard of review were adopted. (LAW-RA)

(11) The policy was *designed* to obtain statements that, although inadmissible in the prosecution's case-in-chief, could be used to impeach suspects who chose to testify in their criminal cases (LAW-RA)

(12) This, in effect, is the reason why the novel was *written*. (LC-RA)

Importantly, the implied agent in these expressions is frequently someone other than the researcher; they are 'attributions' rather than 'averrals', to use the terminology of Hunston (2000). Such attributed statements are particularly prominent in text-based humanities disciplines (Hiltunen 2010, 252), and this is reflected in the lexical patterning of the passive.

The comparison between RAs and the corresponding data from SEs, set out in Figure 7.4, reveals many similarities between the two types of writing. As can be seen, many verbs with high attraction scores in LAW-RA, such as *base* and *make*, demonstrate a similar behaviour in LAW-SE, and the verb *use* in the passive is equally prominent in physics SEs and RAs. However, if we look at individual verbs, differences start to emerge. These are clearly seen Figure 7.5, which shows the attraction and reliance scores for nine prominent verbs, using VERB as the grouping variable. This visualization is useful, as it allows us to observe instances of overuse and underuse with respect to published texts (horizontal axis) and compare the rates of passivization (vertical axis). For instance, while *base* and *associate* are used in similar ways across corpora, *find, give, know,* and *make* appear to be overused in physics student writing with respect to published writing. *Give* is similarly overused in MED-SE with respect to MED-RA, while *perform* and *use* are apparently underused. Interestingly, *see* is overused in literary critical student writing.

These differences suggest that lexical factors play an important role in the use of the passive. As the degree of passivization varies between verbs, then the overall number of passives in a corpus is clearly dependent on the kinds of lexical verbs it contains. Moreover, the fact that we can observe differences between RAs and SEs is interesting, as such differences are potentially relevant to EAP.

There are clearly a number of factors that are potentially responsible for these differences. For example, the overuse of *give* and *find* is partially explained by the type of assignment given to students, which gives rise to statements that would not be equally appropriate in proper research articles. To illustrate, example (13) is part of a longer chronological account of a specific task, which would be out of place in a published research report. In turn, example (14) does

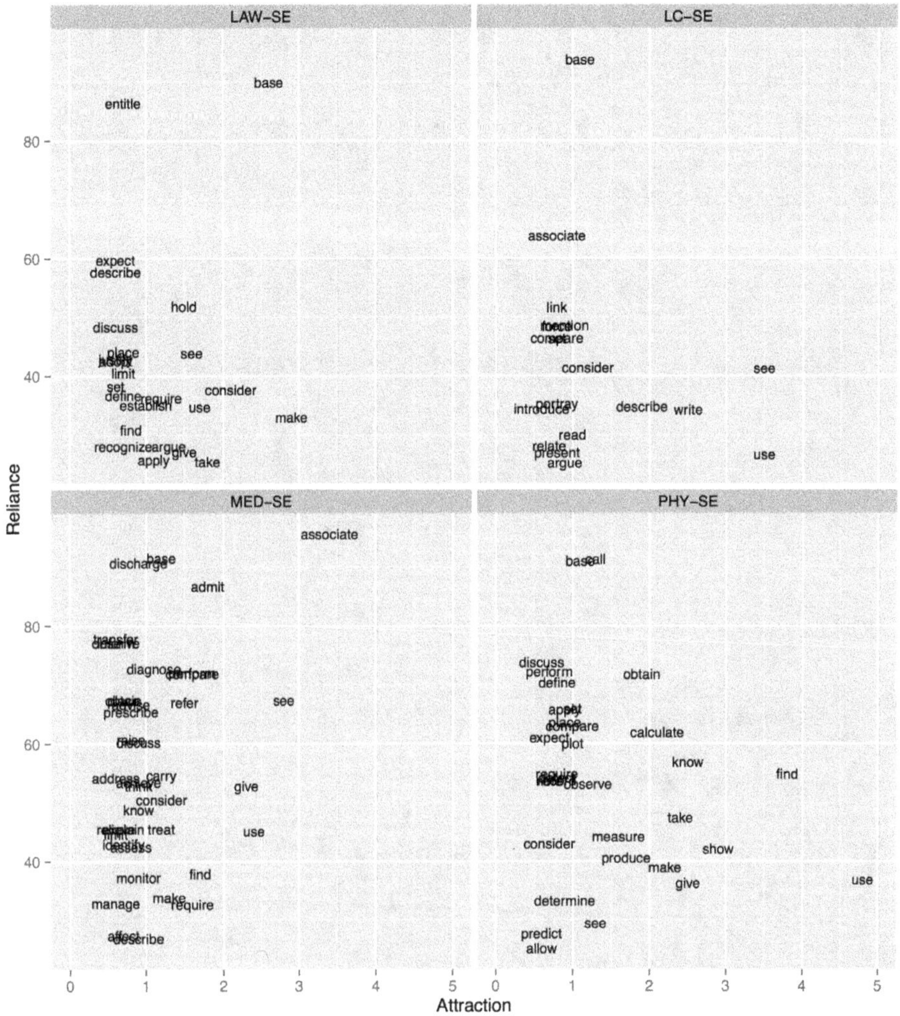

FIGURE 7.4 *Lexical association of the passive in SEs.*

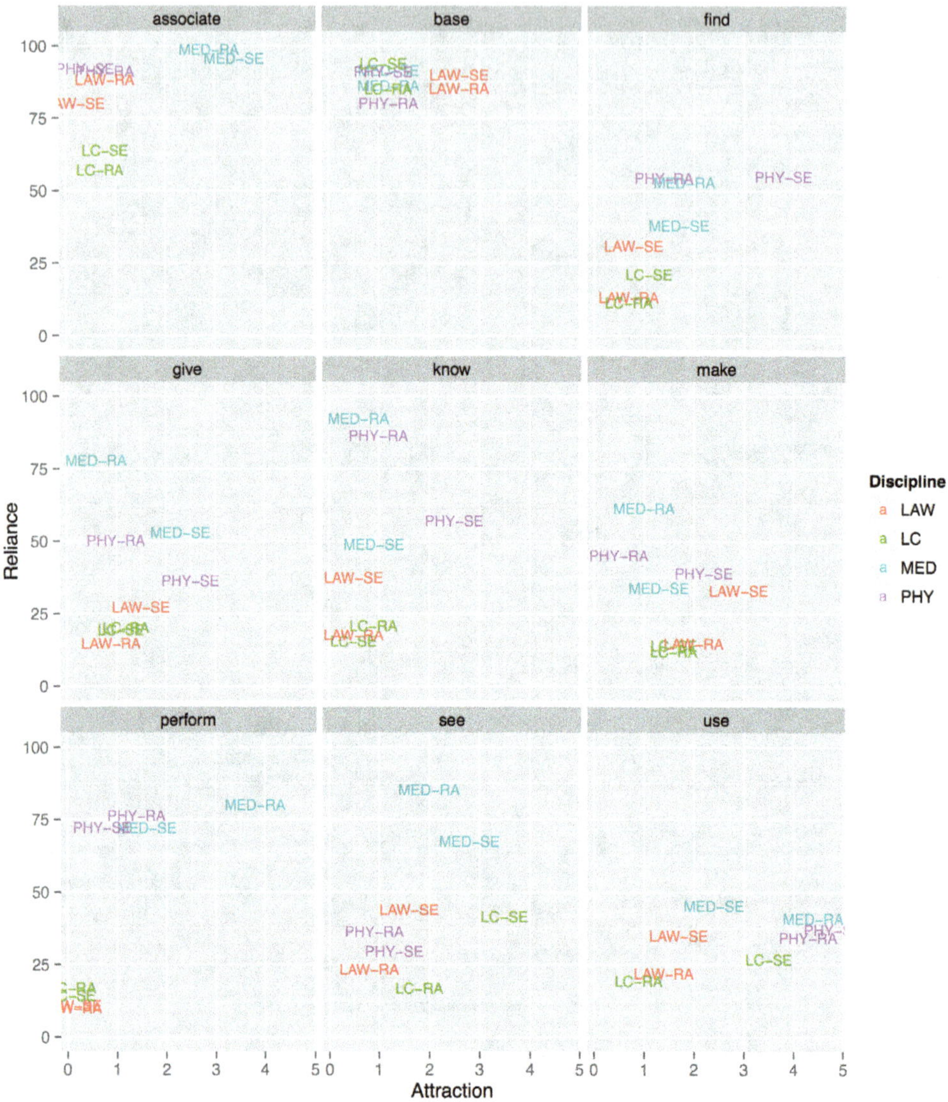

FIGURE 7.5 *Attraction and reliance across subcorpora grouped by* VERB.

not report results, but rather speculates about the kinds of results that could be achieved by modifying the experimental setting.

(13) Here, we *were given* two halides. (PHY-SE)
(14) If such interactions were to be taken into account then it would *be found* that the resistance of material would depend on the magnetic field as well as the temperature. (PHY-SE)

Accordingly, the differences between SEs and RAs observed in Figure 7.5 are not necessarily due to students' difficulties in coping with the communicative demands of the target situation. Instead, SEs are produced in different conditions compared to RAs, and the range of allowable contributions is therefore wider. To assess the pedagogic implications of these findings, it is therefore necessary to carefully consider the role of genre and type of assignment.

Discussion and Concluding Remarks

This study has used a large EAP corpus with a broad disciplinary coverage to investigate the use of passives at a relatively high level of generality. The analysis provides a clear picture of how passives are used in different disciplinary settings: comparing texts representing hard and soft sciences, passives are significantly more frequent in the former. This finding is further confirmed by the fact that similar results are obtained using two different ways of measuring the frequency of the passive. The analysis therefore provides empirical validation for many observations about the passive made in earlier studies, which are usually based on a qualitative investigation of small data sets. In addition, all eight subcorpora contain a considerable number of bare passives, but their relative frequency is consistently higher in RAs.

The analysis of lexical associations indicates that the main explanatory factor is the link between passives and the act of reporting research activities; this interpretation is also consistent with earlier results (e.g. Dorgeloh and Wanner 2003; Wanner 2009). At the same time, the results highlight the importance of lexical patterning for determining the frequency of grammatical constructions such as the passive. The data clearly show that the degree of passivization varies greatly between individual verbs, meanings, and functions, and any account of the passive therefore needs to take account of the full variety of verbs that occur in the corpus. The complex nature of this linkage cannot be fully explored in this study, and future work is thus clearly needed to provide a more complete account on the relationship between voice and lexical choice.

Ideally, such an account would involve a systematic consideration of a number of other textual and linguistic variables, such as TENSE (Shaw 1992) and SECTION (Millar et al. 2013), other indices of self-presentation, e.g. the use of personal pronouns, the use of other reporting strategies, fixed or semi-fixed formulaic expressions involving passive forms (e.g. *as can be seen*, see Hyland 2008), and, finally, the varying proportions of 'averred' and 'attributed' statements between subcorpora (cf. Hiltunen 2010).

More research is also needed to establish the pedagogic relevance of the present findings. The analysis has shown that passives are used differently in student writing compared to research articles, which clearly represent the kind of writing that they aim to master (Tribble 2011). At the same time, such differences cannot necessarily be interpreted as evidence for the claim that students' use of the passive is inadequate. This is because RAs and SEs represent different genres, and variations observed at the level of text may therefore reflect their different communicative purposes. While the present study compares RAs and SEs at the macrolevel, both labels in fact subsume a great variety of subgenres, text types, macrostructures, and rhetorical moves, and investigating them separately is likely to provide further insights into the role of the passive in this register.

Corpus

BAWE *British Academic Written English Corpus*. 2008. Compiled by Hilary Nesi, Sheena Gardner, Paul Thompson, and Paul Wickens. http://www.coventry.ac.uk/bawe.

References

Ball, Catherine N. 1994. "Automated Text Analysis: Cautionary Tales." *Literary and Linguistic Computing: Journal of the Association for Literary and Linguistic Computing* 9/4: 295–302.

Becher, Tony, and Paul Trowler. 2001. *Academic Tribes and Territories: Intellectual Enquiry and the Culture of Disciplines*. Buckingham: Society for Research into Higher Education and Open University Press.

Biber, Douglas. 1988. *Variation Across Speech and Writing*. Cambridge: Cambridge University Press.

Biber, Douglas. 2012. "Register as a Predictor of Linguistic Variation." *Corpus Linguistics and Linguistic Theory* 8/1: 9–37.

Biber, Douglas, Stig Johansson, Geoffrey Leech, Susan Conrad, and Edward Finegan. 1999. *Longman Grammar of Spoken and Written English*. London: Longman.

Bunton, David. 1999. "The Use of Higher Level Metatext in Ph.D Theses." *English for Specific Purposes* 18/S1: S41–S56.

Charles, Maggie. 2007. "Argument or Evidence? Disciplinary Variation in the Use of the Noun *That* Pattern in Stance Construction." *English for Specific Purposes* 26/2: 203–18.

Dorgeloh, Heidrun, and Anja Wanner. 2003. "Too Abstract for Agents? The Syntax and Semantics of Agentivity in Abstracts of English Research Articles." In *Mediating Between Concepts and Grammar*, edited by Holden Härtl, and Heike Tappe, 433–56. Berlin: Mouton de Gruyter.

Dorgeloh, Heidrun, and Anja Wanner. 2009. "Formulaic Argumentation in Scientific Discourse." In *Formulaic Language, Volume II: Acquisition, Loss, Psychological Reality, and Functional Explanations*, edited by Roberta Corrigan, Edith A. Moravcsik, Hamid Ouali, and Kathleen M. Wheatley, 523–44. Amsterdam and Philadelphia: John Benjamins.

Dudley-Evans, Tony, and Maggie Jo St. John. 1998. *Developments in ESP: A Multi-Disciplinary Approach*. Cambridge: Cambridge University Press.

Fløttum, Kjersti, Trine Dahl, and Torodd Kinn. 2006. *Academic Voices: Across Languages and Disciplines*. Amsterdam and Philadelphia: John Benjamins.

Garside, Roger, and Nick Smith. 1997. "A Hybrid Grammatical Tagger: CLAWS4." In *Corpus Annotation: Linguistic Information from Computer Text Corpora*, edited by Roger Garside, Geoffrey Leech, and Tony McEnery, 102–21. London: Longman.

Gilquin, Gaëtanelle, and Magali Paquot. 2008. "Too Chatty: Learner Academic Writing and Register Variation." *English Text Construction* 1/1: 41–61.

Granger, Sylviane. 1983. *The Be + Past Participle Construction in Spoken English: With Special Emphasis on the Passive*. Amsterdam: Elsevier.

Halliday, M. A. K., and J. R. Martin. 1993. *Writing Science: Literacy and Discursive Power*. London: Falmer Press.

Heslot, Jeanne. 1982. "Tense and Other Indexical Markers in the Typology of Scientific Texts in English." In *Pragmatics and LSP: Proceedings of the 3rd European Symposium on LSP, Copenhagen, August 1981*, edited by Jørgen Høedt, Lita Lundquist, Heribert Picht, and Jacques Qvistgaard, 83–104. Copenhagen: The LSP Centre.

Hiltunen, Turo. 2010. "Grammar and Disciplinary Culture: A Corpus-Based Study." Helsinki: Department of Modern Languages, University of Helsinki. http://urn.fi/URN:ISBN:978-952-10-6464-7.

Huddleston, Rodney. 1971. *The Sentence in Written English: A Syntactic Study Based on an Analysis of Scientific Texts*. Cambridge: Cambridge University Press.

Huddleston, Rodney, and Geoffrey K. Pullum, et al. 2002. *The Cambridge Grammar of the English Language*. Cambridge: Cambridge University Press.

Hunston, Susan. 2000. "Evaluation and the Planes of Discourse: Status and Value in Persuasive Texts." In *Evaluation in Text: Authorial Stance and the Construction of Discourse*, edited by Susan Hunston, and Geoff Thompson, 176–207. Oxford: Oxford University Press.

Hyland, Ken. 1996. "Writing without Conviction? Hedging in Science Research Articles." *Applied Linguistics* 17/4: 433–54.

Hyland, Ken. 1999. "Academic Attribution: Citation and the Construction of Disciplinary Knowledge." *Applied Linguistics* 20/3: 341–67.

Hyland, Ken. 2000. *Disciplinary Discourses: Social Interactions in Academic Writing*. Harlow: Pearson Education.

Hyland, Ken. 2005. *Metadiscourse: Exploring Interaction in Writing*. London: Continuum.

Hyland, Ken. 2008. "As Can Be Seen: Lexical Bundles and Disciplinary Variation." *English for Specific Purposes* 27/1: 4–21.

Hyland, Ken, and Polly Tse. 2005. "Evaluative *That* Constructions: Signalling Stance in Research Abstracts." *Functions of Language* 12/1: 39–63.

Leech, Geoffrey, Marianne Hundt, Christian Mair, and Nicholas Smith. 2009. *Change in Contemporary English: A Grammatical Study*. Cambridge: Cambridge University Press.

Mair, Christian. 2009. *Twentieth-Century English: History, Variation and Standardization*. Cambridge: Cambridge University Press.

Millar, Neil, Brian Budgell, and Keith Fuller. 2013. "'Use the Active Voice Whenever Possible': The Impact of Style Guidelines in Medical Journals." *Applied Linguistics* 34/4: 393–414.

Nesi, Hilary. 2008. "BAWE: An Introduction to a New Resource." In *Proceedings of the 8th Teaching and Language Corpora Conference*, edited by Ana Frankenberg-Garcia, Tawfiq Rkibi, Maria do Rosário Braga da Cruz, Ricardo Carvalho, Cristina Direito, and Diogo Santos-Rosa, 239–46. Lisbon: Instituto Superior de Línguas e Administração.

Nesi, Hilary, and Sheena Gardner. 2012. *Genres Across the Disciplines: Student Writing in Higher Education*. Cambridge: Cambridge University Press.

Pullum, Geoffrey K. 2014. "Fear and Loathing of the English Passive." *Language and Communication* 37: 60–74.

Rundblad, Gabriella. 2007. "Impersonal, General, and Social: The Use of Metonymy versus Passive Voice in Medical Discourse." *Written Communication* 24/3: 250–77.

Rundblad, Gabriella. 2008. "We, Ourselves and Who Else?: Differences in Use of Passive Voice and Metonymy for Oneself versus Other Researchers in Medical Research Articles." *English Text Construction* 1/1: 23–40.

Schmid, Hans-Jörg. 2000. *English Abstract Nouns as Conceptual Shells: From Corpus to Cognition*. Berlin: Mouton de Gruyter.

Seoane, Elena. 2006. "Changing Styles. On the Recent Evolution of Scientific British and American English." In *Syntax, Style and Grammatical Norms: English from*

1500–2000, edited by Christiane Dalton-Puffer, Dieter Kastovsky, Nikolaus Ritt, and Herbert Schendl, 191–211. Bern: Peter Lang.

Seoane, Elena. 2009. "Syntactic Complexity, Discourse Status and Animacy as Determinants of Grammatical Variation in Modern English." *English Language and Linguistics* 13/3: 365–84.

Seoane, Elena. 2013. "On the Conventionalisation and Loss of Pragmatic Function of the Passive in Late Modern English Scientific Discourse." *Journal of Historical Pragmatics* 14/1: 70–99.

Shaw, Phillip. 1992. "Reasons for the Correlation of Voice, Tense, and Sentence Function in Reporting Verbs." *Applied Linguistics* 13/3: 302–19.

Svartvik, Jan. 1966. *On Voice in the English Verb*. The Hague: Mouton.

Swales, John M. 1990. *Genre Analysis: English in Academic and Research Settings*. Cambridge: Cambridge University Press.

Swales, John M. 2004a. "Then and Now: A Reconsideration of the First Corpus of Scientific English." *Ibérica* 8: 5–21.

Swales, John M. 2004b. *Research Genres: Explorations and Applications*. Cambridge: Cambridge University Press.

Tarone, Elaine, Sharon Dwyer, Susan Gillette, and Vincent Icke. 1981. "On the Use of the Passive in Two Astrophysics Journal Papers." The *ESP Journal* 1/2: 123–38.

Tarone, Elaine, Sharon Dwyer, Susan Gillette, and Vincent Icke. 1998. "On the Use of the Passive and Active Voice in Astrophysics Journal Papers: With Extensions to Other Languages and Other Fields." *English for Specific Purposes* 17/1: 113–32.

Tribble, Christopher. 2011. "Revisiting Apprentice Texts: Using Lexical Bundles to Investigate Expert and Apprentice Performances in Academic Writing." In *A Taste for Corpora: In Honour of Sylviane Granger*, edited by Fanny Meunier, Gaëtanelle Gilquin, and Magali Paquot, 85–108. Amsterdam and Philadelphia: John Benjamins.

Wallis, Sean, Jill Bowie, and Bas Aarts. 2012. "That Vexed Problem of Choice. Reflections on Experimental Design and Statistics with Corpora." Paper presented at the 33rd Conference of the International Computer Archive of Modern and Medieval English (ICAME 33), Leuven, May 30–June 3. http://www.ucl.ac.uk/english-usage/staff/sean/resources/vexedchoice.pdf.

Wanner, Anja. 2009. *Deconstructing the English Passive*. Berlin: Mouton de Gruyter.

Xiao, Richard, Tony McEnery, and Yufang Qian. 2006. "Passive Constructions in English and Chinese: A Corpus-Based Contrastive Study." *Languages in Contrast* 6/1: 109–49.

CHAPTER 8

Adverbial Hapax Legomena in News Text: Why do some Coinages Remain Hapax?

Antoinette Renouf

Abstract

In recent studies, the author has been working towards a finer definition of neology from a modern diachronic, corpus-based perspective. The focus so far has been on those neologisms which, for various reasons, capture the public and media imagination. Here, attention moves from 'successful' neologisms to the 'silent majority' of neologisms, that is, ones which have not recurred in the corpus (so far). A 'hapax legomenon' is a word occurring once only, with over half the word types in a large corpus of text being of this type. The current study builds on research conducted in 1997–2000 as part of the APRIL project (Renouf and Baayen 1998; Renouf 2010), which was set up to monitor the structure of the lexicon at hapax level, where patterns of productivity are most accessible.

This chapter describes a pilot study of a subset of neologisms passing through a news corpus over time, in an attempt to account for their obscurity. The focus is on adverbs, the least frequently occurring of the open-set grammatical classes. Tentative reasons are proposed for the non-recurrence of these hapax formations, with reference to the presence of certain features. This corpus-driven analysis sheds new light on the evolving lexicon at hapax level.

Keywords

corpus linguistics – lexis – collocation – neology – change – diachrony – hapax legomena – adverb – news text – coinage

Introduction

Since 2011, I have been studying neology from a modern diachronic, corpus-based perspective. By 'modern-diachronic' I mean from 1984 to 2012. Such a brief time-span has been termed 'brachychronic' (Mair 1997), 'short-term' (Mair 2008), and 'short-term change in diachrony' (Kytö et al. 2000, 85).

 | DOI 10.1163/9789004321342_009

My focus so far has been on those neologisms which, for various reasons, capture the public and media imagination, and which recur and increase in frequency and productivity in my journalistic corpus over time. Here, I turn my attention to the 'silent majority' of neologisms which individually have not made an impact in the corpus. These are the 'hapax legomena' or 'singletons', words occurring once only in a finite corpus. This is a provisional status: in an evolving diachronic corpus, a word may recur at a later point. I use the term 'hapax' to refer to an individual word form. Over half the word types in a large body of text, 56% of types in the corpus, are hapax legomena, or 'hapaxes'.

In Natural Language Processing, such words have been traditionally disregarded in large-scale database search in commercial settings, since they are judged by default to be errors or of no linguistic consequence. As the Neocrawler team (<http://www.neocrawler.de/crawler/html/index.php?abfrage=about>) at Munich, led by Schmid, says, "[n]ot all new coinages are here to stay. Indeed many ad-hoc formations, which are created on the fly, are never used a second time—their occurrence may not even be noticed." Yet, ephemerality and percentage errors aside, I see a value in studying these phenomena, sharing with Boussidan the view that "these items may be the first of their kind, either as formal neologies or as indicative of the unfolding of a semantic process. Therefore, they cannot be called 'errors' and are rather 'unusual uses' or idiosyncratic ones. Indeed, among them, many words are simply used once in a specialized article" (Boussidan 2013, 181).

Adverbs constitute the least frequently occurring of the open word classes (noun, verb, adjective, and adverb) in the corpus. This is still a significant class to deal with, and a manual search yields relatively few *bona fide* hapaxes. I examine the adverbs in two data time-chunks, December 1991 and November 2001.

Data

The data from which these sample time-chunks are taken are unbroken flows of news text from *The Independent* and *The Guardian* newspapers from 1984 to 2012 (*The Guardian* 1984–1988; *The Independent* 1989–1999; *The Guardian* from 2000). As of 2012, this corpus contains 1.3 billion word tokens, of which 2.1 million are hapax tokens, constituting only 0.15% of the total number of tokens; that is to say, a hapax legomenon occurs only once in 1,000 running words. On the other hand, the database contains 3.6 million word types, of which 2.1 million are hapax types, constituting 56%, over half, of the total number of types. The corpus is composed of 28 sequential, monthly time-chunks of text. As noted above, the time-chunks selected for this paper are prior to the end date of our evolving corpus, in December 1991 (*The Independent* text) and November 2001 (*The Guardian* text), allowing a time lapse and thus an eventual change in the profile of hapax legomena to have taken place. The final subsets of adverbs for study are those which have by then still not recurred in the corpus.

The chosen time-chunks are not representative of the 28 monthly time-chunks which make up the corpus, since the latter inevitably vary in content, but they do serve as a basis for a range of observations as to the nature of hapax legomena. Where useful, I then draw on the whole corpus to substantiate any observations made.

Analytical Tools

The tools of the AVIATOR project,[1] 1990–1993 (Renouf 1993, 2010; Baayen and Renouf 1996), consist of a series of software filters, through which a chronologically-processed series of newspapers in electronic format are fed. Each word therein, with its context, is matched against an accumulating Master Word Bank and a Master Collocate Bank, to identify new words and word uses. The software filters cumulatively identify candidates for new words, new word combinations, and new word senses, and record an accumulating log of words over time.

For the automatic identification of candidate adverbs, the APRIL[2] and WebCorp Linguist's Search Engine[3] systems each use pre-existing POS taggers. APRIL, 1997–2000 (Renouf and Baayen 1998; Renouf 2010) uses the TnT tagger,[4]

1 The AVIATOR team at the University of Birmingham consisted of software developers Alex Collier (primary), Sue Blackwell, and Eleanor Mundy, Paul Davies as statistician, and myself as Principal Investigator and linguist. Thanks for project funding are due to the EPSRC, DTI, BRS Software Ltd, Collins Publishers, and Nimbus Records.

2 The APRIL team at the University of Liverpool consisted of Alex Collier and Mike Pacey as sequential primary software developers, Andrew Kehoe as GUI developer (in final project year), Paul Davies as statistician, and myself as Principal Investigator and linguist. Thanks for project funding are due to the EPSRC and FT Electronic Publishing.

3 The WebCorp Linguist's Search Engine, or WCLSE, team at Birmingham City University consisted of software developers Matt Gee (primary), Andrew Kehoe, and Jay Banerjee, Paul Davies as statistician, and myself as Principal Investigator and linguist. WCLSE built on the 2000–2003 WebCorp project software and experience. Thanks for project funding for both are due to the EPSRC.

4 TnT, the short form of *Trigrams'n'Tags*, is a statistical part-of-speech tagger, developed by Thorsten Brants in 2000 while at the University of Saarbrücken (<http://www.coli.uni-saarland.de/~thorsten/tnt/>).

also conducting morphological analysis by means of a novel chart parser. Meanwhile, WebCorp Linguist's Search Engine, with its highly-developed graphical user interface (Kehoe and Gee 2009; Renouf and Kehoe 2013), builds on these systems to analyse data and produce textual, numeric, and graphical output to illustrate findings. It uses TreeTagger[5] to apply POS tags.

Method

There are two main tasks involved in carrying out this study. I first identified words which remain hapaxes throughout the corpus. They are largely unknown to tagging systems, so there is a high error rate in classification, and a discrepancy between their analyses. I have thus supplemented the automatic tagging procedures with a manual trawl, cross-checking linguistic and frequency outputs by returning to the original text. This time-consuming process reduces the candidate data immensely, which explains the small *bona fide* hapax inventories finally arrived at. The second task was to identify qualities which might explain why the hapaxes do not recur. The qualities are outlined below.

Baayen and Sproat (1996, 165) state that "the hapaxes of a particular morphological process mostly consist of non-idiosyncratic formations from that process". My corpus has supported this assertion. The subset of *bona fide* hapax adverbs which emerge in the two time-chunks is listed in Tables 8.1 and 8.2. They are largely the result of regular morphological derivation,[6] primarily *-ly* productivity, with contributions from rarer suffixes, *-wards*, *-wise*, as well as *-style*;[7] and one compound adverb. As registered in Table 8.1, there are 15 hapax adverbs in time-chunk December 1991 which remain hapax to the end of 2012. Table 8.2 lists the 26 remaining hapax adverbs in time-chunk November 2001.

---

5 TreeTagger was developed by Helmut Schmid, University of Stuttgart, 1993/1994 and 1995/1996; (<http://www.cis.uni-muenchen.de/~schmid/tools/TreeTagger/>). It was found to cope better than TnT with unknown words when tested against other taggers (<https://sites.google.com/site/casualconc/utility-programs/casualtreetagger#TOC-Checking-unknown-words/>) in the AMALGAM automated tagging programme set up at Leeds by Eric Atwell in the 1990s (<http://www.comp.leeds.ac.uk/ccalas/amalgam/amalgtag1.html>).

6 Acknowledging that there is a long-established school of thought which sees adverb-forming *-ly* as a property of inflection rather than derivation, a theoretical framework on morphological grounds for this has recently been provided in Giegerich (2012).

7 The suffix *-style* stands for a range of formations which attach to independent words to form adverbs (Renouf and Baayen 1998, 181–189) but which are in the process of grammaticalization, and so might still be argued to be independent words, forming compounds and not derived forms.

TABLE 8.1 *December 1991 hapax adverbs*

1. antiquities-wise	6. planlessly	11. soundlie
2. Churchwise	7. post-modernistically	12. strrrrictly
3. escabeche-style	8. screen-right	13. unboringly
4. monocularly	9. self-accusingly	14. undeflatably
5. not-so-subtly	10. self-excusingly	15. white-bonnetedly

TABLE 8.2 *November 2001 hapax adverbs*

1. Aruba-style	10. goatily	19. Moztly
2. burrrrrkwards	11. Freudiantly	20. oh-so-inconveniently
3. Company-wise	12. hallwards	21. Perthonally
4. configurally	13. hot-bloodedly	22. pneumonically
5. cryogenetically	14. impudentlye	23. publiquely
6. Eventwise	15. indirectedly	24. racewise
7. featurally	16. knowledgedly	25. Thimply
8. flowerchild-style	17. life-changingly	26. warmth-seekingly
9. geochemically	18. mooingly	

Pilot Study of Factors which may Cause some Adverbs to Remain Hapax

In journalism, linguistic and socio-pragmatic factors combine to match language to real-world events. Neologistic activity is centred on nouns, since these fulfil a number of roles in news text, primarily naming, characterizing, and establishing ownership of new events and ideas (see Hohenhaus 2007). Adjectives also serve these functions (see the emergence of *toxic*, in 2009), though generally as a modifier in a vogue phrase (such as *big societal, fluffy liberalism, fiscal cliff, troubled families*, or *squeezed middle*) in the period 2010–2012 (Renouf 2014).

Adverbs, on the other hand, are a step removed from real-world concerns. Where they do contribute to topicality, they are likely to maintain the meaning of the base adjectival attribute. Their roles outside the mainstream of journalistic focus are supportive: semantic, stylistic, and deictic. Their predominantly local role means that they make their greatest contribution to nonce-formation in my news text.

Recasting this, Kerremans (2012, 78) says that "whereas neologisms seem to be coined to refer to new objects, events or ideas, nonce-formations or ad-hoc formations predominantly serve poetic, stylistic, [...] deictic or contextual [...] purposes". This would see new nouns as *bona fide* neologisms, and adverbial coinages as ad-hoc devices steered by contextual requirements. Hohenhaus (2007, 19) echoes the contextual imperative, saying that nonce-formations are "ad hoc formations that do not end up in the lexicon (and in many cases could not be listed, because they are too dependent on their context of occurrence)".

This contextual dependency is observably a primary characteristic among my non-recurrent adverbial formations, combined with others which emerge as I explore the data. I operate in the awareness of Hohenhaus' observation that

> some new formations may systematically be excluded from becoming permanent lexical entries [...] Exclusions for this include context-dependency (and non-generic semantic interpretations), certain syntax-like special types of NFs [...] (in addition to 'dummy- compounds' [...] these comprise 'real' phrasal compounds [...] expletive infix formations, and 'identical constituent compounds') [...] and formal deviation. (Hohenhaus 2006, 18)

In this study, I am not in fact interested in hypothesizing why a word does not go on to achieve dictionary status, but only why it does not recur. Often, multiple features will combine to prevent this. Observation of my sample hapaxes has led to the identification of eight features which may explain non-recurrence, which are presented below.

Rare Adjectival Base or Modifier in Derivational or Compounded Adverbial Formation

Hypothesis: A derived or compounded adverbial formation with a rare or context-determined base element is less likely to recur.

The adverbial suffixes *-ly*, *-wards*, *-wise*, and *-style*[8] are widely used in the corpus, are very productive of hapax legomena, and are present in my sample data. In this section, I examine the nature of these derivational formations.

8 As well as others (*-first*, *-ward*, *-ways*, *-wide*, *-long*, *-like*, *-fold*, *-way*, and *-most*) which are not represented by hapaxes in the two data time-chunks.

Adverbial Formations with the Suffix *-ly*

The most common derivational suffix for adverbs is *-ly*. As Nevalainen (2004, 17) states, "its productivity is almost unrestricted: it is possible to form adverbs from practically all adjectives by means of the *-ly* suffix in Present-day English". While there is an inherent inconvenience and complexity to the structure of many adverbs, the process of attaching *-ly* to a base element is a relatively simple adverbialization process, in terms of both morphology and interpretation.

In general language use, formations with *-ly* fall into two main categories: (i) regular aggregations of lexical and morphological elements, and (ii) those with an added stylistic quality and purpose. My sample hapaxes seem to be of the second category:

(1) she showed us into the *goatily* aromatic room where she makes her cheeses. (11/11/01)

(2) the crow proceeded to ram the cow at great speed. It takes a few minutes after waking up for a cow to unlock it's [sic] legs so it had to stand there and *mooingly* take it. (09/11/01)

Examples (1) and (2) present two adverbial coinages with the suffix *-ly*, *goatily* and *mooingly*, which exhibit stylistic interest due to their surprising choice of derived adjectival bases, but which probably do not recur due to their extreme context-dependency.

As a collocate for *aromatic*, *goatily* is not entirely surprising. Though the primary collocates of *aromatic* (2,377 occurrences) are intensifiers—*highly*, *intensely*, and *deeply*—they are followed by *spicily, tangily, pungently, smokily, resinously,* and *grapily*. The coinage *goatily* simply goes a step further in semantic specificity.

In the full text containing *goatily*, three instances of *goats* and two of *goat's cheese* precede its appearance. This could make it temporarily 'available'[9] or activated in the short-term lexicon of the writer, 'priming'[10] the writer to coin *goatily* subsequently.

Progressing to the adverbial coinage *mooingly*, its participial base, *mooing*, occurs 143 times in the full corpus, 25% of which as a pre-modifier, to *cows* (6),

9 Availability is not understood here as 'disponibilité' (Gougenheim et al. 1956).

10 Not 'lexical priming' (Hoey 2005), but perhaps a first step towards it; or perhaps towards 'entrenchment'. Langacker (1987, 59) describes the routinization of lexical retrieval as "a continuous scale of entrenchment in cognitive organization. With repeated use, a novel structure becomes progressively entrenched, to the point of becoming a unit". There has to be a first step.

sound (4), *noises* (3), *sounds* (2), *cow* (2), *cattle* (2), and 25 hapax nouns. Despite this promising morphological ancestry, *mooingly* remains a hapax. This may be because *mooing* is an unlikely base—not only grammatically, as a verbal participle, but also collocationally with the lemma TAKE when meaning 'tolerate', and semantically, since so little can proceed in a 'mooing' fashion.

Adverbial Formations with the Suffix *-wards*

There is only one instance of a hapax with the suffix *-wards* in our sample, shown in (3). The noun *hall* is an unusual nominal base for the suffix *-wards*. The primary sense of *-wards* is 'in the direction' or 'with X as a target', and it assigns the semantics of 'destination' to any attachment.

(3) the admittedly rare pleasure of a cheque arriving that used to send me scurrying *hallwards* at the first footfall of the postie. (01/11/01)

In conventional use, it attaches to nouns naming points of the compass and directions, places, people, and events, often metonymously. However, in the full corpus, it further attaches to a range of stylistically marked and thus humorous exceptions, including nouns naming objects concrete (e.g. *ovenwards*) and abstract (e.g. *rant-wards*), adjectives (e.g. *nude-wards*), and adverbial phrases (e.g. *over-rainbow-wards*).

Equally, the adverb *hallwards* is an unusual collocate for *scurrying* (2,159 occurrences). The word *scurrying* is versatile, being both adjectival and participial and, surprisingly, often used in the domain of musicology. Its commonest right-hand collocates in the corpus are *back* (145 occurrences), *away* (50), *down* (44), *round* (35), and *home* (17). Nevertheless, it does attract a few *-wards* adverbs: *backwards* (4), *goalwards* (2), *eastwards* (2), and *northwards* (1).

There is thus weak collocational precedent in the analogical uses *ovenwards* and *goalwards*, which licences *hallwards* to occur, though not strongly enough to ensure its wider diffusion in the language.

Adverbial Formations with the Suffix *-wise*

As Marchand (1969, 358) put it, "*wise* is being used less and less as an independent word", and he had already classified it then as a 'semi-suffix'. More recently, Sicherl (2009) reports it to be widely accepted as a suffix, reviewing the state-of-the-art as follows:

> [...] the two earlier uses ('manner' and 'dimension') of the suffix *-wise* [...] are [...] regarded as practically unproductive by most authors [...] the 'viewpoint' use seems to be freely productive [...] Any novel

> combinations ending in *-wise* appearing in the English language today therefore tend to be viewpoint adverbs [...] (Sicherl 2009, 170)

Against this terminological background, (4)–(6) show three adverbial coinages ending in the suffix *-wise*. These are indeed viewpoint adverbs, about which Plag (2003, 98) notes that "the scope [...] is not the verb phrase, but the whole clause of sentence". These adverbs generally occupy clause initial or final positioning, as in (4)–(6), but they are also positioned medially elsewhere in the corpus. They each fulfil here the discourse function of specifying the respect in which a preceding statement is to be understood (but with further scope to their deictic role in the full corpus).

(4) The aim is to diversify widely, geographically and *company-wise*. (17/11/01)
(5) He's still quite an inexperienced horse *racewise*, he's only a six-year-old. (26/11/01)
(6) It took the British Rail Pension Fund to keep Sotheby's on the straight and narrow, *antiquities-wise*. (22/12/91)

Context-specificity could be a factor restricting the recurrence of these coinages. The topic focus in each statement is identified through the nominal component in the hapax formation, which is necessarily context-determined.

Another characteristic which could hinder recurrence is the unwieldiness of adverbs ending in *-wise*. An example is *company-wise* in (4), which is morphologically at odds with its conjoined adverbs, *widely* and *geographically*. It can be said to offend the rules of parallelism, where elegance and ease of readability are maintained by the concatenation of matching grammatical structures. In addition, the hapax formation *antiquities-wise* is awkward in having a plural noun as base, though it is licensed "because this [i.e. *antiquities*] is the unmarked form" (Bauer and Renouf 2001). Furthermore, the base form of this adverb, *antiquities*, whilst not rare (2,424 occurrences), is not productive, otherwise yielding only three derived forms: *antiquities-department*, *antiquities-filled*, and *antiquities-smuggling*.

Adverbial Formations with the Suffix *-style*

Adverbs are formed by the attachment to the base word of a second word which, if independent, forms a compound adverb. However, some attaching words are in a state of grammaticalization and tend to function as dependent suffixes. In Renouf and Baayen (1998, 185–188), we examined the 'vogue' adjectival suffixes in British journalism, concluding that *-style*, together with

-effect and *-like*, is a suffix similar to *-type*, on the grounds of pragmatic function (expressing similarity) and high level of productivity. There are indeed 23,437 occurrences of **-style* (lower-case only) in the total corpus, about 75% of which are hapax occurrences.

As shown in (7)–(9), three hapax adverbs ending in *-style* occur in the selected data. They are grammatically conventional, being noun bases with *-style* as an attachment, but their semantics are rather context-specific. The adverbs *escabeche-style* and *Aruba-style* are closely tied to the topics of cooking and weddings, respectively; *flowerchild-style* is closely tied to past reality, evoking earlier styles of behaviour. Their base forms are not very supportive of the recurrence of these formations. The nouns *escabeche* (59 occurrences in 45 texts) and *flowerchild* (2 occurrences) are rare. The proper noun *Aruba* refers to an island which is occasionally referred to (234 occurrences; 157 texts), and has only two derived forms: *Aruba-based* and *Aruba-style*.

(7) olives prepared *escabeche-style*, flavoured with spices, garlic and lemon. (09/12/91)
(8) Tie the knot, *Aruba-style*. A change in the law in Aruba means couples will marry there. (04/11/01)
(9) Pretending that we do, *flowerchild-style*, looks to me like avoiding inconvenient truths. (04/11/01)

Non-Standard Grammar

Hypothesis: An adverbial coinage considered grammatically irregular is less likely to recur.

The adverb *antiquities-wise* in (6) above is the only instance in the selected data of an adverb exhibiting grammatical irregularity, as a noun-noun compound with a pluralized first element. In fact, the use of pluralized first elements is increasingly common (cf. Bauer and Renouf 2001), particularly in cases in which such elements are habitually pluralized when used as referentially independent words. This is the case with *antiquities*. However, to the extent that *antiquities-wise* is perceived as grammatically odd, this is likely to act as a disincentive to its recurrence. In the full corpus, more obvious examples of hapax adverbs displaying base-form ungrammaticality include [adverbs in *-ly*] + *wise*, formations such as *mentally-wise, technically-wise, emotionally-wise, financially-wise, nerdly-wise, olfactorally-wise*; [adjectives in *-al*] + *wise*, such as *legal-wise, social-wise, digital-wise, evangelical-wise, international-wise, professional-wise*; [adjectives in *-ive*] + *wise*, such as *creative-wise*; and [nouns in *-ic*] + *wise*, such as *academic-wise* and *rhetoric-wise*.

Non-Standard Orthography

Hypothesis: An adverbial coinage which exhibits non-standard orthography is unlikely to recur.

Instances of non-standard spelling occur in the hapax adverbial data. There, they represent the phonological characteristics of speech. They are orthographically idiosyncratic, but grammatically and morphologically orthodox.

The items in (10)–(16) are hapaxes but not coinages. Examples (10)–(13) contextualize spoken words in transcription, conveying the pronunciation of, or emphasis placed on, a word by the particular speaker or type of speaker. It represents particular speech characteristics intended to convey aspects of character: Scottish rhotic trill in (10), a nervous habit of speaking while throat-clearing in (11), and instances of lisping in (12)–(13):

(10) 'It is my duty as administrator,' he announces, 'to. hew. *strrrrictly* to the. law.' (08/12/91)
(11) that urgggh areas of the NHS have gone *burrrrrkwards*. (29/11/01)
(12) *Perthonally* we don't think lithping ith in the leatht bit funny. (27/11/01)
(13) and *thimply* don't get the joke. Pleath explain. (27/11/01)
(14) a season under the title Festival of Britten (as groan-inducing as *Moztly* Mozart). (18/11/01)
(15) John [...] do say he will horse whip them *soundlie* when he do catch them. (04/12/91)
(16) For their Sodommerye they use it soe *publiquely* and *impudentlye*. (19/11/01)

In the unlikely event that these precise contexts and thus formations were to recur, it is improbable that identical spellings would ensue. The spelling is arbitrary. The word *str/r/r/r/ictly* is represented by a random number of <r>s, intended to convey visually the physical force or length of the alveolar trill. In 15,916 instances of *strictly* in the total corpus, we find only this instance of multiple <r>s.

Example (14) plays on the title of a music festival, 'Mostly Mozart', exploiting its alliterative and allusive potential. The probable obstacle to its recurrence is not its complexity, but its acknowledged 'groan-inducing' effect on the reader.

Examples (15)–(16) display three quoted cases of obsolete though valid orthography: in (15), a possibly anachronistic cod-formation, and in (16), two *bona fide* instances based on *-ly*. These are not uses but citations. Whether they recur will depend on whether their archaic source texts are known and needed for further quotation for some purpose. On past performance, it seems that this is unlikely.

Semantic Specificity

Hypothesis: An adverbial coinage which is semantically specific is unlikely to recur.

In (17), we see the semantic confection *undeflatably*, coined by the author, Irving Wardle, a writer and theatre critic. It is clear why he coined this epithet: in the context of reviewing a performance of *Toad of Toad Hall*, he was uniquely placed to exploit its two senses, one of literal deflation (a physical characteristic of a toad) and the other of metaphorical deflation (of the sins of pride and conceit associated with this toad). Wardle also employed the adjective *undeflatable* in three subsequent theatre reviews, shown in (18)–(20). The lemma (and metaphor) has clearly established itself in Wardle's repertoire, but it is semantically very restricted.

(17) Nicholas Hytner's recast revival led by Desmond Barrit's *undeflatably* self-satisfied Toad. (01/12/91)
(18) it allows Lady Gimcrack and the *undeflatable* Richard Bonneville to score their own points. (31/03/91)
(19) I never thought to see the *undeflatable* hero of Much Ado played as a low status figure. (11/07/93)
(20) she has comic value as an *undeflatable* punchbag, it is only when Richard starts thumping it that their relationship makes sense. (16/10/94)

Another possible reason for its continuing status as hapax is that of competition (see phrasal formations below). In principle, *undeflatably* has many synonyms. Most of them, though not as semantically multi-layered, are better represented in the full corpus, and could potentially see off or undermine *undeflatably*. These include *unflattenably*, *unpuncturably*, *unsubduably*, *irrepressibly*, *insuppressibly*, *uncontrollably*, *unrestrainably*, *unquenchably*, *unstoppably*, *irrestrainably*, *irredeemably*, and *uncontainably*.

(21) the *unquenchably* inconvenient MP for Linlithgow. (21/08/97)
(22) (Cruise's Vanilla Sky) '*unquenchably* pretentious.' (17/12/01)

However, none of these competitors in the corpus matches the original spirit and wit of *undeflatably*, except *unquenchably* in (21) and (22), which, however, could not be substituted in the *undeflatably* context, since it does not relate to toads. There seem to be few grounds for attributing competitive threat to these equally rare cases, given that Wardle does not appear to favour them in any case.

Genre Specificity

Hypothesis: An adverbial coinage which is genre-specific is less likely to recur.

The term 'genre-specificity' is used here to refer to the restricted semantic, syntactic, pragmatic, and collocational relationship which can obtain for a coinage within a particular journalistic genre. Consider (23) and (24) below:

(23) Lancaster's walls are decked with family portraits. The widow's late husband glares *monocularly* as if he had been married to Maudie Littlehampton. (15/12/91)

(24) Avril Elgar plays the housekeeper as the archetypal simple soul, so snugly, *white-bonnetedly* simple that her simplicity becomes almost self-parodic. (11/12/91)

The hapaxes *monocularly* and *white-bonnetedly* are more than adverbs of manner; they are stylistically and topically intrinsic to their genre and domain of origin. As seen in (23) and (24), their two contexts are rather *recherché*, being extracts of the genre of arts reviews, and of subject domains in the arts: respectively, ballet and theatre. Idiosyncratic language choice is the stuff of theatre criticism. The two hapax coinages refer to props for the worlds of *La Fille mal gardee* [sic] and *The Innocents*, respectively. The adverb *monocularly* is a metonymic reference to an upper-class character in ballet created by Osbert Lancaster. For its part, *white-bonnetedly* is a wilful allusion to a simple girl.

Although they bring sharper definition to the critical content of the reviews, these hapaxes in their stylistically-specific roles make rare partners for other words in their texts. The adverb *monocularly* is entirely strange and unpredictable as a collocational candidate for *glares*. It only makes itself understood in this context by drawing on the reader's awareness both of the meaning of *glares* and of its primary collocating adverbs of theatrical manner: i.e. *angrily*, *balefully*, *unforgivingly*, *accusingly*, and *wrathfully*, and by assuming this meaning by association. It should be allowed, though, that the practised ballet-goer will probably be cognisant of the circumstances of the allusion to Lancaster. Similarly, *white-bonnetedly* is a strange and unpredictable collocate for *simple*, of which the chief adverbial collocates in the general corpus are *relatively*, *quite*, *deceptively*, *fairly*, *pretty*, and *apparently*. Still, *white-bonnetedly* is understandable to the reader in the context of *simple* if the assumption is made, on the basis of its grammar and sentence location, that it is an attribute of *simple* in this particular context of period drama. Again, this is perhaps underestimating the educated reader of arts reviews, for whom this type of stylistic manoeuvre is fairly routine fare. Reader sophistication aside, however, the likelihood of these two items recurring seems small, even in reviews of the same performances.

On the other hand, it must be noted that the base form of these two adverbs bode well for their future appearance, with *monocular* occurring 51 times and *bonneted* 30 times in the full corpus.

Domain Specificity

Hypothesis: A technical adverbial coinage quoted from a specialized textual domain is unlikely to recur in general news text.

The hapax adverbs in (25)–(27) are technical terms of the kind periodically imported into a general news section, often quoted from specialist reports or articles held in archives. Example (25) comes from *The Plague in England*, an archive piece from *History Today*; examples (26) and (27) come from a lecture in the Neurocognitive Development Unit, Institute of Child Health, UCL:

(25) they doubt that plague can be transmitted *pneumonically* indefinitely, being more likely to revert to the less virulent bubonic form. (01/11/01)
(26) Normal controls process faces *configurally*; they look at the whole face and the relationships between the parts. (06/11/01)
(27) By contrast, people with Williams syndrome process faces *featurally*; they focus on single details in a face. (06/11/01)

In addition to their technicality, these terms are elevated in register. They are thus not likely to be needed often in mainstream news text.

Creative Play

Hypothesis: An adverbial coinage coined for purposes of creative play is less likely to recur.

Creative play is, by definition, unlikely to produce coinages which are readily repeated. Its stock-in-trade is originality and marginality. In (28)–(30), the hapax derivations are each puns on or allusions to existing lexis. The adverb *self-excusingly* is licensed by its coordinating phrase, *self-accusingly*, on which it is built by analogy (and possibly in the cause of parallelism). The adverb *screen-right* in (29) is coined in playful contrast to the conventional *stage-left* of theatrical stage directions. In turn, the adverb *warmth-seekingly* in (30) is coined by analogy with *heat-seeking*, of missiles: the suitor is irresistibly drawn to the warmth of the desired one, like a weapon with an infra-red homing mechanism (and apparently about as welcome).

(28) Arts: whether self-accusingly or *self-excusingly* is hard to say. (22/12/91)
(29) Film: a small-holder exited at great speed *screen-right* when a pig reared up. (30/12/91)

(30) I inch *warmth-seekingly* closer to her when she suddenly elbows me. (24/11/01)

These adverbs are also hyphenated, thus more complex than average, and for this reason also statistically less likely to recur. Furthermore, *self-accusingly* and *warmth-seekingly* have marked structures, as synthetic-compound base adjectives, which are phrasal transformations of a longer clause, bringing significant semantic front loading to the adverb. This is in principle unlikely to recur.

Blocking

Hypothesis: An adverbial coinage which essentially carries out the same task as an existing word is unlikely to recur.

In the words of Bauer (2003, 80), "[b]locking refers to the non-existence of a derivative (in the societal sense [...]) because of the prior existence of some other lexeme". However, he concedes (2003, 80–81) that "[b]locking does not entirely prevent the coining of words [...] by individuals [...] All that is blocked is the institutionalisation of these words".

We have already encountered the semantic equivalents *undeflatably* and *unquenchably* (see above). Examples (31) to (34) show four coinages which to some degree also usurp the role of existing words:

(31) a small *indirectedly* elected element. (01/11/01) [*indirectly*]
(32) a *cryogenetically* preserved corpse. (30/11/01) [*cryogenically*]
(33) the user controls a vast and stupid workforce that scurries *planlessly* about a landscape full of obstacles until told how to escape. (23/12/91) [*aimlessly*]
(34) I am trying to make a reputation as someone who writes *unboringly* about the Church of England. (15/12/91) [*interestingly*]

Coinages *indirectedly* and *cryogenetically* in (31) and (32) appear to be accidental or intentional morphological and semantic variants of existing derivations: *indirectedly* echoes *indirectly*, while *cryogenetically* echoes *cryogenically*. In turn, *planlessly* and *unboringly* in (33) and (34) are probably intentional lexical variants of existing adverbs. The former is a marked choice for a semantic slot which could have been occupied by *aimlessly*. The lemma *scurr** does license this semantic direction (among others), collocating with *blindly*, *vainly*, *ineffectively*, *chaotically*, and *futilely*. But why *planlessly*? If it were an issue of style, why not *lunkheadedly* or something more exotic or witty? My conclusion is that it is a semantic choice. The implication is that workers are creatures who need to have plans. Equally, one guesses that *unboringly* in (34) was strategically chosen over the conventional *interestingly* to mean, perhaps mock-modestly, a point midway between *boringly* and *interestingly*.

Fischer (1998, 178–179) observes that "the existence of lexical alternatives that are shorter, structurally less complex, easier to pronounce and with neutral or positive associations can inhibit the institutionalization of a near-synonymous neologism". It is not entirely clear whether these non-recurrent cases are explained fully by this analysis, but *indirectedly* and *cryogenetically* are certainly more cumbersome morphologically than their semantic competitors.

Phrasal Formations

Hypothesis: A multi-word adverbial string is statistically unlikely to recur; increasingly so with increasing length or complexity.

The two hyphenated adverbial phrases in (35) and (36) each happen to be introduced by interactive prefacers, *not-so* and *oh-so*, which are marked stylistically, conveying an implied attitude on the part of the writer:

(35) This divide is subtly, sometimes, *not-so-subtly*, manipulated by nationalists and extremists. (07/12/91)

(36) the accidental photocall: the couple is *oh-so-inconveniently* caught on camera. (19/11/01)

In the case of *not-so-subtly*, the writer could have chosen a morphological formation, *unsubtly*. From the rhetorical perspective, it is understandable in example (35) that *not-so-subtly* is a more effective rebuff for *subtly* than *unsubtly*, but this is because *not-so* is more than the sum of its lexical parts. It is underplayed, implying a judgement or the knowingness that the reality is at odds with the positive surface semantics of the adverb; consider: *not-so-discreetly, privately, surreptitiously, gently, coincidentally, accidentally, seamlessly, neatly.*

In the *oh-so*-adverb formation in (36), *oh* is imitative of a sigh; *oh-so* is an intensifier ironizing excessive emotion. The *oh-so*-adverb usually caricatures the language of a particular person or sector of the population (e.g. *oh-so-not-21st-century*) or ironizes precious or insincere behaviour (e.g. *oh-so-humbly, beatifically, earnestly, subtly, plausibly*).

These phrases themselves occur only once in my corpus, and presumably await the next appropriate context. Meanwhile, the prefacers are extremely productive. The *not-so*-adverb phrase generates 884 types, 67% of which are hapax (with a further 19% dis and tris legomena), while the *oh-so*-adverb phrase generates 455 types, 68% of which are hapax (plus 22% dis and tris legomena).

The more general point here is that multi-word phrases and phrasal strings such as these are statistically improbable, and thus rarely recurrent. There are notable exceptions, where a phrasal string catches on in the imagination of a journalist or the public. Exceptionally, a hyphenated string can extend to strings of tens of words; consider (37) below:

(37) before you can say do-the-podcast-chat-on-the-phone-while-simultaneously recording-yourself-on-an-MP3-player-and-send-us-the-file-over-the-tinterwebs. (20/08/08)

These long strings are composed of any grammatical unit, and function almost exclusively as pre-modifiers to nouns. The closest to an adverbial phrase would probably be in a paraphrase, as here:

(38) Instead, you want to look good in a kind of "I'm-actually-quite-fabulous-give-me-a-rise" way, but not in an "I-will-be-very-grateful-and-will-pay-back-accordingly" way. (06/12/06)

The likelihood of recurrence diminishes statistically as the length increases.

Concluding Remarks

This study has sought to identify reasons for the non-recurrence of all adverbial hapax legomena in my selected data. I have established the following inhibiting qualities, in the order in which they were found:

(a) a rare or context-determined base element;
(b) grammatical irregularity;
(c) non-standard orthography;
(d) semantic specificity;
(e) genre specificity;
(f) domain specificity;
(g) creative play;
(h) competition;
(i) length or complexity, especially of multi-word phrases.

Aside from issues of multiple categorization, I am aware that the qualities of non-standard orthography (c) and length or complexity of multi-word phrases (i) are not of the same kind as the others. Variant spelling could be regarded as being subsumed under the standard orthography of lemmas, while the length of multi-word phrases could be less important than their specificity of meaning and context.

This paper, it is hoped, has gone some way to explaining the lack of productivity of the hapax adverb, based on observations of its immediate and local context, and of the journalistic practices of *The Guardian* and *The Independent* journalists, who are responsible for the adverbial coinages under scrutiny, either as authors of coinages themselves or by quoting other authors (often politicians and celebrities). Predictions cannot be made without knowing the full range of influences on these people, from inter-textual to inter-modal to international ones. As Baayen says (p.c.), "the use of *goatily* might just be the very last event in a long chain of previous events sparked off in a different part of lexical space".

It must be recognized that there is often no apparent reason why a word remains hapax or recurs. Among coinages which are essentially the same, one will recur and another will not. This also raises questions about whether there is really an important difference between hapax, dis and tris and tetrakis legomena. Baayen and Sproat (1996, 162) observe that there is a difference in their productivity profiles, but we find a number of circumstances in the data where recurrent words essentially still constitute a single coinage. In my data such cases include:

(a) polysemous items (*saucewise*, 2 occurrences);
(b) words with literal and metaphorical meaning (*westwardly*, 2 occurrences);
(c) words newly but unwittingly coined by more than one person (*grassily*, 4 occurrences);
(d) words coined and then used by the same person several times in the same text (for example, 4 occurrences of the adverbial phrase *post-Sally* by writer Ann Treneman).

It is impossible to quantify or evaluate these cases without knowing the circumstances of coinage: whether one person has borrowed from another, or several people have unwittingly coined the same adverb. It is likely that where the recurrences are within a specific genre or domain, they have been absorbed into the common parlance of that group of journalists, but there is no straightforward way of establishing this.

Another question arising here is at what point the increasing frequency of recurrence establishes a linguistically significant threshold. My data samples contain adverbs based on nominal and participial compounds: some remain hapax (*life-changingly*, *warmth-seekingly*), while others recur (*heart-swellingly*, 2 occurrences; *skin-pricklingly*, 2 occurrences; *eye-bleedingly*, 24 occurrences). The current study ends at precisely the point where the majority of neologicians and morphologists typically begin work: where new words relinquish their status as nonce-formations and venture out into the larger world of text.

References

AMALGAM. http://www.comp.leeds.ac.uk/ccalas/amalgam/amalgtag1.html.

Baayen, R. Harald, and Antoinette Renouf. 1996. "Chronicling the Times: Productive Lexical Innovations in an English Newspaper." *Language* 72/1: 69–96.

Baayen, R. Harald, and Richard Sproat. 1996. "Estimating Lexical Priors for Low-Frequency Morphologically Ambiguous Forms." *Computational Linguistics* 22/2: 155–66.

Bauer, Laurie. 2003. *Introducing Linguistic Morphology*. 2nd edn. Edinburgh: Edinburgh University Press.

Bauer, Laurie, and Antoinette Renouf. 2001. "A Corpus-Based Study of Compounding in English." *Journal of English Linguistics* 29/2: 101–23.

Boussidan, Armelle. 2013. "Dynamics of Semantic Change. Detecting, Analyzing and Modeling Semantic Change in Corpus in Short Diachrony." PhD diss., Université Lumière—Lyon 2.

Fischer, Roswitha. 1998. *Lexical Change in Present-Day English: A Corpus-Based Study of the Motivation, Institutionalization, and Productivity of Creative Neologisms*. Tübingen: Gunter Narr.

Giegerich, Heinz. 2012. "The Morphology of *-ly* and the Categorical Status of 'Adverbs' in English." *English Language and Linguistics* 16/3: 341–59.

Gougenheim, Georges, René Michea, Paul Rivenec, and Aurélien Sauvageot. 1956. *L'Élaboration du Français Élémentaire. Étude sur L'Établissement d'un Vocabulaire et d'une Grammaire de Base*. Paris: Didier.

Hoey, Michael. 2005. *Lexical Priming: A New Theory of Words and Language*. London: Routledge.

Hohenhaus, Peter. 2006. "Bouncebackability: A Web-as-Corpus-Based Case Study of a New Formation, its Interpretation, Generalization/Spread and Subsequent Decline." SKASE *Journal of Theoretical Linguistics* 3/2: 17–27.

Hohenhaus, Peter. 2007. "How to Do (Even More) Things with Nonce Words (Other than Naming)." In *Lexical Creativity, Texts and Contexts*, edited by Judith Munat, 15–38. Amsterdam and Philadelphia: John Benjamins.

Kehoe, Andrew, and Matt Gee. 2009. "Weaving Web Data into a Diachronic Corpus Patchwork." In *Corpus Linguistics: Refinements and Reassessments*, edited by Antoinette Renouf, and Andrew Kehoe, 255–79. Amsterdam and New York: Rodopi.

Kerremans, Daphné. 2012. "A Web of New Words: On the Conventionalisation of English Neologisms." PhD diss., Ludwig-Maximilians-University Munich.

Kytö, Merja, Juhani Rudanko, and Erik Smitterberg. 2000. "Building a Bridge Between the Present and the Past: A Corpus of 19th-Century English." *ICAME Journal* 24: 85–97.

Langacker, Ronald W. 1987. *Foundations of Cognitive Grammar. Vol. 1, Theoretical Prerequisites*. Stanford, CA: Stanford University Press.

Ljung, Magnus. 1997. *Corpus-Based Studies in English*. Amsterdam and Atlanta: Rodopi.

Mair, Christian. 1997. "Parallel Corpora: A Real-Time Approach to the Study of Language Change in Progress." In *Corpus-Based Studies in English*, edited by Magnus Ljung, 195–209. Amsterdam and Atlanta: Rodopi.

Mair, Christian. 1998. "Corpora and the Study of the Major Varieties of English: Issues and Results." In *The Major Varieties of English. Papers from MAVEN 97, Växjö 20–22 November 1997*, edited by Hans Lindquist, Staffan Klintborg, Magnus Levin, and Maria Estling, 139–58. Växjö: Växjö University.

Mair, Christian. 2008. "Corpora and the Study of Recent Change in Language." In *Corpus Linguistics: An International Handbook*, edited by Anke Lüdeling and Merja Kytö, 1109–25. Berlin: Mouton de Gruyter.

Marchand, Hans. 1969. *The Categories and Types of Present-Day English Word-Formation*. Munich: Verlag C. H. Beck.

Neocrawler. http://www.neocrawler.de/crawler/html/index.php?abfrage=about.

Nevalainen, Terttu. 2004. "Three Perspectives of Grammaticalization: Lexico-Grammar, Corpora and Historical Sociolinguistics." In *Corpus Approaches to Grammaticalization in English*, edited by Hans Lindquist, and Christian Mair, 1–32. Amsterdam and Philadelphia: John Benjamins.

Plag, Ingo. 2003. *Word-Formation in English*. Cambridge: Cambridge University Press.

Renouf, Antoinette. 1993. "A Word in Time: First Findings from Dynamic Corpus Investigation." In *English Language Corpora: Design, Analysis and Exploitation*, edited by Jan Aarts, Pieter de Haan, and Nelleke Oostdijk, 279–88. Amsterdam and Atlanta: Rodopi.

Renouf, Antoinette. 2010. "Identification Automatique de la Néologie Lexicologique et Sémantique: Questions Soulevées par Notre Méthode." In *Actes del I Congrés Internacional de Neologia de les Llengues Romàniques*, edited by M. Teresa Cabré, Ona Domènech, Rosa Estopà, Judit Freixa, and Mercè Lorente, 129–41. Barcelona: Institut Universitari de Lingüística Aplicada. Universitat Pompeu Fabra; Documenta Universitaria.

Renouf, Antoinette. 2014. "Neology: From Word to Register." In *Recent Advances in Corpus Linguistics: Developing and Exploiting Corpora*, edited by Lieven Vandelanotte,

Kristin Davidse, Caroline Gentens, and Ditte Kimps, 173–205. Amsterdam and Atlanta: Rodopi.

Renouf, Antoinette, and R. Harald Baayen. 1998. "Aviating among the Hapax Legomena: Morphological Grammaticalisation in Current British Newspaper English." In *Explorations in Corpus Linguistics*, edited by Antoinette Renouf, 181–9. Amsterdam and Atlanta: Rodopi.

Renouf, Antoinette, and Andrew Kehoe. 2013. "Filling the Gaps: Using the WebCorp Linguist's Search Engine to Supplement Existing Text Resources." *International Journal of Corpus Linguistics* 18/2: 167–98.

Sicherl, Eva. 2009. "The English Suffix *-wise* and its Productivity from the Non-Native Speaker Perspective." *Slovene Linguistic Studies* 7: 169–87.

PART 3

Corpora and Grammar: Examining Grammatical Variation in Space

CHAPTER 9

English in South Africa: The Case of Past-Referring Verb Forms*

Johan Elsness

Abstract

Even though less than 10% of the total population of South Africa are classified as L1 speakers of English, this language nevertheless enjoys a particularly strong position, since it is understood, and largely also spoken, by a substantial proportion of all the four main population groups that make up South Africa. In this article the focus is on White vs. Black speakers. The article surveys the opposition between the two leading verb forms used to refer to past time in English, the present perfect and the preterite, noting that the present perfect tends to be used somewhat more widely in British as compared with American English. An elicitation test carried out with students at the University of Cape Town reveals that Black speakers conform closely to the American norm, while results for White speakers are more similar to those for British English. This is ascribed mainly to the general dominant influence of the American variety throughout the world, counterbalanced by the strong British heritage among the White population, although the possible influence of Afrikaans is also considered. Figures from the *Corpus of Global Web-Based English* are used for comparisons of South African English with American, British, Australian, and New Zealand English.

Keywords

South African English – varieties of English – tense – aspect – present perfect – preterite – corpus – elicitation

* I would like to acknowledge my indebtedness to two anonymous reviewers for the very useful comments they made on an earlier version of this chapter.

 | DOI 10.1163/9789004321342_010

Introduction

In this chapter I look at the special language situation in South Africa, where English has a strong position but is still spoken as L1 only by a minority, even among the White population. The focus is on the variation between the two main verb forms used to refer to past time in English: the present perfect and the preterite. The various population groups and languages are surveyed in the section that follows. Then, the opposition between the two verb forms is reviewed and the results of an elicitation test carried out at the University of Cape Town are presented. Some quite marked differences between White and Black informants emerge, which are compared with similar tests for British and American English, and to some extent even Australian and New Zealand English. Next, data from the *Corpus of Global Web-Based English* show some striking similarities with the elicitation results. The final section summarizes the findings and offers some possible explanations.

Population Groups and Languages in South Africa

By comparison with many other countries, South Africa is characterized by a particularly wide spread of ethnic groups and of languages spoken, in a population totalling slightly more than 50 million. According to the 2011 Census (where the official term for ethnic group, or race, is 'population group'), Blacks make up 79.2% of the total population, Whites only 8.9%. Coloureds account for a further 8.9%, and Indians for only 2.5%.[1]

While only Afrikaans and English had the status of official national languages during the apartheid years, a total of 11 languages, plus sign language, were given that status when majority rule was introduced in 1994. In addition to the two Indo-European languages, these include nine indigenous African languages. All the official languages are set out in Table 9.1, which gives the number of people recorded as speaking each of them as their first language in the 2011 Census. As our focus in the present chapter will largely be on the Cape Town area, in the Western Cape province, figures are given for that province separately, as well as for South Africa as a whole.

1 The remaining 0.5% is accounted for by 'Other'.

TABLE 9.1 *Speakers of the 11 official languages + sign language in the Western Cape and in South Africa as a whole according to the 2011 Census: Raw frequencies, vertical percentages in brackets. Unspecified and not applicable are excluded. From <https://www.statssa.gov.za/Census2011/Products/Census_2011_Census_in_brief.pdf>, pp. 23 25*

First language	Western Cape	South Africa
Afrikaans	2,820,643 (49.7%)	6,855,082 (13.5%)
English	1,149,049 (20.2%)	4,892,623 (9.6%)
IsiNdebele	15,238 (0.3%)	1,090,223 (2.1%)
IsiXhosa	1,403,233 (24.7%)	8,154,258 (16.0%)
IsiZulu	24,634 (0.4%)	11,587,374 (22.7%)
Sepedi	8,144 (0.1%)	4,618,576 (9.1%)
Sesotho	64,066 (1.1%)	3,849,563 (7.6%)
Setswana	24,534 (0.4%)	4,067,248 (8.0%)
Sign language	22,172 (0.4%)	234,655 (0.5%)
SiSwati	3,208 (0.1%)	1,297,046 (2.5%)
Tshivenda	4,415 (0.1%)	1,209,388 (2.4%)
Xitsonga	9,152 (0.2%)	2,277,148 (4.5%)
Other	127,117 (2.2%)	828,258 (1.6%)
Total	5,675,605 (100%)	50,961,442 (100%)

Table 9.1 shows that Afrikaans is spoken as the first language (L1) by very nearly half the population of the Western Cape. In this province Xhosa is the second most common language, spoken by a substantial proportion of the Black population. English is in third place, and it is worth noting that in the Western Cape the number of L1 speakers of English is far less than half the figure recorded for Afrikaans, but then this province includes large rural areas. The position of English is much stronger in Cape Town and other cities. Bowerman (2012, 511) refers to English as "the *de facto* primary official language of the country", and describes it as "extremely pervasive in government, commerce, education and the media". Mesthrie (2012, 493) claims more modestly that a "conservative estimate would be that at least half the present population of 50 million speakers speaks English as an L1 or L2".

The position of English in South Africa is further complicated by the fact that there is a great deal of variation in the kind of English spoken. During the apartheid years it was White South African English (SAE) that had the status of an official language, but even within that variety some marked geographical differences were, and still are, notable, associated with the different characteristics of the various waves of British immigration into South Africa, from the occupation of the Cape in 1795 onwards. Most of these differences concern phonological and to some extent lexical features. The former Natal province (now KwaZulu-Natal) stands out as the area with the English variety most similar to the standard British norm, following an influx in the 1840s and 1850s of settlers who, unlike most of the other British settlers, were largely standard speakers, for example "retired military personnel and financially hard-pressed aristocrats" (Lass 2002, 109). However, a great deal of levelling of such geographical variation has taken place, and Mesthrie (2002, 18) speaks of "the twentieth-century continuum of (white) South African English varieties".

In addition to the White L1 speakers of English there are considerable numbers of English speakers in the other population groups as well. Some of these are also L1 speakers of English, but many are L2 speakers. Among the majority Black population, most people speak L2 English, at various levels of proficiency.[2] However, Mesthrie (2012, 493) draws attention to the fact that many Black children now attend private and government schools formerly reserved for Whites. These Black children learn a kind of English which Mesthrie (2012; see also Mesthrie 2010) describes as a "crossover" variety which shares little with "older" Black SAE. Mesthrie observes that this crossover variety is essentially an L1, and with few exceptions the same as White SAE; thus Mesthrie (2012) decides to focus on the traditional L2 speakers in his treatment of Black SAE.[3]

In a country with such a varied language situation, a great deal of influence must be expected from one language to another. In the case of Black SAE, Mesthrie (2012, 494) discusses the possible influence of Coloured and Indian English in the various provinces, and also of the many indigenous African languages, although he refers to several studies which have failed to detect any clear links between L2 English features and features of the various groups of the respective L1 African languages.[4] Bowerman (2004, 948), in his treatment of White SAE, mentions that morphological and phonological features which are distinctive of this English variety have often been put down to the influence of Afrikaans, but also refers to Lass and Wright (1986) and Mesthrie and West (1995), who point out that many of these features may have survived from Settler English.

2 de Klerk and Gough (2002, 373) maintain that many Blacks speak only a very rudimentary (pidgin-like) form of English, which can hardly be recognized as the variety called Black SAE.

3 Mesthrie (2004, 962) had said of Black L1 speakers of English that "there is currently little to be gained by considering these to be speakers of BlSAfE [Black SAE]".

4 Mesthrie mentions Makalela (2004), de Klerk (2006), and de Wet et al. (2007).

The general impression is that traditional White SAE is now in decline. Bowerman (2012, 517) refers to it as a "waning variety, in terms of both its numerical speech community and its influence"—it has been decimated by emigration and no longer dominates government, education, and the media.[5] Also, speakers of White SAE now mix much more freely with speakers of other English varieties and of other languages, a development which we can assume will lead to a greater influence of those varieties and languages. Instead, the traditional L2 variety of English spoken by many Blacks is now the dominant variety in parliament, political discourse on radio and television, and increasingly also in domains such as tourism and commerce (see Mesthrie 2012, 493). Mesthrie also points out that ordinary speakers do not distinguish between what he takes to be the dominant group of Black L2 speakers of English and "crossover" L1 speakers, but think of themselves as simply speaking English (Mesthrie 2012, 493).

The Opposition Between the Present Perfect and the Preterite in English

The use of the present perfect is more restricted in English than in many other languages, including German and French; hence the acceptability distinction between:

(1)		*I'	ve	seen	him	yesterday
(2)	German	Ich	habe	ihn	gestern	gesehen
		I	have	him	yesterday	seen
(3)	French	Je	l	'ai	vue	hier
		I	him	have	seen	yesterday

In English the present perfect is generally barred in constructions such as (1) with distinct specification of a past time clearly separate from the deictic zero-point. On the other hand, cases of vague past-time specification, for example by means of a temporal adverbial like *just*, leave considerable scope for individual choice between the present perfect and the preterite. In such cases a tendency has often been noted for British English (BrE) to favour the present perfect more than American English (AmE) does.[6] Overall, the present perfect/

5 To some, probably quite small, extent this is counterbalanced by a shift from Afrikaans to English among some White speakers, although Bowerman (2012, 511) sees this as not strictly White SAE but rather the L2 variety Afrikaans English slowly becoming L1.

6 See e.g. Elsness (1997, 2009a).

preterite ratio seems to be higher in BrE than in AmE. However, in most kinds of text the preterite is several times more frequent than the present perfect in all varieties of English. It is the scale of the predominance that varies.

Current relevance has been referred to as a conditioning factor leading to the selection of the present perfect:[7]

(4) We have to leave now—the taxi has arrived.

However, (5) demonstrates that with past-time specification added, the present perfect is likely to be replaced by the preterite:

(5) We have to leave now—the taxi arrived five minutes ago.

This is not to deny that the lack of any clear past-time specification shifts the attention towards the present time sphere, often leading to a current-relevance reading. In cases of conflict, however, temporal specification usually prevails over current relevance.

So far we have been concerned with the situation in Present-day English. Figure 9.1, based on the material first used for Elsness (1997), shows that from a very modest beginning in Old English the present perfect increased consistently up to the beginning of the Modern English period, but then levelled off and has even decreased in frequency over the past couple of centuries, especially in AmE.[8]

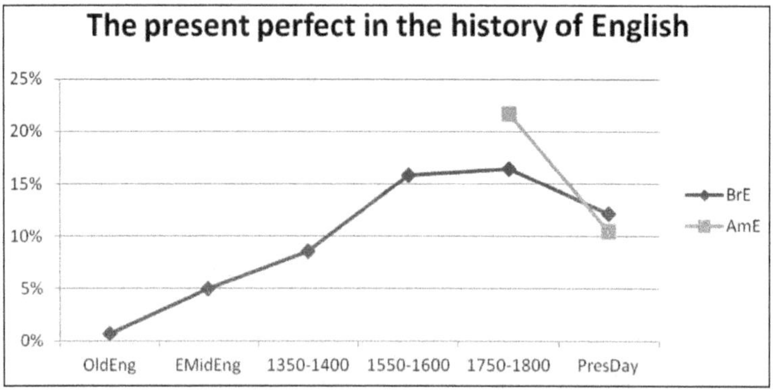

FIGURE 9.1 *The present perfect as a proportion of all past-referring verb forms in the history of English.* HAVE *perfects, active and passive. Progressive forms not included. From Elsness (1997).*

7 For a survey of some of the scholars advocating current relevance as the main conditioning factor for the use of the present perfect in English, see Elsness (1997, 67–69).

8 The development in Late Modern English is discussed in some detail in Elsness (2014).

In the particular case of SAE, White or Black, little work seems to have been done on the perfect/preterite opposition (or other tense-and-aspect matters). In his treatment of White SAE, Bowerman (2004, 949–950) has a section called 'Past *do* + uninflected verb', exemplified by (6) and (7):

(6) Did you bring my books?
(7) Did you have lunch yet?

Example (6) would probably be current in most varieties of English but the combination of the preterite verb form and the adverbial *yet* as in (7) is otherwise strongly associated with AmE.[9] Bowerman notes that this tense usage is often stigmatized as Broad or Afrikaans English, but adds that in his experience it is quite common in what he calls General White SAE (Bowerman 2004, 949). Both the section title and the examples provided by Bowerman suggest that he sees this as typical of interrogative constructions, where he says that this pattern "usually takes the place of present tense *have* + past participle". He ascribes this White SAE tense usage to possible Afrikaans influence, a language that does not distinguish between the preterite and the present perfect: 'Did you bring it?' and 'Have you brought it?' would both be realized as:

(8) Het jy dit gebring?
have you it brought?

Bowerman (2012) claims more generally that the distinction between the two verb forms "is levelled fairly frequently in WhSAfE [White SAE], so that they are sometimes interchangeable" (Bowerman 2012, 517), without confining this observation to interrogative contexts. Afrikaans is again given as a possible influence.

A prominent feature of Kortmann and Lunkenheimer (2012), in which both Bowerman (2012) and Mesthrie (2012) appear, is the long list of WAVE (*World Atlas of Variation in English*) features used to indicate the occurrence or otherwise of various grammatical phenomena in the English varieties described. The list consists of a total of 235 grammatical features and a specification of the possible occurrence of each feature in each variety on a scale where A indicates that "feature is pervasive or obligatory", B that "feature is neither pervasive nor extremely rare", and C that "feature exists, but is extremely rare" (Kortmann and Lunkenheimer 2012, 5).

Two of the WAVE features are of particular relevance to us: feature 99 ("levelling of the difference between present perfect and simple past: simple

9 See e.g. Elsness (1997, 117–118, 224–225; 2009a, 237–238) and Hundt and Smith (2009, 54–55).

past for StE [Standard English] present perfect") and feature 100 ("levelling of the difference between present perfect and simple past: present perfect for StE simple past") (Kortmann and Lunkenheimer 2012, 943). In Bowerman's section on White SAE both these features are recorded with the rating B, that is, levelling both ways of the present perfect/preterite opposition is given as "neither pervasive nor extremely rare". The respective examples are (9) and (10):

(9) Did you ever buy the milk?
(10) I have seen one in Germany last year.

It may further be noted that feature 109 (called "perfect marker *already*") is also given rating B. The example is (11), that is, it is similar to example (7) above, there described as a typical AmE feature, with *already*/*yet* combining with the preterite tense.

(11) Did you eat already?

The same features also appear in Mesthrie's section on Black SAE. Here feature 99 is again given the ranking B, while feature 100 is given C. The respective examples are (12) and (13) (from Mesthrie 2012, 498):

(12) Were you ever in Jo'burg?
(13) My standard nine, I have enjoyed it very much.

The different rankings mean that in Black SAE replacement of the Standard English present perfect with the preterite is taken to be more common than the converse process, while in White SAE levelling both ways is reported as equally common.

Elicitation Test

In the absence of corpus material which would allow for a comparison of SAE with other national varieties (but see the following section) and of internal variation within SAE, we shall consider the results of an elicitation test I carried out at the University of Cape Town (UCT) in 2011.[10] A total of 235 informants took part, all of them students in the Psychology Department. Most participants were in their early twenties. The test was done electronically through

10 This was the same test I had previously carried out in Britain, the US, Australia, and New Zealand. See Elsness (1997, 2009a, 2009b).

a questionnaire sent out to their respective e-mail addresses. The informants gave the following information about their ethnic backgrounds (population groups): White: 113; Black: 65; Coloured: 32; Indian: 16.[11] Under the apartheid regime UCT was a White university, but it now has a very mixed student body, and it can be seen that my informants represented a good spread across population groups, albeit with a White predominance. The informants gave their home language(s) as follows: English: 169; Xhosa: 22; Zulu: 22; Afrikaans: 18; Other, African: 11; Other, General: 22. UCT is an English-language university, and all students speak English, but with a wide range of home languages, as can be seen.

A total of 66 constructions were included in the test. Half of them had preterite verb forms, which in most cases were contrasted with the present perfect (in a few cases with the pluperfect). Informants were asked to indicate their judgment of each construction on a five-point scale: 'Completely unacceptable', 'Dubious', 'Uncertain', 'Fair', and 'Perfectly OK'. In the subsequent analysis these were recoded as numerical values, 1–5.

Findings revealed a great deal of difference between White and Black informants, and our focus will largely be on that division. The detailed results to be presented below are confined to informants giving English as at least one of their home languages, which substantially reduces the number of Black participants (to N=19), although the main trends were the same even without this restriction. Whether all these informants can be considered L1 speakers

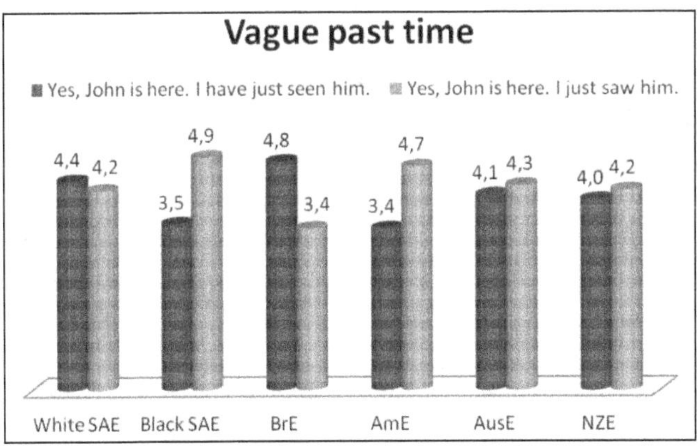

FIGURE 9.2 *Mean scores for the present perfect vs. the preterite in constructions with vague past-time specification. Statistical significance of differences recorded between White and Black SAE: present perfect: p≤0.05; preterite: p≤0.001.*

11 The figures provided here and below do not generally add up to the same total, because some informants left some of the questions unanswered.

of English is still uncertain, but the distinction between L1 and L2 speakers is itself often blurred in South Africa, as we have seen.

In most cases we shall compare SAE only with BrE and AmE, but Figure 9.2 also includes Australian English (AusE) and New Zealand English (NZE), to place the recorded variation in the broader global picture. Constructions with a vague specification of past time are among those where the rivalry between the present perfect and the preterite is at its most open. The expectation that in such cases AmE will favour the preterite more than BrE, and the present perfect less, is amply confirmed by the results with the temporal adverbial *just* in Figure 9.2.[12]

In this case the full, uncontracted form in which the perfect auxiliary appeared may have had some impact on the results: perhaps especially to the AmE informants, the uncontracted auxiliary may have seemed objectionable, leading to a lower mean score for the present perfect alternative.[13] On the other hand, with the irregular verb SEE there is a clear difference between the realizations of the preterite and of the past participle, so that overall the two verb constructions are in any case clearly distinct.

Not surprisingly, both AusE and NZE place themselves somewhere between BrE and AmE, the preterite alternative scoring slightly more highly than the present perfect in both varieties.[14] In the case of SAE, there is a very striking difference between the White and the Black informants. The results for Blacks are very close to those for AmE, the mean score for the preterite construction being very close to the top score 5, and that for the present perfect being considerably lower. This distribution contrasts sharply with that recorded by the White SAE informants, where the score for the present perfect is slightly higher than for the preterite. It can be seen from the caption that for both verb forms this difference is statistically significant.[15]

As noted above, current relevance is often referred to as a major explanatory factor in attempts to describe what distinguishes the present perfect from the preterite in English. In the construction set out in Figure 9.3 the current relevance of the subject referent's past residence in America (Africa)

12 According to the t-test, the differences recorded between AmE and BrE are statistically significant at the 0.1% level for both verb forms.

13 For evidence that in the contemporary language contractions are more common in AmE than in BrE, see e.g. Leech et al. (2009, 257).

14 The perfect/preterite distinction in AusE and NZE is discussed in detail in Elsness (2009b).

15 Here and elsewhere statistical significance was calculated by means of the t-test applied to independent samples, which takes the deviation recorded within each result into account.

seems obvious, and yet a clear and consistent preference for the preterite was recorded.[16] This may be explained at least partly by the fact that in this construction the current relevance is clearly marked, even outside the verb form, and most particularly in that this part of the construction takes the form of a *because*-clause. Hence further marking of such relevance may be seen as redundant. It is also worth noting that even in this case there is a distinct difference in the score given to the present perfect construction, between White SAE and BrE on the one hand and Black SAE and AmE on the other, in line with the general tendency for the present perfect to be more common in BrE. Comparison with the scores for the constructions with *just* set out in Figure 9.2 shows that there is a more consistent preference for the preterite here. That must be because *recently* indicates a more distant past than *just*. Also, the very slight surface difference in the realization of *'s lived* vs. *lived* may have led some informants to think that the difference was immaterial, and hence to mark the simpler alternative, i.e. the preterite, higher; the contrast between *have seen* and *saw* is much more distinct, especially with the intervening adverbial between the auxiliary and the main verb in the perfect construction.

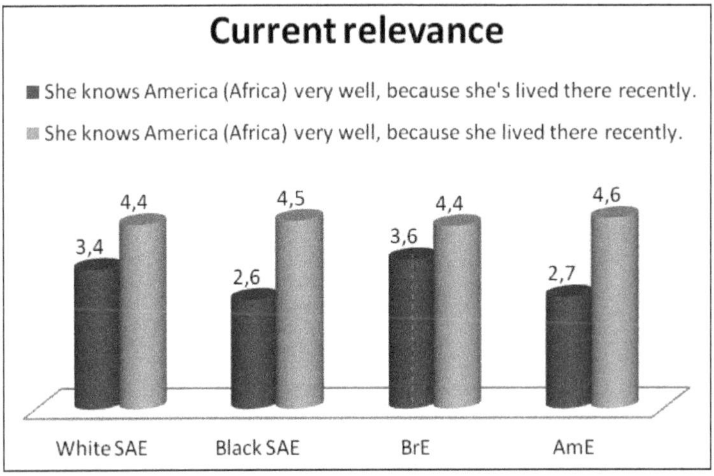

FIGURE 9.3 *Mean scores for the present perfect and the preterite in constructions suggesting current relevance. Statistical significance of differences recorded between White and Black SAE: perfect construction: p≤0.05; preterite construction: n.s.*

16 When this test was applied in Britain, the US, Australia, and New Zealand, the construction included the term *Africa*, which was replaced by *America* when the test was repeated in South Africa.

Current relevance comes up again in the construction presented in Figure 9.4. Here the results are very different: the present perfect alternative consistently gets the higher score, and that score is even higher in Black than White SAE, as well as in AmE compared to BrE. But this is a rather special construction, one special feature being the temporal specifier *ever*: it has frequently been noted (e.g. Elsness 1997, 295) that in combination with that specifier (and also with *never* and *always*) the preterite is often used, even though the temporal reference typically extends all the way up to the deictic zero-point.[17] However, the conditioning factor which seems to prevail in this case is that the sentence form is interrogative, which is an environment where the present perfect has been found to be particularly common, as we will see again below.[18]

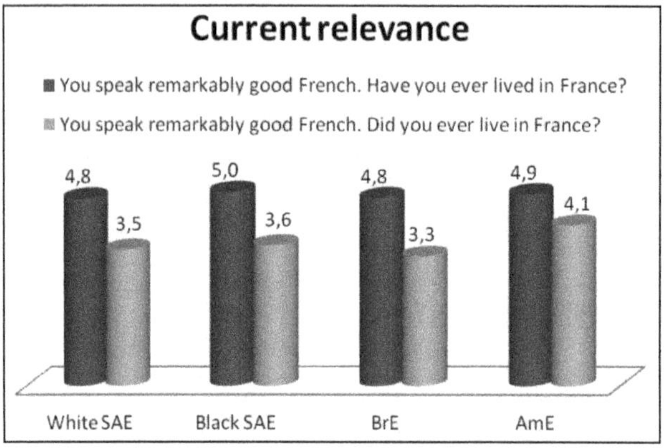

FIGURE 9.4 *Mean scores for the present perfect and the preterite in constructions suggesting current relevance. Statistical significance of differences recorded between White and Black SAE: perfect construction: p≤0.05; preterite construction: n.s.*

The construction set out in Figure 9.5 is also interrogative, with the alternation between the present perfect and the preterite occurring in a tag question, with negative polarity (and also in the preceding main clause). Both constructions

17 For an extensive discussion of the correlation between adverbial and verb form, see Werner (2013, 2014), based on an analysis of the *International Corpus of English* (ICE).

18 See e.g. Elsness (1997, especially pp. 205, 224). My results for White as well as Black SAE run counter to Bowerman's (2004) suggestion, noted above, that in White SAE the preterite commonly replaces the present perfect in interrogative constructions.

were given with contraction of the negative particle, hence both the perfect auxiliary and the preterite form of the auxiliary DO occur in their full forms; but this is unlikely to cause any objection in interrogative constructions, where either auxiliary occurs in pre-subject position, so that the contracted auxiliary is hardly an option. Although all the four varieties register the higher score for the present perfect alternative, the highest scores for the present perfect were again recorded in Black SAE and AmE; hence this is similar to the other interrogative construction considered (cf. Figure 9.4).

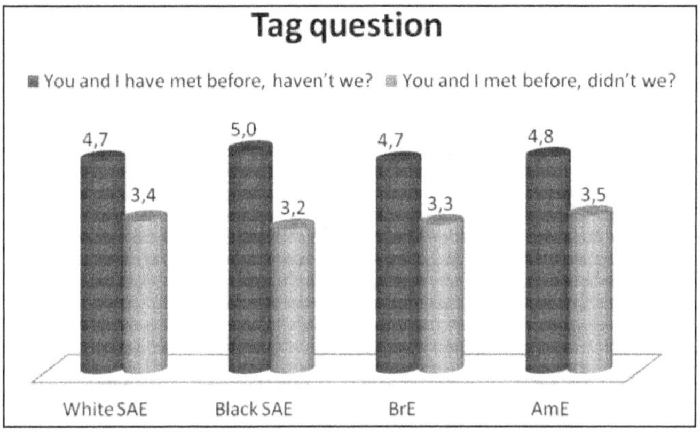

FIGURE 9.5 *Mean scores for the present perfect and the preterite in tag questions. Statistical significance of differences recorded between White and Black SAE: perfect construction: $p \leq 0.05$; preterite construction: n.s.*

The prevailing trend, however, is for the higher preterite score to be recorded in Black SAE, and the higher score for the present perfect in White SAE, as is confirmed by Table 9.2, which gives the number of constructions with each verb form where the difference recorded between White and Black SAE was found to be statistically significant at least at the 5% level.[19] A total of 15 such cases were recorded. The overall tendency can be seen to be very clear.

19 These results are again based on responses only from informants giving English as a home language.

TABLE 9.2 *Higher mean scores according to verb form and ethnic background: Cases where the White/Black SAE difference is statistically significant at least at the 5% level*

	Present perfect	Preterite	Total
White SAE	5	0	5
Black SAE	2	8	10
Total	7	8	15

The two cases where, contrary to the prevailing trend, a perfect construction received a higher mean score from the Black informants are the two interrogative constructions just considered. Furthermore, it is noteworthy that both these constructions are among the few perfect constructions where the score for AmE was higher than that for BrE. A possible explanation may be that in interrogative clauses the temporal reference will often be unequivocally to a period of time extending from the past all the way up to the deictic zero-point.[20] This is precisely the kind of temporal reference for which the present perfect is most obviously the preferred verb form in English. Interrogative constructions may hence be more resistant than other constructions to what is assumed to be the general decline of the present perfect in English (along with negative constructions, for similar reasons). It is highly noteworthy that even in this case Black SAE stays very close to the AmE model. In addition to the temporal reference, the likely realization of the perfect auxiliary may contribute further to the continued preference for the present perfect in these constructions: whereas the auxiliary is increasingly likely to be contracted in writing, to *'ve* or *'s*, and to be reduced in speech to /s/, /z/, or a barely audible /v/, the full form of the auxiliary is still likely to occur in interrogative and negative verb phrases. Thus, the distinction between the realizations of the present perfect and the preterite remains more clear-cut in such cases, which seems to make the distinction more resistant to levelling. The fact that the perfect auxiliary will occur in its full form in such cases may in itself help to make the present perfect more acceptable to many speakers and writers, who might otherwise opt for the preterite in borderline cases, with only a vague specification of past

20 See Elsness (1997, especially pp. 202, 206).

time, either to avoid what is seen as too heavy an auxiliary if it is given in its full form, or because it has been reduced so much as to be felt to be redundant.

Figure 9.6 gives the mean scores for all the present perfect and preterite constructions included in the elicitation test. AmE has the highest score for the preterite and the lowest score for the present perfect; with BrE it is the other way round. In addition to AmE, Black SAE and AusE also have higher scores for the preterite, while White SAE and NZE have higher scores for the present perfect, along with BrE. The tendencies that were noted in Figure 9.2 above are thus confirmed, although the differences between the varieties distinguished were more distinct when only results for the one construction were considered.

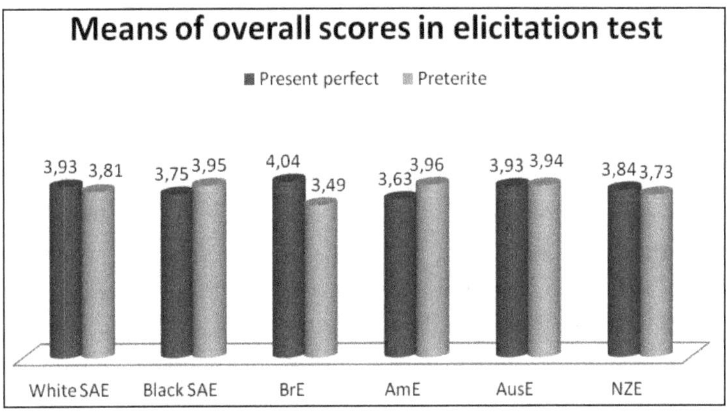

FIGURE 9.6 *Means of overall scores in own elicitation test according to national variety + White/Black SAE.*

Corpus Investigation

SAE is included among a total of 20 national varieties of English covered by the huge *Corpus of Global Web-Based English* (GloWbE), which was released by Mark Davies in 2013.[21] The overall size of GloWbE is 1.9 billion words. Figure 9.7 provides the results from all the 20 countries of a search on the string 'have.[VHO] [VVN*]'.

This string represents all occurrences of *have* tagged as the present tense auxiliary immediately followed by the past participle of a lexical verb. Most of

21 Detailed information about this corpus is given at <http://corpus2.byu.edu/glowbe/>.

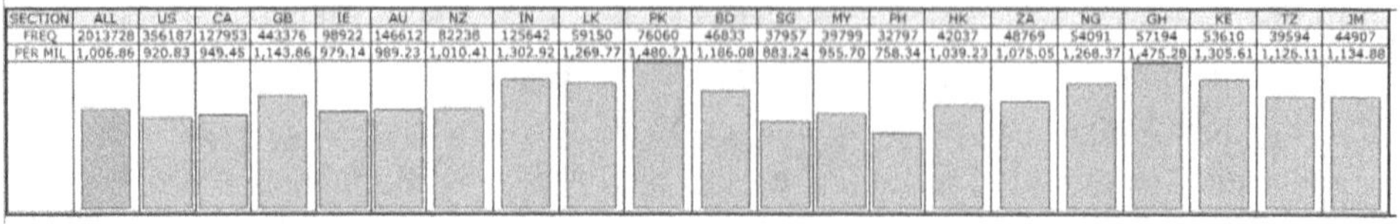

SECTION	ALL	US	CA	GB	IE	AU	NZ	IN	LK	PK	BD	SG	MY	PH	HK	ZA	NG	GH	KE	TZ	JM
FREQ	2013728	356187	127953	443376	98922	146612	82238	125642	59150	76060	46833	37957	39799	32797	42037	48769	54091	57194	53610	39594	44907
PER MIL	1,006.86	920.83	949.45	1,143.86	979.14	989.23	1,010.41	1,302.92	1,269.77	1,480.71	1,186.08	883.24	955.70	758.34	1,039.23	1,075.05	1,268.37	1,475.28	1,305.61	1,126.11	1,134.88

FIGURE 9.7 *Results of search on 'have.[VHO] [VVN*]' in GloWbE. Raw frequencies and frequencies per million words.*

the results will be occurrences of the present perfect of lexical verbs, but constructions with the third person singular auxiliary *has* will not be captured in this initial search, nor will constructions with a contracted auxiliary. These will be included in searches restricted to the language varieties under scrutiny in this chapter, to be presented below. Another restriction is that present perfect constructions with one or more intervening items between the auxiliary and the main verb will not be captured, which means that cases with intervening adverbials, for example, will be omitted. Pilot searches were carried out allowing for one or more intervening items, yielding results which showed more or less the same tendencies. A disadvantage of allowing for intervening items is that a lot of irrelevant hits will necessarily be generated, i.e. cases which are not perfect constructions—the more intervening items allowed, the greater the yield of irrelevant hits. A further disadvantage is that negative and interrogative present perfect constructions will also be included, which will distort the comparison with the preterite of lexical verbs, which does not occur in either negative or interrogative contexts (cf. *I did not think; Did you think?*, with the lexical verb in the infinitive). The restriction to the past participle of only lexical verbs meant that progressive and passive constructions were also excluded, since these have the past participle of the auxiliary BE (*They have been writing; They have been written*). Again this helps in the comparison with the preterite, since the preterite of lexical verbs does not occur in those patterns (*They were writing; They were written*).

Most of the constructions resulting from the search string specified above can be assumed to be occurrences of the present perfect with the restrictions outlined.[22] The results can be seen in Figure 9.7.[23] It can be observed that a great deal of variation emerges. The expected difference between AmE and BrE is confirmed, the frequency of the present perfect being notably higher in the latter variety. As could also be expected, AusE and NZE place themselves some-

22 This was confirmed by a brief look at some of the resulting sentences. For obvious reasons, no attempt at manual post-editing was made with a material of this magnitude.

23 For an explanation of the national codes used in GloWbE, see <http://corpus2.byu.edu/glowbe/?r=y>.

where between AmE and BrE, AusE somewhat closer to the AmE level, NZE closer to BrE. A striking result is that quite a few of the 'new' varieties of English record frequencies well above that for BrE, Pakistani and Ghanaian English topping the list.[24] As regards SAE ('ZA' in the chart), the result can be seen to be slightly lower than that for BrE but higher than for both AusE and NZE. No distinction is made here between White, Black, or any other SAE variety.

Table 9.3 gives more detailed results from GloWbE for constructions which in the vast majority of cases can be assumed to be present perfect forms, in SAE and the four other varieties addressed in this chapter. The first four rows set out the normalized frequencies recorded for each of the two present tense forms of the perfect auxiliary, plus their contractions. The tags following the auxiliaries restricted the searches to cases where the first form actually had the function of a present tense auxiliary, thus excluding the infinitive, for example, and are especially important in the case of *'s*, which by itself may also function as a contraction of *is* or as the genitive ending.

TABLE 9.3 *The present perfect and the preterite in five national varieties in GloWbE. Normalized to frequencies per million words. Ratios between the preterite and the present perfect*

	SAE	BrE	AmE	AusE	NZE
have.[VHO] [VVN*]	1,025.41	1,081.07	911.77	1,029.82	1,051.90
has.[VHZ] [VVN*]	1,075.05	1,143.84	920.83	989.22	1,010.41
's.[VHZ] [VVN*]	21.21	46.96	41.51	37.77	32.73
've.[VHO] [VVN*]	255.90	428.77	460.37	428.20	372.44
Total PERF	2,377.57	2,700.64	2,334.48	2,485.01	2,467.48
[VHZ] got/gotten	22.66	32.57	43.29	32.57	30.74
[VHO] got/gotten	60.58	112.04	87.91	105.67	95.04
PERF w/o got(ten)	2,294.33	2,556.03	2,203.28	2,346.77	2,341.70
[VVD*]	13,389.68	14,362.71	14,621.87	13,292.15	13,194.76
got.[V*D]	262.39	313.58	365.45	304.14	297.09
PRET w/o got	13,127.29	14,049.13	14,256.42	12,988.01	12,897.67
PRET/PERF	5.72	5.50	6.47	5.53	5.51

24 Xinyue and Collins (2012, especially p. 392) also record a great deal of international variation in the frequency of the present perfect in their investigation of the various ICE corpora. Only Indian English comes out with a higher frequency than BrE. Neither Pakistani nor Ghanaian English are represented in their material, however. See also Schmied (1991) and van Rooy (2009) on similarities between different African English varieties.

The construction HAVE *got*(*ten*) can be a problem, since this frequently acts as a set phrase with clear present time reference rather than a genuine present perfect (*How many children have you got?*). Since the occurrence of this idiomatic expression may vary between the national varieties, it was thought best to deduct it from the recorded perfect frequencies. *Got* was therefore also deducted from the preterite figures. The bottom row gives the ratios calculated between the preterite and the present perfect (without *got*/*gotten*).

It should be borne in mind that the figures presented for the present perfect are not the precise frequencies of that verb form, for the reasons discussed above. They can nevertheless be assumed to be a good approximation, and there is little reason to believe that inaccuracies vary much between the national varieties. If we focus on the ratios between the preterite and the present perfect, it can be seen that the expected positions of AmE and BrE are again confirmed: AmE has the highest ratio, BrE the lowest. The pattern for the remaining varieties is also the same as in Figure 9.7 (with frequencies for some of the assumed present perfect forms): AusE is closest to AmE, followed by NZE and then SAE, which is closest to the BrE level.

These results invite comparison with the results of my elicitation test, although such a comparison involves some obvious problems, one being that in the elicitation test results were recorded on a scale from 1 to 5, while the results from GloWbE are frequencies per million words. In an attempt to put the two sets of results on an equal footing, we shall use ratios between the preterite and the present perfect of the means of all the constructions included in the elicitation test (see Figure 9.6 above) and compare those with the ratios based on GloWbE. To further facilitate the comparison, both sets of ratios will be normalized so that BrE=1; moreover, the maximum deviation will be equalized, so that the ratios for AmE will also be the same.[25] The ratios which emerged from this process are set out in Table 9.4 and illustrated in Figure 9.8.

Bearing in mind the various reservations noted above, there can be seen to a striking similarity between the two sets of ratios between the preterite and the present perfect: we have already noted that AmE comes out on top in both cases, and that BrE achieves the lowest scores. Furthermore, AusE is somewhat closer to the AmE level than NZE is in both cases. SAE cannot be brought directly into this comparison, since GloWbE does not distinguish between White and Black speakers, but the overall GloWbE result for SAE can be seen to be somewhat higher than for both AusE and NZE, a result which

25 This was done by adjusting each ratio based on GloWbE according to the following formula: New GloWbE ratio=1+((Old GloWbE ratio -1)*(AmE elicitation result -1)/(Old AmE GloWbE ratio -1)).

conceals the quite marked difference between White and Black SAE uncovered by the elicitation test. The similarity between the two sets of ratios otherwise recorded suggests that the emerging trends may indeed be representative of real underlying differences between the national varieties.

TABLE 9.4 *Adjusted ratios of the preterite to the present perfect in GloWbE and own elicitation test. Both normalized to BrE=1, maximum deviations equalized*

<table>
<tr><th></th><th>White SAE</th><th>Black SAE</th><th>BrE</th><th>AmE</th><th>AusE</th><th>NZE</th></tr>
<tr><td>GloWbE</td><td colspan="2">1.0608</td><td>1.0000</td><td>1.2628</td><td>1.0102</td><td>1.0031</td></tr>
<tr><td>Elicitation</td><td>1.1222</td><td>1.2193</td><td>1.0000</td><td>1.2628</td><td>1.1605</td><td>1.1244</td></tr>
</table>

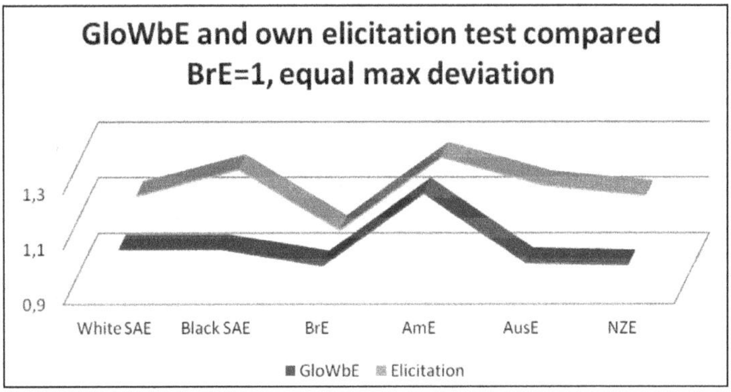

FIGURE 9.8 *Results from GloWbE compared with own elicitation test. Both normalized to BrE=1, maximum deviations equalized. Cf. Table 9.4.*

Conclusion

We have seen that in the main the distribution of the present perfect and preterite verb forms in SAE follows the same pattern as in the other national varieties. Our material has not allowed us to examine any possible geographical variation in the kind of English spoken across South Africa. However, some striking differences have been noted between White and Black SAE. The prevailing trend has been found to be that the present perfect scores more highly in White SAE than in Black SAE, while it is the other way round with the preterite. This puts White SAE more in line with the BrE norm, and Black SAE with AmE. In certain interrogative constructions from the elicitation test the perfect score was higher for Black SAE. It seems that in such constructions the present perfect is more resistant to pressure from the preterite than in other cases, presumably because in many such cases the temporal reference is clearly to past time extending all the way up to the deictic zero-point, which is precisely the kind of temporal reference associated above all with present perfect verb forms. The fact that in interrogative constructions the perfect auxiliary naturally occurs in its full, uncontracted form may also help to uphold the distinction between the two verb forms in these cases. It may be no coincidence that in interrogative constructions the present perfect also scores more highly in AmE than in BrE. This, hence, is a further similarity between Black SAE and AmE.

An important question then arises: why does White SAE keep closer to the BrE norm, and Black SAE to the AmE norm? An obvious answer is the influence of the British heritage on White English-speaking South Africans. Not least under the apartheid regime, traditional, standard BrE was very much the model for SAE. Although in some respects this link has been weakened in recent years, it is no surprise to see that the perfect/preterite opposition remains close to the BrE norm, even among present-day White South Africans.

The possible influence of Afrikaans may be a further explanatory factor, since this language generally uses the present perfect corresponding to both the present perfect and the preterite in English. Quite a few of the White participants in the elicitation test indicated that they spoke Afrikaans (as well as English) at home, and the mean perfect scores for these are in fact somewhat higher, and the preterite scores slightly lower, than for the other White informants, although both differences are too small to be statistically significant.[26]

Nevertheless, as others have warned, it may sometimes be difficult to distinguish between the influence of Afrikaans and the surviving influence of Settler English; this goes for the perfect/preterite opposition too, since the present perfect seems to have been used more widely in earlier English than is the case today (see Figure 9.1 above). It is true that the present perfect scores recorded for White SAE are somewhat lower than those for BrE, but influence from Afrikaans and/or Settler English may help to explain why the present perfect remains notably higher in White compared with Black SAE.

26 Mean present-perfect score for White informants (also) speaking Afrikaans at home (N=13): 4.0112; for other White informants (N=99): 3.9149. The corresponding preterite scores were 3.7770 and 3.8122, respectively.

The influence of the mass media, especially television, may also be playing a role. Since the end of apartheid, former restrictions (from both sides) have been lifted, and both American and British television are now watched a great deal (see Bowerman 2012, 514). American popular culture seems to be especially influential in parts of the Black population, which may further help to explain why Black SAE is so similar to AmE.

More broadly, the fact must not be overlooked that AmE is now the most influential English model world-wide, and has indeed been so for some time. The absence of the special conditioning factors linking White SAE to BrE may be the main reason why the distinction between the present perfect and the preterite in Black SAE has been found to be so close to the AmE norm.

Corpus

GloWbE Davies, Mark. 2013. *Corpus of Global Web-Based English: 1.9 billion words from speakers in 20 countries*. Accessed May 2013. http://corpus2.byu.edu/glowbe/.

References

Bowerman, Sean. 2004. "White South African English: Morphology and Syntax." In *A Handbook of Varieties of English. Vol. 2: Morphology and Syntax*, edited by Bernd Kortmann, Kate Burridge, Rajend Mesthrie, Edgar W. Schneider, and Clive Upton, 948–61. Berlin: Mouton de Gruyter.

Bowerman, Sean. 2012. "White South African English." In *The Mouton World Atlas of Variation in English*, edited by Bernd Kortmann, and Kerstin Lunkenheimer, 511–9. Berlin: Mouton de Gruyter.

de Klerk, Vivian. 2006. *Corpus Linguistics and World Englishes: A Study of Xhosa English*. London: Continuum.

de Klerk, Vivian, and David Gough. 2002. "Black South African English." In *Language in South Africa*, edited by Rajend Mesthrie, 356–78. Cambridge: Cambridge University Press.

de Wet, Febe, Philippa Louw, and Thomas Niesler. 2007. "Human Automatic Accent Identification of Nguni and Sotho Black South African English." *South African Journal of Science* 103: 159–64.

Elsness, Johan. 1997. *The Perfect and the Preterite in Contemporary and Earlier English*. Berlin: Mouton de Gruyter.

Elsness, Johan. 2009a. "The Present Perfect and the Preterite." In *One Language, Two Grammars? Differences Between British and American English*, edited by Günter Rohdenburg, and Julia Schlüter, 228–45. Cambridge: Cambridge University Press.

Elsness, Johan. 2009b. "The Perfect and the Preterite in Australian and New Zealand English." In *Comparative Studies in Australian and New Zealand English: Grammar and Beyond*, edited by Pam Peters, Peter Collins, and Adam Smith, 89–114. Amsterdam and Philadelphia: John Benjamins.

Elsness, Johan. 2014. "The Present Perfect and the Preterite in Late Modern and Contemporary English: A Longitudinal Look." In *Corpus Interrogation and Grammatical Patterns*, edited by Kristin Davidse, Caroline Gentens, Lobke Ghesquière, and Lieven Vandelanotte, 81–103. Amsterdam and Philadelphia: John Benjamins.

Hundt, Marianne, and Nicholas Smith. 2009. "The Present Perfect in British and American English: Has There Been any Change, Recently?" *ICAME Journal* 33: 45–63.

Kortmann, Bernd, and Kerstin Lunkenheimer. 2012. *The Mouton World Atlas of Variation in English*. Berlin: Mouton de Gruyter.

Lass, Roger. 2002. "South African English." In *Language in South Africa*, edited by Rajend Mesthrie. 104–26. Cambridge: Cambridge University Press.

Lass, Roger, and Susan Wright. 1986. "Endogeny vs. Contact: 'Afrikaans Influence' on South African English." *English World-Wide* 7/2: 201–23.

Leech, Geoffrey, Marianne Hundt, Christian Mair, and Nicholas Smith. 2009. *Change in Contemporary English: A Grammatical Study*. Cambridge: Cambridge University Press.

Makalela, Leketi. 2004. "Making Sense of BSAE for Linguistic Democracy in South Africa." *World Englishes* 23/3: 355–67.

Mesthrie, Rajend. 2002. "South Africa: A Sociolinguistic Overview." In *Language in South Africa*, edited by Rajend Mesthrie, 11–26. Cambridge: Cambridge University Press.

Mesthrie, Rajend. 2004. "Black South African English: Morphology and Syntax." In *A Handbook of Varieties of English. Vol. 2: Morphology and Syntax*, edited by Bernd Kortmann, Kate Burridge, Rajend Mesthrie, Edgar W. Schneider, and Clive Upton, 962–73. Berlin: Mouton de Gruyter.

Mesthrie, Rajend. 2010. "Sociophonetics and Social Change: Deracialisation of the GOOSE Vowel in South African English." *Journal of Sociolinguistics* 14/1: 111–46.

Mesthrie, Rajend. 2012. "Black South African English." In *The Mouton World Atlas of Variation in English*, edited by Bernd Kortmann, and Kerstin Lunkenheimer, 493–500. Berlin: Mouton de Gruyter.

Mesthrie, Rajend, and Paula West. 1995. "Towards a Grammar of Proto-South African English." *English World-Wide* 16/1: 105–33.

Schmied, Josef. 1991. *English in Africa: An Introduction*. London: Longman.

van Rooy, Bertus. 2009. "The Shared Core of the Perfect Across Englishes: A Corpus-Based Analysis." In *World Englishes—Problems, Properties and Prospects. Selected Papers from the 13th IAWE Conference*, edited by Thomas Hoffmann, and Lucia Siebers, 309–30. Amsterdam and Philadelphia: John Benjamins.

Werner, Valentin. 2013. "Temporal Adverbials and the Present Perfect/Past Tense Alternation." *English World-Wide* 34/2: 202–40.

Werner, Valentin. 2014. *The Present Perfect in World Englishes: Charting Unity and Diversity*. Bamberg: University of Bamberg Press.

Xinyue, Yao, and Peter Collins. 2012. "The Present Perfect in World Englishes." *World Englishes* 31/3: 386–403.

CHAPTER 10

A Look at Participial Constructions with *Get* in Hong Kong English*

Eduardo Coto-Villalibre

Abstract

English constructions consisting of the verb *get* plus a past participle (e.g. *The whole suburb got destroyed by the fire*) have been the subject of several studies, relating mostly to Present-day English (Chappell 1980; Carter and McCarthy 1999), but also to some ESL varieties, in some of which the construction is said to be particularly frequent (Collins 1996). Recent research (Coto-Villalibre 2014a, 2014b) shows that *get*-constructions form a fuzzy set and can be placed on a gradient depending on their degree of 'passiveness', that is, depending on the number of features they share with traditional *be*-passives.

In this chapter the author examines how this gradient is manifested in a specific ESL variety, namely Hong Kong English. The various characteristics of the *get*-constructions posited on the gradient will be discussed and then compared with the results obtained for British and Indian English in the author's earlier studies. The analysis uncovers the existence of differences between the varieties as regards the information status of subjects, the type of lexical verb involved, and the semantic prosody of the *get*-constructions.

Keywords

central *get*-passives – *get* + V*en* constructions – passive gradient – World Englishes – ICE corpora

---

* For generous financial support I am grateful to the European Regional Development Fund, the Spanish Ministry for Economy and Competitiveness (grants FFI2014-52188-P and FFI2014-51873-REDT), and the Autonomous Government of Galicia (grants GPC2014/004 and R2014/016). Thanks are also due to Teresa Fanego, Elena Seoane, and Paloma Núñez-Pertejo for their feedback on an earlier version of this chapter, as well as to the audience of my presentation at the ICAME34 conference and the two external reviewers of this chapter, who provided me with new ideas that improved its final version.

 | DOI 10.1163/9789004321342_011

Introduction

As we know, passives in Present-day English can select two different verbs, *be* and *get*. But what is a *get*-passive? The change from the active to the passive voice involves a structural rearrangement of the clause elements, where the active subject becomes the passive agent, the active object becomes the passive subject, and the agent, if mentioned at all, is introduced by the preposition *by*. The change from active to passive is illustrated in the following example:

(1) a. The forest fire destroyed the whole suburb. (active)
b. The whole suburb *got destroyed* by the forest fire. (passive)

Though these features apply generally to both *be-* and *get*-passives, research on the latter suggests that *get*-passives, as opposed to *be*-passives, tend to be avoided in formal English while they are recurrent in conversation (Quirk et al. 1985, 161; Biber et al. 1999, 476; Huddleston and Pullum et al. 2002, 1442; McEnery et al. 2006, 112–113), occur only with dynamic verbs, that is, verbs which denote an action and not its outcome (e.g. *cut, play, send, throw, type*) (Huddleston and Pullum et al. 2002, 1442; Alexiadou 2005, 17), and do not normally have an overt agent *by*-phrase (Quirk et al. 1985, 161; Carter and McCarthy 1999, 52; McEnery et al. 2006, 113). Actually, the findings of McEnery et al.'s (2006, 113) study show that in F-LOB, of approximately one million words of British English recorded in the 1990s, the short or agentless form of the *be*-passive is over eight times as frequent as its long or agentful form, while for the *get*-passive the short form is over ten times as frequent as its long form. The contrast in the spoken part of the *British National Corpus* (BNC), of about ten million words (10% of the corpus), is even more marked, where the short forms of *be-* and *get*-passives are over 18 and 37 times as frequent as their long forms, respectively. Moreover, the animate subject of *get*-passives has a higher degree of responsibility for the action described than the subject of *be*-passives, and is also commonly attributed adversative consequences, hence its frequent occurrence with predicates such as *arrest, blame, hit, kill, shoot*, and the like (Hatcher 1949, 436–437; Chappell 1980, 444–445; Arce-Arenales et al. 1994, 14; Rühlemann 2007, 120; Toyota 2007, 148, 153).

The present chapter is part of a larger project (Coto-Villalibre 2014c) which involves a cross-varietal comparative analysis of '*get* + past participle' constructions in East and South East Asian Englishes. In this study, the focus is on *get*-constructions in Present-day spoken Hong Kong English, on the basis of data extracted from the Hong Kong component of the *International Corpus of English* (ICE-HK). I first classify the different *get*-constructions according to their degree of 'passiveness' on a gradient, which ranges from central *get*-passives to borderline constructions with *get*. Then I describe the corpora used in this study and present the results of the analysis. Given the compatibility across the individual corpora in ICE,[1] I compare the findings obtained for Hong Kong English with those obtained for British and Indian English in my earlier research (Coto-Villalibre 2014a, 2014b). The chapter closes with a summary of the main conclusions.

Since I will be comparing Hong Kong English and Indian English, a few words seem in order to describe these two varieties. To begin with, both Hong Kong English and Indian English are English as a Second Language (henceforth ESL) varieties. Schneider (2007) proposes a model of the evolution of Postcolonial Englishes in which he claims that despite all surface differences there is a shared underlying uniform process which conducts their formation, accounts for the similarities between them, and seems to operate whenever there is language transfer. He calls it the 'Dynamic Model' and describes it as a sequence of five progressive stages, a process which moves from the transferring of English to a new territory through a period of vigorous social and linguistic changes to a renewed stabilization of a newly emerged variety. The spread and influence of English in India gained importance during the second half of the eighteenth century, while in Hong Kong this happened in the mid-nineteenth century. Both ESL varieties have reached phase 3 of Schneider's model, known as 'nativization', a stage in which the imported and the local varieties merge and a restructuring of the English language takes place, mainly at the grammatical and lexical levels.

Of great interest for this study is the expression of the passive in the substrate languages influencing English in India and Hong Kong, since this could have a bearing on the results obtained from the corpus. The expression of the passive voice in Hindi, the most widely used substrate language for Indian English, is fairly similar to the passive in English, in that it is also expressed by means of a periphrasis, namely the passive auxiliary *ja* followed by an inflected past participle of the main verb (Sandahl 2000, 101; Kachru 2006, 93). In Cantonese, the most common substrate language for Hong Kong English, by contrast,

1 As mentioned by one reviewer, the comparability among the different ICE corpora is an object of ongoing discussion, since, for instance, there are slight discrepancies as regards the dates of compilation of the different individual corpora, and the number of words of the spoken component varies slightly between varieties. However, these disadvantages are clearly outweighed by the advantages. The ICE corpora are an indispensable source for comparative studies across varieties of English world-wide. The limitations mentioned above are minimized, for instance, by applying normalized frequencies to the varying corpus sizes.

passives are not expressed by means of a periphrasis. In this dialect of Chinese, passives are strongly associated with the expression of adversative meaning (Matthews and Yip 1994, 150). With respect to substrate influence, therefore, we might expect Indian English to be characterized by a fairly frequent use of *get*-passives and Hong Kong English to show a low frequency of *get*-passives, these generally having adversative meaning.

The Gradient

The definition of the English *get*-passive has always been a point of debate. Proof of this are the voices which brand it as "a linguistic puzzle" (Carter and McCarthy 1999, 54), as "a contentious point of discussion" (Chappell 1980, 411), or even as "the subject of widespread disagreement" (Collins 1996, 43). In fact, the term 'passive' itself is misleading, since a large number of *get* + past participle constructions involve types of meanings different from the regular passive functions, despite their formal and semantic similarity. In order to classify these constructions, authors such as Quirk et al. (1985), Collins (1996), and Leech et al. (2009) have placed them on a gradient according to their degree of 'passiveness'. For my purposes, I have used a data-driven gradient, created in light of the data retrieved from the corpora and their detailed analysis. My classification differs from other taxonomies put forward so far in the literature not only as regards the terminology used but also regarding the number and nature of the categories of *get*-constructions posited along the gradient. Thus, we can distinguish five types of *get*-constructions: (i) central *get*-passives, with the auxiliary *get* followed by a verbal past participle; (ii) pseudo *get*-constructions, which lack both an active counterpart and an agent phrase, and are followed by a stative past participle; (iii) adjectival *get*-constructions, whose members exhibit adjectival properties; (iv) idiomatic *get*-constructions (e.g. *get used to*); and, finally, (v) resultative *get*-constructions, with an intervening noun phrase between *get* and the past participle.

Central Get-*Passives*

At the top end of the gradient we find central *get*-passives, the most strongly represented of the five subclasses according to Collins (1996, 49). As mentioned in the introduction, among the features distinctive of *get*-passives are the tendency to occur only with dynamic verbs and to leave the agent *by*-phrase unexpressed; if present, though, their referent is typically animate and human (Quirk et al. 1985, 161; Huddleston and Pullum et al. 2002, 1442; Alexiadou 2005, 17; McEnery et al. 2006, 112–113). Moreover, the animate subject of the *get*-passive is usually responsible for the action described and the passive is also commonly attributed adversative semantics (Hatcher 1949, 436–437; Collins 1996, 52; Carter and McCarthy 1999, 49–50). The whole construction is non-gradable and has an equivalent active counterpart, as illustrated in (2):

(2) a. Commuters are *getting ripped off* by the MTR. (ICE-HK:S2B-007 #62:1:B)
b. The MTR is ripping off commuters.

Pseudo Get-*Constructions*

Further down the scale are pseudo *get*-constructions, which seldom have an active counterpart and in which the possibility of agent addition is very rare, as in (3):

(3) She didn't really want to *get married* at that age. (ICE-HK:S1A-006 #86:1:A)

Collins (1996, 47) classifies the verbs belonging to this category as either reciprocal (e.g. *get divorced* (*from each other*) and *get married* (*to each other*)) or reflexive, including body care verbs or verbs of grooming such as *get changed, get cleaned, get dressed, get shaved,* and *get washed* (*by oneself*). In these constructions, *get* functions as a copular verb and not as a catenative, and is followed by a non-gradable stative past participle (e.g. *married* in (3) above, according to Quirk et al. (1985, 161), means 'in a state of marriage') as its complement, which is therefore adjectival. Nonetheless, these participles do not fulfil all of the properties attributed to adjectives; for instance, they are never gradable (**They got very washed*), *get* cannot be replaced by a lexical copular verb (**They seemed washed,* although *?They seemed married*), and the criterion of coordinating the participle with an adjective is unclear (*?They got washed and ready*). Finally, as in central *get*-passives, *get* puts the emphasis on the subject and on what happens to him/her/it as a result of the action.

Adjectival Get-*Constructions*

Close to the periphery we find adjectival *get*-constructions, whose members are adjectives, derived by lexical-morphological conversion of the V*en* form, and *get* is a copula rather than a catenative, as in (4) below. These constructions fulfil criteria such as the ability to be used attributively (*a bored young fellow*), to be modified by a degree adverb (*so bored*) and coordinated with another adjective (*I got bored and uneasy*), and to replace *get* with a lexical copular verb, such as *become, feel,* or *seem* (*The young fellow seemed bored*).

(4) I *got* so *bored* at home dude like I want to go out. (ICE-HK:S1A-099 #151:1:B)

Although the presence of an agent phrase is hardly possible, since these constructions commonly involve a change of state rather than an agent-motivated event, a reduced number of cases of adjectival constructions might show verbal properties (i.e. an agent-like phrase and an active analogue). Example (5) below, for instance, is verb-like in having an agent-like phrase (*at some of it*) and an active analogue (*Some of it really annoyed you a bit*). Quirk et al. (1985, 168–169) and Collins (1996, 46) refer to them as 'semi-passives' and 'psychological *get*-passives', respectively, and they remark that the use of agent *by*-phrases in these adjectival past participle constructions is very rare, although agent-like phrases introduced by different prepositions seem to be quite common, among them *about, at, over, through, to*, and *with*.[2]

(5) You've *got* really a bit *annoyed* at some of it. (ICE-HK:S1B-076 #162:1:B)

Idiomatic Get-*Constructions*

On the very periphery of the *get*-constructions gradient we find idiomatic expressions where the relationship between the V*en* form and the verb from which it historically derived has been totally lost from sight, as with *get accustomed to* in (6). These constructions are no longer '*get* + past participle' (where *get* could be replaced by *be*), but fixed collocations, as in expressions such as *get fed up with*, *get rid of*, and *get used to* (Collins 1996, 49, Leech et al. 2009, 156).

(6) They *get accustomed to* such kind of environment. (ICE-HK:S1A-043 #588:1:A)

Resultative Get-*Constructions*[3]

Beyond the periphery we find resultative *get*-constructions, where *get* is a main verb followed by a noun phrase, functioning as an object, before the participle. When the intervening NP is a reflexive (example (7)), the construction is explicitly agentive, with the subject referent being involved very directly and

2 Note that these 'semi-passive' constructions, which have been regarded in my previous studies (Coto-Villalibre 2014a, 2014b) as a separate category, have now been fused with adjectival *get*-constructions into one single category. Corpus studies (Coto-Villalibre 2014c) have proved that these constructions whose members exhibit a mixture of verbal and adjectival properties are rather infrequent and marginal.

3 'Resultative *get*-constructions' correspond to 'reflexive *get*-constructions' in my earlier research (Coto-Villalibre 2014a, 2014b). The terminology has been slightly modified to account for examples such as that in (8).

being responsible for the action described. However, there are occasions in which the intervening NP is not a reflexive, but a causative, as in (8).

(7) The candidate can always re-participate and *get* yourself *reelected.* (ICE-HK:S1B-024 #61:1:D)
(8) I *got* my work *published* in the newspaper. (ICE-HK:S1A-013 #207:1:A)

These constructions, which have *get* as a main verb taking non-finite complementation, cannot be considered as *get*-passives, since the passive *get*-construction is a simple catenative with no intervening NP between *get* and the non-finite complement, as in *My work got published* (Huddleston and Pullum et al. 2002, 1443).

A Corpus-Based Study of *Get*-Constructions

The Corpora

Having presented the classification of *get*-constructions and the characteristics of each of the subtypes, I now turn to the empirical part of my study, which involves the identification and analysis of the different *get*-constructions in a corpus of Hong Kong English, in light of the characteristics described above. As these constructions feature mainly in conversation, I concentrated on the spoken part of the Hong Kong component of the *International Corpus of English.* ICE-HK, like the rest of the individual corpora in ICE, contains 500 samples, 300 of spoken English and 200 of written English, of approximately 2,000 words each, leading to a corpus of around one million words. The spoken component consists of dialogues, both private and public, and monologues, both scripted and unscripted, amounting to around 600,000 words.[4]

I began my research by carrying out an automatic search for the different word forms of *get*, namely *get, gets, getting, got,* and *gotten,* followed by a past participle. I entered all the examples into a database and manually identified all the relevant *get*-constructions. Finally, I classified the *get* + past participle constructions following the passive gradient presented above and analysed

4 ICE-HK contains a large number of extra-corpus material, that is, utterances produced by non-corpus speakers. To ensure that only examples from comparable corpus material are included, the *get* + past participle constructions found within the extra-corpus material in ICE-HK were filtered out and the frequencies for the number of *get*-constructions were normalized. I would like to thank Cristina Suárez-Gómez for suggesting me to distinguish between corpus and extra-corpus material.

them according to the defining characteristics of central *get*-passives. Given the compatibility across the individual corpora in ICE, which share a common corpus design and common schemes for textual and grammatical annotation, I used the corresponding parts of ICE-GB and ICE-IND as benchmark corpora by comparing the results obtained in the present study with the findings from my corpus analysis of *get*-constructions in Present-day spoken British and Indian English (Coto-Villalibre 2014a, 2014b).

The Results

The quantitative analysis of the spoken Hong Kong component of ICE yielded a total of 151 tokens of *get* followed by a past participle, whose distribution according to type of construction is shown in Table 10.1.

As can be seen, although almost all constructions occur relatively frequently in the Hong Kong corpus sample, of the five subclasses, the adjectival *get*-construction is the one most commonly represented, closely followed by central *get*-passives and pseudo *get*-constructions. Some striking differences with the other two varieties are noticeable: (i) the number of *get*-constructions (note a normalized frequency of 2.5 per 10,000 words in ICE-HK), which is higher in ICE-GB (3.6 per 10,000 words), and remarkably higher in ICE-IND (5.2 per 10,000 words); and (ii) their distribution, since in the Indian component the most common constructions are central *get*-passives, whereas in the British and Hong Kong components *get*-passives are outnumbered by adjectival *get*-constructions. Therefore, Collins' (1996, 54) assertion that central *get*-passives are especially frequent in Indian English is confirmed in this study. A possible reason for these differences in the use of passives among contact

TABLE 10.1 *Distribution of* get + Ven *constructions according to type of construction*

Type of construction	ICE-HK		ICE-GB		ICE-IND	
	Percentage	Tokens	Percentage	Tokens	Percentage	Tokens
central *get*-passive	23.2	35	23.3	50	40.4	126
pseudo *get*	19.9	30	13.5	29	15.7	49
adjectival *get*	27.1	41	27.0	58	19.9	62
idiomatic *get*	11.9	18	16.7	36	8.0	25
resultative *get*	17.9	27	19.5	42	16.0	50
Total	100 (NF 2.5)	151	100 (NF 3.6)	215	100 (NF 5.2)	312

varieties of English is the influence of the substrate languages. As mentioned in the introduction, the similar passive periphrasis in Hindi may account for the high number of central *get*-passives in Indian English. The lack of such a construction in Cantonese might explain the relatively lower number of these constructions in Hong Kong English.

Actually, application of the chi-square test shows that the differences between ICE-IND and ICE-HK on the one hand, and ICE-IND and ICE-GB on the other, concerning the number of central *get*-passives are statistically significant (chi-square value 50.3, p<0.0001, df=1 and chi-square value 31.96, p<0.0001, df=1, respectively; note that for df=1 the chi-square reported is the Yates chi-square, corrected for continuity). Furthermore, percentage deviation indicates that the observed chi-square frequency in ICE-IND is 79.1% greater than that expected on the basis of the null hypothesis.

The Agent *By*-Phrase

Although the presence of an agent *by*-phrase was listed as one of the defining criteria of central *get*-passives (for passive constructions in all languages, by definition, involve an agent), ICE-HK contains just three tokens of agent *by*-phrases, two of these occurring in central *get*-passives and the other in a resultative *get*-construction, as examples (9) and (10) illustrate. A similar pattern is also visible in the British and Indian components, with only eight and seven agent phrases, respectively. This confirms the ideas voiced by Quirk et al. (1985, 161) and Carter and McCarthy (1999, 52) that *get*-passives, and *get*-constructions in general, are predominantly agentless, mainly because of the low information value of the agent.

(9) In fact he gets himself that far under that he's stuck <,> *he gets caught* ***by the top of his whither of his pommel*** <,> and he couldn't go any further <,> (ICE-HK:S2A-010 #50:1:B)

(10) All you have to do is to find some way to present the facts to picture reality *The key is to get your reality accepted* ***by others*** (ICE-HK:S2B-036 #103:2:A)

The long passive (where the agent phrase is overtly expressed) retains all the information that would be conveyed in its corresponding active counterpart. The function of long passives, therefore, is not that of eliding information, but that of rearranging the order of constituents in the clause, mainly for reasons of the length and information status of such constituents (Seoane 2009). Accordingly, I examined the length of the subject and the agent *by*-phrase in the agentful constructions of the three varieties and found that the choice of the long passive can to a large extent be accounted for by the principle of end-weight formulated in Quirk et al. (1972), according to which long and heavy elements tend to be placed at the end of the clause, as in example (9) above. In fact, in most of these agentful constructions the agent phrase is longer than the subject in terms of number of words. The differences between the three varieties arise when focusing on the information status, the definiteness, and the animacy of subjects and agents in these agentful constructions. As regards the information status of these constituents, both subjects and agents tend to provide given information in ICE-GB and ICE-IND. The general tendency, however, is maintained in ICE-HK, where subjects tend to have a higher degree of givenness than agent *by*-phrases, which usually convey new information, retaining the unmarked given-before-new order of constituents in clause structure. Concerning the definiteness of these constituents, there is a disparity among and within the three varieties, as the four possible combinations do occur: definite-definite, definite-indefinite, indefinite-definite, and indefinite-indefinite. As far as the animacy of the subjects and agents is concerned, the unmarked order of subject animate—agent inanimate does hold for most long passives in ICE-IND and ICE-HK, whereas in ICE-GB the proportion of long passives that topicalize a patient noun phrase whose referent is higher than the agent in the animacy hierarchy, and of the constructions where both subjects and agents are equally human and animate or inanimate, is much the same.

The Dynamicity of the Verb Category

Since the semantic type of verb used may favour the use of one particular *get*-construction over another, I analysed the verb type distribution in my corpus sample according to Biber et al.'s (1999, 360ff.) verb classification, which distinguishes seven major semantic domains: activity verbs (*buy*, *put*, *send*), communication verbs (*ask*, *tell*, *write*), mental verbs (*know*, *see*, *think*), verbs of facilitation or causation (*allow*, *cause*, *enable*), verbs of simple occurrence (*become*, *happen*, *occur*), verbs of existence or relationship (*appear*, *exist*, *seem*), and aspectual verbs (*continue*, *finish*, *start*). The analysis concludes that the great majority of the verbs occurring with *get*-constructions in the three corpora are activity verbs (70% in ICE-GB, 73% in ICE-IND, and 74% in ICE-HK), that is, verbs which denote an action and not its outcome. This overwhelming frequency of activity verbs was expected since, in general, the category of activity verbs occurs much more frequently than any other verb category and they are particularly common in conversation (Biber et al. 1999, 365–366).

If we compare Tables 10.2 to 10.4 below we see that the majority of activity verbs in *get*-constructions occur in central *get*-passives (32 of 112 in ICE-HK, 46 of 151 in ICE-GB, and 110 of 229 in ICE-IND), while the majority of mental verbs appear in adjectival *get*-constructions (21 of 34 in ICE-HK, 31 of 53 in ICE-GB, and 38 of 64 in ICE-IND). In other words, *get*-passives, as opposed to *be*-passives, tend to occur with activity verbs, which are the dynamic verbs *par excellence* (Huddleston and Pullum et al. 2002, 1442). On the contrary, mental verbs yield stative participles or adjectival *-ed* forms, which favours an adjectival analysis. The semantic categories of communication verbs, aspectual verbs, and simple occurrence verbs (in ICE-IND) were recorded to a lesser extent, while not a single instance of causative or existence verbs was found. This is not surprising, since causative verbs are relatively rare and *get* is not possible with verbs which report a state of existence or a relationship that exists between entities.

TABLE 10.2 *Distribution of* get + Ven *constructions according to verb type in ICE-HK*

Type of construction	Activity	Mental	Communication	Aspectual
central *get*-passive	32	0	2	1
pseudo *get*	30	0	0	0
adjectival *get*	20	21	0	0
idiomatic *get*	8	10	0	0
resultative *get*	22	3	2	0
Total	112	34	4	1

TABLE 10.3 *Distribution of* get + Ven *constructions according to verb type in ICE-GB*

Type of construction	Activity	Mental	Communication	Aspectual
central *get*-passive	46	0	4	0
pseudo *get*	27	0	0	2
adjectival *get*	27	31	0	0
idiomatic *get*	25	11	0	0
resultative *get*	26	11	2	3
Total	151	53	6	5

TABLE 10.4 *Distribution of* get + Ven *constructions according to verb type in* ICE-IND

Type of construction	Activity	Mental	Communication	Simple Occurrence	Aspectual
central *get*-passive	110	7	3	6	0
pseudo *get*	48	0	0	0	1
adjectival *get*	24	38	0	0	0
idiomatic *get*	9	16	0	0	0
resultative *get*	38	3	9	0	0
Total	229	64	12	6	1

Semantics

An examination of the semantics conveyed by all *get*-constructions in ICE-HK yielded the following findings: 53 examples (35%) of adversative connotations, 23 examples (15%) of beneficial implications, and 75 examples (50%) of neutral value for the subject referent. What is meant by neutral value is that there are no beneficial or adversative effects upon the subject, or at least those effects are not clearly visible, as in *get circulated, get displayed, get downloaded, get drafted, get sent, get taped, get translated,* and *get written.* Of interest here is the predilection for semantically neutral implications for the subject (50%) if all constructions are considered together. This tendency is also found to the British (47%) and Indian (60%) components. The predominance of semantically neutral utterances argues against the claims in the relevant literature (Carter and McCarthy 1999, 49; Fleisher 2006, 249; Rühlemann 2007, 120; among others) that *get* + past participle constructions are semantically restricted to a set of verbs with an adversative core meaning. Since passives in Cantonese are commonly associated with adversative meaning (Matthews and Yip 1994, 150), the low proportion of adversative semantics in Hong Kong English attested in the corpus seems to discount substrate influence.

A slightly different picture obtains, however, if we consider each construction individually, as will be seen below. The distribution of the semantic connotations within the different *get*-constructions in the three varieties under study is as follows (compare Figures 10.1–10.3):

(a) Adversative implications are confirmed in central *get*-passives for ICE-HK and ICE-GB (e.g. *get arrested, get burnt, get hurt, get injured, get killed, get stolen, get sued,* and *get yelled down*), while such a tendency is not attested in ICE-IND, which shows a clear predominance of semantically neutral utterances. Adjectival *get*-constructions tend to have adversative semantics in the three varieties under consideration (e.g. *get annoyed, get bored, get depressed, get drunk, get exhausted, get lost, get messed up*, and *get scared*).

(b) Neutral semantics are preferred in pseudo *get*-constructions (e.g. *get dressed, get married*) and idiomatic *get*-constructions (e.g. *get accustomed to, get used to*) in all three varieties, and in resultative *get*-constructions in ICE-HK and ICE-IND (e.g. *he has to get the card encoded, you got your sentence written*).

(c) Beneficial connotations are conveyed to a large extent in resultative *get*-constructions in ICE-GB, as in *get the job done* and *get their money paid.*

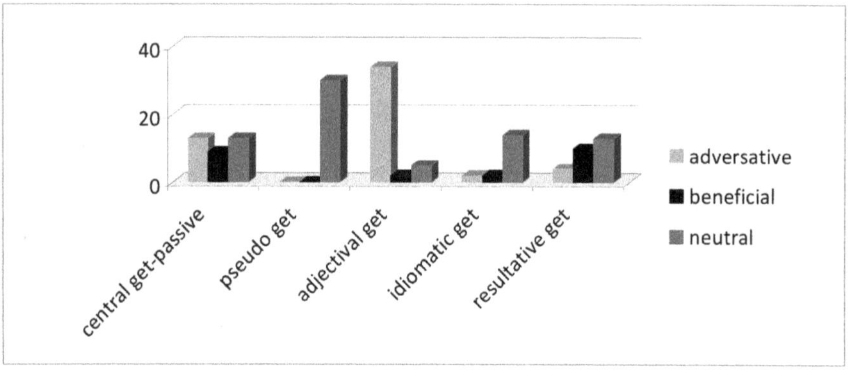

FIGURE 10.1 *Distribution of* get + Ven *constructions according to semantics in* ICE-HK *(tokens).*

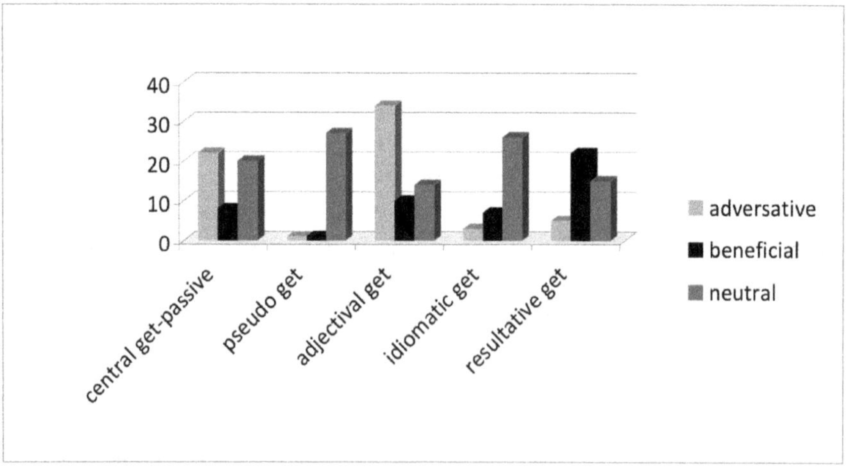

FIGURE 10.2 *Distribution of* get + Ven *constructions according to semantics in* ICE-GB *(tokens).*

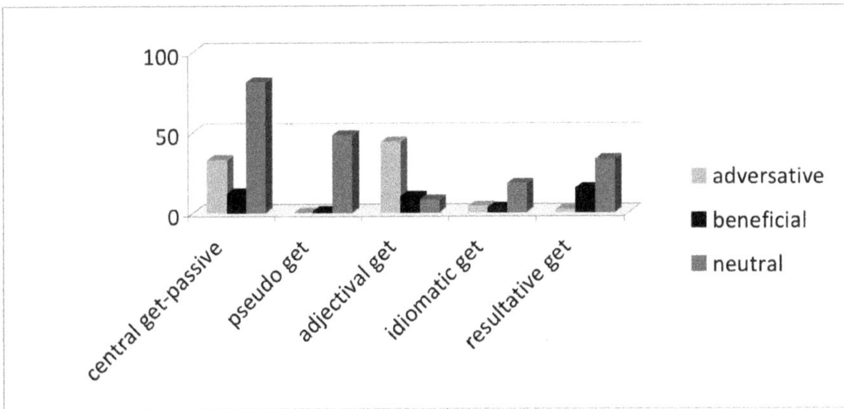

FIGURE 10.3 *Distribution of* get + Ven *constructions according to semantics in* ICE-IND *(tokens).*

The Subject: Degree of Responsibility and Animacy Features

Two aspects of the subject in *get*-constructions have been analysed: on the one hand, whether it can be attributed some degree of responsibility for the action described in the clause, and, on the other hand, its animacy features. As regards the former, the results confirm that in 74% of the occurrences analysed in ICE-HK (the highest percentage of the three corpora) the subject is clearly responsible for initiating the action (example (11) below, illustrating a resultative *get*-construction), whereas in only 18% of the cases the subject is definitely not responsible (e.g. (12)). Cases in which it is not clear whether the subject is in control and in which the context is ambiguous were classified as neutral (8%), as in (13):

(11) Yeah and <.> s [sic] </.> I just want *I just want to* ***get*** *the work* ***done*** Do you have anymore <{> <[> Anymore [sic] </[> <[> Work </[> </{> to do Well yes actually I have two uhm [sic] essays to be handed in next week (ICE-HK:S1A-095 #135:1:A)

(12) But still the major <,> the major problem lies on the staff cost <{18> <[18> <,> </[18> which in a way I'm kind of happy because <,> kind of happy not <.> hap [sic] </.> personally I'm not because *I* ***get*** *my salary* ***cut*** like most of people because as you know the university pays scale is linked with government <{19> <[19> civil </[19> servants <{20> <[20> pays </[20> scale and we have a six percent cut in the next two years (ICE-HK:S1B-072 #110:1:A)

(13) You get the survivors <,,> and then you socialize *you* ***get actualize***[***d***] and <,> whatever it is <,> (ICE-HK:S2A-042 #82:1:A)

The other two varieties share the same disposition as regards the attribution of responsibility to the subject for the action described in the clause. These varieties show a lopsided preference for responsible subjects (67% in ICE-GB and 53% in ICE-IND) over non-responsible subjects (27% in ICE-GB and 45% in ICE-IND), and the neutral cases are always low in number. The same pattern is appreciated as well when concentrating on the individual subclasses of *get*-constructions in the three varieties. As shown in Table 10.5 below, pseudo, adjectival, idiomatic, and resultative *get*-constructions tend to occur with responsible subjects in all varieties.[5] Noteworthy is the fact that central *get*-passives in the three varieties (especially in the Indian component) prefer non-responsible subjects, a finding that clashes with the literature on the topic which states that the subject in *get*-passives is usually attributed some kind of responsibility for initiating the event described in the clause, which is determined both by the meaning of *get* and by features of the context (Hatcher 1949, 437; Huddleston 1984, 445; Toyota 2007, 148). Furthermore, application of the chi-square test shows that the differences observable at first glance between ICE-IND and ICE-HK on the one hand, and ICE-IND and ICE-GB on the other hand, concerning the number of central *get*-passives with non-responsible subjects are indeed statistically significant (chi-square value 60.06, $p<0.0001$, $df=1$ and chi-square value 36.76, $p<0.0001$, $df=1$, respectively). Moreover, percentage deviation indicates that the observed chi-square frequency in ICE-IND is 100.6% greater than what is expected on the basis of the null hypothesis.

TABLE 10.5 *Distribution of* get + Ven *constructions according to subject responsibility in tokens (and percentages)*

Type of construction	ICE-HK		ICE-GB		ICE-IND	
	resp.	non-resp.	resp.	non-resp.	resp.	non-resp.
central *get*-passive	6 (24.0)	19 (76.0)	7 (17.1)	34 (82.9)	14 (11.6)	107 (88.4)
pseudo *get*	29 (96.7)	1 (3.3)	28 (96.6)	1 (3.4)	48 (98.0)	1 (2.0)
adjectival *get*	37 (90.2)	4 (9.8)	36 (65.5)	19 (34.5)	32 (54.2)	27 (45.8)
idiomatic *get*	18 (100)	0 (0)	35 (97.2)	1 (2.8)	24 (96.0)	1 (4.0)
resultative *get*	21 (84.0)	4 (16.0)	38 (97.4)	1 (2.6)	46 (92.0)	4 (8.0)

5 Note that the few examples in which the subject responsibility is neutral are not reflected in the table.

TABLE 10.6 *Distribution of* get + Ven *constructions according to subject animacy in tokens (and percentages)*

Type of construction	ICE-HK		ICE-GB		ICE-IND	
	animate	inanimate	animate	inanimate	animate	inanimate
central *get*-passive	24 (68.6)	11 (31.4)	34 (68.0)	16 (32.0)	32 (25.4)	94 (74.6)
pseudo *get*	30 (100)	0 (0)	28 (96.6)	1 (3.4)	48 (98.0)	1 (2.0)
adjectival *get*	36 (87.8)	5 (12.2)	49 (84.5)	9 (15.5)	48 (77.4)	14 (22.6)
idiomatic *get*	18 (100)	0 (0)	36 (100)	0 (0)	24 (96.0)	1 (4.0)
resultative *get*	26 (96.3)	1 (3.7)	40 (95.2)	2 (4.8)	49 (98.0)	1 (2.0)

As far as the animacy features of the subject are concerned, as a whole *get*-constructions in ICE-HK appear with an animate subject in almost 89% of the cases (the highest ratio of the three corpora) (e.g. (14) below) and this predominance is maintained in each of the five subclasses (see Table 10.6). There are, however, 17 examples (11%) where the subject is inanimate. In most cases where the subject of the *get*-construction is inanimate, some human entity associated with it retains responsibility, is involved in the action, or is affected by the results of the event (e.g. (15)), although there are also cases in which the subject referent does not stand in a direct relationship to any person, as the *MFN* (Most Favoured Nation status) in example (16).

(14) ***We** almost get lost* you know in this in some point because you know we which try to find a nice rock so we can sit down and have our picnic right (ICE-HK:S1A-041 #241:1:A)

(15) <[> No but it's swollen </[> </{> you you [sic] can't sort of see straight It is I mean when ***your eye** get[s] swollen* you it's sort of like you know blocking your vision a little bit say so by by [sic] the time you turn to one angle you see you know there's you you [sic] think that there's something there but it's actually your eyelid (ICE-HK:S1A-100 #280:1:A)

(16) So I think it's a significant situation that we <,> have no choice but to work on it uh [sic] <,> If we don't work on it and and [sic] ***MFN** gets terminated* we may <,> be sorry that we didn't do any lobbying work (ICE-HK:S2A-028 #19:1:A)

This preference for animate and human subjects is also complied with in the case of ICE-GB (87%) and ICE-IND (65%), and applies to all subclasses of *get*-constructions. An exception here is the case of central *get*-passives (to a large extent) in Indian English (25.4%; see Table 10.6 above). The chi-square analysis gives a significant result (chi-square value 64.03, p<0.0001, df=1 and chi-square value 53.89, p<0.0001, df=1, respectively) when comparing the number of central *get*-passives with inanimate subjects between ICE-IND and ICE-HK on the one hand, and ICE-IND and ICE-GB on the other. Furthermore, percentage deviation indicates that the observed chi-square frequency in ICE-IND is 133% greater than expected on the basis of the null hypothesis. This finding, which sets ICE-IND apart, runs contrary to the literature on this topic (Arce-Arenales et al. 1994, 14; Dahl and Fraurud 1996, 58; Toyota 2007, 153), which claims that central *get*-passives do occur predominantly with an animate and human subject.

A remarkable finding is that, although the predilection is clearly for animate subjects, there is a considerable number of inanimate subjects in *get*-constructions, especially in ICE-IND (ICE-HK: 11%; ICE-GB: 13%; ICE-IND: 35%), which argues against Lakoff's (1971, 154–155) oft-quoted claim that *get*-passives cannot take inanimate subjects. The weakening in the restrictions on central *get*-passives to allow the occurrence of inanimate subjects points towards a process of grammaticalization of this type of *get*-construction, which would be subject to fewer restrictions. These findings on the animacy of the subject in *get*-constructions are particularly interesting if historical data are taken into account, since unambiguous *get*-passives with inanimate subjects emerged later than those with animate subjects. In ARCHER, for example, they begin to appear more frequently only in the last subperiod (1950–99), as the following two examples from Hundt (2001, 74) illustrate:

(17) *The dishes* don't get done. (ARCHER, 1978ryan.jo)
(18) *Articles* get written about it. (ARCHER, 1956flem.f9)

As for twentieth-century English, Hundt (2001, 74–75) suggests that the number of *get*-passives with inanimate subjects shows a drastic increase in American English (from three in BROWN (1960s) to 20 in Frown (1990s)) and a slight increase in the British corpora (from six in LOB (1960s) to eight in F-LOB (1990s); see also Toyota 2008, 161). Data from my corpus analysis of Hong Kong English, British English, and especially Indian English seem to reinforce this tendency towards a widespread use of *get*-constructions with inanimate subjects.

Summary of Findings

The overall findings of the analysis of the three varieties are summarized in Tables 10.7 to 10.9 below:

TABLE 10.7 *Overview of* get + Ven *characteristics in* ICE-HK

Type of construction	No agent *by*-phrase	Animate subject	Activity verb	Responsible subject	Adversative semantics
get-passive	+	+	+	–	+
pseudo *get*	+	+	+	+	–
adjectival *get*	+	+	–	+	+
idiomatic *get*	+	+	–	+	–
resultative *get*	+	+	+	+	–

TABLE 10.8 *Overview of* get + Ven *characteristics in* ICE-GB

Type of construction	No agent *by*-phrase	Animate subject	Activity verb	Responsible subject	Adversative semantics
get-passive	+	+	+	–	+
pseudo *get*	+	+	+	+	–
adjectival *get*	+	+	–	+	+
idiomatic *get*	+	+	+	+	–
resultative *get*	+	+	+	+	–

TABLE 10.9 *Overview of* get + Ven *characteristics in* ICE-IND

Type of construction	No agent *by*-phrase	Animate subject	Activity verb	Responsible subject	Adversative semantics
get-passive	+	–	+	–	–
pseudo *get*	+	+	+	+	–
adjectival *get*	+	+	–	+	+
idiomatic *get*	+	+	–	+	–
resultative *get*	+	+	+	+	–

(a) *Get*-constructions occur generally without an overtly expressed agent *by*-phrase; if present, though, its referent is equally distributed as animate and inanimate in Hong Kong and British English, while it is typically inanimate in the Indian variety.
(b) Subjects tend to be animate and human throughout all the subcategories, except for central *get*-passives in Indian English, which tend to occur with inanimate subjects.
(c) As regards the type of lexical verb, there are slight differences between the individual varieties. The three varieties show the same distribution in that central *get*-passives, pseudo, and resultative *get*-constructions, which tend to carry a dynamic past participle, occur primarily with activity verbs, while adjectival *get*-constructions, which tend to take stative past participles or adjectival *-ed* forms, make considerable use of mental verbs. The difference lies, however, in idiomatic *get*-constructions, which tend to occur with activity verbs in British English, and with mental verbs in Hong Kong and Indian English.
(d) Responsible subjects do prevail in most non-central members of the gradient, namely in pseudo, adjectival, idiomatic, and resultative *get*-constructions. Unexpectedly, however, central *get*-passives in all varieties resemble prototypical *be*-passives in having as subject a non-responsible patient of the action, which suggests again a growing grammaticalization of the construction.
(e) The semantic prosody varies depending on the type of construction and the variety of English. Thus, there is a tendency for central *get*-passives (in Hong Kong and British English) and adjectival *get*-constructions to code adversative implications for the subject; for pseudo, idiomatic, and resultative *get*-constructions (in Hong Kong and Indian English) to display semantically neutral connotations; and for resultative *get*-constructions in the British component to occur in beneficial contexts.

Conclusions

The preceding comparative analysis and discussion of *get*-constructions in Present-day spoken Hong Kong English, British English, and Indian English allows us to confirm that most of the prototypical syntactic, semantic, and pragmatic characteristics attributed to central *get*-passives in the relevant literature (Quirk et al. 1985; Collins 1996; Carter and McCarthy 1999; Huddleston and Pullum et al. 2002) can also be observed in the different varieties examined here: most *get*-constructions are agentless, take a dynamic past participle, and have an animate and responsible subject; nonetheless, they tend to convey semantically neutral meanings.

As is frequently the case in contact varieties, the substrate language may influence the form and frequency of particular constructions in the emerging varieties of English. In this particular case, the existence of a similar underlying passive periphrasis in Hindi may exert an influence on the high incidence of central *get*-passives in Indian English.

As already noted in the relevant sections, the differences regarding the predominance of inanimate subjects and agents in the Indian variety and the figures for non-responsible subjects in the three varieties have proved to be statistically significant. The fact that neither subject animacy nor subject responsibility are complied with is consistent with Dahl and Fraurud's (1996, 58) theory that both concepts are closely interrelated, since it is animate human referents which can show volition and intentionality over their actions. Furthermore, the meaning of *get*-constructions has started to shift from primarily adversative semantics to more neutral contexts, this trend being especially observable in the Indian component. These results are striking and unexpected, since Indian English is linguistically very conservative (as British English is among the native varieties). It seems, therefore, that Indian English is leading the way in the proliferation of inanimate subjects and non-adversative implications in *get*-constructions in general, and central *get*-passives in particular, within the outer circle varieties.

Thanks to these differences between the three varieties, notably the loss of subject animacy and responsibility and the loss of adversative semantics, there is evidence that *get*-constructions move along a continuum of prototypicality, that a process of grammaticalization is affecting central *get*-passives, and that some of the features of central *get*-passives commonly attributed to them in the literature apply less clearly to ESL varieties. As a consequence, if this trend continues, central *get*-passives might eventually move closer to other *get*-constructions along the gradient, losing in this way their prototypical or defining characteristics.

Corpora

ARCHER *A Representative Corpus of Historical English Registers* 3.1. 1990–1993, 2002, 2007, 2010. Originally compiled under the supervision of Douglas Biber, and Edward Finegan at Northern Arizona University, and University of

Southern California. Modified and expanded by subsequent members of a consortium of universities. Current member universities are Northern Arizona, Southern California, Freiburg, Heidelberg, Helsinki, Uppsala, Michigan, Manchester, Lancaster, Bamberg, Zurich, Trier, Salford, and Santiago de Compostela. http://www.alc.manchester.ac.uk/subjects/lel/research/projects/archer/.

BNC *British National Corpus*, version 3 (BNC XML Edition). 2007. Distributed by Oxford University Computing Services on behalf of the BNC Consortium. http://www.natcorp.ox.ac.uk/.

Brown *A Standard Corpus of Present-Day Edited American English, for Use with Digital Computers*. 1964, 1971, 1979. Compiled by W. Nelson Francis and Henry Kučera. Brown University. Providence, Rhode Island.

F-LOB *The Freiburg-LOB Corpus* (POS-tagged version). 2007. Compiled by Christian Mair, Albert-Ludwigs-Universität Freiburg, and Geoffrey Leech, University of Lancaster.

Frown *The Freiburg-Brown Corpus* (POS-tagged version). 2007. Compiled by Christian Mair, Albert-Ludwigs-Universität Freiburg, and Geoffrey Leech, University of Lancaster.

ICE-GB *International Corpus of English, the British Component*. 1998. Project coordinated by the Survey of English Usage, University College London. http://ice-corpora.net/ice/icegb.htm.

ICE-HK *International Corpus of English, the Hong Kong Component*. 2002. Project initiated by Philip Bolt and later coordinated by Kingsley Bolton, and Joseph Hung. http://ice-corpora.net/ice/icehk.htm.

ICE-IND *International Corpus of English, the Indian Component*. 2002. Project coordinated by S. V. Shastri, and Gerhard Leitner. http://ice-corpora.net/ice/iceind.htm.

LOB *The Lancaster-Oslo-Bergen Corpus of British English* (POS-tagged version). 1986. Compiled by Geoffrey Leech, Lancaster University, Stig Johansson, University of Oslo (Project leaders), Roger Garside, and Knut Hofland (Heads of computing).

References

Alexiadou, Artemis. 2005. "A Note on Non-Canonical Passives: The Case of the *Get*-Passive." In *Organizing Grammar: Linguistic Studies in Honor of Henk van Riemsdijk*, edited by Hans Broekhuis, Norbert Corver, Riny Huybregts, Ursula Kleinhenz, and Jan Koster, 13–21. Berlin: Mouton de Gruyter.

Arce-Arenales, Manuel, Melissa Axelrod, and Barbara A. Fox. 1994. "Active Voice and Middle Diathesis: A Cross-Linguistic Perspective." In *Voice: Form and Function*, edited by Barbara A. Fox, and Paul J. Hopper, 1–21. Amsterdam and Philadelphia: John Benjamins.

Biber, Douglas, Stig Johansson, Geoffrey Leech, Susan Conrad, and Edward Finegan. 1999. *Longman Grammar of Spoken and Written English*. London: Longman.

Carter, Ronald, and Michael McCarthy. 1999. "The English *Get*-Passive in Spoken Discourse: Description and Implications for an Interpersonal Grammar." *English Language and Linguistics* 3/1: 41–58.

Chappell, Hilary. 1980. "Is the *Get*-Passive Adversative?" *Papers in Linguistics: International Journal of Human Communication* 13/3: 411–52.

Collins, Peter. 1996. "*Get*-Passives in English." *World Englishes* 15/1: 43–56.

Coto-Villalibre, Eduardo. 2014a. "From Prototypical to Peripheral: The '*Get* + V*en*' Construction in Contemporary Spoken British English." In *Diachrony and Synchrony in English Corpus Linguistics*, edited by Alejandro Alcaraz-Sintes, and Salvador Valera-Hernández, 205–31. Bern: Peter Lang.

Coto-Villalibre, Eduardo. 2014b. "*Get* + Past Participle Constructions in Present-Day Spoken Indian English: Exploring the Passive Gradient." In *Current Research in Applied Linguistics: Issues on Language and Cognition*, edited by Paula Rodríguez-Puente, Teresa Fanego, Evelyn Gandón-Chapela, Sara Riveiro-Outeiral, and María Luisa Roca-Varela, 10–30. Newcastle upon Tyne: Cambridge Scholars Publishing.

Coto-Villalibre, Eduardo. 2014c. *A Semantic and Syntactic Approach to* Get-*Constructions in World Englishes*. PhD Diss., University of Santiago de Compostela.

Dahl, Östen, and Kari Fraurud. 1996. "Animacy in Grammar and Discourse." In *Reference and Referent Accessibility*, edited by Thorstein Fretheim, and Jeanette K. Gundel, 47–64. Amsterdam and Philadelphia: John Benjamins.

Fleisher, Nicholas. 2006. "The Origin of Passive *Get*." *English Language and Linguistics* 10/2: 225–52.

Hatcher, Anna G. 1949. "To Get/Be Invited." *Modern Languages Notes* 64/7: 433–46.

Huddleston, Rodney. 1984. *Introduction to the Grammar of English*. Cambridge: Cambridge University Press.

Huddleston, Rodney, and Geoffrey K. Pullum, et al. 2002. *The Cambridge Grammar of the English Language*. Cambridge: Cambridge University Press.

Hundt, Marianne. 2001. "What Corpora Tell us about the Grammaticalisation of Voice in *Get*-Constructions." *Studies in Language* 25/1: 49–87.

Kachru, Yamuna. 2006. *Hindi*. Amsterdam and Philadelphia: John Benjamins.

Lakoff, Robin. 1971. "Passive Resistance." In *Papers from the Seventh Regional Meeting of the Chicago Linguistic Society, April 16–18*, 149–62. University of Chicago: Chicago Linguistic Society.

Leech, Geoffrey, Marianne Hundt, Christian Mair, and Nicholas Smith. 2009. *Change in Contemporary English: A Grammatical Study*. Cambridge: Cambridge University Press.

Matthews, Stephen, and Virginia Yip. 1994. *Cantonese: A Comprehensive Grammar*. London: Routledge.

McEnery, Tony, Richard Z. Xiao, and Yufang Qian. 2006. "Passive Constructions in English and Chinese: A Corpus-Based Contrastive Study." *Languages in Contrast* 6/1: 109–49.

Quirk, Randolph, Sidney Greenbaum, Geoffrey Leech, and Jan Svartvik. 1972. *A Grammar of Contemporary English*. London: Longman.

Quirk, Randolph, Sidney Greenbaum, Geoffrey Leech, and Jan Svartvik. 1985. *A Comprehensive Grammar of the English Language*. London: Longman.

Rühlemann, Christoph. 2007. "Lexical Grammar: The GET-Passive as a Case in Point." *ICAME Journal* 31: 111–27.

Sandahl, Stella. 2000. *A Hindi Reference Grammar*. Leuven: Peeters.

Schneider, Edgar W. 2007. *Postcolonial English: Varieties Around the World*. Cambridge: Cambridge University Press.

Seoane, Elena. 2009. "Syntactic Complexity, Discourse Status and Animacy as Determinants of Grammatical Variation in Modern English." *English Language and Linguistics* 13/3: 365–84.

Toyota, Junichi. 2007. "An Adversative Passive in English: In Search of Origins." In *On Interpreting Construction Schemas: From Action to Motion to Transitivity and Causality*, edited by Nicole Delbecque, and Bert Cornillie, 143–69. Berlin: Mouton de Gruyter.

Toyota, Junichi. 2008. *Diachronic Change in the English Passive*. Basingstoke: Palgrave Macmillan.

CHAPTER 11

Who is the/a/Ø *Professor at Your University*? A Construction Grammar View on Changing Article Use with Single Role Predicates in American English*

Marianne Hundt

Abstract

Predicate nominals designating single role holders like *president, prime minister, queen*, or *pope* allow for variable article use in English. The default should be that single role holders do not combine with the indefinite article because they do not meet the numerical requirement, i.e. they do not constitute sets with more than one member (even if there is a succession of presidents, queens, etc.). Exceptions to the rule are "cases where two salient construals of the role holder designated by the predicate nominal are possible and, consequently two article patterns exist side by side" (Berezowski 2009, 132). These construals are often motivated by extra-linguistic facts, like different religious traditions. But Berezowski's study also shows that there is lexical variation as well as variation according to the copula verb used in the construction. In this chapter, the author uses data from the *Corpus of Historical American English* (COHA) to investigate variable article use with single role predicate nominals in twentieth-century American English. Corpus data show that there is diachronic variation: a general tendency towards greater use of definite and indefinite articles in these constructions. However, there is also considerable lexical variation. Variable rule analysis further shows that different factors (such as copula verb, lexical item, and modification within the noun phrase) play a role in article use, but they do so in varying degrees for different lexical items. A construction grammar account is used to explain how single role predicate construals can be extended to nouns like *teacher* and *father*.

* I would like to thank the audience at ICAME 34 as well as two anonymous reviewers for useful comments on previous versions of this chapter.

 | DOI 10.1163/9789004321342_012

Keywords

variable article use – single role predicate nominals – construction grammar – diachronic variation – American English – constructional bootstrapping

Introduction

In German, predicate constructions like *Sie ist Lehrerin* or *Er ist Anwalt* are grammatical whereas the English equivalents of such copula constructions require the use of an article: *She is **a** teacher, He is **a** lawyer.* However, as is often the case, there are a few exceptions to this rule: for predicate nominals designating single role holders like *president, prime minister, queen*, or *pope* the default is to use a bare NP:

(1) Barak Obama is *president* of the US.
(2) Before Ratzinger was *pope*, he was Prefect of the Sacred Congregation for the Doctrine of the Faith.

But it is also possible to use the definite or indefinite article in such constructions. The following examples from the *Corpus of Historical American English* (COHA) illustrate variation (zero,[1] indefinite, definite) with *professor* in this syntactic environment:

(3) Ralph F. Young *is Ø professor* of history, Temple University, Philadelphia, Pa. (COHA, 2004, MAG)
(4) Noam Chomsky *is a professor* of linguistics at M.I.T., a New Left ideologue (American Power and the New Mandarins), a leading protester against the war in Viet Nam—and a Hedgehog. (COHA, 1970, MAG)[2]
(5) Dr. Norman Lehmer *is the Professor* of mathematics at the University of Southern California. (COHA, 1939, NF)

---

1 Note that the term 'zero' is simply used as a convenient shorthand for 'NP without a definite or indefinite article' here (i.e. a so-called 'bare NP') and that no theoretical claims are made as to the existence of a zero element in the construction.

2 The use of *hedgehog* in this context refers to Chomsky as a political thinker; the distinction between hedgehogs and foxes was first made in antiquity but popularized (in a semi-jocular fashion) in an essay by Isaiah Berlin in 1953 (thanks to Douglas Biber for drawing my attention to Berlin's essay).

At first sight, the use of an indefinite article with *professor* in example (4) seems to imply that there is more than one professor of linguistics at M.I.T., whereas the use of the definite article in example (5) appears to have the opposite effect, i.e. the NP suggests that there is only one professor of mathematics at the University of Southern California. This reading is probably reinforced by the use of a capital <p> in the spelling of *Professor*. Whether the bare NP should be read as a variant of the indefinite or the definite article is a matter of debate (see below). The different readings triggered by the indefinite and definite article may lead to differences in their use with role nouns in predicate constructions: the question is whether all nouns that designate roles equally allow the use of both an indefinite and a definite article when they are used as predicate complements. Another question is whether the two articles have the same semantic effect when they combine with different nouns. This point will be taken up later on in this chapter.

Note that the head noun in examples (1) and (3)–(5) above is post-modified by an *of*-phrase; it is also possible to find examples with pre-modification (6) and, occasionally, a combination of pre- and post-modification (7):

(6) Frank E.A. Sander is *Bussey* professor and associate dean at Harvard Law School. (COCA, 1993, ACAD)

(7) You have been *Disney* Professor *of Archaeology* at Cambridge for eleven years [...]. (BNC, GTA 1543)

The examples with proper names as pre-modifiers do not make use of an article, but article use even in this context is variable, as the following examples show:

(8) Renfrew was formerly *the Disney Professor of Archaeology* at the University of Cambridge and Director of the McDonald Institute for Archaeological Research and is now a Senior Fellow of the McDonald Institute for Archaeological Research. (<http://en.wikipedia.org/wiki/Colin_Renfrew,_Baron_Renfrew_of_Kaimsthorn>; last accessed 15.12.2014)

(9) At one point I observed that, since there is *a Disney Professor of Archaeology* at Cambridge, why didn't we approach the Disney Corporation for funds. (<http://damtp.cam.ac.uk/user/sjc1/talks/after-dinner.ps>, last accessed 15.12.2014)

Finally, there are examples where the definite article is used with role nouns without any modification:

(10) If you go back all of these years that he's been *the pope* and you trace back where Rome, the Vatican is today, compared to then, with the use of the media, [...]. (COCA, 2005, SPOK)

The question whether or not modification of the head noun is a significant factor in the variable use of articles has not been addressed systematically so far. Another open research question is whether article use with nouns like *president* or *professor* is stable across time.

In the next section, I briefly review previous descriptive accounts of variable article use with nouns that designate roles. Then, I provide the theoretical background. The data used for the empirical part of this study are described in the following section, which also details how the variable contexts were defined for data retrieval. Next, I present results on the distributional analysis of variable article use with role nouns. In a second step, I use a multivariate analysis to investigate which factors play a role in the choice of indefinite and definite articles instead of a bare NP. The quantitative findings will be used to account for change across time against the theoretical background provided earlier on. The construction grammar approach to variable use in predicate nominals also allows me to account for extensions of the single role construal to non-prototypical instances. The empirical approach used in this chapter is necessarily selective. In the concluding section, I therefore also outline avenues for future research.

Previous Research on Predicate Nominals with Single Role Holders

The issues that are relevant to the description of variable article use in predicate nominals with single role holders concern the question of definiteness of the NP and uniqueness of the roles. These, in turn, are related to the envelope of variation, i.e. the possibility of the bare NP alternating with a definite and an indefinite article or just one of the two. In addition to the choice of the article, relevant aspects to consider are the range of predicate constructions that allow for variable article use and modification of the head.

Definiteness and Uniqueness

In their description of variable article use with nouns like *president* or *prime minister*, standard reference grammars such as Quirk et al. (1985, 276), Biber et al. (1999, 261–262), or Huddleston and Pullum et al. (2002, 409) all agree in one respect, namely that variation is between the use of the definite article and a bare NP, and that both variants are definite because they refer to a (unique/

specific) individual in a specific situation. Chesterman (1991, 84), who conceptualizes definiteness as gradient, claims that the bare NP is even more definite than the variant with the article because bare NPs are more familiar to the speaker:[3]

> Such observations suggest that null is somehow 'even more definite' than *the*. This hints at a possible explanation for much 'exceptional' usage: forms with null would be conceptually closer and therefore conceptually clearer to the speaker. Since one function of *the* is precisely to delimit a concept, such a function would be redundant in the case of concepts which were adequately delimited already.

A minority view (e.g. Jespersen 1909–49, Vol VII, 451; Hewson 1972, 91–96; Berezowski 2009, 61–64) holds that bare predicate NPs designating roles such as *president* or *pope* are inherently indefinite. Berezowski backs up his argument with a comment in Epstein (1999, 56) on the instantiation of roles:

> A nominal designating a role does not refer to any specific individual but, rather, to a fixed property. At the same time, the individual instantiating the role (the role value) can vary from one occasion to another. (quoted from Berezowski 2009, 63)

As illustrated in examples (3)–(5) above, variation in this syntactic context potentially includes both definite and indefinite articles, and the bare NP variant may thus be definite or indefinite, depending on the context. At times, world knowledge is needed to decide whether the bare NP is a variant of the definite or the indefinite article. A sentence like *He is professor of anthropology at U Mass* can be argued to be ambiguous between a definite and an indefinite reading, i.e. native speakers' interpretation may vary between the readings *He is the professor of anthropology*, if there is only one chair for this field at any one time, and *He is a professor of anthropology*, if there are several. But definiteness can also be a question of the speaker's/writer's point of view rather than having to be necessarily grounded in hard facts. We will return to this point in the qualitative analysis of corpus data.

---

3 For Chesterman (1991, 182), articles range from most indefinite (zero) to most definite (null), with *some, a*, and *the* occupying intermediate points on this gradient. Singular (proper) nouns without an article are examples of the 'null form' whereas the indefinite form of mass and plural nouns is labelled as a 'zero form' in this account (see Chesterman 1991, 16–17).

The discussion about definiteness is closely related to the notion of uniqueness or 'singularity' of the role holder. Both Quirk et al. (1985, 276) and Biber et al. (1999, 261) stress that article use with nouns like *president, chairman*, or *director* is optional in copula constructions because these name a "unique role/task/position". Huddleston and Pullum et al. (2002, 409) are somewhat less committal in their wording: they take NPs that "allow role interpretations" to permit use in bare NPs. This potentially allows for the non-uniqueness of the noun in question, one could argue. Contexts in which a group of people rather than an individual may occupy a certain role were already mentioned above. While at any one time, there is only one pope, king, or queen, one president or prime minister in office, the referents of nouns like *managing director* or *chairman* but also *governor* and *professor* may be somewhat less 'unique' and therefore more likely to license the use of an indefinite article, as the following examples from the *Corpus of Contemporary American English* (COCA) show:

(11) Jim Awad *is a managing director* at Zephyr Management, a good friend of ours. (COCA, 2011, SPOK)
(12) He *is a chairman* of the African-American Studies at Temple University in Philadelphia. (COCA, 1991, SPOK)
(13) He [...] still survives to fight again –and, "incidentally, to show the world how low a blackguard can *become a Governor* [...]." (COCA, 1905, MAG)
(14) John Boice *is a professor* of medicine at Vanderbilt University. (COCA, 2012, SPOK)

According to Berezowski (2009, 114), the variant with an indefinite article is used whenever a referent is construed as a member of a set rather than a single role, e.g. the set of professors of medicine at a university.

Variability: Articles, Constructions, and Modification

None of the reference grammars mentions variation with indefinite *a* as a variant construction. According to Berezowski (2009, 64), singular role holders such as *president, prime minister, queen, pope*, etc. do not typically combine with the indefinite article as predicate nominals because, under normal circumstances, they do not meet the numerical requirement, i.e. they do not constitute sets with more than one member (even if there is a succession of presidents, queens, etc.). If this succession is the topic of discussion, even a noun like *pope* can take an indefinite article, as in Berezowski's example from the *British National Corpus* (BNC), incidentally the only one of its kind attested in the whole corpus:

(15) Was there a Pope Julius II? Indeed, there *was a Pope* Julius II. He held office from 1503 to 1513 and, among other things, he was responsible for building the beginning of the great Church of St Peter's. (BNC, G2Y; quoted from Berezowski 2009, 59)

Note, too, that this occurrence is from an existential construction, which is different from the constructions above in that existential constructions do not allow for variable article use even with singular role holders. It is therefore not only the extra-linguistic context that licenses the use of an indefinite article with *pope* in (15) but the existential construction itself that requires one.

Beyond the function of specifying a member of a set, however, the indefinite article can also be used in contexts where a predicate nominal's special properties are expressed, as in (16):

(16) And I am so privileged to *be a president* of all the Chileans. (COCA, 2010, SPOK)[4]

In other words, both definite and indefinite articles can be used with singular role holders as predicate nominals, at times with specific semantic effects.

As far as the range of syntactic contexts is concerned where article use is described as variable, the reference grammars mention copula verbs like *be* and *become*, but also constructions with *appoint* or *elect*; in addition, article use is said to vary with oblique predicate nominals following *as*, illustrated in the following examples:

(17) [...] *as the Reynolds professor of American studies* at Wake Forest University in Winston-Salem, she has, she said, "a large umbrella." (COCA, 1993, NEWS)

(18) [...] he went south to teach, serving *as a professor of sociology* at Atlanta University from 1897 to 1910 and from 1934 to 1944. (COCA, 1994, MAG)

Quirk et al. (1985, 276) also include appositive constructions among the copular relations, such as:

4 Note that article use in this particular case might also have been influenced by the speaker's first language (Spanish), which would require the use of an article (i.e. [...] ***la/una*** *presidenta de todos los chilenos*).

(19) Anne Martin, (*the*) *star of the TV series* and (*the*) *author of a well-known book on international cuisine*, has resigned from her post on the Consumer Council.

These are not included in the empirical part of my study, but they are relevant to the discussion of variation and change provided later in the chapter. Huddleston and Pullum et al. (2002, 409), finally, also mention constructions with the nouns *position*, *part*, or *role* as contexts in which predicate nominals occur in bare NPs. The question is, however, whether article use in the latter context is variable or not. Quirk et al. (1985, 276, footnote [c]) point out that "the definite article is generally omitted following expressions such as *the post of*, *the position of* and *the role of*". While corpus evidence shows that a definite article is occasionally attested in such predicative constructions, these turned out to be too rare to be included in the empirical part of the study:[5]

(20) Both the candidates have been trying on *the role of the president*. (COCA, 2000, SPOK)
(21) Well, he didn't say I am resigning. He said I am leaving *the post of the president*. (COCA, 1991, SPOK)

The reference grammars do not mention modification as a potential factor influencing variable article use in predicate constructions with role nouns. Berezowski (2009) discusses various kinds of modification in his qualitative analysis of individual corpus examples, but he does not back up his qualitative analyses with numerical evidence on the influence that pre- and post-modification might have on variable article use.

5 The following example is superficially similar, but the context is one of rehearsing and the meaning of 'acting a role' is slightly different from that of actually occupying a role:
(i) Another might spend the day after she's attended a wedding, organizing friends and toys into a wedding party while she takes on *the role of the minister*. (COCA, 1994, MAG)
Two more examples stem from contexts which might have been influenced by language contact:
(ii) The prewar sectarian balance in ALI was also achieved through always electing a Sunni to *the post of the vice-president*, [...]. (COCA, 2000, ACAD)
(iii) [...] the National Alliance will get the prime minister post, and Iraqiya will get *the post of the Parliament speaker*. (COCA, 2010, SPOK)
The author's name of the text from which (ii) is taken is Sami E. Baroudi, and the article is published in *Arab Studies Quarterly*; (iii) is used in a foreign news reportage.

Previous Quantitative Research

On the whole, there is little previous research that takes variation into account from a quantitative point of view: only one reference grammar and a monograph provide numerical evidence on variable article use with single role nouns as predicate nominals. Based on a study of all occurrences of *is + chairman/director* in the *Longman Spoken and Written English Corpus*, Biber et al. (1999, 262) point out that "the pattern with the zero article outnumbers the pattern with the definite article by about 5 to 1". Berezowski (2009) uses BNC data for a quantitative and qualitative analysis of singular role holders as predicate nominals in British English. It becomes clear from Figure 11.1 that the nouns he investigates show a marked preference for the pattern without an article, thus supporting the hypothesis that bare NPs are the dominant variant with role nouns in predicate nominals. However, his data also indicate that the indefinite article is attested with quite a few of the nouns in his sample, such as (*arch-*)*bishop, queen, professor, managing director*, and *captain*. Berezowski's study thus shows that there is an element of lexical variation involved.

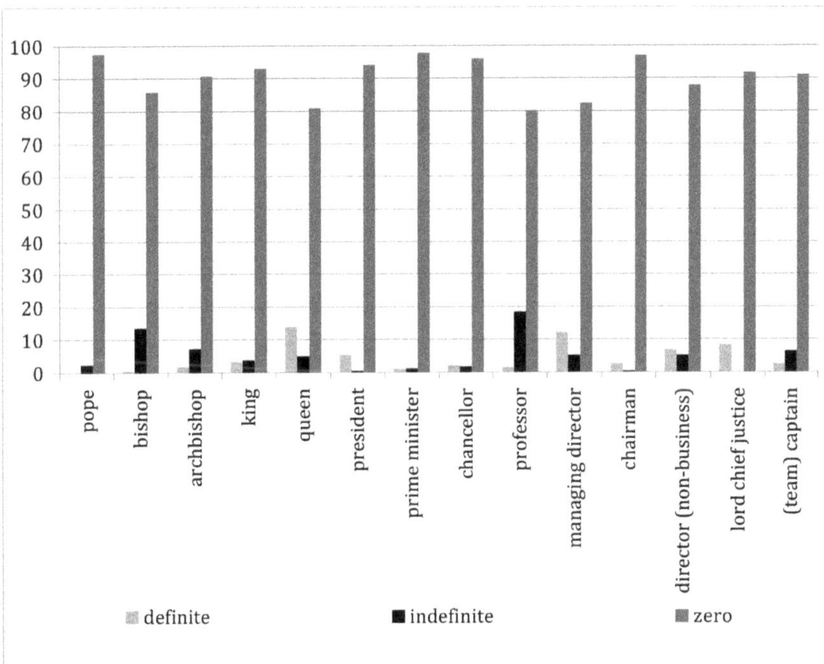

FIGURE 11.1 *Relative frequency (percentage) of* NP *structure for singular role nouns in predicate function in the* BNC *(based on Berezowski 2009, 76, 77, 115, 133).*

Singular Role Holders and Predicate Nominals—A Construction Grammar Approach

Previous research on predicate nominals indicates that semantic aspects as well as choice of lexical head appear to play a role. This suggests that variation and change in patterns like *He is (the/a) professor (of* SUBJECT*) (at X University)* may fruitfully be approached within a cognitive construction grammar (henceforth CxG) approach.[6] Generally speaking, constructions are form-meaning pairings that are attested with sufficient discourse frequency (e.g. Goldberg 2006, 5). These pairings can occur at different levels of abstraction. Predicate nominals, for instance, are one kind of form-meaning pairing. Predicate nominals with singular role holders, in turn, are a subtype of the more abstract predicate nominal construction; patterns with particular singular role holders such as *pope, president*, or *professor* slot into this subtype of the predicate nominal construction but behave in slightly different ways because they are different kinds of singular role holders. Other scholars (e.g. Traugott 2008, 236 or Trousdale 2008, 170) use labels such as 'macro-level' and 'micro-level' to situate constructions on the different levels of abstraction (see also Traugott and Trousdale 2013, 13–17). At the most abstract, i.e. the macro-level, a predicative construction (henceforth PC) consists of a grammatical subject, a copula, and the subject predicate. At this level of abstraction, the slots in the macro-construction are underspecified, i.e. they can be filled by various kinds of NP or copula. On the meso-level, different subtypes of PCs can be distinguished, e.g. existential constructions which have a fixed subject, namely *there*, PCs with subject predicate NPs that refer to a member of a set such as *teacher* and *lawyer*, or those that refer to singular role holders, i.e. sets with only one member. At this level of abstraction, certain construction types require an article (e.g. the existential construction) or allow for variable article use (e.g. non-existential constructions with single role holders). Trousdale (2008, 169) suggests that some meso-level constructions themselves may be more abstract than other meso-level constructions. More recently, Hilpert (2013) points out that these levels are useful heuristic notions rather than a fixed set of hierarchical levels:

> The use of these terms does not imply that the constructional network is viewed as discretely divisible into, say, three or four levels of abstraction. Rather, it is assumed that constructions are mentally represented along a continuum of schematicity. (Hilpert 2013, 5)

6 For different kinds of CxG, see Goldberg (2006, chapter 10).

The meso-level construction that is the focus of this chapter could be labelled as the 'role predicate nominal construction' (*NAME/PRONOUN is (a)/(the) ROLE NOUN*) to distinguish it from the regular predicate nominal construction (e.g. *NAME/PRONOUN is a/the COMMON NOUN*). Language change may affect the micro-level but, in the long term, it may also affect the meso-level (e.g. by blurring the distinction between a role noun and a common noun).

On the micro-level, we find variable syntactic patterns for individual nouns that designate singular role holders, e.g. *X COPULA (the/a) (pre-modification) president (post-modification)*, where elements in brackets are optional. One could argue that the variable patterns with or without articles and/or modification constitute constructional subtypes on the micro-level as the meaning from one subtypes to the next may vary. In other words, the notation with optional elements should really be read as a shorthand way of representing slightly different micro-level constructions.

Constructs, finally, are the concrete realizations (i.e. empirically attested instances) of the more abstract levels above, e.g. *Jean Aitchison is Emeritus Rupert Murdoch Professor of Language and Communication at Oxford University* or *Colin Renfrew is Disney Professor Emeritus of Archaeology and former Director of the McDonald Institute for Archaeological Research at the University of Cambridge*. According to Traugott (2008, 236), constructs are tokens whereas the constructions at the various levels of abstraction are types. As far as the relation of general constructions and more specific constructions is concerned, Goldberg (2013, 22) notes that "grammar also has more specific constructions that serve to override the specifications of the general construction". In other words, inheritance (e.g. of an obligatory article) can be limited.

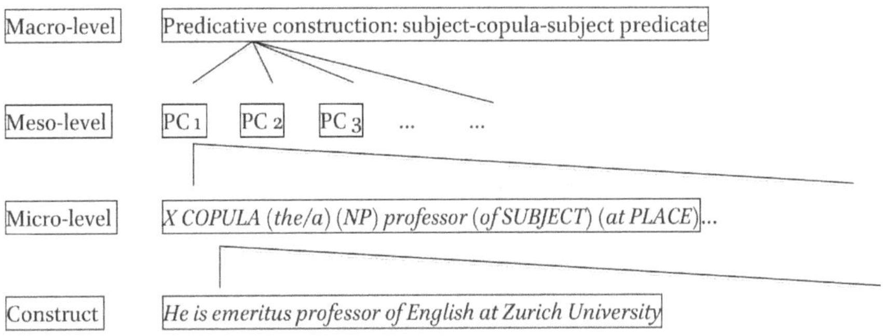

FIGURE 11.2 *A CxG model of predicate nominal constructions (including role predicate nominal constructions).*

Note that the articles at the micro-level for a noun like *professor* are really variable as long as either a post-modifying *of*-phrase is used (see examples (17) and (18)) or the predicate construction includes reference to the place where the professor teaches:

(22) He *is professor* in the Kroc Institute for International Peace Studies at the University of Notre Dame, [...]. (COCA, 2009, MAG)
(23) He *is professor* at King Saud University in Saudi Arabia. (COCA, 2009, SPOK)

In addition to the different levels of abstraction, the notion of 'inheritance' plays an important role in CxG: constructions form part of a constructional network and can inherit information from related constructions in the network (provided they do not conflict with each other). For the micro-level of the CxG model of predicate nominal constructions, this means that the variants with or without a definite or indefinite article inherit properties from the different functions that these articles serve. Within CxG, we expect the variant with the article to have a different meaning from the one without an article; as articles themselves are taken to have meaning(s) (definiteness, member of set), the article is seen as contributing to the meaning of the meso-level constructions (title interpretation vs. common noun interpretation). Epstein (2002) points out that speakers actively employ the different functions of articles to construe referents:

> *Speakers* employ the article to *construct* discourse referents under various conceptual guises, [...] the article is compatible with a range of functions in addition to unique identifiability (familiarity): discourse prominence, role/value status, and point of view shifts. (Epstein 2002, 333; emphasis added)

Data and Definition of the Variable

The approach taken in this chapter starts with the head noun rather than the construction. This means that the focus of the investigation is on lexicogrammatical variation, which, as a general rule, requires the analysis of large corpora whenever content rather than function words are involved. The empirical evidence for this study therefore has to come from sufficiently large corpora. For a diachronic study of twentieth-century American English, COHA provides an ideal source.

The copula verbs included in my study are *be* and *become*. It turned out that instances of single role referents after the conjunction *as* were too infrequent to be included in the analysis. COHA was searched for instances of the copula verbs *be* and *become*, allowing for variable article use and both pre- and post-modification. The searches allowed for one word to occur in pre-head position (in addition to the optional article). Information of variable article use was retrieved for five nouns: *professor, president, governor, manager*, and *director*.

In a second step, I manually removed false positives. Among these are examples that bear only superficial similarity with single role predicate nominals because the head noun is used referentially:[7]

(24) He *is a professor* who is paid a salary for doing nothing. (COHA, 1893, FIC)
(25) It *was the Professor* who spoke,—whom the reader will recognize as myself, [...]. (COHA, 1861, FIC)

The retrieval algorithm also culled instances of existential constructions from the corpus. Since these do not allow for variable article use (see above), they were manually excluded from the analysis. Finally, only some interrogatives were included as relevant data: *who is professor of linguistics at your university*? is a relevant, variable context because it attributes a role to an individual; other interrogatives with *be* such as **where is professor of linguistics* do not attribute a role, do not allow for bare NP use, and were therefore also excluded from the counts.

Results

In this section, I present results both on the overall distribution of forms and the multivariate analyses. A total of 3,543 concordance lines for *professor, president, governor, manager*, and *director* were included in the analyses. The overall picture across all nouns does not appear to be very striking (see Figure 11.3), but it proves significant in a chi-square test at $p<0.001$. In other words, bare NPs decrease somewhat whereas definite articles show a moderate increase.

However, the results across all nouns mask quite considerable variation between individual lexical items. In the following analyses, the nouns will therefore be treated separately.

7 These particular instances are from the pre-1900 part of the corpus and stem from a more comprehensive search conducted for this noun.

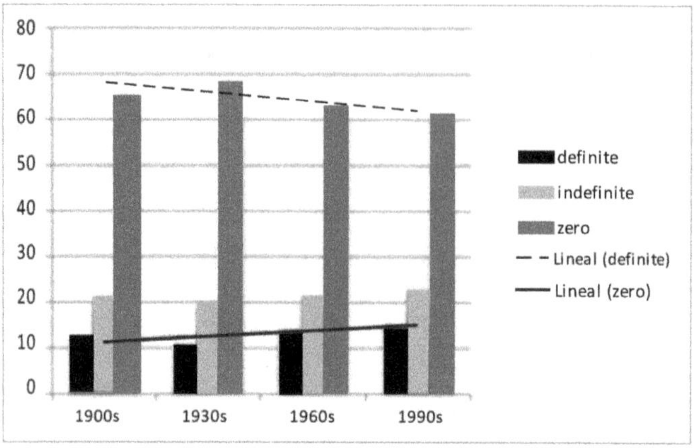

FIGURE 11.3 *Variable article use (percentage) with single role predicate nominals in* COHA *(Period 1, N=589; Period 2, N=933; Period 3, N=1,161; Period 4, N=860).*

Distributional Analysis of Articles Across Time

Figure 11.4 shows the development for *professor*. The trendline indicates that indefinite articles, the dominant pattern from the beginning, show an overall increase with this noun in twentieth-century American English at the expense of the bare NP. Indefinite articles increase particularly when the NP is post-modified.

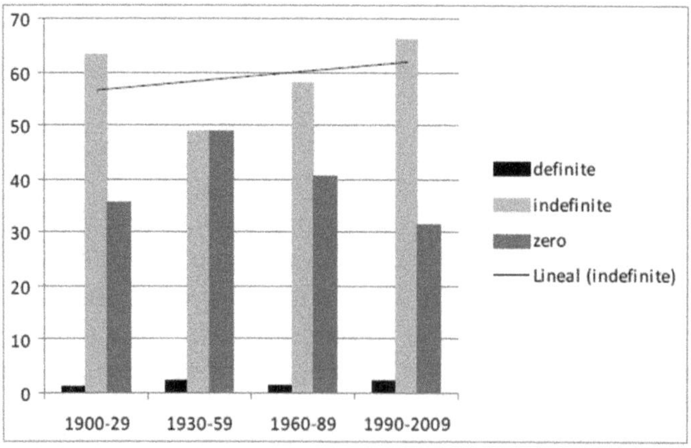

FIGURE 11.4 *Variable article use (percentage) with predicate nominal use of* professor *in* COHA *(Period 1, N=87; Period 2, N=135; Period 3, N=207; Period 4, N=215).*

Figures 11.5 and 11.6 show that *president* and *governor* both prefer the bare NP as predicate nominals; moreover, the change across time appears to be minimal and might turn out to be below the level of statistical significance. For both nouns, the more common variant is the one with the definite article whereas the indefinite article is an extremely rare option. In some (but not all) instances, the use of the indefinite article goes hand in hand with a specific semantic effect. In (26) and (27), the role of president is contextualized as one in a series of presidents. In (28) and (29), additional pre-modification indicates that special properties are assigned to the head of the NP, i.e. the focus is on the *kind of* president/governor rather than the role, making the use of the article obligatory.[8] The same semantic effect is achieved in (30), but without making the indefinite article obligatory.

(26) For the benefit of the non-Americans present, Lincoln *was a president* of the U.S.A., the Great Emancipator [...]. (COHA, 1937, MAG)
(27) [...] in America every boy may some day hope to *become a president* of the bank for which he works as a clerk. (COHA, 1962, FIC)
(28) But in the long run, Roosevelt *was a war President.* (COHA, 1992, MAG)
(29) Hiram Slater *was a pro-choice governor*, and this was a pro-choice crowd. (COHA, 1904, MAG)
(30) Mr. Pompidou will aim to *be a president* of the majority in Parliament. (COHA, 1932, MAG)

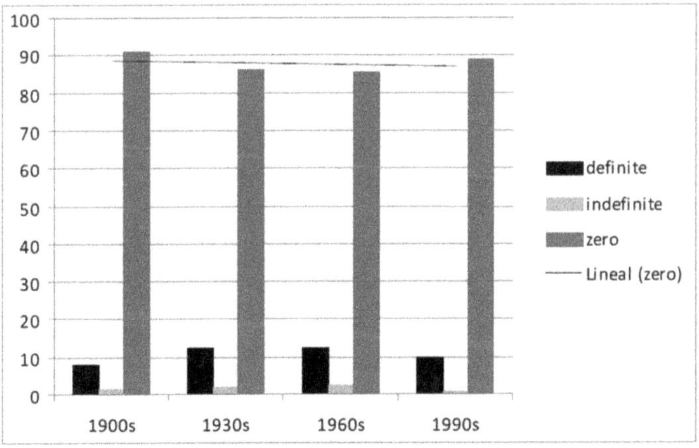

FIGURE 11.5 *Variable article use (percentage) with predicate nominal use of* president *in* COHA *(Period 1, N=141; Period 2, N=265; Period 3, N=342; Period 4, N=231).*

8 Note that these instances are not included in the variable rule analysis below.

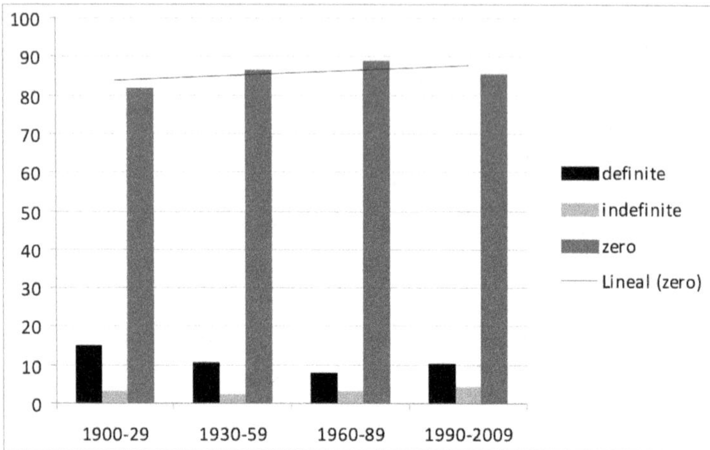

FIGURE 11.6 *Variable article use (percentage) with predicate nominal use of* governor *in* COHA *(Period 1, N=158; Period 2, N=158; Period 3, N=160; Period 4, N=69).*

Figure 11.7 summarizes the diachronic development for *manager*, which shows a preference for the bare NP in the first half of the twentieth century, but a preference for the use with either a definite or an indefinite article in the second half of the twentieth century. Bare NPs without any modification, in particular, appear to give way to usage with *a* or *the*; examples (31) to (34) illustrate typical examples from the beginning and the end of the twentieth century:

(31) [...] he would be the right man. Gordon Hart should *be manager*. (COHA, 1920, FIC)
(32) Frank Fenton *was manager* and he insisted on securing the most desirable table for them [...]. (COHA, 1922, FIC)
(33) "[...] she'd *be the manager* and I'd be the cook." (COHA, 2004, FIC)
(34) [...] I decided to turn my life around and *become a manager*. (COHA, 1990, FIC)

Figure 11.8 shows that *director* undergoes a reverse development from *manager* in that bare NPs become the dominant variant across time while instances with the indefinite article show a marked decrease; predicate nominals with definite *the* increase moderately. In this case, it appears that post-modification may play a role, i.e. there seems to be a trend from (35) to either (36) or (37):

(35) He *was a Director* of the German Exchange Bank. (COHA, 1904, NEWS)
(36) Kaplan *is director* of clinical dermatology at the University of California [...]. (COHA, 1996, MAG)
(37) Heather Weiss *is the Director* of the Harvard Family Research Project. (COHA, 1995, MAG)

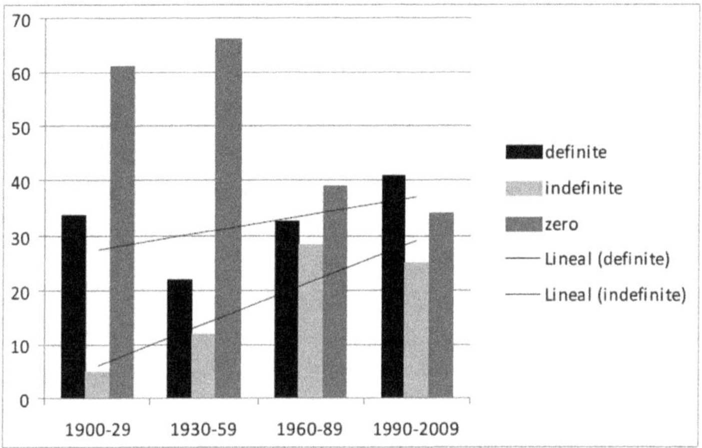

FIGURE 11.7 *Variable article use (percentage) with predicate nominal use of* manager *in* COHA *(Period 1, N=80; Period 2, N=151; Period 3, N=113; Period 4, N=88).*

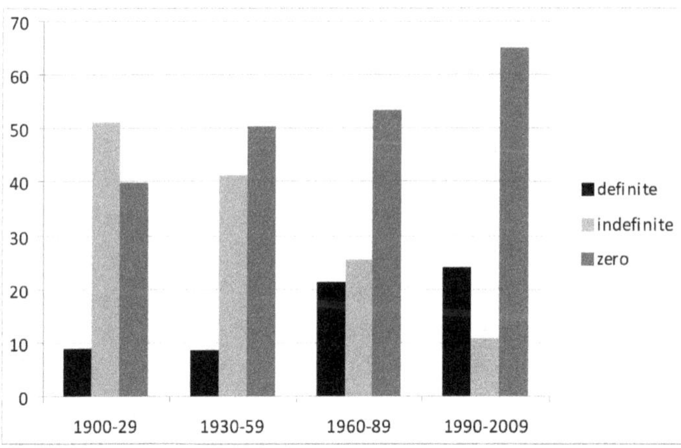

FIGURE 11.8 *Variable article use (percentage) with predicate nominal use of* director *in* COHA *(Period 1, N=123; Period 2, N=224; Period 3, N=339; Period 4, N=257).*

The question is whether the trends that are apparent from the graphs and the examples given above will also prove to be statistically significant. Moreover, only a multivariate analysis can reveal which factors (period, modification, type of construction) influence the choice of bare NP against definite or indefinite article with individual nouns.

Multivariate Analysis of Variable Article Use in Twentieth-Century American English

Since definite articles are a rare minority variant with *professor*, only the indefinite article and the bare NP were included in the multivariate analysis. For the analysis of *president* and *governor*, indefinite articles were excluded on account of their low frequency. All three variants (bare NP, definite, and indefinite article) are regularly used with *manager* and *director*. However, as VARBRUL only allows for a binomial analysis, the analysis compared bare NPs against those with an article (either definite or indefinite).

In the following analyses, variable article use was coded as the dependent variable. In addition, one external variable (subperiod) and two internal grammatical variables (modification, copula) were included. In variable rule analysis, these independent variables are referred to as 'factor groups'. Due to the sparseness of data, the factor group 'modification' only distinguishes between 'none' and 'modification' (subsuming instances of pre- and post-modification). The factor group 'copula' (or VP) distinguished between BE and BECOME. The factors are ranked according to their range, which is calculated by subtracting the lowest factor weight in the factor group from the highest weight; the highest range is typically the strongest constraint. Only statistically significant factor groups are included in the following tables.

Table 11.1 shows that with *professor* modification is even more important than diachronic change: overall, indefinite articles are most likely to occur with *professor* in predicate nominals that are neither pre- nor post-modified. Diachronic change also proved to be a significant factor, with the factor weights indicating that there is a relatively steady increase of indefinite articles from the beginning to the end of the twentieth century.

With *president* and *governor*, it is the definite article that is the alternative option alongside the dominant use of the bare NP. Tables 11.2 and 11.3 show that there is no significant change over time and that we are dealing with stable variation in the twentieth century. For both nouns, the choice of verb is the most important factor: definite articles are significantly more likely to be used after BE than BECOME. But there is one difference: with *president*, the definite article is also more likely to be used in post-modified NPs than without modification, whereas modification of *governor* is not a significant factor.

TABLE 11.1 *Variable rule analysis of contributing factors to the probability of indefinite article use with* professor *in* COHA

Input: 0.611
Overall proportion: 58.0
Total N = 653

	Factor weight	%	N
Modification			
none	.84	88.4	137
modification	.37	48.6	242
Range 47			
Period			
1900–1929	.36	47.7	51
1930–1959	.40	50.0	66
1960–1989	.52	58.8	120
1990–2009	.62	67.6	142
Range 26			

TABLE 11.2 *Variable rule analysis of contributing factors to the probability of definite article use with* president *in* COHA

Input: 0.102
Overall proportion: 11.2
Total N = 962

	Factor weight	%	N
VP			
BE	.55	13.2	95
BECOME	.34	5.4	13
Range 21			
Modification			
modification	.58	14.7	77
none	.40	7.1	31
Range 18			

TABLE 11.3 *Variable rule analysis of contributing factors to the probability of definite article use with* governor *in* COHA

Input: 0.109
Overall proportion: 11.5
Total N = 531

	Factor weight	%	N
VP			
BE	.58	13.3	55
BECOME	.31	5.1	6
Range 26			

With *manager*, all three factor groups turned out to be significant (see Table 11.4): diachronic variation is the most important; there is no difference between modification and choice of verb in terms of range, but modification gets an overall higher factor weight. Articles show a significant increase from the first to the second half of the twentieth century. In addition, articles favour NPs without modification and the copula BE over BECOME.

As with *manager*, all factor groups are also significant with *director*, but in a different order (see Table 11.5): the strongest constraint is modification, followed by the period and choice of verb. In other words, unmodified *director* fosters the use of an article. Diachronically, the use of articles decreases over time. Finally, we are more likely to see *director* used with an article than in a bare NP when it follows BE rather than BECOME.

Discussion

Prototype Effects, Construal, and Diachronic Change

Corpus evidence from COHA has shown that there is diachronic stability in variable article use with prototypical role nouns such as *president* and *governor*. In addition, BE is a more prototypical verb overall in the predicate nominal construction than BECOME. With the exception of *president* and *governor*, modification does not have a strong effect on facilitating the use of an article in single role predicate nominals. Some of the variation observed may also have

TABLE 11.4 *Variable rule analysis of contributing factors to the probability of definite* OR *indefinite article use with* manager *in* COHA

Input: 0.482
Overall proportion: 48.4
Total N = 432

	Factor weight	%	N
Period			
1900–1929	.40	38.8	31
1930–1959	.35	33.8	51
1960–1989	.62	61.1	69
1990–2009	.69	65.9	58
Range 34			
Modification			
none	.64	61.3	57
modification	.46	44.8	152
Range 18			
VP			
BE	.53	51.7	185
BECOME	.35	32.4	24
Range 18			

to do with speaker choice (Epstein 1996, 2002) in the construal of uniqueness. This is likely to account for diachronic change in variable article use of the less prototypical role nouns: construal may change over time, a change that may reflect cultural aspects beyond the purely linguistic reasons for change. In other words, the role of a professor may simply have come to be viewed as less unique over time, licensing the more frequent use of the indefinite article which refers to an individual as a member of a group: the construal with the indefinite article instead of a bare NP emphasizes the ordinariness of the role of professor. It may also be the case that in the past there were more situations with only one chair per subject or department, making reference to this one person more unique rather than referring to one of a set of professors.

TABLE 11.5 *Variable rule analysis of contributing factors to the probability of definite* OR *indefinite article use with* director *in* COHA

Input: 0.463
Overall proportion: 45.9
Total N = 943

	Factor weight	%	N
Modification			
none	.80	78.8	130
modification	.43	38.9	303
Range 47			
Period			
1900–1929	.59	60.2	74
1930–1959	.52	49.6	111
1960–1989	.52	46.6	158
1990–2009	.41	35.0	90
Range 18			
VP			
BE	.53	48.2	375
BECOME	.38	35.2	58
Range 15			

Corpus evidence thus supports a view of gradient membership in the single role category: prototypical members of the category are those roles which permit only one person to occupy the position/office at any one point in time, such as *president* or *pope*. These seem to be limited to variability between bare NP and definite article when they are used as predicate nominals (also diachronically). Somewhat less prototypical members are nouns designating professions like *professor*, which are also terms functioning as titles. As seen above, Huddleston and Pullum et al. (2002, 409) maintain that bare NP use of nouns as predicate complements is limited to nouns which permit role interpretation. However, this is apparently not limited to offices that are filled by a unique individual. The evidence provided in this chapter suggests that some nouns may be more prototypical as single role holders, namely *president* or *governor*; others, like *professor* and *manager*, have come to be used less often with a bare NP, which could reflect a change in people's perception of these positions. Finally, a noun like *director* has come to be viewed more as a single role holder over time, it seems.

Analogical Change and Constructional Bootstrapping

Initially, I pointed out that nouns like *lawyer* or *teacher* require an article when they are used as predicate nominals. However, corpus data show that these nouns can also be used in the role predicate nominal construction:

(38) She *was lawyer* for a state House committee, then went to Washington in 1983 and joined Citizen Action, a grass-roots policy group. (COCA, 1993, NEWS)

(39) I *was teacher* and a preacher, and that put me way up on the pedestal to parents. (COCA, 2007, SPOK)[9]

It may thus no longer be the uniqueness of the referent and his/her role that determines grammatical behaviour. It appears that bare NP use of nouns as predicate complements has come to be extended to title nouns more generally than single roles. If it is title nouns rather than single role status that licenses bare NP use of predicate complements, we can account for the spread (by analogical extension) of the pattern to so-called pseudo-titles (and beyond).

Analogical change has been linked to the question of actualization, how a change proceeds in step-wise fashion after reanalysis has taken place. According to De Smet (2012, 603),

> [t]he general answer [...] is that actualization is strongly guided by appearances. The more familiar or the less conspicuous some innovation looks, the more likely it is to manifest itself. What looks familiar is, in turn, determined by a multiplicity of (possibly superficial) similarity relations that link a reanalysed item's potential new uses to existing older uses. [...] The claim that actualization proceeds through similarity-based generalizations gives center stage to analogy as the main mechanism determining the course of events.

9 Note that Clyne (2003, 153) attributes bare NP use with occupational terms like *teacher* as predicate nominals in the Tarrington-Tabor (Western Victoria) area of Australia to structural influence of German. On this evidence, it is possible that language contact in the US may have supported analogical extension of bare NP use to such occupational terms, too.

If we combine De Smet's idea about actualization explicitly with CxG,[10] we can postulate that these 'older uses' are established constructions into which lexical items undergoing change are slotted. I suggest the term 'constructional bootstrapping' for this process. In the case of role nouns in predicate constructions it might be the prior use of the nouns as pseudo-titles. The similarity between title constructions like *President Obama* and single role predicate nominals is semantic and formal: titles and roles often refer to 'unique' individuals and both constructions (typically) lack a determiner. A noun such as *doctor,* for instance, is established in the title construction and from there could spread by analogy to the single role predicate nominal construction in its bare NP variant:

(40) My father *was doctor* to the County Farm, our local home for old people without money. (COCA, 2000, FIC)
(41) For a time he *was doctor* to the Hell's Angels. (COCA, 1996, SPOK)

In a similar fashion, *lawyer* and *teacher* can be used as pseudo-titles in the title construction in (42) and (43), and from this pattern, usage can be extended to the single role predicate nominal construction (38) and (39):

(42) And feminist *lawyer Gloria Allred* says we shouldn't even be doing this program about it. (COCA, 1995, SPOK)
(43) *Teacher Catherine Oppenheimer* is more interested in energy and characterization—at which most children excel—than in the steps. (COCA, 1990, MAG)

Finally, even a noun like *father* may proceed along a similar path, first as a pseudo-title (44) and then as a single role predicate nominal (45):

(44) Thirty-two-year-old *father* of two Sean Dickey says his marriage is going downhill […]. (COCA, 2002, SPOK)
(45) A widower, he *is father* of an adult son and daughter. (COCA, 1997, MAG)

In some constructs, the role interpretation is made explicit, and (46) even combines a professional and an interpersonal role, putting a noun that can

10 De Smet situates his work within usage-based models of grammar, including Croft's (2001) and Goldberg's (2006) construction grammars, and Langacker's (2000) notion of similarity between constructions, but does not explicitly claim that he is working within CxG himself.

function as a pseudo-title alongside one that does not permit usage in the title construction quite so easily:

(46) I also think it was completely inappropriate for Howard K. Stern to have a sexual relationship with his client. He shouldn't have *been lawyer* and *lover*. He should have chosen one. (COCA, 2007, SPOK)[11]

A possible bridging context may be prototypical title uses of the nouns in predicate nominal constructions, as illustrated in (47) and (48):

(47) Before coming to Armstrong, she taught for more than 35 years in private and public education in Savannah, Georgia, where she *was Teacher* of the Year in 1995–1996. (COCA, 2012, ACAD)

(48) [...] he *was father* of the year. (COCA, 2004, FIC)

Extension of bare NPs to nouns that do not typically occur in the single role predicate construction is also supported by examples where the abstract role function of a noun is contextually foregrounded, as in (49) and (50):

(49) [...] someone who has just been a lawyer very recently remembers what it's like to represent people, remembers what it is like *to be lawyer*, [...]. (COCA, 1998, SPOK)[12]

(50) The research also suggests the need to reconceptualize the *roles* and relationships within the educative process, challenging the notion of who is *teacher*, who is expert. (COCA, 2003, ACAD)

---

11 Interestingly, *lover* is only attested in conjunction with other nouns as a role predicate nominal in COCA:

(iv) [...] he had been *lover, protector and friend*. (COCA, 1993, NEWS)

(v) At once, she is a promise of romantic fulfillment and of down-to-earth fun; she is *lover and pal*, straddling dream and reality. (COCA, 2000, NEWS)

Note that *lover* is also attested a little earlier on its own as a pseudo-title:

(vi) She and *lover* Lindsey Buckingham joined Mac in' 75. (COCA, 1990, NEWS)

12 One reviewer suggested that there might be non-native speaker influence in this example. Closer examination shows that this is not the case: the speaker is Spencer Aronfeld, a US lawyer, who—judging by spoken material available on sources such as YouTube—clearly seems to be a native speaker of US English. In other words, even though some of the data discussed in this paper may appear odd to native speakers of English, they are not automatically the result of transcription errors or non-native speaker influence.

In other words, the change starts locally by slotting ordinary nouns like *lawyer* and later *father* into a title noun construction. From this construction, spread into neighbouring constructions (by similarity) is possible. Thus, constructional bootstrapping is incremental. The important thing is that the micro-level rather than the constructional macro-level plays a central role. Essentially, my argument is that a version of CxG which distinguishes different constructional levels allows us to detail how lexical items change their distributional properties, i.e. gradually change from one category into another. The question is whether the spread to the title noun construction always precedes the use in a single role predicate construction. Corpus data show that this may not necessarily be the case. The earliest title use of *lawyer* in COHA, for instance, dates from 1823:

(51) I know that you are a favourite with Dr. Plumber, and *lawyer Kidder*. (COHA, 1843, FIC)

The two uses of *lawyer* as a predicate nominal in a bare NP from COHA are fairly early attestations from the beginning of the twentieth century, but they do not antedate the pseudo-title use of *lawyer*:[13]

(52) Of the period of storm and stress at home, from 1848 to 1869, when he *was lawyer, author, journalist, editor, soldier, politician*, when he wrote his Meister Karl, first translated Heine, and sprang into fame as Hans Breitmann, the letters are almost as silent. (COHA, 1905, MAG)
(53) I could be disbarred if I *was lawyer* for both sides. (COHA, 1914, FIC)

With *teacher*, however, the bare NP is attested as a predicate nominal (54) before it is used as a pseudo-title (55):

13 The following example shows that *lawyer* is used in a bare NP as a predicate nominal, but the context is a generic one and does not refer to an individual. It is therefore more likely that the bare NP is licensed by the generic meaning of the example than the grammatical, and there is no obvious connection with the status of a particular role in this context:
(vii) Whether a man *be lawyer*, farmer, or mechanic, matters not, if he be intelligent and respectable. (COHA, 1835, FIC)
Also excluded as an early use of a bare NP of a single role predicate nominal is a non-standard example from a novel with likely influence of language contact:
(viii) Den he shake my hand—say he always bin lub me—will take me to country whay brack man is gentleman and hab white wife, and *is lawyer*, and school mosser, and preacher, and hab white man for dribe he carriage. (COHA, 1845, FIC).

(54) He *was teacher* of the Negro free-school when he died. (COHA, 1827, FIC)
(55) It may be doubted if *Teacher Willwell* or Pastor Harold had prepared him for the emergency. (COHA, 1850, FIC)

In other words, the two syntactic environments may be equally likely to act as bootstrapping constructions for the extension of syntactic properties of title nouns to pseudo-titles. But chronology does not have to be a problem for analogical extension. De Smet (2012, 609) points out that

> [...] sometimes most of an item's new uses following reanalysis appear more or less simultaneously or, in any case, in too quick a succession to make confident claims about the order of first appearances (which, in such cases, corroborates the idea that actualization captures a set of changes that, at a more abstract level, belong together). Even if the order of first appearances is unclear, however, different uses gain acceptability at a different pace or at different times, as reflected in their usage frequencies. Therefore, steps in the actualization process are not necessarily to be seen as the abrupt introduction of surface innovations, one after the other, but can also manifest themselves as gradual and potentially overlapping probabilistic shifts in the acceptability of an item's various new uses.[14]

Thus, the order of steps may differ for individual nouns: the locus of change could be different, i.e. *lawyer* could have acquired bare NP usage in the title construction whereas *teacher* could have developed its bare NP use in the role predicate nominal construction and then spread to the title construction.

Constructional bootstrapping also plays a role on the level of the micro-construction, i.e. collocational preferences. According to De Smet (2012, 625), collocations foster analogical extension because they provide familiar environments:

> Apart from determining the broad direction of actualization, similarity also has more subtle effects on the actualization [...]. Particularly, it is found that actualization exploits existing collocations. New steps in the actualization process are easier to take if the result resembles some established cooccurrence pattern.

14 Opposite trajectories of change are found for *fun* and *key* as adjectives, with *fun* starting off from predicative use and spreading to attributive contexts and *key* acquiring its adjectival function in attributive function and spreading to predicative contexts (see De Smet 2012, 621–625).

With roles in predicate nominals, typical patterns of pre- or post-modification would serve the same bootstrapping function at the micro-constructional level. Further research will have to show whether *father* is more likely to be used as a pseudo-title when post-modified by a prepositional phrase (as in (44) and (45)). Similarly, collocational patterns like BE *X to a Y* (see (56) and (57)) and BE *not X enough to V* (see (58)) may have played a role in the extension of the single role predicate nominal construction to non-prototypical nouns.[15]

(56) For a long time I *was reporter to a journal*, […]. (COHA, 1854, FIC)
(57) He would not, for example, *be lover to a woman* whose husband had introduced him to her […]. (COHA, 1941, FIC)
(58) He *was not hypocrite enough to say*, "I do love you;" (COHA, 1867, FIC)

Finally, more abstract co-occurrence patterns such as lists might also help in the analogical extension of bare NP use to nouns that typically require an article in title or single role predicate constructions. In addition to example (46), which joins *lawyer* and *lover* in a short list, the following examples of the single role predicate construction (see (59) and (60)) and the pseudo-title construction (see (61) and (62))[16] would support such a view:

(59) Whether a man *be lawyer*, *farmer*, or *mechanic*, matters not, if he be intelligent and respectable. (COHA, 1835, FIC)
(60) Banker Stevens, 57, *is golfer, fisherman, Republican, Methodist*. (COHA, 1928, MAG)
(61) […] a preliminary list of ten amateurs from whom the cup-receiver will be picked: # *Golfer* Robert Tyre Jones Jr. # *Marathoner* Clarence De Mar # *Swimmer* Helene Madison # *Tennis Player* Helen Wills Moody # *Track &; Fielder* Barney Berlinger # *Girl Sprinter* Stella Walsh # *Swimmer* Ray Ruddy # *Poloist* Thomas Hitchcock Jr. # *Shot Putter* Harlow Rothert # *Sprinter* George Simpson #. (COHA, 1930, MAG)
(62) […] *Financier* James B. Brown of Kentucky. # *Banker* Herbert L. Clark of Philadelphia. # *Surgeon* John B. Deaver of Philadelphia. […] # *Copperman* Daniel C. Jackling of San Francisco. # *Philanthropist* Eldredge R. Johnson

15 On variable article use in comparative constructions, see also Jespersen (1933, section 13.5); I am grateful to John Payne for pointing this out to me. Another context mentioned by Jespersen, i.e. BE *less X than Y* (e.g. *He is less statesman than philosopher*), is not attested in either COHA, COCA, or the TIME magazine corpus.

16 For a more detailed study of pseudo-title nouns in Late Modern American English, see Hundt and Payne (2014).

of New Jersey. # *Engineer* Charles Franklin Kettering of Dayton, Ohio. # *Lawyer* Alexander Lincoln of Boston. [...] # *President* William M. Sloan of the American Academy of Arts &; Letters (Manhattan). # *Merchant* Percy Straus of Manhattan [...]. (COHA, 1928, MAG)

Note, however, that the conjoins in example (39) are bare NP (*teacher*) and an NP with an indefinite article (*a preacher*), so variable article use is also possible in coordinate NPs or lists, it appears.

Conclusion and Outlook

The corpus data investigated in this study provide empirical evidence that there is diachronic variation in the use of articles in role predicate nominals (with the exception of more prototypical title nouns such as *president* and *governor*). The present chapter proposes a usage-based account of language change that includes probabilistic modelling of construction-internal factors, such as the presence or absence of modification.

The results of the corpus analyses suggest that role nouns are a prototypically structured category. The CxG approach allows us to account for (lexical) variation in variable article use of role predicate nominals. It also explains how constructional change, in this case, is likely to affect the micro-level of representation rather than the meso-level (as in Hilpert 2013, 209). With single role predicates, we see change that affects the likelihood of individual nouns (*professor* vs. *director*) to be construed as unique roles or common nouns. In the long run, however, these local changes may result in a convergence of the meso-level constructions (role predicate nominal construction and 'regular' predicate nominal construction). Thus, the CxG approach is a suitable framework here, allowing for analogical extension of the role predicate nominal construction to atypical (i.e. non-role or pseudo-role) nouns. Adapting ideas from De Smet (2012), I argued that this may work via constructional bootstrapping with title noun constructions, and possibly other collocations. However, constructional bootstrapping is a hypothesis that needs to be tested against historical corpus data. In particular, it remains to be shown which other constructions may have served as bootstrapping contexts. A methodological issue is how we might discover these in a more systematic way than the one taken in this chapter. The idea that constructional bootstrapping plays a role in constructionalization and analogical extension of constructions to atypical environments may find support in research on language acquisition. Abbot-Smith and Behrens (2006), who studied the emergence of passive constructions in speakers of German, found that the acquisition of the *sein*-passive was supported by the prior acquisition of the *sein* copula, i.e. acquisition of one pattern was aided by a supporting construction. Moreover, acquisition supported by this kind of 'constructional conspiracy' (their term) was characterized by a sudden increase in frequency to adult-like rates rather than the slower acquisition rates typical of acquisition without constructional support.

In this chapter, I took a noun-based approach to the construction by searching for head nouns that are known to show variable article use in the single role predicate construction. It would also be possible to start from a construction as a frame and investigate the range of nouns that are attested with a bare NP, e.g. by searching for constructions of the type [*proper name*] *works/worked as* [*role noun*]). Such a search reveals that nouns like *valet, night janitor, superintendent,* and *watchman* are all possible in the single role referent predicative construction:

(63) He *works as valet* for a big, thickset, friendly-faced engineer whose friends and helpers all call him The Chief. (COHA, 1929, MAG)
(64) He *works as night janitor* at Loyola High School [...]. (COHA, 2000, FIC)
(65) [...] he *works as superintendent* of security at an auto plant. (COHA, 1990, MAG)
(66) Although the father *works as night watchman* of an office building, he has no job security. (COHA, 2001, MAG)

Future research on variable article use and diachronic change should thus involve the following triangulation: it should start with a word-based approach in a particular syntactic environment in order to explore constructional variance and diachronic change, move on to the construction-based approach to establish a broader range of lexical items that slot into a construction, and then use the word-based approach again to establish the range of constructions in which bare NPs are used and how they spread from one construction to another. Finally, it might also be fruitful to extend the study back into the nineteenth century.

Corpora

BNC *British National Corpus*, version 3 (BNC XML Edition). 2007. Distributed by Oxford University Computing Services on behalf of the BNC Consortium. http://www.natcorp.ox.ac.uk/.

COCA Davies, Mark. 2008–. *The Corpus of Contemporary American English: 520 million words, 1990-present*. http://corpus.byu.edu/coca/.

COHA Davies, Mark. 2010–. *The Corpus of Historical American English: 400 million words, 1810–2009*. http://corpus.byu.edu/coha/.

References

Abbot-Smith, Kirsten F., and Heike Behrens. 2006. "How Known Constructions Influence the Acquisition of Other Constructions: The German Passive and Future Constructions." *Cognitive Science* 30/6: 995–1026.

Berezowski, Leszek. 2009. *The Myth of the Zero Article*. London: Continuum.

Biber, Douglas, Stig Johansson, Geoffrey Leech, Susan Conrad, and Edward Finegan. 1999. *Longman Grammar of Spoken and Written English*. London: Longman.

Chesterman, Andrew. 1991. *On Definiteness: A Study with Special Reference to English and Finnish*. Cambridge: Cambridge University Press.

Clyne, Michael. 2003. *Dynamics of Language Contact: English and Immigrant Languages*. Cambridge: Cambridge University Press.

Croft, William. 2001. *Radical Construction Grammar: Syntactic Theory in Typological Perspective*. Oxford: Oxford University Press.

De Smet, Hendrik. 2012. "The Course of Actualization." *Language* 88/3: 601–33.

Epstein, Richard. 1996. "Viewpoint and the Definite Article." In *Conceptual Structure, Discourse and Language*, edited by Adele E. Goldberg, 99–112. Standford: Center for the Study of Language and Information.

Epstein, Richard. 1999. "Roles, Frames and Definiteness." In *Discourse Studies in Cognitive Linguistics*, edited by Karen Van Hoek, Andrej A. Kibrik, and Leo Noordman, 53–74. Amsterdam and Philadelphia: John Benjamins.

Epstein, Richard. 2002. "The Definite Article, Accessibility, and the Construction of Discourse Referents" *Cognitive Linguistics* 12/4: 333–78.

Goldberg, Adele E. 2006. *Constructions at Work: The Nature of Generalization in Language*. Oxford: Oxford University Press.

Goldberg, Adele E. 2013. "Constructionist Approaches." In *The Oxford Handbook of Construction Grammar*, edited by Thomas Hoffmann, and Graeme Trousdale, 15–31. Oxford: Oxford University Press.

Hewson, John. 1972. *Article and Noun in English*. The Hague: Mouton.

Hilpert, Martin. 2013. *Constructional Change in English: Developments in Allomorphy, Word Formation and Syntax*. Cambridge: Cambridge University Press.

Huddleston, Rodney, and Geoffrey K. Pullum, et al. 2002. *The Cambridge Grammar of the English Language*. Cambridge: Cambridge University Press.

Hundt, Marianne, and John Payne. 2014. "How Weird Are Teenagers? Variation and Change in the Use of Noun-Name Collocations." Paper presented at the Eighteenth International Conference on English Historical Linguistics (ICEHL 18), Leuven. 14–18 July.

Jespersen, Otto. 1909–49. *A Modern English Grammar on Historical Principles*. 7 vols. London: Allen and Unwin.

Jespersen, Otto. 1933. *Essentials of English Grammar.* London: Allen and Unwin.

Langacker, Ronald W. 2000. "A Dynamic Usage-Based Model." In *Usage-Based Models of Language*, edited by Michael Barlow, and Suzanne Kemmer, 1–63. Stanford: CSLI Publications.

Quirk, Randolph, Sidney Greenbaum, Geoffrey Leech, and Jan Svartvik. 1985. *A Comprehensive Grammar of the English Language*. London: Longman.

Traugott, Elizabeth C. 2008. "Grammaticalization, Constructions and the Incremental Development of Language: Suggestions from the Development of Degree Modifiers in English." In *Variation, Selection, Development. Probing the Evolutionary Model of Language Change*, edited by Regine Eckardt, Gerhard Jäger, and Tonjes Veenstra, 219–50. Berlin: Mouton de Gruyter.

Traugott, Elizabeth C., and Graeme Trousdale. 2013. *Constructionalization and Constructional Changes*. Oxford: Oxford University Press.

Trousdale, Graeme. 2008. "A Constructional Approach to Lexicalization Processes in the History of English: Evidence from Possessive Constructions." *Word Structure* 1: 156–77.

CHAPTER 12

Clause Fragments in English Dialogue*

Jill Bowie and Bas Aarts

Abstract

Participants in dialogue often use clause fragments, such as *At Camberwell* or *A cheap bottle*, which are structurally incomplete but in fact make complete contributions to the discourse. Their interpretation depends on their links to other structures in the context. The hypothesis that will be explored in this chapter is that just a few different kinds of grammatical link are exploited recurrently to serve a wide range of discourse purposes. Based on systematic analysis of a set of data drawn from the dialogues in the ICE-GB corpus, we argue that two frequent grammatical sub-types can be distinguished, which we label 'extensions' and 'matches'. Extensions are interpretable as added constituents of antecedent structures in context, while matches are interpretable as alternative constituents of antecedent structures. These antecedents may be uttered by either the same speaker or another speaker. We show how fragments fulfil a wide range of discourse functions and contribute to discourse cohesion. Our study also provides evidence against what we call the 'strict ellipsis' account of clause fragments, which claims that the 'missing' material can be recovered directly from the preceding context. We use authentic corpus examples, rarely considered in ellipsis debates, to show that such an account is untenable.

Keywords

fragments – ellipsis – spoken discourse – non-sentential utterances – dialogue – theticals – clause fragments

* We are grateful to two anonymous reviewers and to Tania Kuteva for their helpful comments on an earlier draft of this chapter.

 | DOI 10.1163/9789004321342_013

Introduction

Standard grammatical analyses tend to focus on the written ideal of a sentence, taken as comprising a complete main clause or a coordination of main clauses. However, spontaneous spoken discourse contains many instances of clause fragments like those in (1)–(5), drawn from the ICE-GB corpus (the British component of the *International Corpus of English*; Nelson et al. 2002):

(1) At Camberwell (S1A-015 #74)
(2) Well at least ten or twenty people (S1A-007 #247)
(3) Oh very yes yeah (S1A-095 #247)
(4) Not if you've had lunch (S1A-006 #29)
(5) An awfully long time anyway (S1A-007 #82)

Taken out of context, these examples are incomplete and impossible to interpret, but in context they can be interpreted through links to other structures as conveying propositional meanings, thereby making complete contributions to the discourse. For instance, (1) occurs in the following context:

(6) A: Is Bim *at the Slade* now or not? Did he ever get there?
B: **At Camberwell**
(S1A-015 #72–74)

To interpret B's fragment we need to link it to the phrase in italics within A's first question, and judge it to replace that phrase, giving the meaning 'Bim is at Camberwell now', and thus indirectly answering A's first question.

Empirical research is needed to investigate how clause fragments like those above are interpretable by exploring what kind of grammatical links, in a sense to be explained below, are established to other structures in the discourse context. While generative grammarians have taken an interest in fragments (as discussed in Culicover and Jackendoff 2005, 233ff.), they have typically relied on invented examples. Relevant empirical research has been done within the approach of Conversational Analysis (e.g. Schegloff 2000; Szczepek 2000a; Sidnell 2012). However, the scope of these studies is often defined in discourse-functional terms, so from a grammatical viewpoint they typically look at subsets of the relevant data and are more concerned with functional aspects. In contrast, our aim is to take a grammatical perspective and generalize across the different discourse functions that clause fragments can fulfil. Related empirical research has also been done by researchers on automatic dialogue processing, notably by Fernández et al. (2007) on 'non-sentential utterances' in dialogue in the *British National Corpus* (an unparsed corpus). They propose a practical taxonomy of 15 types, such as 'check question', 'short answer', and 'plain affirmative answer'. However, this line of research does not address the issue of recurrent grammatical linkage types, either.

In this chapter we explore the hypothesis that just a few different kinds of grammatical link are exploited recurrently to serve a wide range of discourse purposes. The article draws on data from the spoken dialogues in ICE-GB, a parsed corpus, to catalogue the kinds of links that we encounter in authentic texts, and describes the nature of these links. We distinguish two frequent grammatical subtypes: extensions, which link on the syntagmatic dimension, and are interpretable as added constituents of antecedent structures in context; and matches, which link on the paradigmatic dimension, and are interpretable as alternative constituents of antecedent structures in context. The distinction is then generalized to cover antecedent structures from either the same speaker or from another speaker. Each grammatical subtype can be used to perform a wide range of discourse actions. A second aim of the chapter is to provide evidence against what we call the 'strict ellipsis' account of clause fragments, which claims that where gaps occur in clause fragments these can be recovered directly from the preceding context.

We begin by defining clause fragments and describing the collection and analysis of data from ICE-GB. We then present more detailed qualitative discussion of the two major fragment types, namely extensions and matches. We then argue against the 'strict ellipsis' account and offer some conclusions.

Defining Clause Fragments

First, it is necessary to define 'clause fragment' and distinguish it from other kinds of non-sentential unit found in spoken discourse. A frequent kind is the single-word discourse marker (DM) such as *Oh, Yes, Hi*. Clause fragments differ from these in containing 'lexico-grammatical content'. This content typically takes the form of a phrase which is not integrated into any clausal structure, despite having the grammatical potential to be a clause constituent. For instance, the prepositional phrase *At Camberwell* in (6) stands alone as a response, without being integrated into any clause, but has the potential to function as a clause constituent—for instance, as a locative complement in *Bim is at Camberwell now*. Often the phrase is concatenated with one or more DMs, as in (2) and (3) above: *Well at least ten or twenty people*

(DM *Well* + NP) and *Oh very yes yeah* (DM + AdvP + DM + DM). We also find subordinate clauses, as in (4), *Not if you've had lunch*; and concatenations of phrases, as in (5), *An awfully long time anyway* (NP + AdvP).

Clause fragments can be defined as non-sentential units of discourse which:

(a) depend on grammatical links to surrounding structures for their interpretation (being interpretable, for example, in terms of post-modifier or adjunct function in an antecedent structure); and
(b) make a complete contribution within their discourse context, by performing an act within the discourse (such as answering or asking a question, agreeing or disagreeing), and typically by conveying a propositional meaning.

These criteria exclude the following types of unit:

(a) DM-only units, e.g. *Wow*; *Hi*; *Okay*; *Oh no*;
(b) elements such as vocatives or DMs which occur as part of a linear sequence through loose attachment rather than grammatical linkage, e.g. *Oh* and *Jo* in *Oh, did you want to see me, Jo?*;
(c) incomplete utterances (cut-offs and trail-offs, i.e. anacolutha), e.g. *So they –*; *And I still uh –*; and
(d) 'free-standing' constructions, e.g. *What about Sam?*; *The sooner the better*; *Morning*; *Thanks*.

The latter category includes a wide range of conventionalized structures that do not conform to canonical sentence form (see e.g. Culicover and Jackendoff 2005, 236–237). These are sometimes labelled as 'minor sentences' or 'irregular sentences'; they do not require linking to another grammatical structure in context in the same way that *At Camberwell* does in (6) above.

Also excluded are elliptical responses with subject and tensed verb, as in (7) below, as we take these to be elliptical main clauses:[1]

(7) B: Is he taping it now?
C: **Yes he is.**
(S1A-049 #141–2)

1 Examples like (7) could perhaps be seen as representing one end of a spectrum, rather than as a completely separate phenomenon from fragments. However, as they are more straightforward instances of ellipsis and have received coverage elsewhere (including in corpus studies, e.g. Greenbaum and Nelson 1999), and as they are clearly distinguishable in formal terms from our fragments, we excluded them from our study.

In contrast, we do not analyse clause fragments as elliptical clauses. Generative analyses (typically based on introspective data) have often treated fragments as 'underlyingly' clausal in form, but it seems preferable to avoid positing extensive 'invisible' syntactic structure, following Culicover and Jackendoff (2005). These authors give invented examples for which a strict ellipsis account is simply unworkable. We return to this point later on in the chapter.

Nonetheless, we still need to explain how fragments like (1) to (5) can be interpreted: as Culicover and Jackendoff note, they are semantically 'orphans' which need to be integrated into a propositional structure. Conversational participants are able to carry out this integration by drawing on their understanding of the potential that isolated phrases have to function as grammatical constituents. It is for this reason that we describe the linkages involved as 'grammatical'. This is not intended to exclude the use of pragmatic inferencing by participants in arriving at interpretations, in combination with their use of grammatical knowledge. We recognize that more 'purely' pragmatic links also play a role in dialogue, but these are beyond the scope of this chapter, as is theoretical discussion of the disputed boundary between syntax and pragmatics (see e.g. Blakemore 2006, in relation to parentheticals).

Collection and Analysis of Data

The Data

ICE-GB, the British component of the *International Corpus of English*, comprises one million words of British English from the early 1990s, and includes written material, spoken monologues, and spoken dialogues. The data for this study are drawn from the spoken dialogues, which comprise around 376,000 words from a range of text categories, as shown in Table 12.1. The largest category is that of private direct (face-to-face) conversation, which contributes nearly half the data. The other categories are private telephone conversations and a range of different 'public' genres, such as broadcast discussions.

All texts in ICE-GB, including the dialogues, are fully parsed. They are divided into 'parsing units' (PUs): sentences of written text or their rough equivalents in spoken texts (in the dialogues, 58% of PUs take the form of a main clause, while 35% are 'non-clauses'). Each PU is represented as a grammatical structure in the form of a tree diagram, where the constituent nodes have grammatical labels for function, form, and additional features. The grammatical trees are fully searchable with the corpus exploration software ICECUP (*International Corpus of English Corpus Utility Program*; Nelson et al. 2002). The spoken texts have audio recordings aligned with the transcribed units, so the researcher can listen to segments of talk while perusing the transcription.

TABLE 12.1 *Text categories in* ICE-GB *dialogue*

Text category	Words	%
direct conversations (private)	185,208	49%
telephone calls (private)	20,419	5%
broadcast discussions	43,920	12%
broadcast interviews	22,147	6%
business transactions	20,546	5%
classroom lessons	42,210	11%
legal cross-examinations	21,179	6%
parliamentary debates	21,060	6%
Total dialogue	376,689	100%

An initial set of 89 clause fragments was collected by examining three entire continuous extracts (of around 2,000 words each) from the category of private direct conversation, using the transcriptions and audio recordings.[2] A preliminary analysis of types was developed based on this set. In order to test this analysis, we then collected a sample of examples from across the dialogues in the corpus, so as to include more speakers and text categories. This required several steps: using grammatically specified searches to identify candidate examples (non-sentential units with lexico-grammatical content),[3] reducing the candidate set to a manageable subset by random sampling, and carrying out hand analysis to identify genuine examples. In this last stage, each candidate example was individually examined within its discourse context (using the transcripts and audio recordings). Incomplete utterances and 'free-standing' constructions were excluded, in accordance with the definition of clause fragments provided above. (DM-only units had already been excluded through the grammatical searches.) Also excluded were examples which could not be analysed (e.g. because of unclear speech). A final set of 134 items was obtained. This gave a combined total of 223 fragments. The collection is strongly weighted

2 The extracts used were S1A-006, S1A-007, and S1A-015.

3 Two grammatical searches were needed: (i) PUs with the form label 'non-clause' and containing at least one immediate constituent with the function label 'element' (i.e. containing phrasal material); and (ii) PUs with the form label 'clause' and the feature label 'dependent' (i.e. subordinate clauses parsed as separate units of discourse).

towards private direct conversation but also includes examples from other text types.

The conventions used in citing examples in following text are noted here. As in the corpus transcriptions, no punctuation is used but the initial word of each PU is capitalized, and two types of pause are indicated: a short pause (lasting for the beat of one syllable) by the symbol <,> and a longer pause by <,,>. We use the forward slash symbol / to indicate the ends of PUs, and curly brackets {} to indicate overlapping speech. We include self-corrections. We add our own glosses for the interpretations of the fragments, in parentheses after the extracts. Finally, we use codes indicating the source text and specific units cited.

Analysing Clause Fragments

It was noted in the introduction that clause fragments depend on links to surrounding structures for their interpretation. On the grammatical dimension, we can make a major division between links on the paradigmatic and syntagmatic axes, adapting the Saussurean distinction for the analysis of spoken language flow, as in Blanche-Benveniste (1990).[4]

Paradigmatic links involve alternative possibilities for the same grammatical 'slot', as in (8) (repeated from (6) above with punctuation replaced by PU markers):

(8) A: Is Bim *at the Slade* now or not / Did he ever get there /
B: **At Camberwell** /
('Bim is at Camberwell now.')
(S1A-015 #72–4)

As mentioned above, we can interpret B's fragment by linking it to the phrase in italics within A's first question, and judging it to replace that phrase, giving the meaning 'Bim is at Camberwell now'. In grammatical terms, this can be analysed as a 'matching' type of link (following Culicover and Jackendoff 2005, 257): the fragment can be 'matched' to *at the Slade* as an alternative possibility which could fill the same grammatical-function 'slot' within that structure, namely that of locative complement.

Syntagmatic links involve dependencies between elements which combine within the same structure, where they fill different slots:

4 Blanche-Benveniste (1990) focuses on speech from a single speaker rather than exchanges between speakers.

(9) A: Does he farm his land <,,> /
B: Uh no / Not really / **In a half-hearted way** /
('He farms his land in a half-hearted way.')
(S1A-073 #180–183)

(10) [context: discussion of recording equipment]
A: That looks [unclear-word] if somebody comes down and starts <,,> /
C: What / **Swearing and cursing** /
('That looks [?] if somebody comes down and starts swearing and cursing.')
(S1A-007 #185–187)

In (9) the bolded fragment links to A's structure by 'extending' it, adding an adjunct to the clause.[5] In (10) the bolded fragment links to A's preceding structure by 'completing' it, supplying the missing complement of *starts* and using present-participial verb forms to fit this grammatical context. C offers her completion as a guess at the kind of objection A was intending to raise (though it is apparent from C's tone and the context that she is dismissing his objection rather than endorsing it).

Combinations of matching and extending also occur:

(11) A: I had it in that garage for *nearly thirty years* /
B: Did you really /
A: **An awfully long time anyway** /
('I had it in the garage for an awfully long time, anyway.')
(S1A-007 #80–82)

Here A, after B's response *Did you really*, downgrades his original claim about duration to a vaguer one. The NP *an awfully long time* matches to his earlier NP *nearly thirty years*, while the adverb *anyway* extends the clause as an adjunct.

Along the discourse-pragmatic dimension, a basic distinction is that between other-speaker (OS) and same-speaker (SS) linkages. Examples (8) to (10) showed OS-links: the fragments uttered by one speaker link back to a structure uttered by a different speaker. Such OS linkages are perhaps the more obvious examples of clause fragments. However, we also find SS links which show some parallels to OS links. Example (11) shows an SS linkage with an intervening brief response from another speaker. As another example, consider the stretch of speech from B in (12), comprising four units in the corpus:

5 This type is termed 'sprouting' by Culicover and Jackendoff (2005), following Chung et al. (1995), but 'extending' seems more transparent.

(12) B: My sister and I were going to get a picture of of she and I done /
Well we've been meaning to do it through this friend of mine who's a photographer for about <,,> four years /
Just never got round to it /
For my mum and dad /
('My sister and I were going to get a picture of she and I done for my mum and dad.')
(S1A-015 #48–51)

Here, the bolded fragment can either link back to *We've been meaning to do it* [...] *for about <,,> four years*, or link back across further intervening material to extend *My sister and I were going to get a picture of she and I done*, in both cases by adding a clausal adjunct. A hearer may not retain the exact form of the earlier structure in memory, but would nonetheless arrive at an understanding that the intended beneficiaries of the planned action were the speaker's parents. ss-linked fragments vary as to what separates the antecedent structure and fragment, ranging from further ss talk, to a short os response (e.g. *Oh*; *Yeah*), a longer contribution from os, an exchange sequence, or just a break in prosody. There is in fact a fuzzy analytical boundary between ss-linked fragments and elements treated as loosely attached parts within a single unit of utterance. Various kinds of loose attachments such as parentheticals, afterthoughts, and dislocations have been discussed in the literature, and are grouped together by Kaltenböck et al. (2011) as 'theticals' which show special properties not adequately captured in standard grammatical accounts (see also e.g. Dehé and Kavalova 2007 and Dehé 2014 on parentheticals). Elements parsed in ICE-GB as loose attachments *within* parsing units have not been included in the present study; the relationship between fragments and various types of theticals is an area for further corpus research. It is not obvious without further empirical research which is the best way to classify all these phenomena; our approach here is to start with a defined subset whose members seem to show shared properties.[6]

For convenience, we will use the labels 'match', 'extension', and 'completion' to refer to fragments which engage in matching, extending, and completing links respectively. The term 'antecedent (structure)' will be used for the structure

6 An anonymous reviewer suggests that we remove the fuzzy boundary between ss-linked fragments and loose attachments by altering our definition, for instance by requiring that there be a change of speaker or intervening material between fragment and antecedent. However, in our view doing this would mean losing sight of the parallels that we see between os and ss instances and between instances with and without intervening material.

TABLE 12.2 *Definitions of fragment types*

Fragment type	interpretable as …
match	an alternative constituent of an antecedent structure in context
extension	an added constituent of an already complete antecedent structure in context
match-and-extension	a combination of match and extension constituents
completion	a constituent which completes an incomplete antecedent structure in context

in context to which the fragment links. The distinction between match and extension is inspired by that between 'matching' and 'sprouting' made by Culicover and Jackendoff (2005) in discussing 'bare argument ellipsis' in speaker exchanges—our OS-linked fragments. For SS continuations, a similar distinction has been made between 'replacements' and 'increments' by the conversation analysts Couper-Kuhlen and Ono (2007). We apply the distinction more generally, to cover both OS and SS linkages, and to include examples where antecedent and fragment are separated by considerable intervening talk.

Table 12.2 gives summary definitions of the different types of clause fragments on the grammatical dimension. Each type can be OS-linked or SS-linked on the discourse-pragmatic dimension.

Table 12.3 shows the classifications made for the fragments in our collection. The majority of examples are matches or extensions. Overall, matches are considerably more frequent than extensions, and OS links are considerably more frequent than SS links (but note the comments above about the fuzzy boundary for SS links). Only 7 examples (all SS ones) are not assigned to a defined category.[7]

Clear instances of OS completions are few in the data, rather surprisingly. Possible instances may sometimes be obscured by overlapping or closely sequenced speech. Examples have been discussed in the literature, for instance by Szczepek (2000a, 2000b) in her work on collaborative productions. The rarity of SS completions in the data is less surprising, as a completing element is likely to have been parsed as part of a single larger PU to make it complete, even if the completion is separated from the rest of the structure by a pause or by SS parenthetical material (or possibly even by a minimal, backchannel OS response).

7 Some of the percentages appear not to total correctly, but this is due to rounding.

TABLE 12.3 *Types of fragment in collection*

	OS	SS	TOTAL
match	95 (42.6%)	41 (18.4%)	136 (61%)
extension	41 (18.4%)	21 (9.4%)	62 (27.8%)
match-and-extension	5 (2.2%)	7 (3.1%)	12 (5.4%)
completion	5 (2.2%)	1 (0.4%)	6 (2.7%)
other	0 (0%)	7 (3.1%)	7 (3.1%)
Total	146 (65.5%)	77 (34.5%)	223 (100%)

The figures reported above are intended simply to give a rough indication of relative frequencies of fragment types in dialogue. Proportions are likely to vary with text type (or genre), but this can only be tested with a much larger study which systematically compares different text types. It also seems likely, however, that numerous other factors will affect the proportions—such as number of participants, relationships between participants, interaction styles, and even the type of topic(s) under discussion—making for a more complex picture.

In the next two sections we report in detail on the two most frequent types, extensions and matches. The main aim is to survey the territory, providing a qualitative description of the kinds of examples that occur. Any comments on relative frequencies are made on the basis of the collection described above; however, we also cite some examples from elsewhere in the corpus or from the literature, in order to achieve fuller descriptive coverage.

Extensions

We have seen that an extension is a fragment which can be interpreted as an added constituent of an already complete antecedent structure in the context. In this section we discuss extensions by another speaker and by the same speaker.

Other-Speaker Extensions

In a further grammatical analysis of extensions, we can identify the grammatical functions that these added constituents can be interpreted as filling within the antecedent structure. We find instances of identifiable functions at the level of the clause or the phrase, and other examples where the functions are harder to identify.

Clausal Extensions

The most common function in our data is that of clausal adjunct (or 'adverbial'). More than half the 41 examples of OS extensions in the collection have this function. Examples of this type have various formal realizations: PPs, subordinate clauses,[8] and AdvPs are common, but NPs also occur. They express a range of meanings, including time, reason, modality, condition, manner, and degree. They occur with a range of different types of discourse-exchange functions, but nonetheless can all be seen as involving extension in *grammatical* (rather than discourse-actional) terms. We illustrate some of this range of possibilities below. We also note various kinds of 'adjustment' to the antecedent structure which are needed to reach an interpretation.

Example (13) involves a question–answer exchange, while (14) and (15) involve statement–question exchanges seeking clarification and further information respectively:

(13) =(9) A: Does he farm his land <,,> /
B: Uh no / Not really / **In a half-hearted way** /
('He farms his land in a half-hearted way.')
(S1A-073 #180–183)

(14) A: I'm going to try and have Wednesday off /
B: Yeah <,> / **This week** /
('You are going to try and have Wednesday off this week?')
(S1A-061 #1–3)

(15) A: How long did you do English for /
A: Uh I did it for about half a term <,,> /
B: **When** /
('When did you do it (for about half a term)?')
(S1A-006 #1–3)

Interpretation of these examples requires adjustment of illocutionary force (question to statement or vice versa) and sometimes of the person of pro-

8 There are good arguments that the subordinate clauses in question should in fact be analysed as PPs headed by prepositions taking clausal complements (Huddleston and Pullum et al. 2002). However, as the analysis is not at stake here, we use the more familiar term, as in the ICE-GB grammatical analysis (based on Quirk et al. 1985).

nouns (*I* to *you*). A fragment can also answer a question expressed indirectly by a subordinate interrogative clause:

(16) B: I don't know *if it would be cheaper to do it in her name* / but I don't think /
A: No / Not if / **Not if we're using your no claims bonus** <,,> /
('It would not be cheaper to do it in her name if we're using your no claims bonus.')
(S1B-080 #278–282)

The interpretation here involves an adjustment which 'extracts' the subordinate clause in italics and makes it a main clause.[9] This kind of example is evidence against a 'strict structural ellipsis' account, to which we return later on.

In the following examples, fragments are used to express disagreement (17) or agreement (18) with a statement uttered by the other speaker:

(17) C: It could just get nicked /
A: No / **Not if if we put it somewhere special like** <,> /
I haven't thought of it yet /
('It wouldn't get nicked if we put it somewhere special.')
(S1A-030 #186–188)

(18) [context: two friends are discussing plans for an outing]
A: Well Xepe seems to love this idea of having a picnic but I'm not too sure about {this} /
B: **{Not} if you've had lunch** /
('Having a picnic is not a good idea if you've had lunch.')
(S1A-006 #28–29)

Note that the disagreement in (17) involves contrasting polarity (positive–negative), while the agreement in (18) is expressed by the matching polarity (negative–negative). In (18) B seems to be supporting A's objection to Xepe's idea. Here a strict ellipsis account would again certainly not work. We return to examples (16) and (18) below.

So far we have discussed examples where the discourse exchange involves 'reverse directionality' of address (Lerner 2004; Sidnell 2012): the speaker of the fragment is responding in some way to the speaker of the antecedent structure (e.g. by answering, questioning, agreeing, or disagreeing). We also find examples where the directionality of address stays the same: where there is

9 The interpretations offered are intended as glosses of the meanings arrived at, rather than indications of hidden underlying structures.

'co-construction' by two speakers addressing one or more others. Examples from the literature often involve 'co-telling', where two speakers who both have knowledge of something are telling about it to another who lacks that knowledge, as in (19):

(19) Cathy: She had this big hairy mole you know those kinds really gross ones
Cindy: **on her neck**
Terri: Oh how disgusting
('She had this big hairy mole on her neck.')
(quoted from Lerner 1992, 263; some transcription details omitted[10] and a gloss added)

In our data there is a rather different kind of example, involving 'co-arguing' rather than co-telling:

(20) A: You can't blame her for that really {can you} /
B: **{If you} gave it to her {Dad}** /
A: {No} /
('You can't blame her for that if you gave it to her.')
(S1A-007 #17–19)

The first comment is addressed by A to her husband, following a sequence where he has been expressing his annoyance that he is now unable to use something that he gave a while ago to a neighbour. A makes the point that it is unreasonable to blame the neighbour for this. B, their daughter, chimes in (in overlap with A's tag question) to support her mother's point, adding the vocative *Dad* which is appropriate from her point of view. In overlap with this vocative, her mother chimes in with *No* to support her daughter's addition. Out of context, one might take B's conditional clause to be of the free-standing kind used to make a suggestion ('I suggest you give it to her, Dad'; see Mato-Míguez, this volume). However, the context makes it clear that he has already given it to the neighbour (to his regret), supporting our co-construction interpretation where B's clause is linked to A's preceding utterance.

As well as clear instances of adjunct function, we also find a few examples where the fragment is more closely related to the verb of the antecedent structure and so more complement-like in function, if we allow for optional clausal

10 We have omitted some of the details of pronunciation and delivery for the sake of simplicity, as the transcription conventions used are different and the details are not at issue here.

complements and consider other criteria for complement status. For instance, Huddleston and Pullum et al. (2002, 219–228) discuss multiple criteria. For them the most important one is licensing, that is, that a complement depends on the presence of an appropriate verb which licenses it, i.e. the verb is subcategorized to take that kind of complement. Consider (21):

(21) A: Uhm <,,> well I've learnt it /
B: **From him** /
A: Yeah /
('Have you learnt it from him?')
(S1A-015 #197–199)

Here B's question fragment *from him* expresses the semantic role of 'source', which is somewhat restricted in the verbs it can occur with, though it is not obligatory to express it with *learn*.[11]

Phrasal Extensions

Extensions at the level of the phrase are also found, although there are only a few in the collection. The following examples involve extensions to noun phrases:

(22) [context: A tells about a lunch given by her doctoral supervisor]
B: Was she cooking it yeah /
A: **Yeah and her husband** /
('She and her husband were cooking it.')
(S1A-039 #48–49)

(23) B: Do you send electronic mail to people that you know though /
A: **Yes and that I don't know** /
('I send electronic mail to people that I know and that I don't know.')
(S1A-015 #9–10)

In (22) we have an NP coordinate which extends the subject NP. Note that adjustment is required to 'insert' the coordinate to arrive at the interpretation. In (23) A adds a coordinate relative clause which extends the post-modification of the head noun *people*.

The following examples involve extension to adjective phrases:

11 Examples where fragments fill an obligatory complement are of course classified as completions since they link to structurally incomplete antecedents.

(24) B: Is uh <,> Giles being energetic about life at the moment /
A: **Oh very yes yeah** /
('Giles is being very energetic about life at the moment.')
(S1A-095 #246–247)

(25) Mike: I'm a committed kinda guy [pause]
Jess: Uh huh [pause] **To everything?**
Mike: Everything
('Are you committed to everything?')
(quoted from Stivers 2010, 2779; some transcription details omitted[12] and a gloss has been added)

In (24), the interpretation requires 'insertion' of *very* into pre-modifying position before the head *energetic*. Example (25) is an interesting one from the literature, where greater adjustment is required for the interpretation, involving 'extraction' of *committed* from its pre-modifying position to a predicative function in the proposition: we would not normally say *Are you a committed-to-everything kinda guy?* (although it is not impossible), but would more naturally say *Are you committed to everything?*

In examples (24) and (25), the speaker could alternatively have used a fragment which included a phrasal head as well as a modifier: *Oh very energetic* in (24) and *Committed to everything?* in (25). These would achieve a very similar effect, but would be analysed grammatically as matches, since they match to phrases in the antecedent structure (with adjustment to predicative function again needed for *committed*). For the examples involving coordination cited earlier, we can also compare possible match alternatives where the entire coordinated structure is uttered instead of just a second coordinate, e.g. *she and her husband* instead of just *and her husband* in (22).

Other Kinds of Extension

We also find examples which are less straightforward to analyse as clausal and phrasal extensions than those discussed above. These often involve loosely linked fragments introduced by elements such as *like*:

(26) [context: B is talking about Edam cheese]
B: I mean it's {all right} thinly sliced with a with an apple I suppose /
A: {Uhm} / **Like Gruyère** /
B: Well that's entirely a different thing /
(S1A-061 #355–358)

12 As in example (19), we have omitted some of the details of pronunciation and delivery for the sake of simplicity. The question mark (used in the original) indicates rising intonation.

(27) A: But I still got I got some even larger ones at Bow but I left those behind in the attic when we sold <,,> /
C: **Along with the other things you left there** <,> /
A: **Such as what** <,> /
(S1A-007 #145–147)

These fragments seem structurally more ambiguous, making it less obvious at what level in the sentence they attach. In (26) A offers a comment, which B rejects, that there is a similarity between Gruyère and Edam, but it is not clear whether this fragment links loosely to B's preceding description of Edam at a clausal level ('Edam is all right thinly sliced with an apple, I suppose, like Gruyère') or at a phrasal level to the subject ('Edam, like Gruyère, is all right thinly sliced…'). In (27), which incidentally shows how several fragments can occur in succession, forming a chain of links, C's fragment serves to comment that A also left other things behind, and we could interpret her phrase as linking loosely to *those* as a post-modifier, i.e. 'but you left those, along with the other things you left there, behind'. Alternatively, we can interpret it as a peripheral extension of the clause *I left those behind…*, i.e. 'but you left those behind in the attic when we sold, along with the other things you left there' (with pronoun adjustment). A's subsequent question *Such as what?* then links loosely to the NP *the other things you left there.*[13]

Same-Speaker Extensions

Among the 21 SS extensions in the collection, there are also instances of clausal extension by adjuncts (e.g. of time, place, reason), phrasal extension by coordinates, and other looser linkages. In about half the examples there is intervening material from OS, SS, or both speakers, while in other instances there is just an intervening pause or break in intonation. In discourse terms, SS extensions seem to simply continue the speaker's preceding act (e.g. statement, question, directive), modifying the propositional content in some way.

The following example was cited as (12) above as one involving considerable intervening SS material; the fragment adds a clausal adjunct, which indicates the beneficiary of the intended action referred to in the first unit:

13 An anonymous referee suggests that maybe the fragments in examples (26) and (27) should be explained by making reference to pragmatic links, but it is not clear what such an account would look like, and how it could be implemented. We conclude that although we are dealing with structural ambiguities here, a grammatical account of these examples is still feasible.

(28) =(12) B: My sister and I were going to get a picture of of she and I done /
Well we've been meaning to do it through this friend of mine who's a photographer for about <,,> four years /
Just never got round to it /
For my mum and dad /
('My sister and I were going to get a picture of she and I done for my mum and dad.')
(S1A-015 #48–51)

In the following examples, there is intervening material from another speaker (the first two turns in (29) were cited as (18) above):

(29) [context: two friends are discussing plans for an outing]
A: Well Xepe seems to love this idea of having a picnic but I'm not too sure about {this} /
B: {Not} if you've had lunch /
A: **Because I'll have eaten anyway** /
('I'm not too sure about this because I'll have eaten anyway.')
(S1A-006 #28–30)

(30) [context: B is describing the location of a cafe]
B: It was just by the market <,> just down some steps /
B: It was just you know the market in Cambridge it was yeah /
A: What in the Kite <,> /
B: I don't know /
A: **Or in the middle of town** /
B: In the in the middle of town /
A: Oh right /
('(Was it) in the Kite or in the middle of town?')
(S1A-015 #260–266)

In (29) A seems to extend his earlier statement without taking account of B's intervening comment. His fragment adds a clausal adjunct expressing reason. In (30) A adds a PP coordinate which extends his previous PP fragment *What in the Kite*, linking across an intervening *I don't know* from B.

We noted above that there is some analytical fuzziness with SS-linked elements as to when to treat the added element as a fragment unit separate from the antecedent and when to treat it as an attachment inside the antecedent. Compare the following examples where, in each case, the bolded unit seems to be tacked on as an afterthought by the speaker, following a pause and an intonational break:

(31) B: You're all wonderful in your own way <,> /
Except Luke <,> /
('You're all wonderful in your own way, except Luke.')
(S1A-069 #76–77)

(32) B: He's going hill-walking / No / He's not /
He's going walking that's all <,> **next week** /
('He's going walking next week.')
(S1A-017 #279–282)

Similar examples have been discussed in the Conversation Analysis literature as 'increments' or 'extensions' (Schegloff 2000; Ford et al. 2002). In (31) the bolded unit has been parsed as a separate unit in the corpus, while in (32) it has been included within a clausal unit despite the prosodic break (and the intervening comment clause *that's all*). Further research is needed to investigate the exact nature of this boundary area, looking also at elements like that in (32) which have been analysed as internal attachments. The relevant point here is simply that there are grammatical parallels between OS and SS fragments—we find similar extension types for both. It is noteworthy that speakers can interpret links between antecedent and fragment/attachment across various different kinds of 'break' between them, whether a prosodic break, a change of speaker, or intervening talk.

Matches

A match can be interpreted as an alternative constituent of an antecedent structure in the context. In this section we discuss OS matches and SS matches.

Other-Speaker Matches

OS matches are the most frequent kind of fragment in our collection, with 95 examples (43%). They match to constituents with a wide range of functions in antecedent structures (e.g. predicative complement, direct object, subject, clausal adjunct, complement of preposition in PPs with various functions). Rather than looking at these grammatical functions, it seems more revealing to consider the lexical-semantic relationships between the fragment and the constituent to which it matches, and to illustrate the wide variety of discourse acts that matches are used to perform. Note that there is often a chain effect, whereby one match fragment links to another fragment which in turn links to a larger antecedent structure, or where there is a longer sequence of fragments before the ultimate link to a larger structure; we have analysed such examples in terms of the immediate link in the first instance.

One common use of matches is to answer *wh*-questions, which involves a semantic relationship of 'filling in' the value of a variable. (33) shows a straightforward example; the italics indicates the constituent to which the fragment matches:

(33) A: *What time* is it <,>/
B: **Twenty past eight** /
('It is twenty past eight.')
(S1A-047 #1–2)

A less straightforward example is shown in (34); here C answers an indirect question posed by a subordinate clause within B's utterance:

(34) [context: A and B are discussing a form that C, their daughter, has to complete]
A: Well she probably has to put the number of people occupying the whole property <,> {presumably} /
B: {Well I} don't suppose she knows *how many people* are living in the whole property /
C: Me? /
B: Mhm /
C: **Well at least ten or twenty people** <,,> /
('At least ten or twenty people are living in the whole property.')
(S1A-007 #243–247)

Here it appears from the audio recording that C has temporarily left the scene, and contributes from a distance, first checking that *she* is intended to refer to her. Her answer repeats the head word *people* from the *wh*-phrase, as well as filling in the missing numerical value. Note that the interpretation involves 'extraction' of the embedded subordinate clause: a literal ellipsis account here would give the wrong result.[14]

Matches are also found in various kinds of responses to *yes/no* questions. The following examples show different kinds of semantic relationship between the matched elements:

---

14 We saw a somewhat similar example of adjustment with an extension fragment in (16).

(35) B: Have you / have you still got the other two then / the other two / well *the other two lodgers* /[15]
A: **The other two lodgers** yes /
('I have still got the other two lodgers.')
(S1A-091 #325–329)

(36) [context: ITV interview; A is the interviewer]
A: Robert Runcie it's it's wonderful meeting you just at this point after *ten years* is it {when} you were just leaving St Albans <,,> /
B: {Yes} / **Just over ten years** /
('It is just over ten years.')
(S1B-041 #49, 51, 53)

(37) A: Is Bim *at the Slade* now or not / Did he ever get there /
B: **At Camberwell** /
A: Oh Camberwell /
('Bim is at Camberwell now.')
(S1A-015 #72–5)

In (35) A uses exact repetition of *the other two lodgers* to support her positive-polarity response: B seemed to be uncertain of the term *lodgers*, but A's response affirms its appropriateness. In (36) Runcie responds to the interviewer's parenthetical question by repeating the matched phrase with slight modification (*just over ten years* instead of *ten years*). In (37) (partially repeated from (8)), B's fragment includes a replacement value for *the Slade*, from which a negative answer to A's first question (and presumably the second also) can be deduced (and A then acknowledges this information in a further fragment).

Another use of matches is posing questions, in order to seek further information or clarification, or to challenge what the OS has said:

(38) [context: discussion of gardening, using glass panes to protect young seedlings]
A: I'm peeved about that giving her *that window* / I was a fool / I was wasn't growing seeds then of course /
C: **What window?** /
('What window are you peeved about giving her?')
(S1A-007 #7–10)

15 The corpus division into units seems anomalous here, as self-corrections are generally included within the same parsing unit as the corrected elements.

(39) [context: A is explaining how he injured his foot]
A: Uhm I was *on the way to the pub* one evening and {stone cold sober} decided to leap over this little wall <,> /
B: {**On the way to the pub not on the way back**} /
('You were on the way to the pub not on the way back?')
(S1A-047 #266, 277)

We could gloss C's question in (38) simply as 'What window do you mean?'. However, in the specific context of A's statement it is more likely that C is asking which window A was annoyed about giving away. The reason is that C's fragment repeats the head noun *window*, and substitutes a contrasting term in the determiner slot—replacing *that*, which indicates definite reference, with a *wh*-form, to indicate that clarification is needed. In (39) B issues a joking challenge to A's claim to have been on the way to the pub when the mishap occurred, humorously implying that A may have been under the influence of alcohol at the time.[16]

Matches can also be used to indicate agreement or disagreement with the OS, as in the following exchange with a sequence of matches:

(40) B: I don't want great big life-size photographs of *relatives* hanging on the wall thank you /
C: **Especially not that side of the family** <laugh> /
A: **Any side of the family thank you from that era** /
(C: 'You/We especially don't want photographs of that side of the family.')
(A: 'I/We don't want photographs of any side of the family from that era.')
(S1A-007 #160–162)

Here C expresses agreement with B's feelings about the photographs of relatives but indicates she finds it especially applicable to a particular side of the family. Her fragment in fact combines matching with extending, as *especially* functions like an added clausal adjunct. A, in contrast, insists that it is applicable to *any* side of the family from that era. Note the chain of lexical-semantic relationships between *relatives*, *that side of the family*, and *any side of the family*.

Matches are also used to express acknowledgement of, or reaction to, what the OS has said. We saw an example in (37) above, where A acknowledges the

16 This fragment is analysed as a match rather than an extension: the speaker has repeated the original PP and added a coordinate PP introduced by *not*, and the whole coordination can be interpreted as filling the function of the original PP.

new information that Bim is at Camberwell (rather than the Slade) by combining the discourse marker *Oh* with simple repetition of the focal term (*Oh Camberwell*). Another example is given below, where the first fragment is the OS match and the second (*Her own mother*) is analysed as an SS match to the first:

(41) A: *She* called Karen a dirty Jewess /
B: **Her mother** / Her own mother /
('Her (own) mother called her a dirty Jewess!')
(S1A-036 #22, 24–25)

Here it is evident from the audio recording that B is reacting with outrage to what she has been told; she does so by using alternative referential expressions which stress the relationship between the two people in the situation described, as this makes it all the more shocking.

The above examples have illustrated a range of lexical-semantic relationships between the matched elements. Lexical repetition is commonly found. Of the 95 OS match examples in the collection, around a quarter involve simple repetition and another quarter involve other kinds of repetition. We have seen examples of repetition with addition by coordination or modification (e.g. *ten years* changed to *just over ten years* in (36)), and of partial repetition with substitution to express a contrast (e.g. *that side of the family* changed to *any side of the family* in (40)), or to fill in a value (e.g. *how many people* changed to *at least ten or twenty people* in (34)). We have seen other instances with no repetition, but still involving clearly identifiable semantic relationships between matched elements (e.g. *what time* and the time specification *twenty past eight* in (33); *relatives* and the semantically similar term *family* in *that side of the family* in (40); *she* and the coreferential expression *her mother* in (41)).

These lexical-semantic relationships help to make dialogues cohesive. Quite often the relationships occur in chains, giving a layering effect, as seen in (40) above. This means that a fragment quite often matches most immediately to another fragment, rather than to a clausal antecedent. Another example of chaining is set out in (42) below, with the matching elements bolded and aligned to show their paradigmatic relationships more clearly.

(42)				
	B: Have you got	**any**	**white**	**wine** /
	A:	**Any**	**what** /	
	B:		**White**	**wine** /
	A: Do we have to take	**a bottle of**		**wine** /
	B: Yeah	**A cheap bottle** /		
	(S1A-038 #208–213)			

Same-Speaker Matches

For SS matches we see patterns of lexical-semantic relationships which are often similar to those seen in OS matches, including repeated elements and semantically related elements. Around half the 41 examples in the collection involve some repetition, sometimes simple repetition, but most often repetition with some alteration. In terms of discourse acts, SS matches often serve simply to emphasize or modify in some way part of the speaker's own prior utterance:

(43) A: It's all frosted glass / It's *{almost} opaque* /
B: {Oh} / Oh /
A: **Almost opaque** <,,> /
(S1A-007 #43–47)

(44) A: Well I quite like that *sort of quininey taste* that grapefruit has /
Slightly bitter taste you know /
(S1A-009 #60–61)

In (43) we have a simple repetition, whereas in (44) the matched elements provide alternative, semantically compatible descriptions of the taste of grapefruit.

In other instances, SS matches are part of a chain that ultimately links back to an OS antecedent, as with the bolded fragment below:

(45) [context: discussion of family forebears]
A: Because the same era would've been horse copers on your mother's side /
[5 intervening turns]
C: What's *a horse coper* /
A: Well *a horse breaker* /
B: No / I don't know that they all were / I mean that {was just} an uncle /
A: {**A sort of** <,>} **glorified gipsy** /[17]
(S1A-007 #164, 170–176)

Here C, after several intervening turns, asks for clarification of A's term *horse coper*. The latter first responds with the fragment *Well a horse breaker*, and then, after some intervening talk from B, offers the alternative description

17 In the corpus the bolded fragment is divided into two separate units, broken after the pause; we have joined them into a single unit as the division seems erroneous, and added an indication of the overlap we hear.

A sort of glorified gipsy. The latter fragment links back to his own earlier fragment and beyond that to C's question. Again, the two descriptions are compatible; they can be put together to form an idea of what a horse coper is.

Another example of chaining is given in (46):

(46) B: No I mean Auden was extraordinarily ugly /
A: *When he was young* /
Only *when he was old* because he had this skin disease /
B: **When he was old yeah yeah** / but never never /
He always he was always fairly ugly /
(S1A-015 #58–63)

Here A first challenges B's initial statement with an extension, *when he was young*, interpretable as a temporal adjunct ('(Are you saying) Auden was extraordinarily ugly when he was young?'). He then utters a fragment with a contrasting SS-matched component, *when he was old*, accompanied by extending adjuncts ('Auden was only ugly when he was old because he had this skin disease'). B then utters an OS-matched fragment, repeating *when he was old* to indicate partial agreement, before going on to express the contrasting opinion that Auden was always ugly.

We see with SS matches, as we did for SS extensions, a blurred analytical line between fragments linking to separate antecedent structures and peripheral attachments within host structures. In about half the 41 examples in the collection, there is intervening talk from OS, SS, or both speakers—often a short OS reaction such as *oh*, *really*, *yes*. In other instances there is no intervening talk, and judgements about breaks in rhythm or intonation can be fine. There is also a fuzzy area concerning the recognition of peripheral attachments as belonging to particular grammatical constructions. For instance, in (47) the bolded element has a match relationship to the subject *they*, clarifying its reference:

(47) A: *They*'ve got a pet rabbit <,> **{Laura} and her boyfriend Simon** /
B: {Oh mmm} /
(S1A-017 #128–129)

On the audio recording A's clause *They've got a pet rabbit* sounds intonationally complete and there is a distinct pause before he adds *Laura and her boyfriend Simon*. B's minimal response overlaps with the start of this addition. In this case the matching element is parsed in the corpus as a 'detached function' element within the clause. It can be taken as an instance of the grammatical construction recognized in the literature as 'right dislocation' (e.g. Geluykens 1994), which typically involves a relationship of coreferentiality between a pronominal constituent in the clause and an NP loosely attached at the end of the clause. However, we could also see it as one subtype of a broader range of loosely attached matching elements (compare (44), for instance). Couper-Kuhlen and Ono (2007) have a broader category of this kind called 'replacement', which includes right dislocations but also similar examples with phrase types other than NPs; they cite an example *I'd like to be like that / **Bilingual**,* where the adjective *bilingual* is added after a pause and intonational break, and 'replaces' (or matches) *like that* in predicative complement function. Further corpus study is needed to examine the boundary line between SS-linked match fragments and loose attachments.

Against a 'Strict Ellipsis' Account

Earlier in the chapter we mentioned work by Culicover and Jackendoff (2005), who argue against what we have called the 'strict ellipsis' account, i.e. "the idea that underlying every elliptical utterance has to be a Sentence, i.e. a tensed clause" (2005, 236). In support of their argument Culicover and Jackendoff first cite numerous made-up free-standing examples of what they call "nonsentential utterance types" which they argue "cannot be derived in any useful sense from sentences" (2005, 236).[18] Here follows a selection: *Hello; Off with his head!; Seatbelts fastened!; How about going to the movies?; John drunk?; Excuse me, doctor; One more step and I'll shoot.*

One major argument against positing a full underlying clausal analysis for such structures is that "[f]or the theorist to introduce an underlying verb, whether contentful or semantically empty, only to delete it in the course of the derivation, simply begs the question" (2005, 237). Culicover and Jackendoff argue that such utterance frames can be learnt: a child only needs to acquire their structure and meaning, and "[t]here is no point in requiring the child also to learn a derivation of the surface frame from an abstract full sentence that explains nothing further about the interpretation" (2005, 237).

These examples are described as 'free-standing' because their interpretation does not depend on a link to an antecedent structure. They differ from clause fragments in that regard, and we therefore excluded such examples as type (d) when presenting our definition of clause fragments. However, the free-standing types establish that non-sentential utterance structures are

18 In doing so, they acknowledge earlier work by Shopen (1972) and Fillmore et al. (1988).

needed in the grammar in any case, opening the way for an analysis of fragments which similarly "posits no more syntactic structure than appears at the surface" (Culicover and Jackendoff 2005, 235). To account for fragments, Culicover and Jackendoff put forward a modified version of the "direct interpretation hypothesis", a term coined by Merchant (2001), which holds that "the unexpressed parts of the fragment's interpretation are supplied not through underlying syntactic structure but via direct correspondence with the meaning of the antecedent sentence" (2005, 234–235).[19] Culicover and Jackendoff propose a mechanism they call "indirect licensing" to account for the semantic and syntactic relationship of the fragment to its antecedent. They point out that a strict ellipsis account runs into problems when the interpretation of the fragment requires 'adjustment' of aspects of the antecedent (e.g. illocutionary force, the use of *you* vs. *I*/*me*, the embedding of clauses).

Although it is not our aim in this chapter to offer a full critique of the strict ellipsis account, our exploration of corpus data lends credence to an account like Culicover and Jackendoff's, as our discussion of authentic examples in this chapter will have made clear. Consider again examples (16) and (18), repeated here as (48) and (49):

(48) =(16) B: I don't know *if it would be cheaper to do it in her name* / but I don't think /
A: No / Not if / **Not if we're using your no claims bonus** <,,> /
('It would not be cheaper to do it in her name if we're using your no claims bonus.')
(S1B-080 #278–282)

(49) =(18) [context: two friends are discussing plans for an outing]
A: Well Xepe seems to love this idea of having a picnic but I'm not too sure about {this} /
B: **{Not} if you've had lunch** /
('Having a picnic is not a good idea if you've had lunch.')
(S1A-006 #28–29)

As we have already noted above, the disagreement in (48) involves opposite polarities (positive–negative), while the agreement in (49) is expressed by identical polarities (negative–negative): this requires 'adjustment' of the antecedents by 'inserting' negation at a higher level. Notice also that grammatically in (48) the antecedent involves an *if*-clause complementing the verb *know*,

19 Merchant himself favours a 'strict ellipsis' account, which he calls the 'deletion hypothesis'. For recent work, see van Craenenbroeck and Merchant (2013), and Xiang et al. (2014).

whereas A's response is paraphrased by turning that interrogative subordinate clause into a declarative main clause (within which a conditional *if*-clause functions as an added adjunct). In (49) B seems to be supporting A's objection to Xepe's idea: the intended interpretation is not 'You're not too sure about this if you've had lunch', but rather something like 'Having a picnic is not a good idea if you've had lunch'. Thus, for an ellipsis account to work in examples like (48) and (49) there would have to be considerable syntactic and pragmatic adjustment.

Conclusion

In this chapter we have focused on clause fragments as a subset of non-sentential utterances which are distinguishable by grammatical and discourse criteria, and which are worthy of attention in terms of their linkage to antecedent structures in context. Examples were identified in the ICE-GB dialogues through a combination of grammatical searches and hand analysis of examples in their discourse contexts. We argued that two frequent grammatical subtypes can be distinguished: extensions, which link on the syntagmatic dimension, being interpretable as added constituents of antecedent structures in context, and matches, which link on the paradigmatic dimension, being interpretable as alternative constituents of antecedent structures in context. Each type can link to either a same-speaker or an other-speaker antecedent structure, and each can fulfil a wide range of discourse functions. Through grammatical fitting to antecedent structures and lexical-semantic relationships to constituents in antecedent structures, fragments contribute to discourse cohesion. In the case of linkages involving a same-speaker antecedent, we have seen that there is a fuzzy boundary between fragments, seen as separate but linked units, and loose attachments, seen as parts of single larger units. Further corpus research is needed to investigate the boundary area between fragments and loose attachments. Finally, based on authentic corpus examples we also argued that a 'strict ellipsis' account of clause fragments is untenable.

Corpus

ICE-GB *International Corpus of English, the British Component*. 1998. Project coordinated by the Survey of English Usage, University College London. http://ice-corpora.net/ice/icegb.htm.

References

Blakemore, Diane. 2006. "Divisions of Labour: The Analysis of Parentheticals." *Lingua* 116: 1670–87.

Blanche-Benveniste, Claire. 1990. "Un Modèle d'Analyse Syntaxique 'en Grilles' pour les Productions Orales." *Anuario de Psicología* 47: 11–28.

Chung, Sandra, William Ladusaw, and James McClosky. 1995. "Sluicing and Logical Form." *Natural Language Semantics* 3: 239–82.

Couper-Kuhlen, Elizabeth, and Tsuyoshi Ono. 2007. "'Incrementing' in Conversation: A Comparison of Practices in English, German and Japanese." *Pragmatics* 17/4: 513–52.

Craenenbroeck, Jeroen van, and Jason Merchant. 2013. "Ellipsis Phenomena." In *The Cambridge Handbook of Generative Syntax*, edited by Marcel den Dikken, 1427–520. Cambridge: Cambridge University Press.

Culicover, Peter W., and Ray Jackendoff. 2005. *Simpler Syntax*. Oxford: Oxford University Press.

Dehé, Nicole. 2014. *Parentheticals in Spoken English: The Syntax–Prosody Relation*. Cambridge: Cambridge University Press.

Dehé, Nicole, and Yordanka Kavalova (eds.). 2007. *Parentheticals*. Amsterdam and Philadelphia: John Benjamins.

Fernández, Raquel, Jonathan Ginzburg, and Shalom Lappin. 2007. "Classifying Non-Sentential Utterances in Dialogue: A Machine Learning Approach." *Computational Linguistics* 33/3: 397–427.

Fillmore, Charles J., Paul Kay, and Mary C. McConnor. 1988. "Regularity and Idiomaticity in Grammatical Constructions: The Case of *Let Alone*." *Language* 64/3: 501–39.

Ford, Cecilia E., Barbara A. Fox, and Sandra A. Thompson. 2002. "Constituency and the Grammar of Turn Increments." In *The Language of Turn and Sequence*, edited by Cecilia E. Ford, Barbara A. Fox, and Sandra A. Thompson, 14–38. Oxford: Oxford University Press.

Geluykens, Ronald. 1994. *The Pragmatics of Discourse Anaphora in English: Evidence from Conversational Repair*. Berlin: Mouton de Gruyter.

Greenbaum, Sidney, and Gerald Nelson. 1999. "Elliptical Clauses in Spoken and Written English." In *The Clause in English: In Honour of Rodney Huddleston*, edited by Peter Collins, and David A. Lee, 111–25. Amsterdam and Philadelphia: John Benjamins.

Huddleston, Rodney, and Geoffrey K. Pullum, et al. 2002. *The Cambridge Grammar of the English Language*. Cambridge: Cambridge University Press.

Kaltenböck, Gunther, Bernd Heine, and Tania Kuteva. 2011. "On Thetical Grammar." *Studies in Language* 35/4: 852–97.

Lerner, Gene H. 1992. "Assisted Storytelling: Deploying Shared Knowledge as a Practical Matter." *Qualitative Sociology* 15/3: 247–71.

Lerner, Gene H. 2004. "On the Place of Linguistic Resources in the Organization of Talk-in-Interaction: Grammar as Action in Prompting a Speaker to Elaborate." *Research on Language and Social Interaction* 37/2: 151–84.

Merchant, Jason. 2001. *The Syntax of Silence*. Oxford: Oxford University Press.

Nelson, Gerald, Sean Wallis, and Bas Aarts. 2002. *Exploring Natural Language: Working with the British Component of the International Corpus of English*. Amsterdam and Philadelphia: John Benjamins.

Quirk, Randolph, Sidney Greenbaum, Geoffrey Leech, and Jan Svartvik. 1985. *A Comprehensive Grammar of the English Language*. London: Longman.

Schegloff, Emanuel A. 2000. "On Turns' Possible Completion, More or Less: Increments and Trail-offs." Paper presented at the Euro-Conference on Interactional Linguistics, Spa, September 16–21.

Shopen, Timothy. 1972. *A Generative Theory of Ellipsis*. PhD diss., UCLA.

Sidnell, Jack. 2012. "Turn-Continuation by Self and by Other." *Discourse Processes* 49: 314–37.

Stivers, Tanya. 2010. "An Overview of the Question–Response System in American English Conversation." *Journal of Pragmatics* 42/10: 2772–81.

Szczepek, Beatrice. 2000a. "Formal Aspects of Collaborative Productions in English Conversation." *InLiSt—Interaction and Linguistic Structures* 17. http://www.inlist.uni-bayreuth.de/issues/17/index.htm.

Szczepek, Beatrice. 2000b. "Functional Aspects of Collaborative Productions in English Conversation," *InLiSt—Interaction and Linguistic Structures* 21. http://www.inlist.uni-bayreuth.de/issues/21/index.htm.

Xiang, Ming, Julian Grove, and Jason Merchant. 2014. *Ellipsis Sites Induce Structural Priming Effects*. Ms., University of Chicago.

PART 4

Corpus Insights into the Pragmatics of Spoken English

CHAPTER 13

The Expression of Directive Meaning: A Corpus-Based Study on the Variation between Imperatives, Conditionals, and Insubordinate *If*-Clauses in Spoken British English*

Beatriz Mato-Míguez

Abstract

Directive meaning in English has usually been associated with imperative clauses (e.g. *Move your head a little*), which can be used for a wide range of directive illocutionary acts (commands, requests, wishes). Conditional clauses are also often employed to code directives in uses where conditional meaning is marginal, if present at all, as in *If you move your head a little, I will examine you*. From conditional clauses of this kind, it appears that another type of clause has emerged and become specialized in directive function, the so-called insubordinate *if*-clause (*If you could move your head a little*), which seems to have undergone the process known as 'insubordination' (Evans 2007). This article examines the variation between the different ways of expressing directive meaning in English, looking at evidence from the *Diachronic Corpus of Present-Day Spoken English*. It offers data on the frequencies of use of the various types of clauses under study and analyses the specific illocutionary force conveyed by each of them.

Keywords

insubordination – insubordinate *if*-clauses – imperative clauses – conditional clauses – illocutionary force – directives – spoken English

* For generous financial support I am grateful to the following institutions: European Regional Development Fund, the Spanish Ministry of Economy and Competitiveness (grants FFI2014-52188-P and FFI2014-51873-REDT); the Directorate General for Scientific and Technological Promotion of the Regional Government of Galicia (grants R2014/016 and GPC2014/004); and the Spanish Ministry of Education (grant FPU AP2010-4570). I am also grateful to Teresa Fanego and María José López-Couso as well as two anonymous referees for their comments on earlier versions of this chapter.

 | DOI 10.1163/9789004321342_014

Introduction

The study reported on in this chapter forms part of a larger project on the characteristics of insubordinate *if*-clauses in contemporary English. Insubordination can be defined as "the conventionalized main clause use of what, on prima facie grounds, appear to be formally subordinate clauses" (Evans 2007, 367). Since earlier studies (Stirling 1999; Mato-Míguez 2014) have shown that insubordinate *if*-clauses are typically used to convey directive meaning, it seems necessary to analyse and compare their particular uses and frequencies with those of other types of clauses which can be employed with the same illocutionary force, in particular with imperative clauses, the most common option to express a directive (see, for example, Quirk et al. 1985, 827ff.). Prototypical conditional clauses with directive meaning also need be taken into consideration given that it is in clauses of this type where insubordinate *if*-clauses seem to have their origin. The data discussed in this study are extracted from the *Diachronic Corpus of Present-Day Spoken English* (DCPSE; Aarts and Wallis 2006; 885,000 words). In what follows, I first characterize the different types of clauses under study, namely imperative clauses, conditionals, and insubordinate *if*-clauses. I then proceed to the corpus study, the analysis of the data, and the discussion of results. The final section summarizes the main findings and puts forward some questions for future research.

Characterization of Imperative Clauses, Conditional Clauses with Directive Meaning, and Insubordinate *If*-Clauses

Imperative Clauses

Imperative clauses are described by Huddleston and Pullum et al. (2002) as "a grammatically distinct class of clause whose members are characteristically used to issue directives" (2002, 853). Formally, they differ from declarative clauses in that they usually lack an explicit subject and have a verb in the base form, as in (1), or an auxiliary such as *do* in the base form followed by the infinitive of the main verb, as in (2) (cf. Quirk et al. 1985, 827). Cases with an explicit subject are also possible, as in (3), but this is an optional rather than an obligatory element. The addition of *you* in such instances, according to Huddleston and Pullum et al. (2002, 926), has an emotive effect. In Quirk et al.'s view (1985, 828) the presence of *you* frequently expresses strong irritation or insistence, but can also be used to distinguish the addressee of the action. Another way of making an imperative more insistent or persuasive is by adding *do* before the verb, but only in cases in which the subject is not explicit, as is the case in (2).

(1) Tell me the truth.
(2) Do tell me the truth.
(3) You tell me the truth.

The imperative verb has no tense distinction and does not allow for the presence of modal auxiliaries. Its uses are restricted to predications that enable a dynamic rather than a static interpretation. Moreover, since imperatives refer to an action in the immediate or remote future, they are incompatible with time adverbials referring to past or habitual actions, such as *yesterday*, *usually*, etc.

English imperative clauses can also be formed with the auxiliary *let* preposed to the verb, followed by a subject in the objective case (Quirk et al. 1985, 829), as in (4).

(4) Let's go outside.

Following Huddleston and Pullum et al. (2002, 934–937), three subtypes of *let*-imperatives can be distinguished:

(a) 'first person inclusive *let*-imperatives' where the speaker proposes an action to be carried out together with the addressee, which the addressee can accept or reject, as in (5). According to Collins (2004, 300–301), this *let* has been bleached of its propositional content and serves merely as a marker of illocutionary meaning.

(5) Let's have a break.

(b) 'first person inclusive *let*-imperatives' which are used as expository directives, typically to guide the reader/hearer through an argument, as in (6) (cf. Huddleston and Pullum et al. 2002, 936; Collins 2004, 309ff.). Collins states that these clauses offer a "less authoritarian tone than ordinary imperatives without *let*" (2004, 310), while Huddleston and Pullum et al. (2002, 936) indicate that in cases in which *us* is contracted to *'s*, the directive is less formal.

(6) Let me remind you again how much more different things were in Russia. (from Collins 2004, 310)

(c) 'open *let*-imperatives', as in (7), where *let* is commonly followed by a noun phrase with third person reference. These clauses are used to define a situation the speaker hopes for or thinks to be advisable. They can therefore be used in cases where the speaker refers to an audience rather than to a specific addressee, for example, in newspaper editorials. These uses of *let* are often paraphraseable by *should* or *may* and, as is the case in 'first person inclusive *let*-imperatives', *let* serves as an illocutionary marker rather than to the definition of the referred future action.

(7) Let that be a lesson to you.

Only subtypes (a) and (b) of *let*-imperatives have been taken into consideration in the present chapter. Open *let*-imperatives have been disregarded here since they do not imply directive meaning; the speaker does not instruct any interlocutor to carry out an action. As a matter of fact, Huddleston and Pullum et al. (2002, 934) consider them as "somewhat peripheral members of the speech act category of directives".

As regards the semantics and pragmatics of imperative clauses, Schwager (2006, 241) maintains that the label 'imperative' is taken to denote one of the language form types at sentence level, namely the one whose tokens are prototypically used for requests or commands. As such, they are paralleled by declaratives (used for assertions), exclamatives (for exclamations), and interrogatives (for questions). Portner (2004, 237–238) states that the difference between commands and requests has to do with pragmatic or sociolinguistic issues. Thus, while orders occur when the basis is social authority, requests occur when no social authority is invoked, and the basis is the speaker's or addressee's benefit. As will be seen below, orders and requests are not the only types of speech acts related to imperative clauses, although they are the most common ones and, by far, the most difficult to distinguish.

Conditional Clauses with Directive Meaning and Insubordinate If*-Clauses*

Earlier studies on insubordinate *if*-clauses (cf. Stirling 1999; Mato-Míguez 2014) have shown that constructions of this kind are generally used to express directives. These clauses seem to have emerged from conditional clauses[1] whose meaning is barely hypothetical, as exemplified in (8) to (10).

1 Although no solid evidence of the origin of insubordinate *if*-clauses in English has yet been provided, recent research (cf., for example, Kaltenböck 2014) points in this direction. Also in favour of such a view is the fact that optative *if*-clauses (e.g. *If only you'd told me earlier*) have followed the same process of insubordination from conditional clauses. In addition, conditional clauses are a useful device for issuing directives and softening the face-threatening effect

(8) If you could open your mouth, I will examine you.
(9) If you could open your mouth, that would be nice.
(10) If you could open your mouth.

As Traugott et al. (1986, 7) recognize, "it is invariably found that some sentences with the formal markers of conditionality are semantically and pragmatically only marginally conditional or not conditional at all". This applies to both prototypical conditional clauses with directive meaning, as in (8) and (9), and insubordinate *if*-clauses, as in (10), whose use is related to the issuing of offers, requests, or orders, rather than with the expression of conditional meaning. In such uses, conditionals have been shown to reduce the strength of the imposing force of imperatives since they allow the speaker to sound less intrusive on the hearer's will (Ford 1997, 401). In Brown and Levinson's view, requests and orders, i.e. cases in which the "S[peaker] indicates that he wants H[earer] to do, or to refrain from doing, some act A" (1987, 66), are viewed as a threat to the negative face wants of the addressee, given that the speaker is intruding into the hearer's freedom of action. In situations like this, conditional clauses offer redressive action, that is, an action that attempts to counteract the potential face damage of the addressee by modifying or adding some element that indicates clearly that a face threat is not intended. The indirectness of conditional clauses redresses these potential face-threatening acts and offers the addressee the option to choose if he/she wants to accept the act proposed by the speaker. As regards insubordinate *if*-clauses (cf. (10)), although they are now a distinct type of clause, as will be commented on below, the fact that, arguably, they originate in full conditionals makes them another suitable strategy to avoid face-threatening acts.

Ford and Thompson (1986, 365) discuss the use of insubordinate *if*-clauses to express polite requests, considering that this may be due to the hypotheticality involved in conditionals and also to the fact that they seem to imply alternatives. A consequent clause is very difficult to supply in many of the examples provided by Ford and Thompson, the response from the addressee often reflecting the understood intent of the utterance, as in (11).

---

of this type of act (cf. Brown and Levinson 1987) to the point that expressions of the type *if I may*, *if you would* have become conventionalized as markers of politeness when trying to avoid damage to the face of the hearer. Finally, cross-linguistic evidence (cf., for example, Lombardi Vallauri 2004 for Italian or Schwenter 1996, forthcoming for Spanish *si*-clauses) also seems to indicate that these clauses have emerged from conditionals.

(11) M: But if you'll call Irey over and get together with him on Tuesday or Wednesday, whenever you fellows are ready I'm ready.
J: Yes, all right, that's fine, (from Ford and Thompson 1986, 365)

If-clauses unconnected to a main clause are also discussed in Ford's (1993, 49–50) study, in cases such as (12), which expresses an offer which is contingent on the hearer's choice.

(12) A: Well if you want me (to) give you a ring tomorrow morning.
B: Tch! Well y-you know, let's, eh- I don't know. I'll see maybe I won't be in. (from Ford 1993, 50)

Clauses of this kind, labelled by Ford as "conditional clauses without apodosis", and equivalent to what I am calling insubordinate *if*-clauses, encode options, i.e. they are issued in situations in which the hearer doubts whether or not to accept what is being proposed. In Ford's view, "when one makes an offer [...] an *if*-clause is a workable format for suggesting the plan of action and at the same time displaying a recognition, or conceding to the fact, that the plan is contingent and the other party may prefer another option" (1993, 139). The answers and reactions of the hearers indicate that these *if*-clauses are not considered as ungrammatical or incomplete, thus suggesting the ongoing conventionalization of these structures.

The literature discussed in the preceding paragraphs only comments on insubordinate *if*-clauses in passing, with no further consideration on their pragmatic and/or grammatical features. It is Stirling (1999) who first provides an in-depth analysis of directive insubordinate *if*-clauses ('isolated *if*-clauses' in her terminology) in Australian English. Considering her data, Stirling states that "the speaker uses the isolated *if*-clause with the illocutionary force of a directive, most frequently a request (but in some cases more appropriately categorised as a suggestion)" (1999, 278). Let us consider example (13):

(13) D: Deep breaths... If you'd like to move your head a little. Thank you. (from Stirling 1999, 278)

This use of insubordinate *if*-clauses with directive meaning corresponds to one of the mechanisms of indirection for directives considered by Brown and Levinson (1987, 227), namely ellipsis. If the missing material were reconstructed in Stirling's examples, it would have to do either with the wish of the speaker for the act to be performed or with the ability or readiness of the hearer to perform it. According to Stirling (1999, 281), this relates to the difference between an assertion and an *if*-clause: whereas the former expresses the meaning 'I believe that X', the latter conveys the meaning 'I believe that there is some possibility that X'. The use of an *if*-clause, then, allows the speaker to express that he/she is giving the hearer the option to perform or not what he/she is requesting.

Mato-Míguez (2014) investigates the uses and characteristics of directive insubordinate *if*-clauses in spoken British English, with data from the DCPSE (Aarts and Wallis 2006). The corpus yielded a total of 3,019 occurrences of *if*. Repetitions of the conjunction and *if*s that do not introduce any clause were discarded, leaving a total of 2,867 *if*-clauses. Of these, the vast majority did not convey directive meaning, prototypical conditional clauses in directive function representing only 0.59% of the tokens analysed (17 examples), and directive insubordinate *if*-clauses amounting to 2.02% of the total (52 examples). The majority of examples of directive insubordinate *if*-clauses in the corpus showed a modal verb, mostly one expressing ability or possibility (*can, could, may, might*) in the past form. This is not at all surprising, given that modals are usually associated with particular pragmatic uses, such as requests or offers, where the past forms tend to have implications of politeness (cf. Quirk et al. 1985, 220).

Also relevant in the discussion of directive insubordinate *if*-clauses is their status as either grammatically complete or incomplete utterances. The absence of a main clause may lead to the classification of these clauses as incomplete statements. Following Matthews' (1981, 40–42) definition of incomplete utterances as cases in which the speaker reformulates an utterance in progress or one which is interrupted by another speaker, we would clearly not consider insubordinate *if*-clauses as incomplete in this sense, that is, as grammatically incomplete. All the examples identified as belonging to this category in this study seem to be intended to be complete. Moreover, ellipsis, understood along the lines of Quirk et al. (1985), Huddleston and Pullum et al. (2002), and other standard reference grammars, that is, as a process of reduction through the omission of some elements, does not apply here either. Let us consider the characteristics for elliptical clauses summarized in Quirk et al. (1985, 888):

(a) The ellipted words are precisely recoverable.
(b) The elliptical construction is grammatically 'defective'.
(c) The insertion of the missing words results in a grammatical sentence with the same meaning as the elliptical sentence.
(d) The missing expression is recoverable from the context.
(e) The missing words are present in the text in exactly the same form.

The conversational contexts of the insubordinate *if*-clauses analysed in this chapter do not provide us with any element that could constitute their main clause; in other words, they are uttered as independent speech acts. As regards criterion (c), since no main clause can be retrieved from the previous discourse, we cannot know if the resulting sentence would have the same meaning; we assume that the main clause would refer to the speaker's attitude towards the act proposed, i.e. wish, gratitude, etc. (e.g. 'I would be grateful if…'). Concerning Quirk et al's criterion of the defectiveness of elliptical constructions, this is not the case of the structures under consideration here; they are used to issue directive meaning and the action proposed is understood and/or performed by the hearer.

Further evidence supporting the status of insubordinate *if*-directives as non-subordinate is reflected in the fact that they can be coordinated with clauses which are clearly independent in status, as in (14), and, more importantly for the purposes of this chapter, they are also used in combination with imperative clauses issuing commands, thus softening their imposing nature, as in (15).

(14) A: So if you if you will go downstairs and then you could look through these two postgraduate guides (DCPSE DI-A08 0135)
A: Uhm and then I'll show you where the others are

(15) A: Keep the bike leaning towards you slightly not on your hip but towards you
A: If you'd like to take a right-hand circle <,> quite tight <,> quite gently (DCPSE DI-F22 0021)
A: Now use the brake if necessary to stop it <,>

Insubordinate *if*-clauses clearly illustrate Evans' (2007, 367) notion of 'insubordination'. Insubordinate clauses usually preserve features of prototypical subordinate clauses, such as the retention of the subordinating conjunction clause-initially. Yet, as they get reanalysed as independent constructions over the course of time, their functions extend beyond those of subordinate clauses. Insubordination represents a frequent cross-linguistic phenomenon, as suggested by the proliferation of recent work examining the characteristics of different types of insubordinate constructions in various languages (see, among others, D'Hertefelt 2013 on conditional clauses in Germanic languages; Gras 2013 on non-subordinating uses of subordinators in Spanish; Sansiñena et al. 2013 on complementizer initial responses in various European languages; Schwenter 1996, forthcoming on independent *si*-clauses in Spanish; and Brinton 2014 on English exclamatory *as if*-clauses).

In terms of diachronic formation, insubordinate clauses follow four steps (Evans 2007, 370ff.):

(a) Subordinate construction with explicit main clause.
(b) Ellipsis of the main clause. Here conversational inferences determine exactly the type of clauses that can be restored.
(c) Conventionalization of ellipsis. At this stage, some of the reconstructions that could be possible in terms of syntax are excluded by convention. Thus, the subset of possible restored material is narrowed down. Consider, for example, (16) below, where the restoration is limited to a positive rather than a negative consequence in the *if*-offer.

(16) If you would maybe like to wash your hands. (from Evans 2007, 373)
[that would be very nice of you]
[you can do it here]
[*you cannot do it]

(d) Conventionalized main clause use of formally subordinate clause. In the final step, the construction has become fully grammaticalized and has a meaning of its own; the ellipsed material cannot be restored.

The insubordinate clauses under analysis in this chapter seem to be placed somewhere between stages (c) and (d), since it has become clear that they do not need a main clause to constitute an illocutionary act. In addition, if we were to reconstruct their main clauses, not all types of clauses would be allowed.

In terms of the range of functions insubordinate clauses may serve, Evans (2007, 386ff.) discusses the following:

(a) Interpersonal coercion, not only in commands but also in threats, warnings, permissives, and abilitatives. Most insubordinate clauses are found in situations where the speaker is concerned with interpersonal control, primarily the imperative in all its forms.
(b) Modal framing; for example, in the expression of deontic and evidential meaning, and in the evocation of quotation or belief.
(c) Marking of discourse contexts; these include negation, reiteration, and contrastive statements, all of them highly presuppositional.

The clauses discussed in this chapter clearly fit into the first of Evans' categories. As recognized by him, "the most common function of insubordinate conditionals is to express polite requests" (2007, 380).

Directives in English: A Corpus Study of the Uses of Imperatives, Conditional Clauses, and Insubordinate *If*-Clauses

As seen above, imperatives, conditionals, and insubordinate *if*-clauses belong to three distinct types of clauses whose pragmatic uses seem to be somewhat related. We now move on to explore their distribution and uses as represented in a corpus. For this purpose I have used as my data source the DCPSE, a parsed corpus of spoken English containing more than 400,000 words from the *London-Lund Corpus* (LLC) and 400,000 words from the British component of the *International Corpus of English* (ICE-GB). The *London-Lund Corpus* is the spoken part of the *Survey of English Usage Corpus* collected in the 1960s. In turn, the ICE-GB is composed of spoken and written texts, dating from the early 1990s, distributed over 32 text categories. The resulting DCPSE contains data from the following text categories: face-to-face conversation, both formal and informal (categories A and B, respectively); telephone conversations (C); broadcast discussion (D); broadcast interviews (E); spontaneous commentary (F); parliamentary language (G); legal cross-examination (H); assorted spontaneous speech (I); and prepared speech (J). The sentence IDs for each example show the following structure "DI-F22 0017" if the example belongs to the ICE-GB component and "DL-F22 0017" if the example belongs to the LLC component, where the first three codes identify the text type the token belongs to, the next figure represents the number of the recording, and the last one stands for the turn of the example in the conversation.

I extracted all imperative clauses, including *let*-imperatives but disregarding those clauses in which *let* functions as an ordinary lexical verb in any of its forms and is paraphraseable by 'allow', and also all those clauses introduced by *if* which could be interpreted as either conditional structures with directive meaning or directive insubordinate *if*-clauses.[2] The overall results are summarized in Table 13.1.

2 The corpus yielded a total of 1,843 prototypical conditional clauses, most of which (1,826; 99.08%) did not convey directive meaning.

TABLE 13.1 *Directives in the DCPSE*

Conditional structures with directive meaning	Insubordinate *if*-clauses	Imperative clauses	
		Let-imperatives	Other imperatives
		253	55
17	52	308	

As shown in Table 13.1, the most common form of directives in the spoken British English material analysed is *let*-imperative clauses. Interestingly, the corpus contains almost the same number of imperative clauses other than *let*-clauses and of insubordinate *if*-clauses. This was not to be anticipated, since the former construction has been established in the language much longer than insubordinate *if*-clauses, and so speakers were expected to use the former pattern more frequently than the latter. In the remainder of this chapter I examine how these four types of clauses are distributed as regards their illocutionary force and whether each type has specialized for certain communicative purposes.

Distribution of Imperatives, Insubordinate If*-Clauses, and Conditional Structures with Directive Meaning According to Illocutionary Act*

After analysing their conversational contexts, imperatives, whether with *let* or others, conditional structures with directive meaning, and insubordinate *if*-clauses were classified according to their illocutionary force. For this I followed the typology of speech acts in Huddleston and Pullum et al. (2002, 929–930) (see also Quirk et al. 1985, 831–832; Davies 1986; Downing and Locke 2006, 211). Of the various types of illocutionary acts identified by these scholars, the clauses at issue here occur in the corpus in five of them: orders, requests, offers, instructions or expository directives, and suggestions.[3] More specifically, I have classified as orders those cases in which the hearer is required to comply with the action proposed; failure to comply is not allowed or is likely to provoke a rebuke. In the category of requests, I have included examples in which the option of not complying is given, but it is assumed that the hearer will carry

3 No examples of the remaining illocutionary acts identified by Huddleston and Pullum et al. (2002, 858–863) and other relevant literature, i.e. permission and acceptance, were recorded in the data analysed.

out what is being asked. Since the boundary between orders and requests is not always clear, and the difference between ordering and asking something is scalar, for the correct identification of these two illocutionary forces I have ultimately relied on Lakoff's Idealized Cognitive Model (1987, chapter 4), as revised by Pérez Hernández and Ruiz de Mendoza (2002; see also Takahashi 2012). Idealized Cognitive Models (ICMs) are complex structured systems of knowledge that help structure mental spaces. As Lakoff puts it, "a mental space is a medium for conceptualization and thought. Thus any fixed or ongoing state of affairs as we conceptualize it is represented by a mental space" (1987, 281). The role of ICMs is to provide the background knowledge that we need to recruit in order to structure mental spaces. Pérez Hernández and Ruiz de Mendoza (2002, 264) have formulated the particular ICMs for requests and orders, taking into consideration the assessment of the cost and/or benefit the action involves to the speaker and to the hearer, the assessment of the degree of optionality conveyed by a speech act, i.e. the degree to which the speech act restricts the addressee's freedom to decide whether or not to carry out the action, and the assessment of the power relationship that holds between the speakers. The formulation of the ICMs of ordering and requesting can be summarized as follows:

TABLE 13.2 *ICM of orders and requests according to Pérez Hernández and Ruiz de Mendoza (2002, 264)*

ICM of orders	ICM of requests
The action represents a cost to the hearer and a benefit to the speaker. They show low optionality, that is, politeness is usually lacking. The speaker is usually more *powerful* than the hearer.	The action represents a cost to the hearer and a benefit to the speaker. The level of optionality is high, since they show politeness. Power relationships do not apply to requests.

As to the categorization of the other directive types found in the corpus, I have classified as offers (also called invitations) cases in which the hearer can choose whether or not to accept what is being proposed, the speaker having an initiating and enabling role, but the benefit of accepting what is being offered residing with the addressee. In the case of instructions or expository directives, compliance with the action is in the interest of the hearer, but it is needed in order to achieve a particular goal. Finally, I have classified as suggestions those examples in which compliance is presented as being in the interest of the addressee and where the speaker proposes a course of action the hearer is free to comply with or not.

Table 13.3 provides the distribution in the corpus of imperatives, *let*-clauses, insubordinate *if*-clauses, and conditional structures with directive meaning according to illocutionary force.

TABLE 13.3 *Distribution of* let-*clauses, imperatives, insubordinate* if-*clauses, and conditional structures with directive meaning according to illocutionary act in the* DCPSE

Type of clause		Type of illocutionary act				
		Order	Request	Offer	Instruction/ expository directive	Suggestion
Imp. clauses	*Let* imp.				124 (79.5%)	129 (100%)
	Other imp.	15 (53.6%)	12 (25.5%)	6 (35.3%)	22 (14.1%)	–
Insubordinate *if*-clauses		13 (46.4%)	23 (49%)	11 (64.7%)	5 (3.2%)	–
Conditional structures with directive meaning		–	12 (25.5%)	–	5 (3.2%)	–
Total		28 (100%)	47 (100%)	17 (100%)	156 (100%)	129 (100%)

In the following sections, I proceed to the analysis and exemplification of the use of *let*-clauses, imperatives, insubordinate *if*-clauses, and conditional structures with directive meaning according to the type of illocutionary force identified.

Orders

In orders, a sense of obligation, no matter its degree of strength, to carry out the action proposed is said to be involved on the part of the hearer. Examples

(17) and (18) illustrate the use of an imperative clause and an insubordinate *if*-clause issuing orders. In (17) the power relationship between the speaker and the hearer is clear, since the speaker is superior in status to the addressee, the latter being an employee. Similarly, in (18), where the hearer has to fill in a form so that his personal details are registered correctly, there is also some sense of obligation.

(17) B: I thought the <unclear-word> were so small <unclear-word> <unclear-word><unclear-word>
B: no
B: so we'll have one last drink
B: *Supply us some more drinks while we are about it* (DCPSE DI B40-0058)
A: yeah

(18) A: OK <,> I presume you've changed address since last year
B: Yes
A: In which case we'd better get you to fill in one of these forms <,,>
A: *If you put your new uhm address there no there and the old address and your name* (DCPSE DI-A20 0280)
B: OK
A: Just name and address <,,>
A: OK thanks very much <,,>

Requests

As shown in Table 13.3, the proportion of insubordinate *if*-clauses issuing requests (49%; cf. (19)) is considerably higher than that of imperatives (25.5%; cf. (20)), and the difference is even higher if we consider *if*-clauses as a whole (74.5%). The use of *if*-clauses (both full conditional structures and insubordinate *if*-clauses) is likely related to issues of politeness, since conditional clauses and insubordinate *if*-clauses seem to imply an option with alternatives; the hearer is given the option of not complying with the action proposed, although it is assumed that the addressee will grant the speaker's request (cf. Huddleston and Pullum et al. 2002, 930). In cases in which the request is made by means of a conditional structure, as in (21), the main clause *we would be most grateful* expresses nothing but the feeling of gratitude the speaker would have if the request was made possible.[4]

4 As pointed out by an anonymous reviewer, the fact that the *then*-clause is rather empty may explain the relative infrequency of full conditional structures for this use.

(19) A: uhm what sort of time
B: Any time <,,>
B: I'll fit in with you <,,>
A: *uhm uhm if you can make it about three* (DCPSE DL-C03 0445)
B: three <,> and where do I go to<,>
A: it's l s uh do you know PanamErican College

(20) A: oh hello <,> you found your way
A: Emma smith
B: yes thanks
B: yes
A: Mike Millican
A: *do come in* (DCPSE DL-A14 006)
A: *Do hang up your coat if you'd like to*<,> (DCPSE DL-A14 0007)

(21) B: so *if we could borrow these and have a look through them and uh then let you have them back we would be most grateful* <,> (DCPSE DL-B14 0098)
A: hm hm hm well the Only thing that an uh is an I'm Anxious about is I do want them back
B: oh surely there would be no question about that

Offers

Like requests, offers are also open to rejection; the addressee can choose whether or not to accept what is being proposed, as shown in (22) and (23), with an imperative and an insubordinate clause, respectively. This may explain the higher proportion of insubordinate *if*-clauses issuing offers (64.7%) than imperatives (35.3%), as they leave the hearer more freedom of choice.

(22) C: I'm sure it was much much <,> cos it sounded so like mush mush you know as in driving sleigh dogs across the frozen wastes <,<<,> <laugh>
B: *Darling have some cherries* (DCPSE DL-B22 0893)
D: *have a handful* (DCPSE BL-B22 0894)
A: wooh suhp
B: it's a very nice supper Jo thank you very much indeed
A: special little pile of cherries he says grabbing a few more
C: hm I agree thank you Jo
D: take several
B: very nice supper indeed

(23) C: we'll have to discUss your finAncial situation in more detail
B: yes
C: uhm <,> if you come Over to TUEsday *if you want to come up to my house and have a cOffee* (DCPSE DL-C04 0229)

B: uhm
C: and or a <,> shErry and have a nAtter abOUt it I'll be vEry wIlling to do that with you that's After six <,>
B: that would be vEry nice that's ch tomOrrow then

Instructions and Expository Directives

As shown in Table 13.3 above, this is the only type of illocutionary act for which the four types of structures under investigation are used in the corpus. However, whereas all the examples recorded of *let*-clauses are used as expository directives[5] to guide the hearer through an argument and engage the active participations of the addressee, as in (24) and (25), the other three clause types are employed to issue instructions.

(24) Let's now talk about the second area where Lord Scarman made recommendations the procedures for dealing with complaints against the police (DCPSE DI-D13 0112)
(25) Let's view uhm example one (DCPSE DI-B60 0134)

For the issuing of instructions, imperative clauses clearly predominate over conditional structures and insubordinate *if*-clauses (14.1% vs. 3.2% for each of the latter two types). Interestingly, of the 32 examples found for this category, 27 cases are issued in the same conversational exchange where insubordinate *if*-clauses and imperatives co-occur. As expected, given the more polite nature of insubordinate *if*-clauses, the conversational exchange starts with insubordinate *if*-clauses and the speaker then switches to imperative clauses. This is shown in (26).

(26) A: Now before we start the engines up I would like you all to go to your machines <,> and we will wheel them around the course so that you get the feel of them <,,>

---

5 Insubordinate *if*-clauses can also be used with this same purpose of guiding the hearer through an argument, as shown in (i) and (ii) from the *Corpus of Spoken Professional American English* (Barlow 2000):
(i) *If we could step back for a minute*, and then we'll come back to your questions on any of these subjects. I would like to just take a couple of minutes to put what has happened the last couple of days in the broader context of the President's policy toward this region.
(ii) The student and their parents would be involved in that. *If we could turn to the comments*. Just real quickly because we are running out of time.

A: Right
A: We're going to do this one at a time <,>
A: *If you'd like to go to your machines* (DCPSE DI-F22 0017)
A: *and Gareth if you'd like to lead* <,,> (DCPSE DI-F22 0018)
A: Right now *take the bike off its side stand and hold its weight on the handlebars* <,> (DCPSE DI-F22 0019)
A: *Keep the bike leaning towards you slightly not on your hip but towards you* (DCPSE DI-F22 0020)
A: *If you'd like to take a right-hand circle <,> quite tight <,> quite gently* (DCPSE DI-F22 0021)
A: Now *use the brake if necessary to stop it* <,> (DCPSE DI-F22 0022)
A: *Apply it very slowly* <,> (DCPSE DI-F22 0023)
A: No not not too jerkily
A: That was too hard a snatch
A: *Treat it very gently* (DCPSE DI-F22 0026)
A: That's much better <,>

Later in the conversation, the speaker changes the topic and again makes use of an insubordinate *if*-clause to express the first directive, then shifting to imperative clauses:

(27) A: *And if you go straight into a left hand circle keeping the bike leaning towards you all the time* <,> (DCPSE DI-F22 0031)
A: That's it
A: *Put it on full lock* <,> (DCPSE DI-F22 0033)
A: You'll clear the bikes
A: That's lovely
A: And back to its starting position <,>
A: *Apply the brake very smoothly and put it back on its side stand* (DCPSE DI-F22 0037)
A: That's the way
A: Lovely

The corpus yields another similar example in which an insubordinate *if*-clause is issued first to formulate an instruction, which is later reinforced by an imperative clause. This is (28).

(28) A: It's on the next one as well <,,>
A: That makes you <,,>
A: *if you could keep it in* (DCPSE DI B36-0234)

B: Yes
A: Yeah
B: *Keep in that <,> place* (DCPSE DI B36-0237)
B: Yeah
B: Sort of
A: Yes
B: Plane <,,>
A: Flat
A: No
A: It's because you're not singing it in the same place <,,>

Cases of conditional structures expressing instructions are of the type shown in (29), in which participant A is giving a direction to participant B by means of an *if*-clause which seems to have no conditional meaning. Note that the presence of the shop is not dependent on the hearer's walking in that direction.

(29) A: What was that <,> building on the corner <,> just past Chapel Street on the right where it used to be Lyon's <,,>
A: What was it called the <,>
A: Well it w it wasn't called Lyon's Corner House but it was
B: Chapel Street
A: Well you know Chapel Street
B: Yeah up at Islington
A: Yeah <,>
A: *If you go on a bit you come to <,> a corner shop a big which used to be a big Lyon's <,> with a* (DCPSE DI-B06 0008)
A: Oh you don't know oh
B: Well as I say I don't know it <,,>

Suggestions

The most frequent type of directive in the corpus is the use of a first person inclusive *let*-imperative with the force of a suggestion for joint future action. In fact, this is the only type of clause employed in the material analysed for directives of this type, although imperative clauses can also be used with this illocutionary force (e.g. *Wait until the price is right*). According to Collins (2004, 304), *let*-clauses of this kind are only marginal members of the directive class since their illocutionary meaning results from the combination of the directive force of an imperative and the assertive force of a suggestion. In these "assertive directives" *let's* is used to mitigate the threatening nature of the act proposed. Examples (30) and (31) illustrate this use of *let*-imperatives:

(30) Well let's leave it at that twenty-fourth of March nineteen ninety-two (DCPSE DI-B60 0159)
(31) So let's play Trivial Pursuit as well after or something (DCPSE DI-B40 0124)

Summary of Findings and Proposals for Further Research

The data examined in this chapter testify to the fact that in spoken British English different types of clauses expressing directive meaning have somehow specialized for certain pragmatic uses. Beginning with *let*-imperatives, although they are usually classified and considered as belonging to the directive class, speakers seem to resort to them when trying to issue suggestions rather than proper directives. Their use as expository directives is also very common. On the other hand, imperatives, conditional clauses, and insubordinate *if*-clauses seem to serve the same range of pragmatic purposes. Focusing on imperatives and insubordinate *if*-clauses, whose use is more common in the corpus than that of conditionals, they are used with almost the same frequency. That said, there seems to be a clear tendency for insubordinate *if*-clauses to code requests, rather than other categories of directive speech acts, probably because their historical origin renders them especially suitable as a more polite option. Issues of politeness also seem to account for the fact that insubordinate *if*-clauses are used first in conversational exchanges where they co-occur with imperatives, so as to prevent a potential face-threatening act.

Although the results of this study point to a specialization of imperatives and insubordinate *if*-clauses for certain directive categories, further research is needed in order to confirm these provisional results. First, the sample analysed needs to be expanded and diversified, so as to include, for instance, data from other varieties of English, this in order to check whether similarities and/or differences in usage across varieties can be discerned or not. Secondly, since polite requests and commands can also be coded as interrogative clauses, the sample should also be enlarged to include this type of clause. This would enable me to provide an overall picture of directive forms in English, and of their use in terms of politeness and indirection.

Corpora

DCPSE Aarts, Bas, and Sean A. Wallis. 2006. *The Diachronic Corpus of Present-Day Spoken English*. Survey of English Usage, University College London. http://www.ucl.ac.uk/english-usage/projects/dcpse/.

CSPA Barlow, Michael. 2000. *The Corpus of Spoken Professional American English*. Rice University. http://www.athel.com/cpsa.html.

References

Brinton, Laurel. 2014. "The Extremes of Insubordination: Exclamatory *As If!*" *Journal of English Linguistics* 42/2: 93–113.

Brown, Penelope, and Stephen C. Levinson. 1987. *Politeness: Some Universals in Language Usage*. Cambridge: Cambridge University Press.

Collins, Peter. 2004. "*Let*-Imperatives in English." *International Journal of Corpus Linguistics* 9/2: 299–319.

Davies, Eirlys. 1986. *The English Imperative*. London: Croom Helm.

D'Hertefelt, Sarah. 2013. "Independent Conditional Clauses in Germanic Languages." Paper presented at the Complex Sentences International Workshop (CSI), University of Leuven, November 16–17.

Downing, Angela, and Philip Locke. 2006. *English Grammar. A University Course*. 2nd edn. London: Routledge.

Evans, Nicholas. 2007. "Insubordination and its Uses." In *Finiteness: Theoretical and Empirical Foundations*, edited by Irina Nikolaeva, 366–431. New York: Oxford University Press.

Ford, Cecilia E. 1993. *Grammar in Interaction: Adverbial Clauses in American English Conversations*. Cambridge: Cambridge University Press.

Ford, Cecilia E. 1997. "Speaking Conditionally: Some Contexts for *If*-Clauses in Conversation." In *On Conditionals Again*, edited by Angeliki Athanasiadou, and René Dirven, 387–413. Amsterdam and Philadelphia: John Benjamins.

Ford, Cecilia E., and Sandra A. Thompson. 1986. "Conditionals in Discourse: A Text-Based Study from English." In *On Conditionals*, edited by Cecilia E. Ford, Elizabeth C. Traugott, Alice ter Meulen, Joseph Reilly, and Charles A. Ferguson, 353–72. Cambridge: Cambridge University Press.

Gras, Pedro. 2013. "Insubordination and the Development of Pragmatic Categories: Evidence from Non-Subordinating Uses of Subordination Markers in Spanish." Paper presented at the Complex Sentences International Workshop (CSI), Leuven, November 16–17.

Huddleston, Rodney, and Geoffrey K. Pullum, et al. 2002. *The Cambridge Grammar of the English Language*. Cambridge: Cambridge University Press.

Kaltenböck, Gunther. 2014. "On Insubordination: Form, Function and Development of Insubordinate *If*-clauses." Paper presented at the Third Conference of the International Society for the Linguistics of English (ISLE 3), University of Zurich, August 23–27.

Lakoff, George. 1987. *Women, Fire, and Dangerous Things: What Categories Reveal about the Mind.* Chicago: University of Chicago Press.

Lombardi Vallauri, Edoardo. 2004. "Grammaticalization of Syntactic Incompleteness: Free Conditionals in Italian and Other Languages." *SKY Journal of Linguistics* 17: 189–215.

Mato-Míguez, Beatriz. 2014. "*If You Would Like to Lead*: On the Grammatical Status of Directive Isolated *If*-Clauses in Spoken British English." In *Diachrony and Synchrony in English Corpus Linguistics*, edited by Alejandro Alcaraz-Sintes, and Salvador Valera-Hernández, 259–83. Bern: Peter Lang.

Matthews, Peter H. 1981. *Syntax*. Cambridge: Cambridge University Press.

Pérez Hernández, Lorena, and Francisco Javier Ruiz de Mendoza. 2002. "Grounding, Semantic Motivation, and Conceptual Interaction in Indirect Speech Acts." *Journal of Pragmatics* 34/3: 259–84.

Portner, Paul. 2004. "The Semantics of Imperatives within a Theory of Clause Types." In *Proceedings of the 14th Semantics and Linguistic Theory Conference*, edited by Robert B. Young, 235–52. Ithaca, NY: CLC Publications.

Quirk, Randolph, Sidney Greenbaum, Geoffrey Leech, and Jan Svartvik. 1985. *A Comprehensive Grammar of the English Language*. London: Longman.

Sansiñena, María Sol, Bert Cornillie, and Hendrik De Smet. 2013. "Between Subordinate and Insubordinate. Complementizer-Initial Responses in English, French, German and Spanish." Paper presented at the Complex Sentences International Workshop (CSI), Leuven, November 16–17.

Schwager, Magdalena. 2006. "Conditionalized Imperatives." In *Proceedings of Semantics and Linguistic Theory XVI*, edited by Masayuki Gibson, and Jonathan Howell, 241–58. Ithaca, NY: CLC Publications.

Schwenter, Scott A. 1996. "The Pragmatics of Independent *Si*-Clauses in Spanish." *Hispanic Linguistics* 8: 316–51.

Schwenter, Scott A. Forthcoming. "Independent *Si*-Clauses in Spanish: Functions and Consequences for Insubordination." In *Dynamics of Insubordination*, edited by Nicholas Evans, and Honore Watanabe. Amsterdam and Philadelphia: John Benjamins.

Stirling, Lesley. 1999. "Isolated *If*-Clauses in Australian English." In *The Clause in English: In Honour of Rodney Huddleston*, edited by Peter Collins, and David A. Lee, 273–94. Amsterdam and Philadelphia: John Benjamins.

Takahashi, Hidemitsu. 2012. *A Cognitive Linguistic Analysis of the English Imperative: With Special Reference to Japanese Imperatives*. Amsterdam and Philadelphia: John Benjamins.

Traugott, Elizabeth C., Alice ter Meulen, Joseph Reilly, and Charles A. Ferguson. 1986. "Overview." In *On Conditionals*, edited by Cecilia E. Ford, Elizabeth C. Traugott, Alice ter Meulen, Joseph Reilly, and Charles A. Ferguson, 3–20. Cambridge: Cambridge University Press.

CHAPTER 14

Taboo Language and Swearing in Eighteenth- and Nineteenth-Century English: A Diachronic Study Based on the *Old Bailey Corpus*

Bianca Widlitzki and Magnus Huber

Abstract

Most studies of the history of taboo language and swearing in English provide only a general historical sketch and tend to focus on written language. By contrast, our study takes a qualitative and quantitative look at spoken language. It is based on the 14-million-word *Old Bailey Corpus 1720–1913*, a corpus of court proceedings with detailed sociolinguistic mark-up. Our findings show that swearing occurred mostly in reported speech. Overall, bad language declined over the two centuries and its concealment in print increased. This was most likely caused by the growing social pressure on both the genre of trial proceedings and the individual speaker. Also, the functions of swearing changed drastically: while curses (e.g. *Damn you!*) declined sharply, slot fillers (e.g. *bloody*) increased noticeably. Surprisingly, female speakers used taboo language more frequently than males, possibly because women were more often the target of curses and name-calling than men. In addition, bad language of both higher-class and female speakers was less often obscured in print, perhaps because editors wanted to expose speakers who, according to the discourse of purity, were least associated with swearing, and at the same time hoping to increase sales through the shock-value of offensive language, especially when used by these groups.

Keywords

taboo language – swearing – censoring – *Old Bailey Corpus 1720–1913* – discourse of purity – gender – social class – historical sociolinguistics – Late Modern English – trial proceedings

 | DOI 10.1163/9789004321342_015

Defining Swearing and Linguistic Taboo

This chapter investigates the forms, functions, frequency, and social distribution of taboo and swearwords in eighteenth and nineteenth century English, as well as editorial interference in their representation in print. So-called 'bad language' can take many forms, which are often difficult to categorize. For our purposes, we adopt the definition of swearing proposed in Ljung (2011). It has the major advantage of covering diverse expressions used to swear while at the same time clearly delimiting the category of swearing. According to Ljung (2011, 4), any utterance must fulfil four criteria to count as swearing:

(a) Swearing is the use of utterances containing taboo words.
(b) The taboo words are used with non-literal meaning.
(c) Many utterances that constitute swearing are subject to severe lexical, phrasal, and syntactic constraints, which suggests that most swearing qualifies as formulaic language.
(d) Swearing is emotive language: its main function is to reflect, or seem to reflect, the speaker's feelings and attitudes.

Taboo words are socially unacceptable expressions (cf. Hughes 2006, 262–263). They can be used for swearing but the mere presence of a taboo word does not on its own constitute a case of swearing, as the following examples illustrate:

(1) Fuck you!
(2) They're not just friends—they're obviously fucking.

Example (1) meets all four criteria of swearing. Most importantly, the taboo word *fuck* is used, but not in its literal sense (criteria (a) and (b)). In addition, the construction is formulaic (criterion (c)): it is not possible to substitute any word with a similar meaning for *fuck*, like **Shag you!* or **Have sex with you!* Finally, the example is a case of emotive language use (criterion (d)), i.e. it is easy to imagine that someone might be venting their anger by using the expression.

In example (2) a taboo word is present (*fucking*), but the utterance as a whole does not meet criteria (b) to (d) for swearing. To begin with, the verb *fuck* is used in its literal sense here (≠ criterion (b)). In addition, this is not a case of formulaic language: it would be entirely possible to substitute, for example, *They're obviously having sex (with each other)* for *They're obviously fucking* (≠ criterion (c)). Lastly, this utterance does not function as a vehicle to reflect feelings and attitudes in the way that in (1) does (≠ criterion (d)).

Swearing and linguistic taboo in English have been the subject of a number of linguistic studies—both from a synchronic (e.g. Jay 1992, 2000; Allan and Burridge 2006) and a diachronic (e.g. Montagu 1967; Hughes 1991, 2006; McEnery 2006) perspective. The historical studies are mostly intended as general overviews: Montagu (1967) traces swearing from antiquity to the twentieth century and Hughes (1991, 2006) provides an extensive social history of 'bad language' in the English-speaking world. In placing its focus on sociolinguistic aspects, especially on the public perception of bad language from 1586 to the present, McEnery (2006) is an exception. English swearing is also discussed in a recent cross-linguistic study (Ljung 2011), which compares swearing in 25 languages.

Our investigation aims to describe the use and representation of bad language in eighteenth- and nineteenth-century English. In contrast to the aforementioned diachronic studies, it specifically focuses on spoken language (as recorded in trial proceedings) and addresses the issue of the representation of such language in the text type of trial proceedings. Of particular interest to us are:

(a) Changes in the sociolinguistics of swearing: were there gender and/or social class differences, and how did they change over the two centuries?
(b) Changes in the categories: what types of expressions were used to swear? What functions did they fulfil? Can change be observed?
(c) Changes in the (written) representation of taboo/swearing: how was bad language dealt with in the written medium? What does this reveal about (language) attitudes in British society at the time?

Data and Methodology

The Old Bailey Corpus

The *Old Bailey Corpus* (OBC; Huber et al. 2012) serves as a basis for the present study. It consists of selected *Proceedings of the Old Bailey*, London's central criminal court (cf. Hitchcock et al. 2014). Containing 415 proceedings between the years 1720–1913, it provides c. 750,000 words of direct speech per decade and amounts to about 13.9 million words of spoken English.[1]

1 The data used in this article come from the pre-publication version of the OBC, which with 407 proceedings is slightly smaller than OBC version 1.0, 2013-06-04 (415 proceedings).

A particular strength of the OBC is the detailed annotation of every speaker turn for sociobiographical (gender, social class, age), pragmatic (role in the court proceeding), and textual variables (the shorthand scribe, printer, and publisher of individual proceedings), which allows the study of eighteenth- and nineteenth-century English in its social context. Although trial proceedings cannot be expected to be one hundred per cent faithful to the spoken word, the verbatim passages of the *Proceedings* are a reasonably close representation of what was said in the courtroom.[2]

The *Proceedings* as such started out as a private enterprise in 1674: publishers sent shorthand scribes to report on criminal trials and subsequently sold their accounts to a public that showed an enormous interest in crime literature (Emsley et al. 2014). From the 1720s onwards, an increasing amount of verbatim material was reported in the *Proceedings*, which makes them suitable for studies of spoken interaction of the time.

In the last quarter of the eighteenth century, the City of London gained more and more control over the content and publication of the *Proceedings*. From 1778, they were required to provide a "true, fair and perfect narrative" of all the trials at the Old Bailey (CLRO 1778, fols. 142–143, as cited in Devereaux 1996, 468).

Identifying Bad Language in the Old Bailey Corpus

As what is considered offensive language varies historically and is relative at any point in time (i.e. there is a cline between offensive and non-offensive), we opted for a data-driven approach for the identification of swearing and taboo in the OBC. The practice of avoiding taboo language most strongly in the press and other printed publications (Hughes 2006, 463) was, in fact, an advantage: the *Proceedings* were expected to deliver an accurate account of the trials but at the same time were not to be obscene (Devereaux 1996, 491). To solve this dilemma, concealment strategies were employed, i.e. the items in question were either half-spelled (3) or completely replaced by asterisks or dashes (4).[3] This was a frequent strategy for publications at the time (McArthur 1996, 55).

(3) You b—y rat! (OBC t18920404-397)[4]

(4) the deceased said he would knock his * * * face in (OBC t18920307-358)

2 Cf. Huber (2007, 2010) for an evaluation of the *Proceedings of the Old Bailey* as a source of spoken language.

3 We also came across a case of concealment by re-spelling: *bougre* for *bugger* (OBC t17700221-6), but for obvious reasons such cases are hard to find.

4 Material quoted from the OBC is referred to by the trial identifier, which is composed of a *t* (for *trial*), followed by the date of the publication of the *Proceedings* (yyyymmdd), and the consecutive trial number of the sessions (-xx).

As the *Proceedings* were targeted at a middle- and upper-class readership (Shoemaker 2008, 565), it is reasonable to assume that they approximated the values of their readership and reflected the dominant social ideology at the time. We therefore decided to take our cue from the publisher's view on what was 'inappropriate' language and considered any word taboo that was at least once censored in some way in the OBC. We are fully aware that this ignores those words that were never censored but that may nevertheless have been considered offensive at the time, such as the following:

(5) a. [...] he said to me, "You *cur*, I will teach you". (OBC t19090518-61)[5]
b. get you gone, you *dog* (OBC t17230828-12)
c. he called him a *hound* [...] (OBC t19020909-580)
d. You *Puppy*, what do you meddle with the Girl for? (OBC t17230530-43)

However, we take the fact that the expressions in (5a–d) and others were never concealed in the OBC as an indication that, while these words may have been considered impolite, they were not felt to be exceptionally insulting. We did not, therefore, consider them further in our analysis.

We operationalized the data-driven approach by searching for the replacement strategies, i.e. conducting searches (using regular expressions) in the OBC for all plausible combinations of letters and asterisks, letters and dashes, and asterisks and dashes on their own. This yielded a list of 2,447 censored items. The full forms of these words were then individually reconstructed from the context and collected in a list.[6] This list was afterwards used as input for a second corpus search, which yielded another 2,095 instances of uncensored swearing or taboo.

Coding the Tokens

Our token list is organized by individual words. This means that examples such as *you damned bitch* are counted twice, once under *damned* and once under *bitch*. While it is possible to argue that *damned bitch* as a whole constitutes one instance of swearing, its components *damned* and *bitch* contrast in form (adjective—noun), function (modifying element—epithet), and in terms of the theme that is referenced (religion—animals). They are therefore best treated individually.

Each token in the final list of 4,542 items was coded for the following parameters: degree of censorship (partial concealment, complete concealment,

5 Italics represent our emphasis, also in other examples.

6 320 (partly) censored swearwords could not be disambiguated. This problem is obvious where items have been completely replaced (*you* ***), but spellings like *this b—idiot* also cause problems because *b*—can stand for a number of items, including *bloody* and *blasted*.

no concealment), year of utterance, gender (female, male), and social class. The social class membership of speakers in the OBC is indicated using the HISCLASS scheme (van Leeuwen and Maas 2011), which is based on the *Historical International Standard Classification of Occupations* (HISCO; van Leeuwen et al. 2002). In its extended scheme, HISCLASS differentiates between 13 social classes, but for our purposes we merged these into two classes: higher (comprising classes 1–5 and including the non-manual professions) and lower (comprising classes 6–13 and including the manual professions).

A total of 4,080 of the 4,542 retrieved items met the definition of swearing given above, the rest were taboo words. The swearwords were additionally coded for themes and functions, following the 'typology of swearing' proposed in Ljung (2011): the themes are the different taboo areas employed in swearing, while the notion of function refers to the purpose that a swearing expression fulfils (Ljung 2011, 29).

The swearing expressions in the OBC reference the following themes: animals (e.g. *dog*), bodily functions and excretions (e.g. *turd, shit*), family (e.g. *son of a whore*), body parts (e.g. *arse*), religion (e.g. *devil, damn*), and sex (e.g. *bugger, fuck*).

As for functions, a major distinction needs to be made between stand-alone expressions and slot fillers. The latter are parts of larger swearing expressions and can take various forms, ranging from traditional degree modification (*It's bloody awful*) to more complicated expressions (*What the hell is going on?*) (Ljung 2011, 30). Stand-alones can be divided into more specific subgroups. After adapting Ljung's cross-linguistic typology for the Late Modern English context, we distinguish between name-calling, expletive interjections, curses, and oaths. Name-calling is "a type of insulting illocutionary act" that makes use of epithets, i.e. negative evaluative nouns, and is "addressed to people who have incurred the speaker's dislike" (Ljung 2011, 124). *You fucking bastard!* would be an example. In contrast, expletive interjections like *Zounds!* are not addressed to anyone, but basically cathartic (cf. Jay 1992, 104). Oaths, in their original function, serve "to swear by something or somebody to back up the claims made by the speaker by taking God or some other venerable being (or the attributes associated with such entities) as witness that the claim is true" (Ljung 2011, 30). It is important to distinguish formal from non-formal oaths. Swearing exclusively makes use of the latter (Ljung 2011, 100–101). These may be formally similar to formal oath-taking (e.g. involve expressions like *I swear to God that I'll…*) but are not actually intended as appeals to a higher power, as all swearing is non-literal. Similarly, curses can be serious or non-serious. Serious cursing presupposes that speakers are convinced that their uttering the curse will "call down evil on somebody" (Ljung 2011, 31). The curses in our data retain to a large extent the form of serious curses (such as (*God*) *damn you!*), but are not intended in this vein. Montagu (1967, 64) summarizes this development as follows: "In societies in which the oath and curse have outlived whatever spirit was once imparted to them, sportive capital has been made of the residue".

Results and Discussion

Swearing and Taboo in Court

The 4,542 retrieved tokens are proof that offensive language was used in the Old Bailey, but a closer look reveals that they are almost exclusively reported in quotes rather than actively used in the courtroom. (6) illustrates a rare counter-example:

(6) *Prisoner*. I did not run.
Prosecutor. You are a saucy lying B—. (OBC t17340424-6)

However, such outbursts are very rare in the OBC. Mostly, speakers in court restrict themselves to reporting past uses of bad language—largely that of others, rarely their own.

Endeavouring to keep bad language out of the courtroom, speakers sometimes resort to vagueness, as in (7) below. The witness acknowledges that offensive language was used, but is saved from having to repeat it in court. Note that he explicitly states that he considers the exact words inappropriate for a courtroom setting.

(7) After that they called the old gentleman names not fit to be mentioned in Court. (OBC t18720610-469)

Alternatively, speakers use euphemisms and sometimes mark them metalinguistically, as in (8). Interestingly, there are cases when even these euphemistic expressions are subject to editorial censorship, as in (9), indicating that the signified rather than the signifier is taboo. Strictly speaking, euphemisms are alternatives to taboo or otherwise "dispreferred expressions" (Allan and Burridge 2006, 32) and therefore by definition not in the same category as tabooed expressions. Nevertheless, we retained those cases in our token list for the simple reason that the printers and publishers at the time obviously considered them offensive enough to be censored.

(8) [...] she said the Money was not in her Pocket, but it was in her Privy Parts (but she made use of the plain Name.) (OBC t17241014-68)

(9) he then charged him with having put his hand into his breeches, and felt his p—e p—s. (OBC t17970712-55)

In general, the use of bad language is not particularly remarked upon where it occurs in the process of gathering evidence, but sometimes we find metalinguistic comments. The speakers in (10) address the notion of what constitutes "disgusting language", and (11) contains an apology for the verbatim reporting of bad language (*your Lordship will excuse me*):

(10) *Q.* What do you mean by disgusting language? *A.* She called her all the blackguard names she could think of—I call "long cow" disgusting. (OBC t18651218-127)

(11) a gentleman [wanted] to know whether I had married one Mrs. Ann Hatfield to one Mr. Remye, I said I had, he said with an oath (your Lordship will excuse me) I am glad of it, for I did not think any body would have had her she is so d—n ugly. (OBC t17440912-54)

This behaviour clearly indicates people's awareness of the force of such language.

Overall Development: Taboo and Swearing in the OBC

Figure 14.1 shows the overall number of taboo and swearwords normalized to one million words in four subperiods of the OBC.[7] Less and less offensive language is reported over the course of the almost 200 years investigated here: we can observe a drastic reduction from 735.2 swearwords pmw in the beginning to a little more than a fifth of this in the last period.

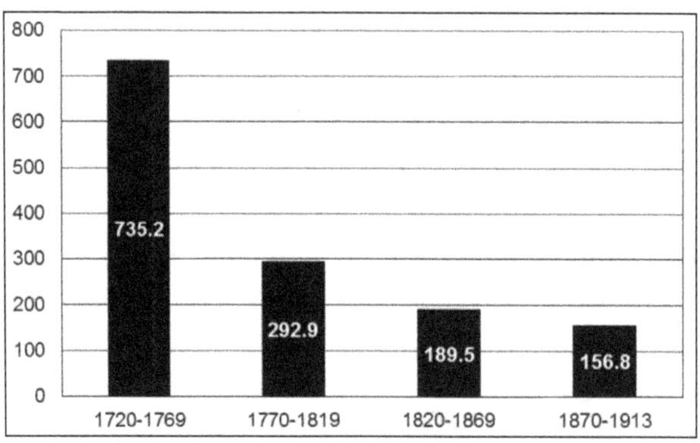

FIGURE 14.1 *Swearing/taboo pmw (N=4,542; all differences p<0.001).*

7 p-values in this article were calculated using either Rayson's (2014) log-likelihood calculator or Preacher's (2001) chi-square calculator.

The major decline in the frequency of bad language took place in the second half of the eighteenth century (from subperiod 1 to subperiod 2), the time when the City of London started to expand its control over the *Proceedings*. The development of the *Proceedings* into an official record imposed on them a standard of linguistic respectability which must have been responsible for the suppression in print of a lot of swearing that did in fact take place in the courtroom. The 'gentrification' of English in the eighteenth century probably also contributed to this development: McIntosh (1998, vii, 1–10) has shown that over the course of the century, several factors (the emergence of a mature print culture, standardization, prescriptivism, the re-articulation of gender roles, and the New Rhetoric) colluded to change English prose from oral, informal, and colloquial to polite, gentrified, and written.[8] That official records were subject to such censorship becomes clear from observations like the following, where a policeman remarked that a swearword had been omitted in the deposition before the magistrate:

(12) I am sure he said he would blow my blasted brains out—I said so before the Magistrate, but I noticed that the word "blasted" was not put down. (Hitchcock et al. 2014; OBC t18730303-223)

The observed decline of swearing and taboo in the OBC is probably also the result of growing social pressure on the speakers. The late seventeenth and early eighteenth centuries saw "a social and moral revolution occurring which [...] established a discourse of purity as a discourse of power" (McEnery 2006, 2). This discourse of purity was especially promoted by a number of religious societies like the Society for the Reformation of Manners and the Society for the Promotion of Christian Knowledge, established by middle-class reformers in the late seventeenth century (McEnery 2006, 87). One of their goals was the eradication of swearing, which they pursued with a mix of methods including prevention (e.g. via education), prosecution (by making use of blasphemy laws and laws against cursing and swearing), and propaganda.

Although these societies faded by the 1730s, their work had a lasting impact as they "established a set of attitudes to bad language that would endure and strengthen throughout the following 300 years" (McEnery 2006, 115). Their campaigns (and those of other like-minded reformers) stigmatized users of

8 We are grateful to an anonymous reviewer for bringing McIntosh (1998) to our attention. A similar development can be observed in negative contractions in the *Proceedings*, which show a sharp decline in the second half of the eighteenth century, presumably because they were felt to be too colloquial (Huber 2010).

bad language as irreligious, lower-class, and uneducated (McEnery 2006, 115). This may have led people, especially those who wished to avoid any association with the lower classes, to use less bad language—if not in all areas of life, then certainly in formal and official contexts such as the courtroom.

The societies' moralistic campaigns and the prevailing social climate also produced the popular belief that women avoided bad language, and femininity became partly "defined by a purity of discourse" (McEnery 2006, 115). Consequently, society would have expected women to use less bad language than men during the period under consideration. However, this is not reflected in our data, as Figure 14.2 shows.

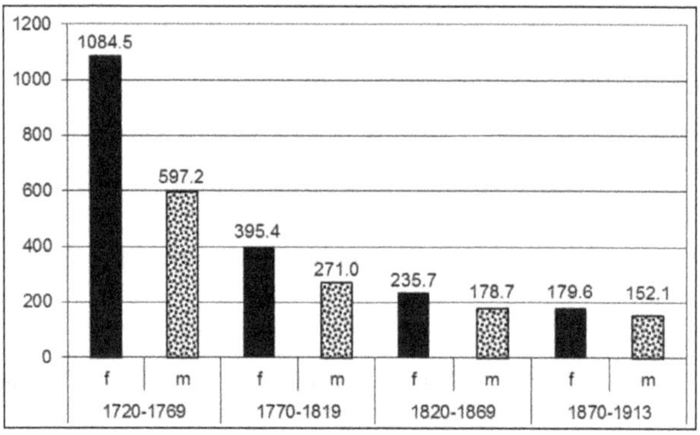

FIGURE 14.2 *Swearing/taboo pmw by gender (N=4,298; f-m differences in 1720–1769 and 1770–1819 p<0.0001; 1820–1869 p<0.01; 1870–1913 n.s.).*

Significantly, more swearwords are reported by women than by men in the first three subperiods. In the 1720–1769 subperiod, male speakers use only a little over half as many swearwords/taboo items as women. Although the difference between the genders grows smaller over the two centuries investigated here, women are consistently in the lead. This result is unexpected in light of the attitudes to bad language in the eighteenth and nineteenth centuries mentioned above—even more so because the OBC consists of speech produced in a courthouse. Whether women adhered to socially expected behaviour or not in their everyday life, we would certainly expect them to do so more rigorously in such a public, official setting.

The discrepancy between females and males is partly explained by the fact that women simply report more speech (as opposed to actions) in their contributions to the trial proceedings. The rates for three common reporting verbs are: SAY (f 10,678 pmw, m 9,993 pmw, p<0.0001), TELL (f 3,333 pmw, m 3,028 pmw, p<0.0001), and ASK (f 6,938 pmw, m 28,751 pmw, p<0.0001). That is, women on average report about 9% more verbal goings-on than men, and this of course increases their rate of bad language.[9] However, since the overall rate of swearwords is 486.9 pmw for women and only 280.5 pmw for men (i.e. only 57.6% of that of women), this explanation only accounted for a proportion of the observed gender differences.

Figure 14.3 considers the data from another perspective, applying the lens of class rather than gender. Comparing the amount of swearing and taboo language produced by higher-class speakers (HISCLASS 1–5 = non-manual professions) with that of lower-class speakers (HISCLASS 6–13 = manual professions), we see that lower-class speakers consistently use more bad language than the higher classes. While the amount of swearing decreases over time in both groups, a remarkably low level is reached by the higher-class speakers already in the second subperiod (158.9 swearwords pmw). This is lower than the lowest figure for the lower class (189.2 swearwords pmw in 1870–1913).

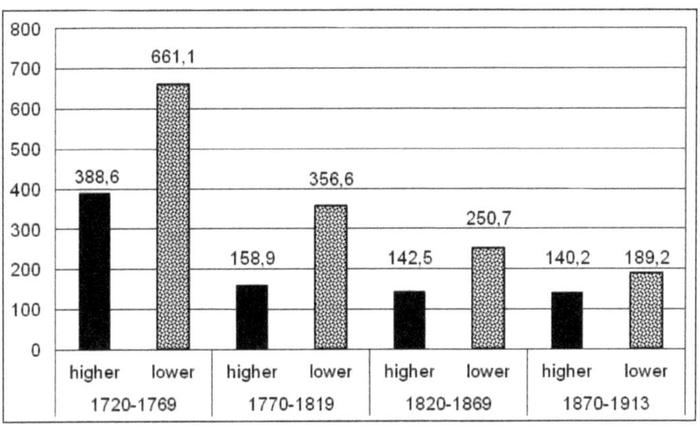

FIGURE 14.3 *Swearing/taboo pmw by social class (N=2,041; all h-l differences p<0.0001, except 1870–1913 p<0.01).*

9 We would like to thank an anonymous reviewer for raising this point. A cross-tabulation of gender with social class yields the following figures for SAY/TELL/ASK: (female-higher 18,634 pmw, female-lower 15,870 pmw, male-higher 15,329 pmw, male-lower 15,212 pmw). That is, it is specifically the higher class members who account for the overuse of reporting verbs by females, whereas higher and lower class males as well as lower class females show lower and very similar rates.

Figure 14.3 confirms that Late Modern assumptions about swearing and social class membership are reflected in the OBC. However, Figure 14.3 also raises the question of whether the gender differences that we observed earlier are actually masked class differences. As there is an unequal distribution of genders across the classes in the OBC (58% of the words uttered by females are from members of lower social classes, while for the males the proportion is only 29%), this possibility needs to be investigated.

Table 14.1 cross-tabulates class and gender for the whole period, 1720–1913.[10] Figure 14.4 is based on these figures and reveals that the rate of bad language is similar for higher- and lower-class females. That is, the higher percentage of lower-class speakers among the women cannot explain the unexpectedly high rate of swearing and taboo words for women (cf. Figure 14.2).

TABLE 14.1 *Swearing/taboo pmw by class and gender (N=2,016; differences involving higher-class males p<0.0001, otherwise n.s.)*

	female	male
higher	89 (333.2 pmw)	1,007 (169.2 pmw)
lower	116 (314.9 pmw)	804 (333.2 pmw)

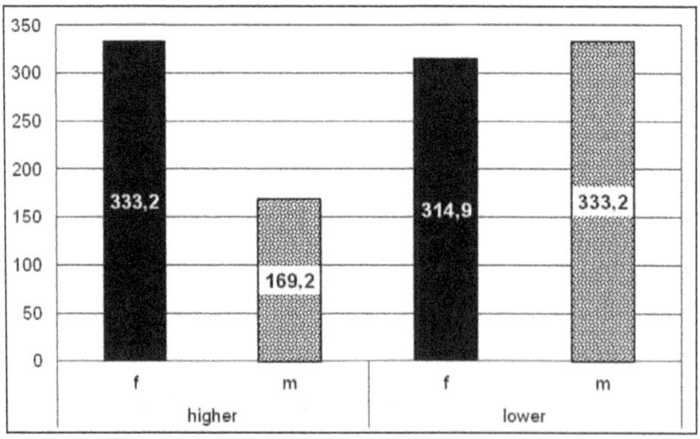

FIGURE 14.4 *Swearing/taboo pmw by class and gender (N=2,016; differences involving higher-class males p<0.0001, otherwise n.s.).*

10 There are too few tokens for which both gender and class of the speaker are known to break the figures down by subperiods.

Rather, one can see immediately that it is the higher-class males who are responsible for the observed differences between the classes and between the genders. Among the higher-class males are the judges and lawyers. Since these professions would have used very little bad language, it is entirely likely that they are the reason for the surprisingly low amount of offensive language among the higher-class males. However, excluding judges and lawyers from the calculation results in only a very moderate increase of bad language in higher-class males, to 203.2 pmw. This group remains the one that reported by far the least swearing. One reason for this could be that the gentrification of English prose started with higher class males and only later affected the other groups.

Alternatively, the fact that bad language was not actively used in the courtroom may obscure the social (and gender) dimension of swearing: trial participants merely reported others' use of bad language, and it may be that women and higher-class speakers were simply more exposed to it and/or reported it in more detail because they were outraged by it—or at least expected to be.

Changes in the Categories: Functions and Themes of Swearing

As mentioned initially, the utterances categorized as swearing are quite diverse, realizing different themes and fulfilling varied functions. Table 14.2 summarizes the functions of swearing in the OBC.[11] As Table 14.2 shows, cursing is by far the most frequent function: 41.2% of all swearing is cursing. In contrast, oaths only constitute a small proportion, with 5.7%. The other functions (expletive interjections and name-calling among the stand-alones, as well as the slot fillers) have rather similar proportions, ranging between roughly 15% and 20%. Note that the same swearword can fulfil different functions. For example, *God* can be used as a curse (13), an expletive (14), an oath (15), and a slot filler (16):

(13) [...] God damn her soul and body [...] (OBC t17321011-38)
(14) [...] oh, my God, the sheets are gone [...] (OBC t17860719-66)
(15) [...] I swear by the God of heaven and earth [...] (OBC t18000528-128)
(16) [...] you and my lord mind nothing but that G—d d—d tea kettle [...] (OBC t17550301-1)

11 The category 'other' comprises marginal functions such as 'unfriendly suggestions' (e.g. *Go to hell!*) as well as tokens that could not be unambiguously categorized.

TABLE 14.2 *Functions of swearing in the* OBC *(categories adapted from Ljung 2011)*

Function	Example	No. of tokens
stand-alones		3,438 (84.3%)
oaths	*by* ***God****, I'll shoot!* (OBC t17330404-51)	229 (5.7%)
curses	***Blast*** *your eyes and limbs* (OBC t17500425-14)	1,681 (41.2%)
expletive interjections	*Oh* ***Christ!*** *It is a wicked shame.* (OBC t18970914-617)	657 (16.1%)
name-calling	*Get up, you* ***son of a bitch!*** (OBC t18741123-32)	829 (20.3%)
other		42 (1.0%)
slot fillers	*What* ***the devil*** *do you think!* (OBC t18390513-1530)	642 (15.7%)
Total		4,080 (100%)

Figure 14.5 shows the diachronic development of the individual functions of swearing, as a percentage of the total of all functions. From the point of view of change in frequency, they fall into three broad groups: (a) fall → curses, (b) static → expletives and oaths, and (c) rise → slot fillers and name-calling. Curses, which make up the biggest group of swearwords, are in fact only frequent in the first two subperiods, where more than half of all swearing expressions are curses (56.3% in 1720–1769; 53.6% in 1770–1819). After that they hardly play a role: the proportion of cursing drops to a mere 2.9% in the last period. Oaths and expletive interjections do not undergo any drastic changes, and name-calling rises moderately from 20.1% to 29.9%. Most striking is the development of slot fillers, which is inversely proportional to that of curses: from subperiod 3, slot filling becomes the most frequent function of swearwords, rising up to 46.9% in the last subperiod.

Evidence from the OBC thus indicates that the extensive use of slot fillers seems to be a relatively recent phenomenon in English. Andersson and Trudgill (1990, 62–63) refer to "five levels of interruption" that reflect the degree to which swearing can intrude into the grammatical patterns of a language (from least to most): separate utterance < adsentence < major constituent < part of constituent < part of a word. Slot fillers as part of a constituent represent a

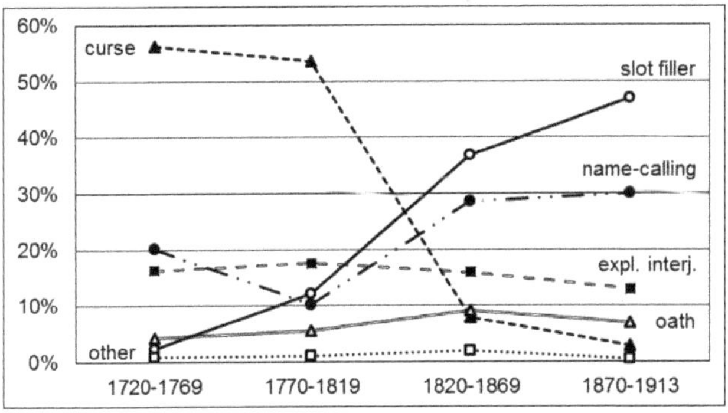

FIGURE 14.5 *Diachronic development of functions of swearing (N=4,080).*

greater intrusion than stand-alones. It is probable that their steady rise was a precursor to even greater intrusion on the word level in more recent history, as in expletive infixation (*abso-bloody-lutely*) in Present-day English.

Discussing the history of English swearing, Hughes (1991, 237) argues that a major shift started in Middle English, which led to the present situation where "various forms of personal abuse, or swearing *at*, have assumed the dominant mode, while asseveration and the invocation of higher powers, or swearing *by* and *to*, have correspondingly diminished". Looking at the above data, we can see that oaths, the most typical instance of 'swearing by/to' had already fallen victim to this shift by 1720. The only remaining swearing constructions of any importance in the 'by/to' category are curses, which frequently refer to higher powers, either explicitly (*God damn your eyes!*) or implicitly (*Damn you!*). Their drastic decline, combined with the accompanying rise in name-calling, the typical form of 'swearing at', lends support to the idea of a general shift in the modes of swearing.

Hughes further remarks that the thematic focus in swearing changed from religious matters to sexuality, bodily functions, and national and racial insults, which he takes to reflect increasing secularization (1991, 237). Figure 14.6 traces the thematic focus of swearing in the OBC, showing the proportions of individual themes as a percentage of all swearing in four subperiods.

The sharp decline of the religious theme (from 79.3% to 27.3%) corroborates Hughes' observation. This drop is compensated by the rise of the family theme (*bastard, son of a bitch/whore*) and *bloody*. There is also a slight rise in the amount of sex- and sexuality-related swearwords to 8.8% in the last subperiod. The other functions remain more or less stable at below 10%.

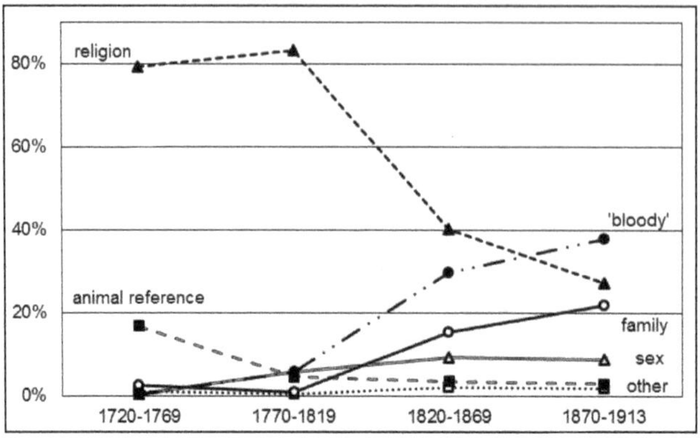

FIGURE 14.6 *Themes used in swearing (N=4,080).*

Bloody is an interesting case. We created this separate category because classification of this word is made difficult by its uncertain and disputed etymology. Several explanations have been put forward (cf. OED s.v. *bloody*, adj., n., and adv.), including that it relates to oaths referring to the blood of Christ or that it emerged out of a contraction of *by our Lady* (the Virgin Mary), but secular etymologies are also plausible. If *bloody* were added to the religious swearwords, the decline of the religious theme would be less than 15% overall, but still noticeable. There is good reason to keep *bloody* separate from this category, though: a more recent theory on its etymology suggests that intensifying *bloody* had strong religious associations during the Reformation but that these soon faded in favour of negative moral evaluation independent of religion (Biscetti 2008, 68).[12] It is possible that the secularization of swearing was both the cause and the effect of the semantic reinterpretation and functional change from a religious swearword (*by our Lady*) to a secular one (*bloody*). Secularization may have helped the phonological erosion of *by our Lady* to *bloody*, and the accompanying loss of semantic transparency of a formerly religious swearword may in turn have contributed to the secularization of swearing.

12 We are grateful to the volume editors for drawing our attention to Biscetti (2008). According to Biscetti (2008, 59–61), prosecuted Protestants began to use the phrase *bloody drunk* with reference to Catholic priests. At a time when alcohol abuse was widespread among the clergy and Protestants were persecuted for rejecting the Catholic dogma of transubstantiation, according to which consecrated wine is substantially transformed into Christ's blood in the Eucharist, calling a Catholic priest *bloody drunk* (i.e. 'drunk on mass wine/Christ's blood') was both sarcastic and sacrilegious.

Representation in Print

The overall aim of the editors of the *Proceedings* was to preserve what was originally said in the courtroom while at the same time conforming to the expectations of society and the authorities concerning the purity of language. One of the editorial strategies to achieve the latter was to obscure bad language in print: in the *Proceedings*, 55% of all swearwords and taboo items (2,447/4,542) are orthographically concealed, by the replacement of some or all of the letters of the word by dashes or asterisks. Complete concealment is extremely rare (only 40 words = 0.9%), presumably because it impedes comprehension more than the practice of half-spelling words. Therefore, complete and partial concealment will be aggregated as 'censored' in the following.

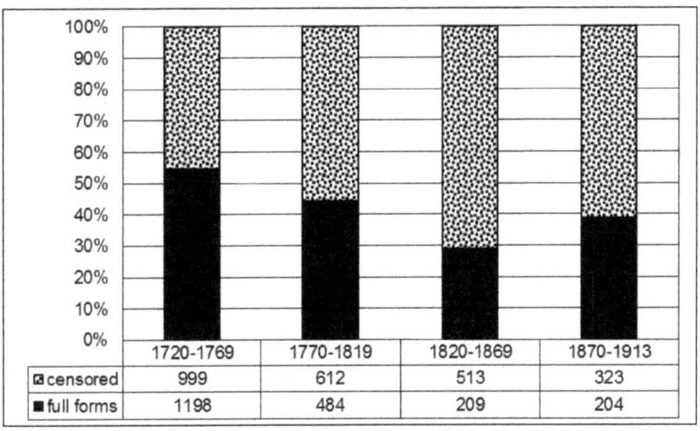

FIGURE 14.7 *Censoring of swearing/taboo in print (N=4,542; all differences p<0.001 except 1770–1819 vs. 1870–1913 n.s.).*

We have seen above that less and less swearing was reported in the *Proceedings* over the eighteenth and nineteenth centuries (see Figure 14.1). Figure 14.7 demonstrates that, in addition, bad language was also subject to increasingly strict censoring in print, with the percentage of orthographically full forms (indicated by the lower part of the bars) dropping by more than 25 percentage points up to subperiod 3. This development agrees with McEnery's (2006, 99) observation that the eighteenth and nineteenth centuries were characterized by a discourse of purity and that "the public expression of such [bad] language via the mass media became an area of concern for the state". As mentioned before, the City of London gained more and more control over the *Proceedings* from the mid-eighteenth century, which led to increasing pressure on editors to suppress and conceal swearing and taboo words.[13]

Our data suggest that the highest impact of public disapproval on the representation of bad language in print was felt only about a century after the major activism of the Society for the Reformation of Manners and other societies in the early eighteenth century. The rise of full forms from subperiod 3 to subperiod 4 may indicate a fading of the moral legacy of these societies. Another factor contributing to this change may be that after a period of increasing municipal control over the *Proceedings* from about 1750 onwards, which resulted in an increasingly formal representation in print of informal spoken language, the portrayal of the spoken word became more faithful again in the second half of the nineteenth century. As part of this trend, interference in the form of censoring bad language receded. The development of negative contraction in the *Proceedings* lends weight to this observation: while contraction must have become more and more frequent in spoken language, a sharp drop can be observed in the (printed) *Proceedings* of the second half of the eighteenth century, followed by a resurgence of contracted forms in the second half of the nineteenth century (Huber 2010, 69; see also footnote 8 above).

The discourse of purity that emerged in the eighteenth century linked swearing particularly to lower-class men (McEnery 2006, 167). It will be interesting to see in what way the gender and social class of the speakers correlate with the degree of censoring in the *Proceedings*. Figure 14.8 shows the editorial censorship by speaker gender, where the lower parts of the bars show the orthographic full forms and the upper parts the censored forms (partial or complete concealment).

According to the tenets of the discourse of purity, society expected swearing more from men, yet men's bad language was consistently more censored in the *Proceedings* (except in the 1870–1913 subperiod, where the gender difference is not significant). Surprisingly, editors and presumably the public tolerated the use of swearing and taboo words more when it came from women and felt less need to conceal it.

---

13 Such pressure was already felt in the early eighteenth century: in 1725, the City authorities condemned the verbatim account of the statement of an Irishman (t17250407-66) as "lewd and indecent" (Emsley et al. 2014).

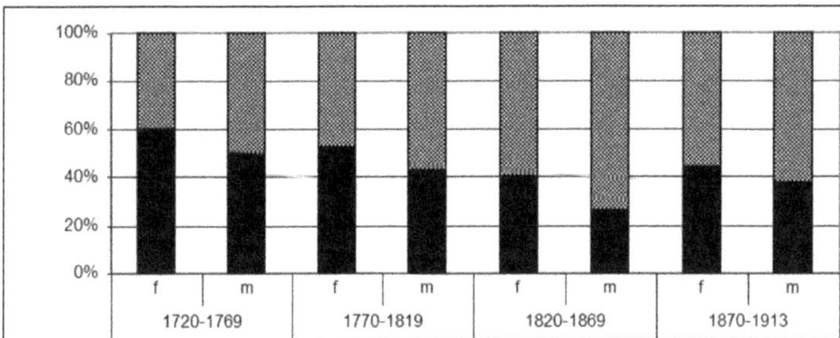

	f	m	f	m	f	m	f	m
	1720-1769		1770-1819		1820-1869		1870-1913	
censored	263	672	100	488	92	412	48	272
full forms	388	678	110	365	61	148	38	163

FIGURE 14.8 *Censoring in print by gender (N=4,298; all f-m differences within subperiods p≤0.01, except 1870–1913 n.s.).*

Figure 14.9 visualizes censorship by the speaker's social class, with the full forms again represented by the lower part of the bars.

Except for 1720–1769, the differences are not significant within the subperiods, but for the entire 1720–1913 period there is a significant class difference (p<0.05): again contrary to expectations, higher-class speakers' bad language was less censored than that of the lower classes. That is, bad language was more tolerated when it came from the mouth of a higher-class speaker.

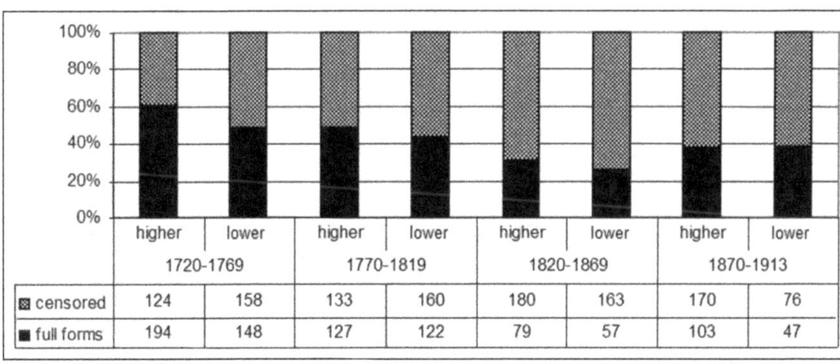

	higher	lower	higher	lower	higher	lower	higher	lower
	1720-1769		1770-1819		1820-1869		1870-1913	
censored	124	158	133	160	180	163	170	76
full forms	194	148	127	122	79	57	103	47

FIGURE 14.9 *Censoring in print by class (N=2,041; all h-l differences n.s., except 1720–1769 p<0.01).*

Table 14.3 cross-tabulates censoring by speaker gender and class to test for interactions between these social categories. Since there are only 2,016 tokens for which both the gender and the class of the speaker are known, we do not distinguish subperiods here.

TABLE 14.3 *Full forms by gender and class (N=2,016; female h-l p<0.01, male h-l p=0.06, higher f-m p<0.0001, lower f-m p=0.06)*

	female	male	Total
higher	60/89 (67.4%)	437/1007 (43.4%)	497/1096 (45.3%)
lower	56/116 (48.3%)	314/804 (39.1%)	370/920 (40.2%)
Total	116/205 (56.6%)	751/1811 (41.5%)	867/2016 (43.0%)

The class and gender differences in Table 14.3 are significant (some marginally so at p=0.06) and demonstrate that the gender differences in Figure 14.9 are not masked class differences, and vice versa: female as well as higher-class speakers' bad language is consistently less censored. Two thirds of the taboo expressions and swearwords of female higher-class speakers remain uncensored, but less than half of those of females from the lower classes. The trend is the same for male speakers, although the percentages are lower and the difference between the classes is not as pronounced.

Since the discourse of purity associated bad language with lower-class males, we would have expected a higher rate of concealment of the bad language of women as well as that of higher-class speakers in the *Proceedings* (as swearing was deemed especially improper for these groups). In order to explain the unexpected findings of Figure 14.8 and Figure 14.9 it is helpful to consider that by far the most instances of bad language uttered in the Old Bailey are actually reported rather than actively used in the courtroom (see above). To ascertain the gender of the speaker who had originally uttered the swearword or taboo item (rather than those of the speaker who reported them in the courtroom), we recoded by hand a random sample of 500 out of all the 2,016 tokens for which information on both gender and class was available.[14] The procedure

14 A sample of 500 out of a total population of 2,016 gives a confidence level of 95%, with a confidence interval of 3.8. Unfortunately, there were not enough contextual clues to

is illustrated in (17), from the testimony of Catherine Harvey, a woman with a lower-class background:

(17) [...] he *up* [sic] with his fist and struck me in the mouth—Margaret Hilligan, who was sitting alongside me, said, "*George, don't strike her*"—he said, "*You b—wh—e, I will strike you too*". (OBC t18490226-752)

The passages in italics are not originally Harvey's words but those of the witness Margaret Hilligan and those of the defendant George Wortley. The only one (reported to be) swearing in this exchange is Mr Wortley, so *b—wh—e* was recoded as coming from a man rather than a woman. Figure 14.10 contrasts the rate of censoring (a) by the gender of the speaker reporting the swearword in the courtroom (reporting speaker) and (b) by the gender of the speaker who originally uttered it (original speaker).

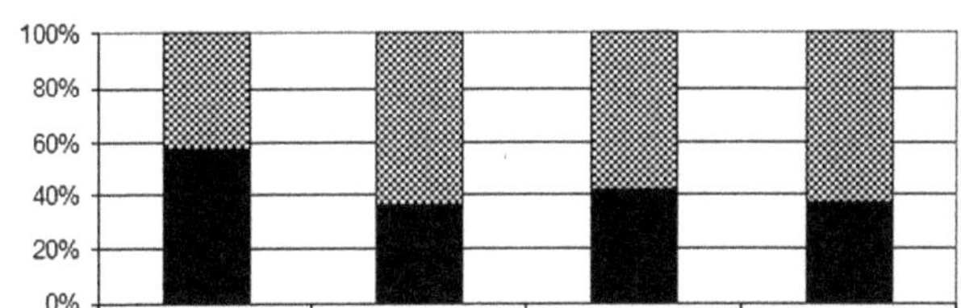

	reporting speaker		original speaker	
	f	m	f	m
censored	20	288	48	258
full forms	27	165	35	152

FIGURE 14.10 *Censoring in print by gender, 500 sample (differences for reporting speaker p<0.01, for original speaker n.s.).*

When basing the calculations on the gender of the original speaker rather than on that of the person reporting the use of bad language in the courtroom, the difference in percentage points becomes smaller (21.0 > 4.2) and not significant. If the editors were indeed deliberately shaping the representation of different social groups' use of bad language, they must have been guided by the social characteristics of those reporting it in the courtroom, i.e. by those traits that were more immediately accessible to the court scribe. It may well be the case that in their unexpected practice of censoring women and the

ascertain the social characteristics of every original speaker in this sample. While the gender could be reconstructed in 493 of the 500 cases, the social class is only known for 210. The latter is too low a number to perform a statistically valid sample analysis, so we can only consider gender here.

higher classes less, editors exploited societal expectations. According to the discourse of purity, swearing and taboo words would have been more shocking when coming from these groups, which were assumed to use bad language the least. Particularly during the eighteenth century, when the publication of the *Proceedings* was still a commercial enterprise, spelling these groups' taboo and swearwords out made their language more shocking and sensationalist and would possibly have increased sales of the *Proceedings*.[15] There is also a psychological factor: since swearing was more shocking when performed by women or higher-class speakers, the editorial non-approval of such unladylike or ungentlemanly conduct may have resulted in exposing and condemning such shocking language by leaving it uncensored.

Conclusion

Our investigation of swearing and taboo in the eighteenth and nineteenth centuries reveals interesting developments on both the level of use and the level of representation in print. As for use, the results from the OBC indicate shifts in the themes and functions of swearing. The cursing function declines drastically, while slot fillers exhibit the most dramatic rise. The dominance of religious swearing is challenged; for instance, the family theme gains popularity. We consider this part of a larger process of increasing secularization.

Bad language in the *Proceedings*, which is mostly found in reported speech, declines in frequency throughout the two centuries and is increasingly concealed in print. This is likely due to the prevailing social climate that increasingly condemned swearing and put growing pressure on both the publishers of the *Proceedings* and the individual speakers.

In light of this, two findings are surprising: more taboo language is reported by females than by males, and bad language is less often censored when uttered by higher-class or female speakers. There is reason to believe that this is the result of interference by scribes or publishers. The reason for this editorial reshaping of what was originally said may have been the attempt to increase the publication's entertainment value by highlighting behaviour that is shocking in its unexpectedness. It is also possible that the editors considered swearing by these groups especially rude and employed the lack of concealment as a way to expose and condemn it.

In future work, it would be interesting to further explore the functioning and patterns of this kind of censorship, e.g by investigating concealment or the

15 Traugott (2011, 70) observes that the earlier *Proceedings* sought "to contradict the expected norms of civil and polite audiences" also by their choice of topics (rape, incest, etc.).

lack of it with regard to speakers' roles in the courtroom (e.g. did defendants swear more than witnesses?) or by (groups of) swearwords (e.g. are religious swearwords censored more than secular ones?). The latter could also provide insight into the perceived offensiveness of an item. On the level of use, the inclusion of uncensored swearwords would constitute a fruitful extension of the investigation.

Corpus

OBC *The Old Bailey Corpus. Spoken English in the Eighteenth and Nineteenth Centuries*. 2012. Compiled by Magnus Huber, Magnus Nissel, Patrick Maiwald, and Bianca Widlitzki. http://www1.uni-giessen.de/oldbaileycorpus.

References

Allan, Keith, and Kate Burridge. 2006. *Forbidden Words: Taboo and the Censoring of Language*. Cambridge: Cambridge University Press.

Andersson, Lars, and Peter Trudgill. 1990. *Bad Language*. Oxford: Blackwell.

Biscetti, Stefania. 2008. "The Diachronic Development of the Intensifier *Bloody*: A Case Study in Historical Pragmatics." In *English Historical Linguistics 2006. Selected Papers from the Fourteenth International Conference on English Historical Linguistics (ICEHL 14), Bergamo, 21–25 August 2006. Volume II. Lexical and Semantic Change*, edited by Richard Dury, Maurizio Gotti, and Marina Dossena, 53–74. Amsterdam and Philadelphia: John Benjamins.

Corporation of London Records Office (CLRO), *Journals of the City Lands Committee* 70, November 13, 1778.

Devereaux, Simon. 1996. "The City and the Sessions Paper: 'Public Justice' in London, 1770–1800." *Journal of British Studies* 35/4: 466–503.

Emsley, Clive, Tim Hitchcock, and Robert Shoemaker. 2014. "The Proceedings—Publishing History of the Proceedings." *The Old Bailey Proceedings Online, 1674–1913 (version 7.0)*. Accessed February 23, 2014. http://www.oldbaileyonline.org.

Hitchcock, Tim, Robert Shoemaker, Clive Emsley, Sharon Howard, Jamie McLaughlin, et al. 2014. *The Old Bailey Proceedings Online, 1674–1913 (version 7.0)*. Accessed January 31, 2014. http://www.oldbaileyonline.org.

Huber, Magnus. 2007. "The Old Bailey Proceedings, 1674–1834. Evaluating and Annotating a Corpus of Eighteenth- and Nineteenth-Century Spoken English." In *Annotating Variation and Change*, edited by Anneli Meurman-Solin, and Arja Nurmi. http://www.helsinki.fi/varieng/journal/volumes/01.

Huber, Magnus. 2010. "Trial Proceedings as a Source of Spoken English. A Critical Evaluation Based on the Proceedings of the Old Bailey, 1674–1913." In *Proceedings Anglistentag 2009 Klagenfurt*, edited by Jörg Helbig, and Rene Schallegger, 65–78. Trier: Wissenschaftlicher Verlag Trier.

Hughes, Geoffrey. 1991. *Swearing: A Social History of Foul Language, Oaths and Profanity in English*. Oxford: Blackwell.

Hughes, Geoffrey. 2006. *An Encyclopedia of Swearing: The Social History of Oaths, Profanity, Foul Language, and Ethnic Slurs in the English-Speaking World.* Armonk and New York: M.E. Sharpe.

Jay, Timothy. 1992. *Cursing in America. A Psycholinguistic Study of Dirty Language in the Courts, in the Movies, in the Schoolyards, and on the Streets*. Amsterdam and Philadelphia: John Benjamins.

Jay, Timothy. 2000. *Why We Curse. A Neuro-Psycho-Social Theory of Speech.* Amsterdam and Philadelphia: John Benjamins.

Ljung, Magnus. 2011. *Swearing: A Cross-Cultural Linguistic Study.* Basingstoke: Palgrave Macmillan.

McArthur, Roshan. 1996. "Taboo Words in Print." *English Today: The International Review of the English Language* 47/3: 50–8.

McEnery, Tony. 2006. *Swearing in English: Bad Language, Purity and Power from 1586 to the Present*. London: Routledge.

McIntosh, Carey. 1998. *The Evolution of English Prose, 1700–1800. Style, Politeness, and Print Culture*. Cambridge: Cambridge University Press.

Montagu, Ashley. 1967. *The Anatomy of Swearing*. New York: Macmillan.

OED = *Oxford English Dictionary*. http://www.oed.com.

Preacher, Kristopher J. 2001. "Calculation for the Chi-Square Test: An Interactive Calculation Tool for Chi-Square Tests of Goodness of Fit and Independence [Computer software]." http://quantpsy.org.

Rayson, Paul. 2014. "Log-Likelihood Calculator [Computer software]." http://ucrel.lancs.ac.uk/llwizard.html.

Shoemaker, Robert. 2008. "The Old Bailey Proceedings and the Representation of Crime and Criminal Justice in Eighteenth-Century London." *Journal of British Studies* 47/3: 559–80.

Traugott, Elizabeth C. 2011. "Constructing the Audiences of the Old Bailey Trials 1674–1834." In *Communicating Early English Manuscripts*, edited by Päivi Pahta, and Andreas H. Jucker, 69–80. Cambridge: Cambridge University Press.

van Leeuwen, Marco H. D., and Ineke Maas. 2011. *HISCLASS: A Historical International Social Class Scheme*. Leuven: Leuven University Press.

van Leeuwen, Marco H. D., Ineke Maas, and Andrew Miles. 2002. *HISCO: Historical International Standard Classification of Occupations*. Leuven: Leuven University Press.

CHAPTER 15

The 'Humour' Element in Engineering Lectures Across Cultures: An Approach to Pragmatic Annotation

Siân Alsop

Abstract

Humour is one of the most difficult pragmatic devices for lecturers and students to engage with, and for researchers to identify systematically. Humour does not always travel well across cultures. It can cause particular problems of miscommunication for the lecturers delivering and for those students receiving it in unfamiliar cultural contexts. This paper demonstrates the use of pragmatic annotation for mapping the distribution, duration, and specific function of humour based on nine attributed types. The analysis looks at 76 English-medium lectures from the UK, Malaysia, and New Zealand, which form part of the *Engineering Lecture Corpus*. Differences in preferred humour type, amount, and laughter response rate are evident across the three cultural subcorpora. In the increasingly globalized academic setting, understanding of such cultural differences is important to all academics and students *on the move*.

Keywords

lectures – humour – pragmatic annotation – engineering – laughter

Introduction

Alongside queuing and politeness, dry humour is often flagged up as a particularly British trait—one which students visiting from overseas are explicitly warned may be baffling to them (University of Sheffield International Student Support 2013). Current internationalization drives in universities result in increased staff and student mobility. In turn, in different cultural settings, the need to understand the nature and extent of potentially tricky pragmatic devices (such as humour) grows.

 | DOI 10.1163/9789004321342_016

The *Engineering Lecture Corpus* (ELC) is a cross-cultural corpus of English-medium lectures gathered from three research sites in the UK, Malaysia, and New Zealand. The UK and New Zealand lectures are delivered by speakers of English as a first language and the Malaysian lectures are delivered by speakers of English as a second language. The level and content of the lectures is comparable across the three subcorpora. The ELC is annotated for various pragmatic features, including humour, to enable regional investigation of variation in academic practice. In the corpus, nine types of humour are manually identified. Indexing the humour episodes gives an overview of occurrence and distribution, which serves to guide a more fine-grained investigation into their function. The aim of identifying and characterizing humour in the ELC is to determine whether there is any difference in its use when the discipline, level, and language medium are constant, but the educational context differs.

Literature Review

Modelling Humour Theoretically

Discussions of humour and laughter in the academic context commonly draw on and extend theoretical models based on classical philosophy (superiority/hostility), cognitive science (incongruity), and physiological or psychoanalytic studies (relief). From a linguistic point of view, these theories are not necessarily exclusive; incongruity can often explain *how* humour occurs, while theories of superiority or hostility explain *why* it occurs and the notion of relief can account for its effect.

Superiority/hostility theories consider humour or the resulting laughter to be indicative of triumph. The teller gains success through the identification of weakness or failings in an 'other'. The roots of such thinking can be traced back to Plato and Aristotle (Attardo 1994, 50; Meyer 2000, 312; Glenn 2003, 19; Partington 2006, 232). Hobbes treated laughter as a sign of social superiority, describing it as "the sudden glory arising from some conception of some eminency in ourselves, by comparison with the infirmity of others, or with our own formerly" (cited in Morreall 1983, 5; Raskin 1985, 36). Listeners as well as tellers can gain a feeling of superiority through recognizing humour.

Superiority/hostility can also be an abrasive form of humour, causing conflict, not consensus (Martineau 1972, 103). In this case elements of malice, disparagement, or derision are central to boosting the teller's sense of power through attacks on individuals, groups, or on the self.

In terms of the mechanism of humour, incongruity theories identify particular cognitive demands: incompatible frames of reference (or planes; Koestler

1989) or schema/scripts (Norrick 1986, 229) are received, semantic processing stumbles over competing meanings, commonality is sought and, if the contradiction can be resolved, new meaning arises. The absurdity of competing frames causes discord in expectations and humorous results (Attardo 1994, 230; Ross 1998, 7). The process is distinguished from simple associative thinking because incongruity lies in the "sudden bisociation of an idea or event with two habitually incompatible matrices" (Koestler 1989, 51), or a shift of mode, narrative, role, or register (Partington 2006, 25). At the pragmatic level in terms of speech act theory, incongruous humour marks a gap in the sense and the force of an utterance (cf. Austin 1962; Searle 1969) and flouts the cooperative principle (cf. Grice 1975). It can also occur at the level of register by mixing styles or references (Ross 1998; Lee 2006).

The subconscious process of combining incongruous planes creates an emotional reaction. Relief theory emphasizes this response, as the moment of realization/resolution of incongruity results in release. Laughter is most simply considered to be the expression of "suddenly perceived incongruity" (Schopenhauer 1966, 59), and built-up tension "gushes out in laughter" (Koestler 1989, 51) acting as a vent through which constraint is relieved (Morreall 1983, 20), or through which the forbidden or suppressed is released (Freud 1976, 183). Successful humour and a laughter response are commonly linked (Raskin 1985, 4). After the resolution of incongruity, then, a physical response is expected.

At this level of effect, there is some agreement across frameworks that humour and laughter can modify behaviour and regulate the unacceptable. Control is explicitly identified as a function of humour and laughter (Martineau 1972; Stebbins 2012). Morreall (1983, 5) notes that classical thought viewed laughter as a "social corrective to get wrongdoers back into line". Bergson echoes the notion of laughter as a "social corrective" through which humiliation is intended, and which is devoid of sympathy (1899, cited in Raskin 1985, 17). Certain types of humour and laughter can indicate social hierarchy, a form of aggression towards those of lower status. Hostile joking can serve the purpose of aggressiveness, satire, or defence (Freud 1976, 97).

Humour has specific functions in particular settings. In interactions between journalists and White House spokespersons, for example, Partington (2006, 226) found that sudden bisociative switches were "performed for a precise rhetorical purpose": persuasion. Meyer (2000, 310) concurs that the recurring presence of humour in rhetoric attests to this persuasive function. Here focus shifts from theoretical concepts to function as a pragmatic device in spoken genres. Within academic institutional discourse, particular humour types perform specific, often very different, communicative functions. They can enable rapport-building, construct in-group cohesion, mitigate conflict, or model identities (Martineau 1972; Partington 2006; Kotthoff 2007; Norrick and Spitz 2008; Nesi 2012; Reershemius 2012; Stebbins 2012). Identifying where and to what extent specific functions of humour occur enables a better understanding of the dynamics of the academic lecture across cultural settings.

Humour Across Cultures

Understanding humour is considered to be one of the most complex cultural adjustments. We learn what to laugh about from our family, peers, and culture (Norrick 1986, 228), so although humour as a field of investigation is regarded as central to understanding communication (Attardo 2003, 1292), it is often specific to certain cultures and attitudes and may not travel well across these boundaries (Ross 1998, 2; Zhang 2005; Lee 2006, 49; Chafe 2007, 127). Studies of Chinese students in New Zealand, for example, report that lecturers' humour style can be difficult to understand (Holmes 2004, 299; Andrade 2006, 139), and Chinese students attending lectures in a British University were reported to completely miss some attempts at humour, which resulted in alienation (Wang 2014). Yusoff (2010, 38) found that misunderstanding humour contributed to problems in the socio-cultural adjustment process for international students in a Malaysian public university, and in a report on the needs of international students in New Zealand, Butcher and McGrath (2004, 544) identify humour as an area of particular concern.

Humour is also mentioned in the support materials for international students visiting British universities. Warnings are issued that immediate comprehension should not be expected, especially of irony and sarcasm, which are "definitely not cross-culturally funny at first" (University of Sheffield International Student Support 2013). Careful listening for cues indicating wit, self-deprecation, disparagement, and teasing are advised to cope with the ever-present discourse feature of humour (Cardiff University Careers Service 2009, 13; University of Northampton Student Services 2012, 20–21).

Moreover, studies of the reception of academic language confirm that it is not always the technical jargon that students struggle with, but rather getting used to the pragmatic applications of everyday language (Ehlich 1999, cited in Reershemius 2012, 856). Lee (2006, 57, 60) observes that it is particularly the use of incongruous registers or references in humour that international students find difficult to comprehend, or completely fail to decode. Self-effacing humour is also identified as problematic for students with different cultural norms for public speaking.

Humour in Spoken Academic Discourse

Linguistic research in spoken academic discourse shows that humour is used as a pragmatic device in academic lectures and presentations. In the *Michigan*

Corpus of Academic Spoken English (MICASE), one of the largest corpora of English-medium academic speech, 'humor' was originally identified as one of 25 relevant linguistic/pragmatic functions and discourse features. It was excluded from the final set of features for pragmatic annotation only because there were too many instances of humour in MICASE to encode (Maynard and Leicher 2007, 109, 112).

Also using MICASE, Lee (2006) discusses the discoursal and rhetorical functions of humour in spoken academic discourse, and its impact on pedagogy in higher education. Lee applied a "broad brush" approach to the definition of humour when identifying the occurrence of laughter by producer or receiver (2006, 52). Speech events are ranked for humour density by calculating the normalized number of laughs per minute or per 1,000 words to create a 'laughter index', and humour categories are determined through a qualitative analysis of a sample of humour-dense speech events. Mastery of the range of categories is deemed to be a skilled and powerful rhetorical device in the academic setting, which occurs more often than may be expected, and may be difficult for international students to fully grasp.

Nesi (2012) looks specifically at 'laughter episodes', largely from the cross-disciplinary *British Academic Spoken English* (BASE) corpus: 160 lectures from the arts and humanities, life sciences, physical sciences, and social sciences. Like Lee, humour was retrieved from the structural mark-up of laughter. Episodes are analysed in light of notions of Politeness Theory (Brown and Levinson 1987), 'face' (Goffman 1967), social management, and anxiety management. Six humour types performing a variety of different functions are identified: lecturer-student teasing, lecturer error, lecturer self-deprecation, black humour, disparagement of out-group members, and register and wordplay.

Reershemius (2012) studies humour in research presentations, drawing on a subcorpus from the GeWiss (*Gesprochene Wissenschaftssprache kontrastiv*) corpus of spoken academic discourse. The subcorpus comprises 1,800 minutes of presentation speech divided equally between speakers from England, Germany, and Poland. In the first instance of quantitative analysis, humour was again identified based on the presence of mark-up for laughter. All data were then revisited for a qualitative analysis, looking for occurrences of humour based on the presence of laughter in context. Findings reveal cultural differences in distribution and function. The British presenters studied identified humour as a means of pushing genre boundaries, and applied it more frequently than their German counterparts.

Common practice in spoken corpora, then, is to recover humour via the structural mark-up of laughter. Schopenhauer (1966), Raskin (1985), and Koestler (1989) expected a laughter response to humour, and following this, the analyses of Lee (2006), Nesi (2012), and Reershemius (2012) rely heavily on this vocal indicator. Laughter and humour may be understood as part of the feeling of 'nonseriousness' (Chafe 2007). Their conflation, however, is potentially erroneous (Glenn 2003, 18–19; Partington 2006, 231), because laughter and humour "are by no means coextensive" (Attardo 2003, 1288). Laughter may also indicate other states such as embarrassment, anxiety, relief, or repair (Ross 1998, 1; Meyer 2000, 311; Swales 2004, 165).

Data and Methodology

The ELC contains 76 transcripts of English-medium lectures delivered at three universities in different parts of the world, as shown in Table 15.1. Although we do not have exact figures, the majority of the students in each setting were local, as these are undergraduate programmes that do not attract international students. The audience was predominantly male in the UK and New Zealand context. In the Malaysian context there appear to be more females, although they are still in the minority.

TABLE 15.1 *ELC holdings*

identifier	1001–1030	2001–2018	3001–3028
origin	Coventry University, United Kingdom (UK)	Universiti Teknologi, Malaysia (MS)	Auckland University of Technology, New Zealand (NZ)
number of lectures	30	18	28
token size	265,000	129,000	171,000
number (gender) of speakers	5 (5 male)	9 (2 female, 7 male)	4 (4 male)

The video data were transcribed locally in plain text, and mark-up was then added to create a corpus of Text Encoding Initiative (TEI)-compliant XML files. Finally, inline XML was used for the 'pragmatic annotation' (cf. Maynard and Leicher 2007) of the corpus. Humour was annotated regardless of whether there was any record of laughter in the surrounding context. Enough context was included to allow the indexed chunks of text to make sense as stand-alone units.

The process of pragmatic annotation of the ELC entailed close, multiple readings of all the transcripts, with reference to the video footage. Three iterations of inter-coder reliability testing were undertaken, involving raters with expert competencies in linguistics and pragmatics, and with subject and cultural awareness. Differences were resolved, if necessary, by adjusting the working list of pragmatic categories. This list was originally derived from Nesi and Ahmad's (2009) list, but was gradually refined to better reflect the occurrence and weight of pragmatic categories in the corpus as a whole.

Humour in the ELC was tested based on whether the text was 'funny' in some way (does the incongruity/relief cause amusement?) and whether there was an additional non-explicit message of some sort. In the current 2014 working list there are nine attributes to the humour element: bawdy, black, disparaging, ironic/sarcastic, joke, playful, self-deprecating, teasing/mock-threatening, and wordplay. The aim was not to identify and describe all possible types of humour, only those that are interesting and recurring.

Umbrella categories in the ELC (such as humour) describe discourse function, and the attributed types refer to content. For example, text annotated as "humour type=bawdy" will feature content that is bawdy. Where partial overlap in content type occurs, such as humour that is mainly bawdy but has an aspect of mock-threat, the annotation reflects the main type identified.

The annotation excludes humour episodes that make explicit reference to the artificiality of the setting, such as the camera or operator, as in (1):

(1) [lecturer] there's a very old saying about lectures it is there is only one thing more boring than a lecture and it's
[student] a lecturer
[students] [laughter]
[lecturer] no it's not a lecturer [laughter] it's a video of a lecture (UK, 1029)[1]

Such instances are a direct consequence of the data collection process and tend to occur at the beginning or end of lectures.

The annotation also excludes humour that arises externally to language, such as an unexpectedly ringing phone. In some studies unintentional humour is identified as a separate category, for example 'howlers' in student writing (Ross 1998, 12). Humour in the ELC is restricted to the deliberate and the

1 Each lecture was assigned a unique identifier based on subcorpus membership; the 30 lectures from the UK are numbered 1001, 1002, 1003 [...] 1030, the 18 lectures from Malaysia 2001–2018, and the 28 lectures from New Zealand 3001–3028 (see Table 15.1).

linguistic—the "humour-creating manoeuvres" (cf. Fillmore 1994) that the lecturer makes through language choice.

Results

The data show that humour of some type is more likely to occur in the UK ELC lectures than in the lectures from Malaysia or New Zealand. Using a token count, humour makes up 3.37% of the UK subcorpus, 2.42% of the Malaysian subcorpus, and 1.92% of the subcorpus from New Zealand. A further breakdown into types is given in Figure 15.1. There are an average of ten humour episodes per lecture in the UK subcorpus, compared to five in the lectures from Malaysia, and four from New Zealand. The average lecture length in tokens varies across subcorpora (UK: 8,830; MS: 7,160; NZ: 6,100) due to factors such as time length, speed of delivery, and time allotted for non-verbal tasks. However, humour is most frequent in the lectures from the UK whether measured by token count or by number of episodes.

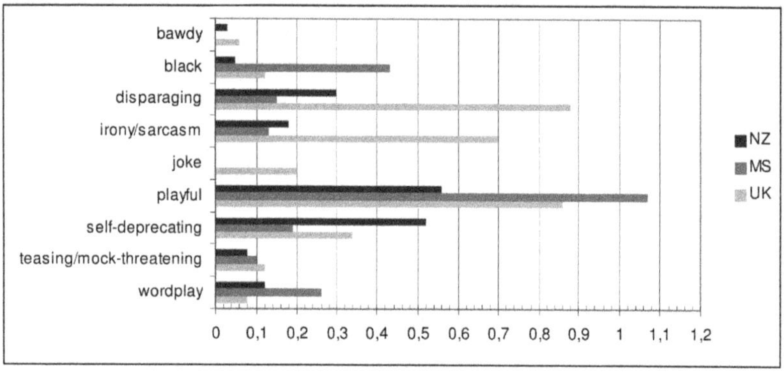

FIGURE 15.1 *Breakdown of humour type normalized (by tokens) as a percentage of each subcorpus.*

Playful humour is the most popular type across subcorpora, and occurs relatively most often in the Malaysian lectures. Black humour and wordplay are also relatively most frequent in the Malaysian subcorpus. By contrast, bawdy humour does not occur at all in the Malaysian subcorpus. Disparaging and ironic/sarcastic types are significantly more common in the UK lectures; jokes are only found in the UK lectures. Teasing/mock-threat has low occurrence across all three subcorpora. Finally, self-deprecation is relatively most frequent in the New Zealand lectures.

Where and for how long each humour episode occurs is plotted in Figure 15.2.

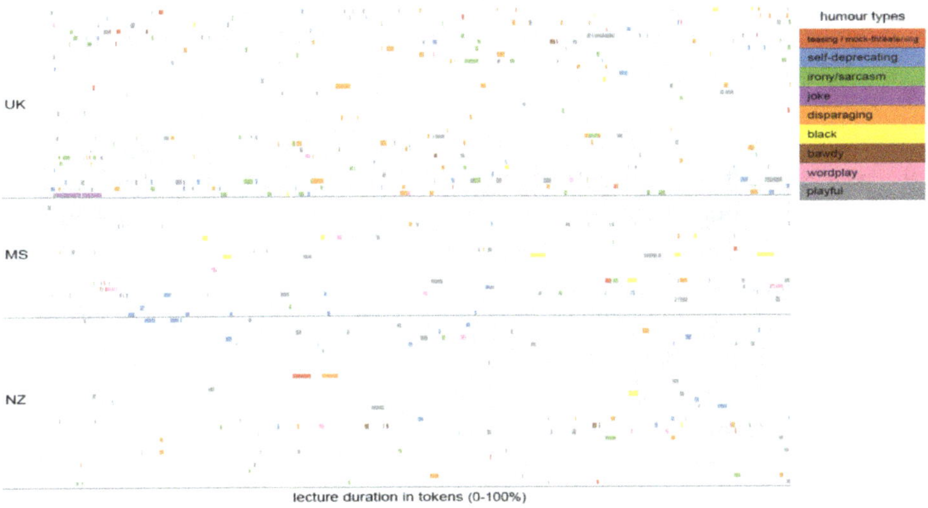

FIGURE 15.2 *Dispersal and duration of humour types in three components of the* ELC.

The ELC data support the hypothesis that not all humour elicits laughter, and not all laughter indicates humour. Both phenomena can occur separately or in conjunction, but the relationship is not dependent.

A total of 78 instances of non-humour-related laughter were identified. Lecturer error is a common cause, but attempts to save face through humour are not always made, and so laughter functions only as a tension release. Recurring themes include calculation errors (1006, 2005, 3007) and mistakes with acronyms (2007). Student discomfort also triggers laughter as a means of release only: poor attendance (1014), failure to grasp concepts (1008, 3014), surprise (1021), and embarrassment at incorrect coursework (1030) all lead to laughter. Technical equipment failure causes laughter outside the remit of our definition of humour (1012, 3013), and there were a number of non-linguistic humorous occurrences such as ringing phones (1005, 3005), dropped objects (1024, 2008), and, for one unfortunate lecturer, electric shocks (3001—multiple).

There was some unexplained laughter where the cause could not be recovered from the video data. Some events happened off camera (1010, 1014, 1015, 3028) or were inaudible (1020, 1025, 2005, 3005), and it was not possible to ascertain whether the resulting laughter was triggered by humour. In other cases the motivation for laughter was clear, but the episode was not categorized as humour because it was not deliberate. The use of certain terminology, such as "wide flanges" (1026) and "lubrication" (3019), for example, provoked a 'juvenile' response, as did reference to the use of urine as first aid (2010). A notable laughter response was received in one lecture from New Zealand, as illustrated in (2):

(2) [lecturer] [...] I would get my hammer ready because I must press fit the bush in the housing so I I whack [hammering action] that in there and then I do expect when I put [points to board] my shaft in the bush it should just
[students] [laughter]
[lecturer] slightly slide in (sigh) oh man
[students] [laughter]
[lecturer] [researcher name] say something
[students] [laughter]
[researcher] it's the language
[lecturer] it's the language yeah exactly yeah ambiguity of language (NZ, 3019)

This example contains both laughter and two competing planes: engineering equipment/sexual innuendo (*bush, housing, shaft*). However, there is no deliberate incongruity; the long-suffering lecturer repeatedly tries to use the terminology seriously. With increasing frustration he eventually admonishes the students: "you guys can't go on laughing forever four years when we're talking about shafts it's just what they're called" (3019). This elicits even more laughter.

Less than 40% (191/489) of humour episodes identified in the ELC elicited a laughter response (LR). In Table 15.2, LR is defined as the identification of at least one vocal description of laughter from either speaker or audience during the episode, whereas NLR means that there is no vocal description of laughter.

As shown in Table 15.2, different types of humour elicit different LR rates, which again differ across cultural components. Self-deprecating humour, for example, does not elicit laughter in almost three quarters of occurrences overall, particularly in lectures from the UK (NLR=84%). Irony/sarcasm is generally met with even less laughter (82% NLR overall and up to 90% NLR in the UK lectures). The Malaysian lectures, however, show a LR in two thirds of occurrences of irony/sarcasm. The same pattern emerges in disparaging humour: overall there is no LR in two thirds of cases overall, but the Malaysian lectures

TABLE 15.2 *Humour episodes (by occurrence) accompanied by speaker/audience laughter (LR) or not (NLR)*

		bawdy		black		disparaging		irony/sarcasm		joke		playful		self-deprecating		teasing/ mock-threat		wordplay		Total
		LR	NLR	LR	NLR	LR	NLR	LR	NLR	LR	NLR	LR	NLR	LR	NLR	LR	NLR	LR	NLR	
UK	raw	1	4	7	2	44	19	62	7	4	0	41	40	26	5	11	4	6	1	284
	%	20	80	78	22	70	30	90	10	100	0	51	49	84	16	73	27	86	14	
MS	raw	0	0	5	5	2	5	3	6	0	0	16	34	4	4	3	2	3	3	95
	%	0	0	50	50	29	71	33	67	0	0	32	68	50	50	60	40	50	50	
NZ	raw	4	0	0	2	10	3	7	3	0	0	14	26	17	8	3	1	5	3	106
	%	100	0	0	100	77	23	70	30	0	0	35	65	68	32	75	25	62	38	
Total	raw	5	4	12	9	56	27	72	16	4	0	71	100	47	17	17	7	14	7	485
	%	56	44	57	43	67	33	82	18	100	0	42	58	73	27	71	29	67	33	

reverse this and show a 71% LR. Bawdy, joke, teasing/mock-threatening, and wordplay types show a general pattern of NLR in over half of all occurrences. Significant variation exists, however, in the case of playful humour, which has an overall LR of 58%. The lowest LR rate was recorded in the UK lectures (29%) and the highest response is again in the Malaysian subcorpus where laughter accompanied humour in well over half of all occurrences (62%). It is possible that the lower overall incidence of humour in the Malaysian subcorpus makes students more disposed to laugh when it does occur, although we have not definitive proof of this.

Humour Types

Playful and Joke

In the ELC the most common humour type identified is playful, which also elicits the highest LR. Conflation of humour and joking is common. Even the lecturers refer to "a little bit of a joke" (1001) or add "just joking" (2001) when instances are actually identified as playful humour, which is defined as good-natured (uncritical, untargeted) banter intended only to amuse, entertain, and establish good rapport. In (3), for example, play is introduced as the lecture theatre becomes a gambling arena:

(3) we'll say fun-sized Mars bar if you hav- if you write something down but get the wrong answer family pack Mars bar double whammy if you don't even try it and because no one complained this is a formal wager (UK, 1005)

Elements of mock-threat and self-deprecation are detectable, but play is the primary intention. This type of humour is constructive and cohesive, and builds the positive face of the group. Although the play is mildly coercive, there is no explicit threat.

A similar pattern exists in most of the playful humour identified, as in (4):

(4) anyone give me a common problem with timber floors they squeak you know why they squeak is it the little rodents inside them (UK, 1009)

Incongruity exists in the unexpected script (gambling/small mammals), but there is no punchline and no resolution. The playful type emerges as a catchall for episodes that are humorous but serve no particular function. Unlike other types identified, the lecturer does not appear to be positioning themself, the audience or a third party, or playing to a script. The listener needs no particular skill to decode the humour, and it is not exclusive.

Unlike playful humour, jokes in the ELC are narrowly identified as a structured oral genre with a set-up and punchline (cf. Raskin 1985, 99; Kotthoff 2007, 268). They seem to function as a time-out. Incongruity accords with the disjunctor model in which one coherent script is developed, and a second, disturbing, script is then activated by a disjunctor. Coherence is restored by a connector (Attardo 1994, 95). An example is given in (5):

(5) at ten o'clock the second lecturer came and he said you know seeing these TV sets reminds me of that um story about ah how we're heading towards an automatic world you know the people are in the plane and the voice comes over the tannoy ah this is a fully automated flight ah we took off ten minutes ago and there is not a single crew member on board this plane everything is automatic but all the systems have been designed to be sophisticated and um fail-safe so be assured that nothing can go wrong uh go wrong uh go wrong uh go wrong (UK, 1030)

The two compatible scripts are the achievement/danger (of automation). The set-up conjures a sophisticated and reliable automatic world. The punchline begins on the second repetition of *go wrong*, which activates a script for faulty machinery stuck on a loop and the potential disaster heralded by onboard announcements. The abrupt switch forces reconsideration of the verity of information taken at face value. Bisociatively the listener must process competing scripts and arrive at the new meaning that automated announcements cannot be trusted. Through jokes, as in playful humour, the lecturer intends only to amuse: the telling is not overly pedagogic, complex, or motivated by control or positioning.

Irony/Sarcasm

In contrast, the main functions of irony/sarcasm are behaviour modification and self-aggrandisement. Irony violates Grice's first maxim: "[d]o not say what you know to be false" (1975, 46). In doing so its purpose is to deliver an implicit message. Saying the opposite of what is meant masks the intention to criticize or self-promote. The presence of at least one of the conditions of failed expectation, pragmatic insincerity, negative tension, and presence of a victim (Campbell and Katz 2012, 459) are likely but not prerequisite in the ELC examples.

As the advice literature to visiting students predicts, a disproportionate amount of this humour type occurs in the UK subcorpus (0.70%; MS 0.13%; NZ 0.18%). Sometimes the incongruity is obvious, as in (6) and (7):

(6) and the formula for calculating bending stress [writes on board] M over Z don't worry its only two weeks ago we were doing it I don't find it embarrassing at all you shouldn't (UK, 1009)

(7) there's delta and there's rectangular and obviously those words are quite similar so it's easy to er be confused when you look at the words (UK, 1029)

Only very occasionally is irony/sarcasm explicitly signalled, however, for example by the use of *not* in (8) and the metastatement at the end of (9).

(8) it's really important I can tell you're very excited to do this group work *not* (NZ, 3028)

(9) the code gives us a very useful set of equations *I say useful cynically* (UK, 1020)

Generally, irony is easy to misinterpret because there is no change in tone or facial indicator to signal that the meaning is not literal. Moreover in the UK lectures 90% of instances of irony/sarcasm did not receive a laughter response. From context, it can be surmised that the function of ironic utterances such as those in (10a–c) is to correct behaviour. The lecturer is really telling his audience to work harder, pay attention, ask questions.

(10) a. we have been working hard on those questions in the book haven't we (UK, 1002)
b. whenever you're ready thank you (UK, 1006)
c. no question oh very good yeah (MS, 2008)

Aside from the student audience, irony is also used to mock other professionals, as in (11) and (12):

(11) does not make sense but hey this is out of the [name removed] book must be right yeah (NZ, 3019)

(12) every time there's an earthquake in the world lots of engineers fly out there on gallivanting holidays in all the distraught local population taking photos of how their structures have failed (UK, 1026)

The recognition of incompetency or questionable ethics through irony elevates the lecturer above their peers.

To a lesser extent, irony/sarcasm is also used to establish solidarity, especially through implied syllabus critique. Ironic descriptions of current lecture content as "the sexy stuff" (1022), and statements such as that in (13) re-position the lecturer from authority figure to sympathizer.

(13) today you're going to get another portfolio question from me whoohoo (UK, 1005)

Irony/sarcasm type episodes are the lowest in average length (25 tokens) of all types. As illustrated by Figure 15.2, these episodes regularly punctuate the lectures, especially in the UK subcorpus. In general the lecturers weave in these short sharp digs to make subtle corrections to behaviour and to reinforce a position of authority/superiority.

Teasing/Mock-Threatening

Nesi (2012, 88) identifies lecturer-student teasing either as a face-threatening act that challenges competence or as flattery that rewards 'typical' student behaviour: drinking and hangovers, over-sleeping, a lack of hard work. For Eisenberg (1986, 182), teasing is a device used by adults either to control or to have fun with children. Similar patterns exist in the ELC, where teasing a specific audience member both confirms their adherence to the 'typical' student script and also admonishes this as the lecturer assumes the role of impatient parent. Consider (14):

(14) I can see that you're drifting away people are not listening very much so I'm going to ask you some questions and try and wake you up I'll ask you a question and then I'll wait and I'll pick on somebody who looks most sleepy (NZ, 3011)

Teasing tends to take the form of gentle mockery of an audience member or the audience, whereas mock-threat manifests in exaggerated threats made in jest to underline a requirement or concept.

Teasing can be closely associated with play through features such as mock challenge, insult through the detraction of valued abilities (Eisenberg 1986, 183–184), and exaggeration (Kotthoff 2007, 274). Teasing/mock-threat in the ELC is differentiated from gentler playful humour if an intended victim/group and some element of exaggerated threat or punishment exists. This type is colourfully exemplified in one of the UK lectures:

(15) kilonewton dot M if I see you write kilonewton slash M I'm going to come round your house with a baseball bat and break your fingers [pause] because that is not the unit of moment that is the unit of load [pause] per metre length do not confuse the two (UK, 1002)

In terms of function, behaviour modification is usually the aim if the recipient of the teasing is present (Eisenberg 1986, 185; Kotthoff 2007, 275). In the ELC the threat is almost always direct and not overheard, as humour is delivered through monologic speech and the lecturer rarely co-opts student conspirators.

More common is the group-threat in which the message is applied to the entire audience or sections of it. The message in this type is always aimed at behaviour modification, such as (16) and (17):

(16) so an- any thoughts on that before I inflict a bit of pain on you (UK, 1017)

(17) if you give me the correct value but it has a plus sign then all my sadistic tendencies come out and I will give you nil points (UK, 1029)

Kotthoff (2007, 274) suggests that teasing usually elicits laughter, but teasing/mock-threat in the ELC is met with a laughter response in less than half of all episodes. The element of threat identified in teasing sets it apart from the more playful banter that elicited high laughter responses. The weight of the implicit messages carried within teasing perhaps inhibits student/lecturer laughter.

Disparaging Humour

Disparaging humour is linked to power. In BASE, the disparagement of out-group members is identified as a particular form of humour that encourages bonding in the lecture theatre, and reinforces in-group identity (Nesi 2012, 86). This type and function is also evident in the ELC, where, for example, lecturers may treat bricklayers (*brickies*) as an outsider group to which neither the audience nor the lecturers belong, for humorous effect:

(18) [lecturer] when we were actually on that job um we bought a load of proper branded super- well mortar plasticiser um which the brickies I don't know they drank it or something
[students] [laughter]
[lecturer] they got rid of it in weeks um i- i- it disappeared in no time I think they used it to wash their hands because it is detergent after all it just disappeared (UK, 1013)

The ELC definition of disparaging humour allows space also for attacks on in-group members. It is distinguished from teasing by the lack of threat and strongly linked to establishing (lecturer) position and superiority in the field of engineering rather than academia. Consider (19) below:

(19) task three was very badly done even [name removed] didn't get the right answer and I would like to explain to him why he didn't get the right answer the rest of you are allowed to listen a lot of you won't understand what I'm saying but what else can I do here (UK, 1030)

The general attack on the audience evokes the script of unintelligent or lazy students, those beyond help. Even the best student must be addressed and his flaws explained. Humour lies in the outrageousness of the implication. The lecturer departs so far from the script of nurturing educator that the shock of his rudeness causes amusement.

This seemingly rough form of disparagement is not uncommon, especially in the UK lectures. Disparagement in general is around three times as likely to occur in the UK subcorpus. Students are admonished particularly for crimes such as giving "stupid" answers (1022), mocked for "brown-nosing" (1029) and for being "a bunch of dippy nonces" (1002). Even pre-emptive disparagement can be found, as shown in (20):

(20) I was waiting for someone to ask if I would kindly derive these two equations and um my answer to that was going to be er A we can't spare the time B you wouldn't understand it so there really isn't any point (UK, 1029)

Yet if there is an element of seriousness in the 'tough love' approach, it seems that the lecturers are playing out the script of site humour—as the abrasive foreman—rather than trying to gain status over the students. The same kind of low register references were evident in the mock-threat humour of UK lectures. When disparagement is directed to others outside the lecture theatre, the level of aggression is maintained in references to other nations (1012, 1013) or other members of staff (1014).

In the lectures from Malaysia and New Zealand, where disparaging humour does occur, it tends to be aimed outside the group, or towards gentler aspects of the 'typical' student script. Focus is on mistakes or poor examples in textbooks (3019, 3021, 3023), bad money management (2007), or lack of experience (2009). As with the teasing and ironic types of humour, direct and biting attacks on students happen more often in the UK lectures, where it seems that any attempt to create in-group cohesion adheres to the wider script of what is to be a young engineer (a form of resilience training), rather than an academic.

Bawdy Humour

Bawdy humour in the ELC also accords with notions of a specific mixed or inappropriate lexis/register which juxtaposes the high and the low (Fillmore 1994; Lee 2006; Nesi 2012). It relates specifically to the vulgar or lewd (direct or implied), and often includes references to sex. It constitutes only 0.06% in the UK and 0.03% in the lectures from New Zealand, with no representation in the Malaysian subcorpus.

Much like disparaging and mock-threatening humour from the UK, the bawdy type seems to echo a form of site humour and relates to behaviour that is out of place in the university setting. Ringing phones make the student particularly fair game for the reception of lewd rebukes, as in (21) and (22).

(21) are we done switched off or inserted on vibrate (UK, 1004)
(22) it's like it's trying to say please insert me in orifice (UK, 1005)

Instances of bawdy humour are also often unprompted, as in (23):

(23) [student] I need glasses though they're on order
[lecturer] it's a bit blurry because of th- there's not enough contrast with the light on but
[student] but I'm just totally blind
[lecturer] okay we won't go into the possible causes for that we'll just let it lie (UK, 1024)

The script shifts seamlessly from housekeeping to masturbation. Jokes often have an element of shock—the taboo or personal attacks—which may cause offence (Ross 1998, 4). The exchange above echoes the set-up and punchline of a joke format, made at the expense of the unknowing co-constructor. There is also an element of teasing as the lecturer directs the humorous attack at a single victim.

In bawdy humour, the conversational tone is lowered sharply as responses are fired back to impromptu situations. By shifting the register quickly between 'man-banter' and the serious work of principles of civil engineering, the lecturer displays full control over language and audience. Connection can be made at the level of the low and inappropriate, and this can also be used to embarrass and establish hierarchy.

Black Humour

Nesi (2012, 88) identifies black humour as a means through which the taboo and embarrassing can be dealt with, particularly in the life sciences. Lecturers in the ELC use it to satirize dark topics, such as the lecturer who explains:

(24) in Japan they call it karoshi that mean death attributed to uh stress at the work place so just like me come here and teach and collapse and pass away (MS, 2010)

This type of humour largely occurs in discussions of health and safety, such as lecture 2010, which accounts for most of the 0.43% black humour in the Malaysian subcorpus. The lecturer provides commentary on a series of images of events with grave consequences, as in (25).

(25) this this slide show how children go to school in India yah and then again from here we can see that er this is quite a hazardous way to cross the river if say er if this is in Malaysia then Sarawak for instance then there'll

be some crocs waiting underneath here so if the any one of the children fall then the croc will surely have a very heavy meal (MS, 2010)

Black humour is used when discussing life-threatening situations, as shown in (26).

(26) immediately after you release the radioactive you must run as fast as possible within one hundred yards around ten second so if you are fat fat okay big size yeah if the the construction area okay not so nice okay it's not easy to run hundred metre within ten second (MS, 2007)

Making light of potential tragedy through black humour emerges as a useful tool for coping with and illustrating the more serious aspects of the physical science of engineering.

Wordplay

The purpose of wordplay is twofold: to gratify the listener and to establish the superiority and skill of the teller. Included in this category are aspects of wit and unusual turns of phrase that cleverly twist the familiar, and incongruous/ambiguous comparisons and contrasts (Ross 1998, 4; Lee 2006, 62). Wordplay in the ELC constitutes a display of wit for amusement where meaning centres on word choice.

In wordplay, bisociation is followed by a punchline that both surprises and resolves the conflict. Koestler's concept of "two strings [that] are tied together by an acoustic knot" (Koestler 1989, 65) is enacted. An example is given in (27).

(27) normally this gets gets machined out you know bored out with a boring tool not a boring tool [laughs] but is er bo- bores out a hole (NZ, 3019)

The homonymic pun relies on ambiguity between a tool that creates a hole and a tool that causes/is attributed with tedium. Humour lies in the absurdity of the clarification between equipment and tedium planes. It could be argued that 'funniness' is limited by the extent of incongruity, which is perhaps reflected by the lack of laughter response. Similar examples of wordplay receive similar responses; as one lecturer laments regarding his pun on the concept of "mating" parts, there's an "opportunity to laugh", but "no laughers today" (3020). Students may be more likely to remember the distinction when the pun is notably bad, and this may offer a pedagogic motivation for its use.

It was hypothesized that wordplay would be a less common humour type in lectures delivered by and to non-native speakers of English because it requires a high level of proficiency to decode the language in the first instance and then to resolve the inherent incongruities—which may also demand culture-specific knowledge. In the ELC, the complexity of this type of humour primarily offers lecturers an opportunity to demonstrate linguistic skill.

Wordplay occurs with most relative token frequency in the Malaysian sub-corpus, however (MS 0.26%; UK 0.08%; NZ 0.12%). The quantitative data suggest that the cognitive load in formulation and processing is not a barrier to its use in this L2 context. The lecturers seemed to gain a certain amount of pleasure from accurately delivering complex and extended sequences, as in (28) below:

(28) if a heat engine is a reversible heat engine if you reverse that reversible heat engine this is a tongue twister here if you reverse a reversible heat engine then it will become a reversible refrigerator (MS, 2018)

Words become a game in which the engineering lecturer demonstrates their grasp of the language and its usage by taking on the role of the knowledgeable English teacher, as in (29).

(29) so circumferential or as call the hoop stress okay stress American call it hoop the British call it circumferential [...] remember hula hoop (MS, 2012)

Common sayings are carefully reconfigured, as (30) illustrates:

(30) an apple a day keeps the doctor away but if the doctor is handsome keep the apple away [...] that's for the girls (MS, 2017)

There is little evidence of culturally-specific themes in wordplay, but some indication of culturally-specific usage, and a definite nod towards the employment of wordplay to establish the script of the skillful academic.

Self-Deprecating Humour

One of the strategic advantages of self-deprecation/denigration is that the revelation of weakness can paradoxically garner respect and trust. Self-denigrating Humor Schema (SHS) is identified as a culturally-specific strategy for developing relationships and dealing with non-serious threats to self-esteem (Niwa and Maruno 2010), or face. It allows for the reduction of tension and the creation of a friendly atmosphere, the construction of cohesion through group laughter, and the approachability of and trust in the teller is increased through risking ridicule (Niwa and Maruno 2010, 80). Such functions are identified in self-effacement and in-jokes in MICASE (Lee 2006) and lecturer self-deprecation and lecturer self-aggrandisement in BASE (Nesi 2012). Although linked to a feeling of non-seriousness without humour by Chafe (2007, 76), in the ELC self-deprecation functions as a non-serious defence mechanism which normally involves a negative reference to the self for comic effect.

This type is most probable, in terms of tokens, in lectures from New Zealand (NZ 0.52%; UK 0.34%; MS 0.19%). Lecturers cover mistakes in calculations with exaggerated jabs at their own inadequacy. One lecturer, for example, repeats in two lectures that "no man is infallible" (1029), "I keep telling you that no man is infallible" (1028) as students point out errors. Lack of preparation is also acknowledged then glossed over with good humour:

(31) I'm not prepared today just I haven't I have been working for the past two weekends [...] I may do the mistakes er purposely or accidentally (MS, 2020)

Self-deprecation is commonly linked to both cognitive abilities and physical attributes. A particular thematic preoccupation is hair (or lack of), particularly in the New Zealand lectures. Reference is made to "the few places I I do have hair left" (3001), "fond memories" of hair combing, (3001), the wonderful hair of others (3002), and pulling out the "few" hairs left (3019).

Explicit reference to the pedagogic role of the lecturer is also made. Lecturers express doubt in their linguistic ability, for example, "I hope I didn't pronounce it wrongly" (2018), or doubts about their own domain-specific knowledge, as in (32):

(32) the only time you shouldn't do that is if you're a hundred percent certain you're gonna get the right answer and I don't think anyone's at that position yet in this room I include me in that (UK, 1004)

Laughter responses for this type of humour are not high (UK 14%; MS 50%; NZ 32%), but the themes of the self-deprecation are lighthearted. In the ELC lectures, fault-picking with the self is delivered with a confidence that suggests power not weakness.

Conclusion

The current conclusions are based on patterns identified from quantitative data with some qualitative analysis. Humour is identified as more common in lectures from the UK subcorpus of the ELC, but there is scope for more detailed qualitative analysis of the features of individual subcomponents, for example, the use of humour in code-switching in the Malaysian lectures. As the corpus expands, we hope to be able to make not only stronger quantitative claims, but also more nuanced qualitative comparisons. The inclusion of further metadata—such as specific figures for the L1 of students and lecturers and the gender status of students—would also give more insight into the reported findings.

In the increasingly globalized field of English-medium lecture delivery, understanding differences in the way pragmatic features such as humour function is valuable to both students and staff. Knowing more about what to expect—as deliverer or receiver—can only enhance the positive communicative effects intended, and reduce unwanted effects such as alienation.

All humour types flout Grice's (1975) maxim of manner; use of language to communicate clearly is not the aim as speakers deliberately subvert conversational expectations. The humour of the ELC lectures relies heavily on switching and incongruity. The same abruptness that echoes throughout Hobbes' "sudden glory" of winning, Koestler's "sudden bisociation" of—and Schopenhauer's "suddenly perceived"—incongruous planes, and Kant's "sudden transformation" to unexpected outcome, is apparent in the ways in which the lecturers modify the behaviour of their students, and establish roles and coherence.

Humour episodes often depend on incongruous slips in expected register as the lecturer departs from the academic to the 'everyday' script. The switch causes surprise and amusement, and can result in laughter. Yet laughter was not found to be a reliable indicator of humour, particularly of types such as self-deprecation and irony.

Both humour type distribution and laughter response rate differ across cultural components. The findings justify the decision to flag up certain problems with humour in the preparatory literature given to international students when they come to UK universities, but they also suggest that humour culture-shock may be multi-directional. Irony in UK lectures, for example, may be difficult for non-UK students to distinguish, but wit and wordplay occur for longer durations in the Malaysian ELC lectures, whilst self-deprecation takes up more space in the New Zealand ELC lectures.

It is impossible to come to any final conclusions about the reasons for these types of variation because it is likely that the students and lecturers themselves cannot really account for their selection of humour types or their decisions to laugh or not to laugh. Moreover, this is a very small sample and there are doubtless individual differences between lecturers regardless of the context in which they are operating. Nevertheless, it does seem clear from this small study that there are differences in lecturing style that are useful to identify and discuss.

Corpora

BASE *British Academic Spoken English Corpus.* Thompson, Paul, and Hilary Nesi. 2001. "The British Academic Spoken English (BASE) Corpus Project." *Language Teaching Research* 5/3: 263–4.

MICASE Simpson, Rita, Sarah Briggs, Janine Ovens, and John M. Swales. (2002) *The Michigan Corpus of Academic Spoken English.* Ann Arbor, MI: The Regents of the University of Michigan. http://quod.lib.umich.edu/m/micase/.

GeWiss *Gesprochene Wissenschaftssprache kontrastiv.* 2009–2013. https://gewiss.uni-leipzig.de/.

ELC *Engineering Lecture Corpus.* In compilation. Compiled by Hilary Nesi, and Siân Alsop. http://www.coventry.ac.uk/research/research-directories/current-projects/2015/engineering-lecture-corpus-elc/.

References

Andrade, Maureen S. 2006. "International Students in English-Speaking Universities: Adjustment Factors." *Journal of Research in International Education* 5/2: 131–54.

Attardo, Salvatore. 1994. *Linguistic Theories of Humor.* Berlin: Mouton de Gruyter.

Attardo, Salvatore. 2003. "Introduction: The Pragmatics of Humor." *Journal of Pragmatics* 35/9: 1287–94.

Austin, John. 1962. *How to do Things with Words.* Cambridge, MA: Harvard University Press.

Bergson, Henri. 1956[1899]. "Le Rire: Essai sur la Signification du Comique." *Revue de Paris,* February 1, February 15 and March 1 Issues. "Laughter." In *Comedy,* edited by Wylie Sypher, 59–190. Garden City, NY: Doubleday.

Brown, Penelope, and Stephen C. Levinson. 1987. *Politeness: Some Universals in Language Use.* Cambridge: Cambridge University Press.

Butcher, Andrew, and Terry McGrath. 2004. "International Students in New Zealand: Needs and Responses." *International Education Journal* 5/4: 540–51.

Campbell, John D., and Albert N. Katz. 2012. "Are There Necessary Conditions for Inducing a Sense of Sarcastic Irony?" *Discourse Processes* 49: 459–80.

Cardiff University Careers Service. 2009. *Career Planning and Identifying Employers for International Students*. Accessed January 1, 2014. http://www.cardiff.ac.uk/carsv.

Chafe, Wallace. 2007. *The Importance of Not Being Earnest: The Feeling Behind Laughter and Humor*. Amsterdam and Philadelphia: John Benjamins.

Ehlich, Konrad. 1999. "Alltägliche Wissenschaftssprache." *Info-DaF* 26/2: 3–24.

Eisenberg, Ann. 1986. "Teasing: Verbal Play in Two Mexicano Homes." In *Language Socialization Across Cultures*, edited by Bambi B. Schieffelin, and Elinor Ochs, 182–98. Cambridge: Cambridge University Press.

Fillmore, Charles J. 1994. "Humour in Academic Discourse." In *What's Going on Here? Complementary Studies of Professional Talk*, edited by Allen D. Grimshaw, and Peter J. Burke, 271–310. Norwood, NJ: Ablex.

Freud, Sigmund. 1976[1905]. *Jokes and their Relation to the Unconscious*. Translated by James Strachey. New York: Penguin Books.

Glenn, Phillip. 2003. *Laughter in Interaction*. Cambridge: Cambridge University Press.

Goffman, Erving. 1967. *Interaction Ritual. Essays on Face-to-Face Behavior*. New York: Anchor.

Grice, Paul. 1975. "Logic and Conversation." In *Syntax and Semantics 3: Speech Acts*, edited by Peter Cole, and Jerry Morgan, 41–8. New York: Academic Press.

Holmes, Prue. 2004. "Negotiating Differences in Learning and Intercultural Communication: Ethnic Chinese Students in a New Zealand University." *Business Communication Quarterly* 67: 294–307.

Koestler, Arthur. 1989[1964]. *The Act of Creation*. London: Arkana and Penguin.

Kotthoff, Helga. 2007. "Oral Genres of Humor. On the Dialectic of Genre Knowledge and Creative Authoring." *Pragmatics* 12/2: 263–96.

Lee, David. 2006. "Humour in Spoken Academic Discourse." *Journal of Language, Culture and Communication* 8/3: 49–68.

Martineau, William H. 1972. "A Model of Social Functions of Humor." In *The Psychology of Humor*, edited by Jeffrey H. Goldstein, and Paul E. McGhee, 101–25. New York: Academic Press.

Maynard, Carson, and Sheryl Leicher. 2007. "Pragmatic Annotation of an Academic Spoken Corpus for Pedagogical Purposes." In *Corpus Linguistics Beyond the Word: Corpus Research from Phrase to Discourse*, edited by Eileen Fitzpatrick, 107–16. Amsterdam and New York: Rodopi.

Meyer, John C. 2000. "Humor as a Double-Edged Sword: Four Functions of Humor in Communication." *Communication Theory* 10/3: 310–31.

Morreall, John. 1983. *Taking Laughter Seriously*. Albany, NY: SUNY Press.

Nesi, Hilary. 2012. "Laughter in University Lectures." *Journal of English for Academic Purposes* 11/2: 79–89.

Nesi, Hilary, and Ummul Ahmad. 2009. "Pragmatic Annotation in an International Corpus of Engineering Lectures." Paper presented at the American Association for Corpus Linguistics Conference, Alberta, Edmonton, October 8–11.

Niwa, Sora, and Shun'ichi Maruno. 2010. "Strategic Aspects of Cultural Schema: A Key for Examining How Cultural Values are Practiced in Real-Life Settings." *Journal of Social, Evolutionary, and Cultural Psychology* 4/2: 79–91.

Norrick, Neal R. 1986. "A Frame-Theoretical Analysis of Verbal Humor: Bisociation as Schema Conflict." *Semiotica* 3/4: 225–46.

Norrick, Neal R., and Alice Spitz. 2008. "Humor as a Resource for Mitigating Conflict." *Journal of Pragmatics* 40/10: 1661–86.

Partington, Alan. 2006. *The Linguistics of Laughter: A Corpus-Assisted Study of Laughter-Talk*. London: Routledge.

Raskin, Victor. 1985[1944]. *Semantic Mechanisms of Humor*. Dordrecht: D. Reidel.

Reershemius, Gertrud. 2012. "Research Cultures and the Pragmatic Functions of Humor in Academic Research Presentations: A Corpus-Assisted Analysis." *Journal of Pragmatics* 44/6–7: 863–75.

Ross, Alison. 1998. *The Language of Humour*. Oxon: Routledge.

Schopenhauer, Arthur. 1966[1959]. *The World as Will and Representation*. Vol. 1, translated by Eric Francis Jules Payne. New York: Dover Publications.

Searle, John. 1969. *Speech Acts*. Cambridge: Cambridge University Press.

Stebbins, Robert. 2012[1980]. "The Role of Humour in Teaching: Strategy and Self-Expression." In *Teacher Strategies: Explorations in the Sociology of the School*, edited by Peter Woods, 84–97. London: Croom Helm.

Swales, John M. 2004. *Research Genres: Explorations and Applications*. Cambridge: Cambridge University Press.

University of Northampton Student Services. 2012. *International Student Handbook*. Accessed January 1, 2014. http://www.northampton.ac.uk/Downloads/2551-international_students_handbook.pdf.

University of Sheffield International Student Support. 2013. *British Humour*. Accessed January 1, 2014. http://www.sheffield.ac.uk/ssid/international/news/british-humour-1.292335.

Wang, Yu. 2014. "Humor in British Academic Lectures and Chinese Students' Perceptions of it." *Journal of Pragmatics* 68: 80–93.

Yusoff, Yusliza M. 2010. "Demographic Differences Among International Undergraduate Students at a Malaysian Public University." *Global Journal of Management and Business Research* 10/2: 36–41.

Zhang, Qin. 2005. "Immediacy, Humor, Power Distance and Classroom Communication Apprehension in Chinese College Classrooms." *Communication Quarterly* 53/1: 109–24.

Index

www.ingramcontent.com/pod-product-compliance
Lightning Source LLC
LaVergne TN
LVHW010623300926
849162LV00001B/48